SCHOOLS AND MASTERS OF FENCING

SCHOOLS AND MASTERS OF FENCING

From the Middle Ages to the Eighteenth Century

EGERTON CASTLE

DOVER PUBLICATIONS, INC.
Mineola, New York

Bibliographical Note

This Dover edition, published in 2003, is an unabridged reprint of *Schools and Masters of Fence: From the Middle ages to the Eighteenth Century,* originally published by George Bell and Sons, London, 1885. For this edition, the bibliography has been moved from the front of the volume and now follows the main text.

Library of Congress Cataloging-in-Publication Data

Castle, Egerton, 1858–1920.
   [Schools and masters of fence]
   Schools and masters of fencing : from the Middle Ages to the eighteenth century / Egerton Castle.
      p. cm.
   Originally published: Schools and masters of fence / Egerton Castle. London : G. Bell, 1885.
   Includes bibliographical references.
   ISBN 0-486-42826-5 (pbk.)
    1. Fencing. 2. Swords. I. Title.

U860.C35 2003
796.86–dc21   2002041609

Manufactured in the United States of America
Dover Publications, Inc., 31 East 2nd Street, Mineola, N.Y. 11501

INSCRIBED TO BARON DE COSSON AND CAPTAIN A. HUTTON,

IN RECOLLECTION OF MANY PLEASANT HOURS SPENT,

WITH THE FORMER AMONG OLD BOOKS AND

OLD ARMS, WITH THE LATTER

IN THE FENCING ROOM,

FOIL IN HAND.

PREFACE.

 WORK of this kind must necessarily contain a great deal of mere compilation, but considering that so little has been written on the subject, and that the early books of Fence are so difficult to find and really such tiresome reading to anyone who seeks intelligible information in their pages, I venture to hope that—however sketchy and superficial—this book may prove of some interest to lovers of ancient arms as well as to the votaries of the fencing school.

Some time ago, my friend Captain Alfred Hutton—a well-known swordsman, who now, however, seems inclined to neglect the sabre and the foil for the brush and maulstick—left under my care a magnificent collection of books treating of the sword and its use, ranging in date from the early sixteenth century to the present day.

Out of these I took sundry notes, at first with a view to future magazine articles, the idea of which was suggested by a clever but unfortunately incomplete notice on early fencing-masters by the late Mr. Latham—whose name is so familiar to all connoisseurs of a good blade—which I discovered in a back number of "Time." Very shortly, however, my plan embraced a wider scope. In a lecture remarkable for its terseness, accuracy, and comprehensiveness, on the "Forms and History of the Sword," delivered at the Royal Institution last year, Mr. Frederick Pollock observed that an account of the development of the fencing art would require, not a discourse, but a book, and that such a book had not yet been written.

Within modest limits I fancied I would make a work of this description out of my notes, when the announcement of the approaching publication of Captain Burton's treatise under the felicitous title of "The Book of the Sword" made me for a time completely abandon the idea. I well knew that Captain Burton never undertakes a subject without exhausting it, and felt sure that the "Book of the Sword" would comprise in itself all that could be said on the topic. When the first part of this immense work appeared,

I was struck however by a passage in the preface which announced the author's intention to neglect all questions of " carte " and "tierce"—notwithstanding his authority as a professed maître d'armes—and to deal with the history of the sword itself rather than with that of the many theories concerning its use.   Perceiving from this that there was still room for a small work on subjects interesting to all frequenters of schools of arms, I forthwith began to arrange my notes into a coherent shape, in which I now present them to the public.

There is little doubt that the French system of fencing can be traced, at its origin, to the ancient Italian swordsmanship ; the modern Italian school of course being derived in an uninterrupted manner from the same source. Either one or the other is followed by all nations in Europe, at least for small-sword or puncturing play; the French, however, having undoubtedly more followers, although it may well be considered an undecided question, from a practical point of view, *i.e. sword,* not *foil* in hand, which of the two systems is the more perfect.

Sabre, spadroon, or rapier-play—all cut-and-thrust play, in fact—derives its leading principles from the more elaborate small-sword fencing, so that a consideration of the development of the latter will be sufficient in the main for the purpose of this sketch.

As Spain produced a school which only flourished in the Peninsula, being even there all but forgotten now, and as Germany and England adopted first the Italian and then the French system, the plan followed in analyzing the most celebrated authors and elucidating their leading principles has been to pay especial attention to the earlier Italian and the later French masters.   On the way many points of interest in the history of well-known schools, and the manners and habits of devotees of the Noble Science of Defence in bygone days, have also been noticed.

The investigation has only been carried to the last years of the eighteenth century, when most of the old traditions of the fencing art were for ever abandoned ; for at that time the fashion of wearing the sword as part of a gentleman's dress was universally discarded, and swordsmanship became consequently no longer an *indispensable* accomplishment.   At the same period, also, the old Compagnie des Maîtres en fait d'Armes in Paris was dissolved by the Revolution, whilst in Germany at nearly all the universities—the great fencing centres of that country—the deadly " Rapier " was relinquished in favour of the comparatively harmless " Schlaeger."

It is true that some improvement—in the *theory* at least—has been introduced into the art of fencing during this century, but the minute points it deals with cannot be interesting to the general reader, besides which, much has been already written on the subject.   On the other hand, the literature of the early history of fencing and fencing schools seems to be very small.

The only authorities that I have been able to find, besides some articles in cyclopædias—all very incomplete and more or less copies of each other— are thirty-eight pages in Posselier's "Théorie de l'Escrime," [1] devoted to a cursory analysis of sixteen authors previous to 1800, and forty pages on the same subject in Marchionni's introduction to his " Trattato di Scherma," [2] a great part of whose text, however, is a mere translation of Posselier's remarks; also the " Bibliographie de l'Escrime " [3] of M. Vigeant, which, without pretending to deal in any systematic manner with the history of fencing schools, is full of most valuable miscellaneous information ; the " System der Fecht-kunst," [4] by Josef Ott, containing a fair amount of useful matter concerning fencing schools; and, lastly, a few notes in Strutt's " Sports and Pastimes " on the justs and tournaments and on the " Corporation of Maisters of Defence."

I owe to the kindness and courtesy of Baron de Cosson, well known as a high authority on the subject of ancient arms and armour, and also to that of Mr. Wareing Faulder, one of the most experienced connoisseurs of such objects, the unhoped-for advantage of having been allowed to arrange for my purpose, in a chronological series, the pick of their magnificent collections of swords, and to have it photographed for publication.

[1] Paris, 1845, 8°.   [2] Firenze, 1847, 8°.
[3] Paris, 1882, 8°.   [4] Olmutz, 1853, 8°.

TABLE OF CONTENTS.

PAGE

DEDICATION 1

PREFACE iii

BIBLIOGRAPHY * xvii

INTRODUCTION.

The Modern Neapolitan School and the old Rapier-play—Object of the work—Fencing in pictures, in historical novels, on the stage—Periods in the history of the Art: the "Sword," the "Rapier," and the "Small Sword"—Modern foil-fencing—Broad principles of the Fencing Art I

CHAPTER I.

The art of individual fighting in the Middle Ages—Tournaments and Schools of Fence—Sword-dancers—Sword-men and gladiators—Sword and buckler and "Swash-bucklers"—Obnoxious nature of early fencing schools—The chartered Corporation of Maisters of Fence under the Tudors—Introduction of Rapier-play in England—National prejudice against the new-fangled weapon—G. Silver's "Briefe sketch of three Italian Teachers of Offence"—Ancient Teutonic schools of fence—The "Marxbruder," the "Federfechter," and the "Luxbrüder"—Ancient fencing schools in Spain—Degrees in arms in the Corporation of Fencing-masters in Spain—Early Italian schools of arms 13

CHAPTER II.

Antonio Manciolino and Achille Marozzo—Classification of cuts—Fanciful guards of the early Italian schools—Marozzo's progression—Practice in the fencing room—Oath exacted from new pupils—Camillo Agrippa's system—Numerical guards and Free use of the point—Giacomo di Grassi—Typical system of early Rapier-play . . 34

CHAPTER III.

Early sixteenth century fencing schools in France and foreign masters—"La noble science des joueurs d'espée" — Henri de Sainct Didier — Mania for duelling under the Valois—Angelo Viggiani—First definition of the lunge 53

* Follows p. 248 in this edition.

PAGE

CHAPTER IV.
Geronimo Sanchez Carranza—The "Father of the Science of Arms in Spain"—
Don Luis Pacheco de Narvaez — Narvaez's progression—Early fourteenth century
fencing schools in Germany—The Schwerdt and the Dusack—Joachim Meyer—
Jacob Sutor—German fencing terms 67

CHAPTER V.
"Vincentio Saviolo his Practise"—The Rapier alone—Rapier and dagger—George
Silver's "Paradoxe of Defence" 79

CHAPTER VI.
Salvator Fabris—"Guardia" and "contrapostura"—Rules for engagement and
disengagement 96

CHAPTER VII.
The Cavalcabos of Bologna—Nicoletto Giganti—The "botta lunga"—Ridolfo
Capo Ferro 105

CHAPTER VIII.
Early years of the "Académie d'Armes"—Italian and Spanish masters of fence
in France—Girard Thibaust d'Anvers—"Académie de l'Espée"—The Mysterious
Circle 120

CHAPTER IX.
Francesco Alfieri — Alessandro Senese—Morsicato Pallavicini — The French
school of the seventeenth century—Le Perche du Coudray—Charles Besnard—The
French foil—Philibert de La Tousche—Jean-Baptiste Le Perche . . . 130

CHAPTER X.
Liancour—"Académies d'Armes" in France—The "Confrérie de Saint Michel"
at Ghent—Labat—Girard 142

CHAPTER XI.
Small-sword fencing and the French "salle d'armes" — Guillaume Danet—The
numerical nomenclature—Danet's theory—La Boèssière—Dissolution of the "Compagnie des Maîtres en fait d'Armes" 158

CHAPTER XII.
The Art of Fence in Spain, in Italy, and in Germany during the eighteenth century
—The Modern Neapolitan School—The Schlaeger 172

CHAPTER XIII.
The Art of Fence in England during the seventeenth century—Gladiators and
stage fights—Sir William Hope—The "Scots Fencing Master"—The "Sword-man's
Vade-Mecum"—The Society of Sword-men in Scotland—"Vindication of the true
Art of Self Defence"—Gladiator's stage fights—Noted Prize-fighting Fencing-masters—
The Practice of the Back Sword—Single-sticks 187

Chapter XIV.

Angelo in Paris and in London—" L'Ecole des Armes "—Angelo's fencing-rooms—
Andrew Lonnergan—Olivier—J. McArthur—Roworth—Practice of the Broadsword and
the Spadroon—Modern English Fencing Schools 212

Chapter XV.

Ancient Swords compared with modern ones—The four periods of the modern
history of the Sword in Europe—Mediæval Swords—The " Rapier "—Component
parts of a complete hilt : Guards and Counter-guards, Quillons, Rings, Pas d'âne and
Knuckle-bow—Various forms of blades : the " Ricasso "—Typical Rapier hilts: bar-, shell-
and cup-hilts—The " Flamberg "—Transition Rapier—The " Colichemarde "—The
Small Sword—Various forms of Broadsword hilts—" Schiavone," " Claymores," and
" Mortuary " Swords—Daggers—" Misericorde," " Main Gauche " and " Stiletto "—
Foils—Rebated Swords and Fleurets—Wasters and Single-sticks 224

Index 249

LIST OF ILLUSTRATIONS.

PAGE

PRACTICE Rapiers, early seventeenth century. (*Heading*) . . 1

Fig. 1.—The Italian Guard, after Rosaroll and Grisetti . . . 1

Fig. 2.—Sbasso e passata sotto, from Rosaroll and Grisetti . . 2

Fig. 3.—Knights contending under "the judgment of God." From a miniature in the Bibliothèque Royale at Brussels. Fifteenth century 14

Fig. 4.—The Long Sword and the Flail in the old German Schools . . 15

Fig. 5.—Sword Dance. From a MS. in the Cotton Library. Ninth century . 15

Fig. 6.—Sword and Buckler. Thirteenth century 16

Fig. 7.—Sword and Buckler Play. Thirteenth century 17

Fig. 8.—Plebii adolescentis in Anglia habitus. From Caspar Rutz, 1557. Showing the sword and hand buckler 18

Fig. 9.—The Long Sword 18

Fig. 10.—Sword and Buckler in Elizabethan days. From Grassi . . 20

Fig. 11.—Sword and Hand Buckler. Fourteenth century. From a MS. in Royal Library of Munich 28

Fig. 12.—From Meyer, 1570. A Marxbruder instructing a Pupil . . . 30

Fig. 13.—"Coda lunga e stretta" and "Cinghiara porta di ferro."—Marozzo . 38

Fig. 14.—"Coda lunga e alta," and "Porta di ferro stretta overo larga."—Marozzo . 39

Fig. 15.—Guardia di testa—Guardia di intrare.—Marozzo . . . 40

Fig. 16.—Coda lunga e larga—Becca possa.—Marozzo . . . 42

Fig. 17.—Guardia di faccia—Becca cesa.—Marozzo . . . 43

Fig. 18.—Prima Guardia.—Agrippa 46

Fig. 19.—Prima Guardia, on a pass.—Agrippa 46

Fig. 20.—Quarta Guardia.—Agrippa 47

Fig. 21.—Seconda Guardia, on a pass.—Agrippa 47

Fig. 22.—Sword and Buckler.—Agrippa 48

Fig. 23.—The Two Swords.—Grassi 50

Fig. 24.—Estocade. From Lacombe's "Armes et Armures" . . . 53

Fig. 25.—Braquemars and Anelace 54

Fig. 26.—Braquemars 54

Fig. 27.—SAINCT DIDIER.—"Tenue et garde du premier coup pour executer et faire le quatriangle, pour le Lieutenant et le Prevost" 57

Fig. 28.—SAINCT DIDIER.—"Ce que doit faire ledit Prevost pour soy deffendre dudit quatriangle, &c." 58

Fig. 29.—SAINCT DIDIER.—"Première opposite et suite du quatriangle" . . 58

PAGE

Fig. 30.—Sainct Didier.—" Le parachevement dudit quatriangle, &c." .   .   .   59

Fig. 31.—Sainct Didier.—" Premier coup tiré sur le maindroit ou estoc d'hault, &c."   59

Fig. 32.—Sainct Didier.—" A prinse faut faire contre prinse, &c."   60

Fig. 33.—Sainct Didier.—" Fin de la contreprinse exécutée par le Lieutenant contre
le Prevost ".   60

Fig. 34.—Prima guardia difensiva imperfetta.—Viggiani   61

Fig. 35.—Seconda guardia alta offensiva perfetta.—Viggiani   61

Fig. 36.—Terza guardia, alta, offensiva, imperfetta.—Viggiani   62

Fig. 37.—Quarta guardia larga, diffensiva, imperfetta.—Viggiani   .   .   .   62

Fig. 38.—Quinta guardia stretta, difensiva, perfetta.—Viggiani   .   .   .   63

Fig. 39.—Sesta guardia larga, offensiva imperfetta.—Viggiani   .   .   .   63

Fig. 40.—Settima guardia stretta offensiva, perfetta.—Viggiani   .   .   .   64

Fig. 41.—Classification of the Guards.—Viggiani   65

Fig. 42.—Spanish Sword.   Early sixteenth century.   From Lacombe's " Armes et
Armures".   67

Fig. 43.—Gaining the advantage by traversing.   Adapted from Girard Thibaust   .   68

Fig. 44.—Rapier-play in German Schools about 1570.—Meyer   .   .   .   74

Fig. 45.—A German Guard with the " Rappir."—J. Sutor   74

Fig. 46.—Meyer's Fencing School   75

Fig. 47.—A German Guard with Sword and Dagger   75

Fig. 48.—The Schwerdt.—J. Sutor   76

Fig. 49.—Practice at the Target with the Dusack.—J. Sutor   76

Fig. 50.—The Dusack.—Countering a cut   77

Fig. 51.—German Dusacks   77

Fig. 52.—The Rappier.—J. Sutor   77

Fig. 53.—Lansquenette or *Landsknecht's* sword found on the north bank of the Thames
near Westminster.   78

Fig. 54.—Saviolo's Guard with the Rapier alone   81

Fig. 55.—Saviolo's Second Guard with Rapier and Dagger   87

Fig. 56.—Ferita di seconda, contra una quarta.—Fabris   98

Fig. 57.—Ferita di quarta, contra una terza.—Fabris   98

Fig 58.—Ferita di quarta contra una seconda.—Fabris   100

Fig. 59.—Ferita di seconda contra una quarta.—Fabris   102

Fig. 60.—A counter, parried with the dagger.—Fabris   103

Fig. 61.—Italian Rapier.   From Lacombe's " Armes et Armures "   .   .   .   105

Fig. 62.—Capo Ferro, 1610.—Prima Guardia ;   Quarta Guardia   .   .   .   108

Fig. 63.—Capo Ferro, 1610.—Seconda Guardia ;   Sesta Guardia   .   .   .   108

Fig. 64.—Capo Ferro, 1610.—Terza Guardia ;   Quinta Guardia   .   .   .   109

Fig. 65.—Capo Ferro, 1610.—The " botta lunga "   113

Fig. 66.—Capo Ferro, 1610.—Time thrust, by a lunge   114

Fig. 67.—Alfieri, 1640.—Time thrust, by a pass   114

Fig. 68.—Capo Ferro.—Time thrust in quarta   115

Fig. 69.—Capo Ferro.—A thrust by a pass, using the left hand to hold the adversary   115

Fig. 70.—Alfieri, 1640.—A time thrust, on the adversary's disengagement, by dropping
under his point   116

Fig. 71.—Capo Ferro, 1610.—Figura che ferisce di quarta nella gola   .   .   116

Fig. 72.—Capo Ferro.—Figura che ferisce di quarta per di sotto il pugnale nel petto   117

Fig. 73.—Capo Ferro.—Figura che ferisce di seconda sopra il pugnale nel petto .   .   117

Fig. 74.—Capo Ferro.—Simple disengagement under the dagger pushed with a lunge .   118

Fig. 75.—Capo Ferro.—A stab with the dagger delivered by a pass .   .   .   118

Fig. 76.—Capo Ferro.—Sword and Cloak   119

PAGE

Fig. 77.—Capo Ferro.—Sword and Buckler 119
Girard Thibaust, d'Anvers. (*Heading*) 120
Fig. 78.—Thibaust's mysterious Circle 123
Fig. 79.—The disadvantage of not stepping correctly across the mysterious circle.—
Thibaust 126
Fig. 80.—Circles Nos. 1 and 2.—Thibaust 127
Fig. 81.—The Sword alone against the Sword and Dagger.—Thibaust . . . 128
Fig. 82.—Time thrust, delivered as the adversary moves his hand to cut at the head.—
Alfieri, 1640 130
Fig. 83.—A thrust timed on the adversary's cut at the knee.—Alfieri . . . 131
Fig. 84.—Sword and Cloak. Paralyzing the adversary's sword-arm by throwing the
cloak over his blade.—Alfieri, 1640 132
Fig. 85.—Time thrust by a *pass* under the adversary's blade.—Alfieri, 1640 . . 133
Fig. 86.—A Counter.—Alfieri, 1640 134
Fig. 87.—Parrying inwards, *passing*, and disengaging under the adversary's dagger.—
Alfieri 135
Fig. 88.—The " estocades de pied ferme, in prime and tierce." From La Tousche . 140
Fig. 89.—Drawing and falling on guard ; two elevations of the hand ; a " pass."—
Liancour 143
Fig. 90.—Thrust in quarte, parried quarte.—A thrust in quinte.—Liancour . . 143
Fig. 91.—Thrust in tierce, parried tierce.—A thrust in seconde.—Liancour . . 145
Fig. 92.—Thrust in quinte, parried " cercle."—A thrust in quarte.—Liancour . 145
Fig. 93.—Thrust in tierce, parried quarte (outside).—Disengagement in quarte.—
Liancour 146
Fig. 94.—Thrust and parry in quarte, with opposition of the left hand.—Labat . 148
Fig. 95.—Thrust and parry in tierce.—Labat 149
Fig. 96.—Thrust in tierce parried by yielding the faible.—Labat 149
Fig. 97.—Thrust in tierce by yielding the faible.—Labat 150
Fig. 98.—Thrust and parry in seconde.—Labat 150
Fig. 99.—Thrust in quarte under the wrist (quinte).—Labat 151
Fig. 100.—Thrust in low quarte, parried by the circle.—Labat 151
Fig. 101.—Flanconnade.—Labat 152
Fig. 102.—Flanconnade parried by the left hand.—Labat 152
Fig. 103.—A pass in quarte, parried in quarte.—Labat 153
Fig. 104.—A " time," taken on a pass by lowering the body.—Labat . . . 153
Fig. 105.—Time, taken on a pass in seconde, by volting.—Labat . . . 154
Fig. 106.—Seizing the hilt by turning the body sideways, on a pass in tierce.—Labat 154
Fig. 107.—Disarming by a heavy parry.—Labat 155
Fig. 108.—Stepping forward with the left foot and seizing the blade.—Labat . 155
Fig. 109.—Coming on Guard, and first motion of the Salute.—Danet . . . 158
Fig. 110.—The Salute, second and third motions.—Danet 159
Fig. 111.—High carte parried carte.—Danet 160
Fig. 112.—Carte parried carte outside.—Danet 161
Fig. 113.—Prime parried prime.—Danet 162
Fig. 114.—Tierce parried tierce.—Danet 163
Fig. 115.—Carte parried low tierce.—Danet 164
Fig. 116.—Seconde parried seconde.—Danet 165
Fig. 117.—Carte parried half-circle.—Danet 166
Fig. 118.—Carte coupée parried octave.—Danet 167
Fig. 119.—Low carte parried low carte.—Danet 168
Fig. 120.—Flanconnade, with opposition of the left hand.—Danet . . . 169

PAGE

Fig. 121.—Quinte parried quinte.—Danet 170
Fig. 122 —Parade de pointe volante.—Danet 170
Coat granted to the *Académie d'Armes de Paris* by Louis XIV. (*Tailpiece*) . . 171
Fig. 123.—The Spanish Guard, according to Danet 175
Fig. 124.—The Italian Guard opposed to the French, according to Danet . . 177
Fig. 125.—The German Guard opposed to the French.—Danet . . . 183
Fig. 126.—Badge of the "Society of Sword-men" in Scotland 199
Fig's Business Card 206
Fig. 127.—The Guard in "Backswording" 208
Fig. 128.—Flip at the head 208
Fig. 129.—Cut at the left side parried 209
Fig. 130.—A Return to the left cheek over the elbow 209
Fig. 131.—A successful flip at the head 210
Fig. 132.—The Outside Guard.—Roworth 215
Fig. 133.—The Inside Guard.—Roworth 216
Fig. 134.—The Hanging Guard.—Roworth 218
Fig. 135.—The Spadroon Guard.—Roworth 219
Fig. 136.—The St. George's Guard.—Roworth 219
Fig. 137 —German Rapier. Early seventeenth century. From Lacombe's "Armes et Armures" 224
Fig. 138.—German Sword, with finger loop. Early sixteenth century . . 232
Fig. 139.—Back Sword, showing the single-edged blade. Sixteenth century . . 242
Fig. 140.—The "Misericorde" 244
Fig. 141.—Spanish Shell Dagger ("Main Gauche"). Close of sixteenth century. From Lacombe's "Armes et Armures" 245

PLATES.

FRONTISPIECE.—An "Espadachin," middle of the seventeenth century. Adapted from a picture by M. Louis Leloir.

CARBON PLATES.
 I.—Swords, early sixteenth century—German swords, sixteenth century—Rapiers . . . . *to face p.* 228
 II.—Rapiers—Basket-hilted Broadswords 232
 III.—Shell-guard Rapiers—Rapiers and Sword—Flambergs . . . 236
 IV.—Daggers—Broadswords, seventeenth century—Transition Rapiers . . 240
 V.—Transition Rapiers—Small Swords—Spanish Swords . . . 244
 VI.—Typical forms of the Sword 246

INTRODUCTION.

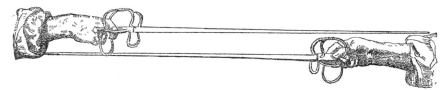

Practice Rapiers, early seventeenth century, showing the manner in which they were held.

HE title of "Maestro di Scherma" inserted after the author's name is a purely honorary distinction, conferred upon him by the courtesy of some Italian fencing-masters under whom he studied the peculiarities of their school.

The Italian mode of fencing retains many of the characteristics of the rapier fence of the seventeenth century, and it was the author's purpose, before investigating the all but forgotten origins of modern fencing, to become thoroughly acquainted with the theory and practice of the Neapolitan method, the only one which has not been swept away by the now ubiquitous French school.

Nevertheless, this book is not a treatise on fencing, and its object is not to fix once more the exact position of "prime" and "quinte" with the foil, nor to prove the possibility of always reposting with a thrust after parrying a cut with the sabre. It is merely the condensed report of a valuable collection of old books left in the author's care, and of many others since discovered in the British

Fig. 1.—The Italian Guard, after Rosaroll and Grisetti.

Museum and foreign libraries, together with an account of the lives and writings of celebrated masters, and of the constitutions of the most important fencing societies.

The author does not profess, however, to analyze closely the contents of *all* the books written on the imperfect play of our ancestors, nor to trace every link in the chain of its development, from the " pancratium " of the fifteenth century, in which wrestling and leaping were of more avail than aught else, to the courteous and academic " assaut " of modern days, where elegance and

Fig. 2.—Sbasso e passata sotto, from Rosaroll and Grisetti. This stroke is essentially the same as some " ferite di prima " taught by the Italian masters of the early seventeenth century.

precision of movements are more highly considered—or ought to be—than superiority in the number of hits.

Such a work would occupy a lifetime and fill a number of thick folios, proving, moreover, quite as useless as those old and ponderous " Fechtbücher " and " Tratados de la filosofia de las Armas " which have been so religiously laid aside for centuries.

But, undoubtedly, the want must be felt of some historical account of the changes in the management of " the white arm," since the days when something more than brute strength became a requisite in personal combat. The subject is full of interest, not only for the fencer who looks upon his favourite pastime as a science, but also in a high degree for the novelist, the painter, the actor, and the antiquarian. The amount of misconception on the subject of ancient sword-play often displayed by some historical painters and novelists is truly incredible. Even in the works of eminent antiquarians such as Ainsworth and even Walter Scott, very seldom guilty of anachronism on any other subject, one reads of duels in the seventeenth century, details of which are evidently borrowed from a modern fencing school.

It can be safely asserted that the theory of fencing has reached all but absolute perfection in our days, when the art has become practically useless. Under the reign of scientific police, arms are no longer a necessary part of a private gentleman's dress, the absurd habit of duelling has happily disappeared, whilst at war, unless it be against savages, more reliance is placed on powder than on " cold steel." It seems, therefore, paradoxical that the management of the sword should be better understood now than in the days when the most peaceable man might be called upon at any time to draw in defence of his life. It is probably this notion which induces most authors to introduce the refinements of modern sword-play into descriptions of duels between " raffinés " or " cavaliers."

The difficulty, first, of getting at the old authors on sword-play, and secondly, when found, of realizing their meaning in the midst of their philosophical digressions, seems to have hitherto prevented the investigation of the subject. A critical examination of the old treatises shows, however, that in the heyday of the duelling mania, more reliance was evidently placed on agility and " inspiration " than on settled principles. It shows, moreover, that most modern ideas of swordsmanship should be dismissed in order to realize what a duel with rapiers in the sixteenth and early seventeenth centuries really was, and how unlikely if not ludicrous are the picturesque descriptions of historical novelists.

Painters must often wish to have some easy means of ascertaining the most usual method of wielding rapier and dagger, colichemardes, or small sword. Indeed, were those old books of fencing, many of which are easily accessible at the British Museum and other great libraries, more often consulted, there would be fewer pictures—even by celebrated artists—representing, for instance, a cavalier attempting to close his hand round the three-inch grip of his rapier, instead of screening it under the guard by locking two fingers round the quillons; or of " mignons " lunging in the most approved modern style and grasping their daggers like stilettos, thumb on pummel, in a manner which would have deprived that weapon of any value, defensive or offensive.

Actors also, who, in every other case, are most particular about historical accuracy, generally dispose of all questions relative to fighting by referring them to the first fencing-master at hand ; and accordingly one sees Laertes and Hamlet with the utmost sangfroid going through a " salute " which, besides being perfectly unmanageable with rapiers, was only established in all its details some fifty years ago. There would indeed be less anachronism in uncorking a bottle of champagne to fill the king's beaker than there is in Hamlet correctly lunging, reversing his point, saluting carte and tierce, &c.— foil fencing, in fact—in spite of the anticipation raised by Osric's announcement that the bout should be played with rapier and dagger.[1]

[1] The introduction in the play of rapier and dagger at the Danish Court during the Middle Ages is, of course, no less an anachronism than that of a small sword bout in the per-

Again, in " Romeo and Juliet " :—

> He tilts
> With piercing steel at bold Mercutio's breast ;
> Who, all as hot, turns deadly point to point,
> And, with a martial scorn, *with one hand* beats
> Cold death aside, and *with the other* sends
> It back to Tybalt, whose dexterity
> Retorts it.[1]

It really seems that a single passage like this (and many such occur in the Elizabethan dramatists), might have suggested the probability of a rapier fight being a very different thing indeed from a modern fencing bout, though certainly not less exciting.

The antiquarian, on his side, will find in the study of swordsmanship the explanation of all the changes in the shapes of guards and blades, and of the differentiation of the sword from the old plain cross-hilted Teutonic " Schwert," through the complicated cut-and-thrust rapier, into either the light triangular small sword or the solid flat sabre.

But it is to the keen swordsman who looks upon foil fencing as the key to all hand to hand fighting, that the historical development of the art offers naturally the greatest interest. It shows him how many generations of practical men were required to elucidate the principles of fencing, and adapt them in the most perfect way to the mechanical resources of the human anatomy, and how utterly unknown many of those principles, which are now looked upon as the A B C of sword-play, were still, in the proudest days of the sword's reign.

The sword is now truly a thing of the past, and elaborate swordsmanship can only be looked upon as a superior kind of pastime, combining mental excitement and bodily exercise—the excitement of a game of skill not entirely independent of chance, together with the delight, innate in all healthy organizations, of strife and destruction—and an exercise necessitating the utmost nervous and muscular tension while it affords the refined pleasure of rhythmical action. But in days gone by the sword was indeed part of the man, and the skilful use thereof, on most occasions, of more import than a good cause. It has often been said that a history of the sword would be a history of humanity, since the latter has ever been a chain of struggles between nations and men ultimately decided by violence. Similarly, it will be found that the changes in the modes of fencing at different periods correspond in a general way to the changes in manners.

formance, but if the actor's part be to carry out the author's ideas, it is certainly a wonder that greater care should never have been bestowed on that scene.
   [1] Act iii., sc. I.

The rough untutored fighting of the Middle Ages represented faithfully the reign of brute force in social life as well as in politics. The stoutest arm and the weightiest sword won the day, even as did the sturdiest baron or the most warlike king. Those were the days of crushing blows with mace or glaive, when a knight's superiority in action depended on his power of wearing heavier armour and dealing heavier blows than his neighbour, when strength was lauded more than skill, and minstrels sang of enchanted blades that nought could break.

Later on, after the Renascence, when life was taken more easily, the depressing armour was discarded in the private walks of life. The discovery of a greater variety of interests and pleasures induced men to lead a more active existence, and they began to walk where before they had ridden in state, reduced the dimensions of their ancestor's sword, and, as the harness of war was now only worn in the camps, came to rely on their agility and cunning to make up for the scantier protection of cloak or hand buckler. Instead of " down right blowes," they devised a multitude of wily attacks, and, in the absence of any very definite mode of self-defence (which had yet to be invented), everyone indulged in as much fantasy in his sword-play as his individual energy allowed him to carry out. The prevailing idea was the discovery of a " botte secrète" and a " universal parry," which was to the fencer of those times what the philosopher's stone was to the alchemist or the Eldorado to the mariner. Those were the days of the " Rapier" and of the companion of its infancy, the dagger. It corresponds in character to the Elizabethan, and, later on, to the " Cavalier" period, often so called in France in contradistinction to the preceding and more " knightly" age. The rapier was as elegant and vicious as its ancestor was sturdy and brutal, its practice as fantastic as the prevailing taste in speech and literature and notions of the outer world.

Afterwards when, in private life, the habit of fighting gradually diminished, and in war firearms came into more general use, the sword lost much of its importance. In the days of the " Grand Monarque," and after the Restoration, it became chiefly an article of dress, for gentlemen only,— like the periwig,—and swordsmanship a courtly accomplishment ranking much in the same category as dancing. A gentleman was then no longer of necessity a soldier, consequently his sword was essentially a " dress sword." From this period dates the absolute distinction between the court and the military sword, both derived from the rapier, while during the process of evolution many leading principles of fencing, applicable to either weapon, were discovered and practically tested.

Through the whole of the eighteenth century, the use of the *small* sword was carefully and almost exclusively cultivated, and the refinements introduced were in due course applied to the other weapons. That was the birth-time of our modern swordsmanship, correct, precise, and elegant, and none the less effective for being less flowery than the rapier-play.

Here, again, it is noticeable how the manner of using the sword in that century reflects some of its chief features. The light, elegant small sword, managed by the wrist and with a comparatively small expenditure of strength, though, at the same time, if anything, even more deadly than the rapier, seems, in truth, a fit weapon wherewith to settle quarrels between bewigged, beruffed, and bepowdered gentlemen, in a courteous and highly refined manner.

Small sword fencing, with its simplified guards, correct attitudes, and regular movements, is obviously characteristic of the age which appreciated the polished and precise style of Addison, Pope, and Hume, just as the wild, impulsive, and imaginative rapier and dagger play, tallies, in our minds, with the involved and hyperbolical speech of Elizabeth and James's courtiers.

The habit of wearing swords in private life, which had become common throughout Europe since the beginning of the wars of religion, went out soon after the French Revolution. The consequence was a very rapid diminution in the number of duels with the sword.[1] The fashion went out first in England, and one may say, perhaps, that such a thing as a duel *with swords* has not taken place between Englishmen since the beginning of this century. On the Continent the practice is still kept up, but in a very desultory manner, and even in France, the once classical land of duellists, fencing is now looked upon merely as a national pastime.

One of the results of neglecting the idea that the foil is but a light substitute for a sword, has been the introduction into foil fencing of complicated attacks and parries, which are really only practicable with featherweight foils, and would defeat their own ends if attempted with any other weapon.

The variety and complication which can be displayed by two expert fencers gives rise to the necessity of a code, based on theoretical reasoning and on the calculation of probabilities, settling the value of hits in case of *double hits*. Such a thing as a double hit in practical fencing ought not to count as really good on either side, the whole art when reduced to its lowest dimension being, as Molière says, " l'art de donner et de ne pas recevoir."

Lightness apart, it is obvious that things are done with a foil which would never be attempted in earnest with a sword. Since the "science of the sword " has become really the science of the foil, the best fencers have

---

[1] A shadow of the old-fashioned mania of " coming to the point " on matters of trivial importance has been kept up at the German universities, although the danger to life and limb was greatly diminished, some forty years ago, by substituting for the old rapier fence the present Schlaeger play, with all its restrictions.

indulged in a play which is artificial, though (when the above-mentioned code relative to hits is closely adhered to) much more perfect. Foil practice may in fact be looked upon as " diagrammatic " fencing, freed of most extraneous, disturbing elements.[1]

In our days it is an art that men can do without, and which indeed most men neglect altogether, at least in our country. But those who do, at any time, devote serious attention to fencing, never seem to lose their taste for it. It is one of those exercises which depend on the cultivation of exact principles from the beginning. Old age may creep on the fencer and diminish the vigour of his limbs and the elasticity of his wrist, but that is amply compensated for, in most cases, by the increased coolness and precision which come of long years of practice. On the other hand, if, trusting to his youth and agility, the beginner does not start by drilling himself into correct action—which admits of all but infinite variety—he will never get beyond a few favourite attacks and parries, which may, however, by constant practice, be performed with intense vigour and rapidity. But as his physical power fails, instead of reaping the benefit of practice, he becomes less and less dangerous to his opponents, and ends by accusing his years and giving up an exercise which might have delighted him to his last days.

The disappointing results of unmethodical fencing are mentioned here to explain how it was that the art so long remained stationary. It will be seen that during the whole of the sixteenth century every other master advocated a different system, consisting of his own favourite tricks. It was only when a sufficient number of schools had been formed, and their tenets set forth by a sufficient number of treatises, that any definite basis to the art of swordsmanship became universally recognized. On those foundations, laid some two hundred years ago by Fabris, Giganti, and Capo Ferro, the science—now so complete—was built by degrees.

Assuming, on the one hand, that the theory of fencing has long since reached its culminating point, and, on the other, that its broad principles apply to every kind of hand to hand fight, with any variety of piercing, crushing, or cutting weapons, and with either one or both hands, a general and elastic statement of those broad principles will not be out of place here.[2]

---

[1] Of course rebated swords and foils have been in use for centuries, but they always *stood* for swords, *sword* play was the object, and few things were attempted with "blunts" that would not be of practical use with "sharps." In our days, however, *foil* play alone is generally the object.

[2] As it was mentioned before, this is not a treatise of fencing. In order, however, to be able to criticise old-fashioned books, generally lacking in explicit technical terms, and often treating of weapons now obsolete, it will be well to lay down definitions which apply broadly to all fencing weapons and which will translate the involved and fantastic expressions of the ancient masters.

A historical sketch of the development of the art can only touch on the most leading principles, but these are quite sufficient for the purpose, as every style depends on the combination and application of *some* or *all* of them.

In such a study, although noticing the practice of very different weapons, foil fencing may be taken as the objective, although it represents by no means a fight with any other form of the "arme blanche."

But, as was said before, the very elaborateness of its practice renders it capable of illustrating all the principles applicable, in various proportions, to other weapons.[1]

There is more variety of play between two weapons of the same kind than between dissimilar ones; many more actions are possible, for instance, with two sabres than with sabre against bayonet, with two small swords than between small and broad swords; therefore, in the enumeration of the fundamental factors of the art of fence, it will suffice to consider the rules of sword fencing as comprising all others.[2]

The "time, distance, and proportion" of the early Anglo-Italian masters of the sixteenth century are still as much as ever the first notions to be grasped. They are now called "time," "measure," and "guard." The very first principle of all fencing is obviously to keep the proper "measure," namely, to keep out of easy reach when on the defensive, and, conversely, never to deliver an attack without being within striking distance. This principle, which savours somewhat of a truism, is, however, much neglected by impetuous and inexperienced fencers. The method of gaining ground, of increasing and decreasing the measure in single combat, is consequently an important point to be noticed among ancient authors. Indeed, our perfect method of lunging and recovering, and only taking such steps as will preserve the same relative position of the feet and body as when on guard, was the last point to be fixed by masters.

The next principle is to keep proper "time," namely, first, to reduce the

---

[1] The duelling sword approaches very nearly to the foil in point of perfection, although any attempt to introduce the complicated play of the latter into a duel would probably be suicidal. The spadroon, or old-fashioned cut-and-thrust sword, lighter than our sabre and heavier than the duelling sword, allowed of still less variety. The broadsword and cutlass, again more ponderous and unwieldy, offer comparatively simple play, and as to the cavalry sabre, the lance, and the bayonet, their possible actions are even more restricted in number. In the case of some specialized ways of fencing, such as the old English "cudgelling" or "back swording," or the German student's "schlaeger," the question of distance or measure becomes of no importance. With the Spanish "navaja" and the South American "machete" most of the art depends on "timing."

[2] Readers happening to be unacquainted with the usual fencing terms, will easily find them in any modern treatise on the art. Mr. G. Chapman's small but comprehensive work on "Foil Fencing" is perhaps the best of that description written in the English language. The same may be said of Mr. Waite's and Captain Burton's treatises on the broadsword. On bayonet exercise there is an excellent work by Captain Hutton.

motions of weapon and body to the strictly necessary, both in number and extent, so as to employ the least possible time in attack and parry ; secondly, to balance those motions carefully with the adversary's, in order to seize at once the least opportunity and to reduce the number of chance hits to a minimum.   It will be seen that, unlike the methods of closing and increasing the measure, the question of time was one of the first to be clearly understood by masters of fence.

Being "on guard" is a notion which has greatly changed its meaning at various times.   In our days a man is said to be on guard when, holding his drawn weapon in front of him, he is in such a position as to be able to deliver every possible attack and come to every possible parry with the least expenditure of energy.   In olden times, as will be seen, the guard was far less comprehensive, for the simple reason that the idea of self-defence was entirely merged in that of offence to the enemy ; and it is only about two centuries ago that parries began to be considered as essentially different from attacks.   The word " guard," therefore, only applied to the preliminary action of an attack—like a position of "assault" in sword exercise—and there were often as many set guards as there were known ways of delivering hits.[1]

Under the word "guard," therefore, will be studied, first, the various kinds of attacks in the early days of fencing, and, later on, its more extended meaning in the perfected rapier and small sword play.   From very eccentric positions, when they were chiefly offensive, guards approximated to our modern attitude in proportion as the question of parrying came to be as much considered as that of attacking.

The definition of guard introduces the questions of " lines," " engagement," and " position of the hand."   These three factors determine the nature of the guard, as they do also that of all attacks and parries, and will consequently be used to explain the meaning of old-fashioned expressions.

The armed hand being kept, when on guard, in front of the body in a position approximately equidistant to all parts which have to be protected, and all parts of the adversary's body which may be attacked, it is convenient, for the purpose of definition, to consider those parts as being either above or below the hand, on the right or on the left of it.   An attack coming above the hand is said to come in a " high line;" below, in a " low line ; " outside the hand, in an " outside line ; " inside, in an " inside line."   Consequently, the expressions, high inside (or outside), low outside (or inside), applied to an attack, define its nature to a great extent.[2]

Every attack has its parry, and four parries, so formed that the length

---

[1] See, for instance, Viggiani's guards from the second to the seventh.

[2] Such a thing as a strictly vertical ascending or descending cut does not really occur, if the whole *trajectory* of the weapon is considered.

of the weapon crosses the " lines " of attack, are, strictly speaking, sufficient to meet the requirements of the defence.[1]

In each of the four lines, the attack and parry can be effected in two positions of the hand, namely, in " supination "—with the nails turned upwards —or in " pronation "—with the nails turned towards the ground. Fencing-masters also speak of the medium position, with the little finger turned towards the ground, but practically this middle position always partakes of either of the two above mentioned.[2]

The point reached or defended is defined according to the line as previously described, but the mechanism of the action differs according to the position of the hand. Consequently, there are eight natural ways of attacking and parrying, namely, two in each line : quarte and prime in the high inside ; sixth and tierce in the high outside ; septime and quinte in the low inside ; seconde and octave in the low outside.

The definition of a good guard has been given as one which offered more or less equal facilities for all attacks and parries ; it may now be added that a most obvious advantage arises from its being such as to close one of the lines. Consequently, there can be as many guards as there are parries, although, in modern days, carte, tierce, and sixth are almost exclusively used.[3]

With these premises it will be possible to give a definition of " engagement " which will not necessitate the notion of *joining* blades, and thus apply to broadsword as well as foil, to ancient swordsmanship as well as modern, to the Italian as well as to French or German schools.

A man may be said to be engaged in a particular guard in a given line when the relative position of his weapon to that of his adversary's is such as to defeat all attacks in that line unless some means be taken to displace the guard and *force* an entrance.

This can be done by *beating* or *binding ;* but the most obvious course

---

[1] Indeed, with all the heavier weapons, broadsword, bayonet, quarter-staff, &c., four parries in the four lines are all that are generally used.

[2] It may be objected that these distinctions do not apply to the broadsword and other cutting weapons except in the supposition that cuts be delivered with the back or false edge. If, however, it be considered that cuts may be delivered obliquely, ascending or descending in each line, as well as horizontally, the distinction between the two positions of the hand becomes obvious ; certain attacks, such as the head cut and cut at the fork, show instances of absolute " pronation " and " supination." Furthermore, in Italian and German sword-play, frequent use is made of the false edge for slicing cuts. It is practically true that, in some of the lines parries cannot be made in both positions, as it would involve the use of the false edge, but *theoretically* they are feasible ; some actions of that kind are even taught in Rowlandson's sword exercise. (*See Bibliography.*)

[3] For instance, in the French school, it is usual to engage carte or sixth ; in the Italian, carte or tierce ; with broadswords, tierce or seconde ; in the old fashion of " back swording," high prime ; in the German " Schlaeger " play, high prime or high septime.

is to change the line of attack by passing the point of the weapon under or over the adversary's armed hand, according as his guard is in a *high* or *low* line ; or by passing over or under the point, in other words *cutting over* or *under*. These two modes of action, as will be seen on a little consideration, apply to all weapons.

One of the most important points in fencing, and one, however, very much neglected by indifferent fencers, is to "keep the opposition" when delivering an attack in any line, namely, to close that line against a possible time thrust of the adversary. Most double hits are the result of a bad " opposition."

" Feints," or menacing in one line with the intention of attacking another, give the offending side some advantage in point of time, provided that they be so pronounced as to compel the defending side to take heed of them, uncovering, in consequence, the part selected for attack. But, on the other hand, the attack, if parried, places the offender at a momentary disadvantage for avoiding the repost.

There is another action, similar to feinting in its ultimate result (although not quite the same as regards its original intention), namely, the *deception* of simple, circular, or compound parries.

There are two ways of parrying. The first, or simple parry, closes the line in which the attack is made, and may be called " opposition ; " the other, or circular parry, forcibly brings back the opposite weapon in the same line, which it closes again.[1]

A universal rule concerning parries of any kind is that, at their termination, that is, at the moment when the adversary's stroke is to be finally thrown aside or stopped, the fort of the weapon should be opposed to the adversary's foible. This opposition, besides minimizing the effort necessary to counteract a hit by affording superiority in leverage, reduces the movements of the weapon and hand to the smallest practical limits.

All these various principles and actions form the basis of the Art of Fencing. Simple and obvious as they are, three hundred years of practical experiments were required for their reduction to a complete system.

In the course of this historical sketch the only points that will be looked for among the old authors are those that have just been defined, to wit :—

Measure and distance—the modes of advancing, retiring, lunging, passing, and traversing.

Time—the relative rapidity of movements of the body compared with those of the weapon.

---

[1] A third description, called " parry by yielding "—which is used to counteract binding—is really but a variety of the latter kind, since it brings the adversary's blade back to the same line again, as in the case of the circular parry, only the circular motion is performed with the fort, whilst the point remains more or less stationary.

Guards—the change in their character from one chiefly offensive to the present.

Attacks—methods of delivering cuts or thrusts, and the gradual simplification of body movements in their performance.

Parries—their ultimate distinction from time hits.

Feints—their comparative simplicity until later times.

Only those books marked in the Bibliography with an asterisk have been analyzed, being chosen as typical of a certain period or as containing some principles previously undiscovered. The arbitrary separation into periods, the first ranging from the early part of the sixteenth century to the first few years of the seventeenth, the second ending with the seventeenth century, and the third merging into our own times, is supported by the prevalence of leading characteristics : the first is the age of the Rapier, before the absolute predominance of the thrust over the cut ; during the second, the art of managing the point underwent a rapid improvement, the Rapier gradually gave way to the small sword, and a special French school developed distinct from the Italian ; the third is the age of the small sword, during which swordsmanship was brought to its present perfection.

More attention has naturally been devoted to the first two periods, as being the least known and the most interesting from an historical point of view. The latter period has been more carefully studied, at least by French authors, and admits of less original investigation. Writers on the Art of Fence have hardly ever found it worth while inquiring into the origins of the methods they expounded.

CHAPTER I.

PARADOXICAL as it seems, the development of the " Art of Fence " was the result of the invention of firearms. Its history need not therefore be taken up higher than the fifteenth century.

The very few writers who have devoted their attention to the subject, generally carry their investigations a great deal too far when they go back to antiquity and expect to find the origin of the science in the works of Polybius or Vegetius.

The ideas of the Greeks and the Romans on such a subject could not possibly persist through the Middle Ages. During that period the habit of wearing plate armour in battle, and, indeed, on most occasions out of doors, caused the sword to be regarded in the light of a weapon of offence only, sufficient reliance being placed on helmet and carapace for protection. On the other hand, unarmoured foot-men, in the impossibility of parrying or withstanding the heavy attacks of an iron-cased antagonist, had to learn either to avoid them by agility or overcome them by skill. So that it may be surmised that as long as the fashion of wearing complete armour prevailed —that is, before the general introduction of gunpowder into warfare—two very distinct schools of fighting existed side by side and with very little in common.

One was that of the noble warrior who cultivated his battering power in the lists and tournaments and the accuracy of his eye by tilting at the ring or quintain, but who otherwise learned little of what would avail him were he deprived of his protecting armour. Indeed, the chivalrous science never had anything but a retarding effect on the science of fence.

The other school, on the contrary, which was adapted to the weapons of the villain or burgess, was much more practical; it induced him to rely to a certain point on his weapons, as well as on general activity, for defence, instead of on the artificial resource of armour. The issue

of a personal combat between two knights was determined, in a great
measure, by the resistance of their armour and, ultimately, by their power
of *endurance*.[1] But a fight between two villains, armed only with clubs,
or with sword and buckler, necessarily admitted of a far greater display of
skill.

A universal feature of the history of all old schools of arms is that
they arose among the middle classes. Whilst the nobleman practised at

Fig. 3.—Knights contending under " the judgment
of God." From a miniature in the Bibliothèque Royale
at Brussels. Fifteenth century.

the barriers, the burgesses and artisans—who also owned weapons, though
of a less noble kind than the knightly sword and lance—learned their use
from jugglers, sword-dancers, or wrestlers, or some ancient veteran well
versed in all the cunning of the art.

Throughout the Middle Ages, when towns managed to obtain a certain
amount of independence, schools were founded where tuition in the art of
fighting with every kind of weapon used on foot could be obtained by any
one possessing the requisite pluck and sinews. On the Continent especially,
where the military value of the middle classes was their chief safeguard against
oppression, a number of " fighting guilds " arose, in which traditions of skill
were handed down through generations ; so that in the course of time it
came to pass that men of all classes who wished to acquire great proficiency
in the use of arms, found it necessary to resort to some such old school of
fence. When " knightly " habits disappeared and were replaced by " cava-

---

[1] See Oliver de la Marche, Froissart, and other chroniclers, *passim*.

lier" manners, the "gentleman" took his lesson in arms from some plebeian fighting-master.

This change in fashion corresponds chronologically with the rising of the sword, as the arm paramount, from the crowd of brutal armour-cracking weapons such as the schwerdt, the voulge, the halbert, the flail, and such like.

With the disuse of total armour, the superiority of the "point" asserted itself, and from the cultivation of the point arose fencing proper. Hence the result that the old fencing schools, which were at the outset altogether popular, ended by being devoted chiefly to the practice of the more aristocratic rapier.

Fig. 4.—The Long Sword and the Flail in the old German Schools.   From J. Sutor.

The materials necessary to the history of the art of fencing in England are very scanty.   Personal combats always were in high favour, both as a means of settling private quarrels and as a violent pastime congenial to the Teutonic character.   In war, our forefathers fought as stoutly with the sword as with all other weapons, but, until the latter part of the sixteenth century, only surmises as to the existence of any *definite system* of swordsmanship can be set forth.

Until that date, woodcuts and miniatures representing fighting or dancing swordsmen, and references to sword and buckler as national weapons, are all the data that can be gathered on the subject.

A kind of "Pyrrhic dance," or display of skill in the management of sword and buckler, was a favourite entertainment in Anglo-Saxon days. This martial exercise was still looked upon as a necessary accompaniment to all festivities in most

Fig. 5.—Sword Dance. From a MS. in the Cotton Library.   Cleopatra, C. viii. Ninth century.

parts of England as late as the fourteenth century, a fact which indicates that it could not have been otherwise than congenial or familiar to the Danish and Norman conquerors.

In most cases, however, the sword dance developed into sham combats, and often into real fights, for the delectation of merrymakers with sportive tendencies.

The distinction between such " cheironomy " and fencing is but slight, and these jugglers or sword-dancers are evidently early instances of those " sword-men " and masters of fence so often mentioned in Elizabethan literature.

These " sword-men," whether jugglers in sport or gladiators in earnest, were, of course, in great request as teachers of the art of handling weapons

dexterously and gracefully by the knightly youth anxious to appear to advantage in the lists, and also by the less aristocratic townsfolk and their prentices, in days when to go unarmed or unpractised was to court violence and robbery. Accordingly, the first regular schools were established by such men, and curious places they must have been!—each master following his particular fancy, and inculcating to all his

Fig. 6.—Sword and Buckler. From a MS. in the Royal Library.   No. 14, E. iii.   Thirteenth century.

pupils what he had found suitable to his particular build and habit.

They were dangerous dens, most of them, inviting the attendance of the pugnacious and dissolute, and had the very worst reputation from the first time they are heard of as institutions.

Men who professed to excel in the practice of fighting could hardly escape the suspicion of making better use of it, for their own ends, than merely teaching the use of the sword in battle or honourable combat ; and, on the other hand, the inducement was great, in those lawless days, to their patrons, noble and otherwise, to employ their capabilities for private vengeance.

People were shy of interfering too openly with these bullies, and many scenes of brutal revelry, as well as darker deeds, must have taken place in comparative safety behind the walls of fence schools.

In London, especially, the conduct of " sword-men " and their scholars was often so obnoxious that regal authority had to intervene, as, for instance, is shown by the following extract from one of those edicts[1] which prohibited at various periods the keeping of schools of arms, and forbade all loyal citizens to " Eskirmer au Bokeler." . . . . " Whereas it is customary for profligates to learn the art of fencing, who are thereby emboldened to commit the most unheard-of villainies, no such school shall be kept in the city for the future, upon penalty of forty marks for each offence.   And all the

---

[1] The fifth of Edward I., A.D. 1286.

Aldermen shall make a thorough search in their several wards for the detecting of such offenders, in order to bring them to justice and an exemplary punishment. And, as most of the aforesaid villainies are committed by foreigners, who from all parts incessantly crowd thither, it is therefore ordered that no person whatsoever, that is not free of the City, shall be suffered to reside therein."

The last part of this extract is remarkable as showing that foreigners were then, as now, to be found among the ardent devotees of the schools. Such edicts were naturally evaded ; fencing schools always reappeared, and were openly frequented. It is, however, probable that many of them, able to give some kind of guarantee for the good character of their attendants took their existence by license.

Fig. 7.—Sword and Buckler Play. Thirteenth century. From a MS. in
the Royal Library, No. 20. D. vi.

But besides these licensed schools, many others were kept surreptitiously, as is shown by such instances as the following, picked out from the records of the city of London :—

"On the 13th day of March, 1311, before Sir Richer de Refham, Mayor of London, appeared, among other delinquents :—Master Roger, le Skirmisour, attached for that he was indicted for keeping a fencing school for divers men, and for enticing thither the sons of respectable persons so as to waste and spend the property of their fathers and mothers upon bad practices." . . .

Notwithstanding the prejudice against them, schools of arms were a necessity for the bulk of a warlike nation, and they continued in existence as a matter of course.

Henry VIII., who was a great lover of all military sports, in order to encourage the practice of martial exercises, instead of suppressing, as his predecessors often attempted to do, the institution of fence schools altogether, incorporated all the most celebrated teachers of defence of the day in a company. And in order to mitigate the evil of independent sword-men, both in their professional teaching and in their private lives, altogether forbade anyone to teach the art of fence on any pretence, in any part of England, if he did not belong to the said company.

In a curious black-letter book entitled " The Third University of

England," and describing the schools and colleges of London in 1615, we find details of the institution of that "Normal" school of fence, and the ordeal that any would-be teacher had to undergo before being "passed" and permitted to call himself a master.

Fig. 8.—Plebii adolescentis in Anglia habitus. From Caspar Rutz's "Omne pene gentium Imagines," 1557. Showing the sword and hand buckler then in fashion.

Fig. 9.—The Long Sword.

"Henry the eighth made the Professors of this art a Company, or Corporation, by letters patent, wherein the art is intituled the Noble Science of Defence.

"The manner of proceeding of fencers in our schools is this : first, they, which desire to be taught at their admission are called Scholars, and, as they profit, they take degrees and proceed to be Provosts of Defence.

"That must be wonne by public triall of their proficiencie and their skill at certain weapons, which they call prizes, and in the presence and view of manie hundreds of people. And at their next and last prize, well and sufficientlie performed, they do proceed to be maisters of the science of defence, or maisters of fence, as we commonly call them. . . . None but such as have thus orderly proceeded by public act and trial, and have the approbation of the principal masters of their company, may profess."

The places where they exercised were commonly theatres, halls, or other enclosures sufficient to contain a number of spectators, as Ely Place in Holborn, the Bell Savage on Ludgate Hill, the Curtain in Hollywell, the Gray Friars within Newgate, Hampton Court, the Bull in Bishopsgate Street, the Clink, Duke's Place, Salisbury Court, Bridewell, the Artillery Gardens, &c.

Among those who distinguished themselves as amateurs in the science of defence are found Robert Greene,[1] " who plaide his maisters prize at Leadenhall," and Tarlton, the comedian, who " was allowed a master " on the 23rd of October, 1587.

This act must have had as an incidental result that of greatly raising the standard of ability among English teachers, and also, by making the " professed" masters jealous of their monopoly, that of reducing the number of interloping swordsmen, whose character partook as much of the " bravo " as of the teacher.

Stow[2] probably refers to members of this corporation when he remarks " the Art of Defence and use of weapons is taught by *professed* masters."

The author of the " Third University of England," who, as was mentioned before, wrote in 1615, mentions a weapon which only came into use in England towards 1580.

" There be manie professors of the science of defence and very skilfull men in teaching the best and most offensive use of verie many weapons, as the long sword, the back sword, *rapier* and dagger, case of *rapiers*, single *rapier*, the sword and buckler or targate," &c.

Although in his days the new-fangled " rapier" had become quite acclimatized in England, in Henry VIII.'s time, and indeed as late as the first years of Elizabeth's reign, it was only known to a few travelled courtiers as an outlandish weapon much used in Italy and Spain, and sometimes in France.

The national weapon was the "sword," with a plain cross hilt, and perhaps a half-ring guard. It was intended mainly for the cut, and usually accompanied by the hand buckler or targate.

Notwithstanding general restrictions, a great deal of obnoxious swaggering was common among the fencing gentry, who were as a rule looked upon with dislike and suspicion by the quieter portion of the community. The contemptuous name of " swashbuckler," applied to obtrusive devotees of the art of fence, graphically described these shady braves, and the clattering noise they created in their brawls, or even when merely swaggering down a narrow street.

It would seem that " swashbucklers " congregated mostly in West Smithfield, the London " Pré au Clercs," one of the few spots where their rioting could be tolerated.[3]

" They got their name," says Fuller,[4] " from swashing and making a noise

---

[1] These details are found in MS. No. 2530. xxvi. D. Sloanian Collection, Brit. Mus.
[2] " Survey of London " (1595).
[3] Justs and tournaments used formerly to take place in Smithfield.
[4] " Worthies of England."

on the buckler, and that of ruffian, which is the same as a swaggerer," because they tried to make the side swag or incline on which they were engaged.

"West Smithfield was formerly called Ruffian Hall, where such men usually met, casually or otherwise, to try mastery with sword and buckler; more were frightened than hurt, hurt than killed therewith, it being accounted unmanly to strike beneath the knee, or with the point. But since that desperate traitor Rowland Yorke first used thrusting with rapiers, swords and bucklers are misused."

Smithfield is also mentioned by Ben Jonson, in the introduction to "Bartholomew Fair," as the common resort of sword and buckler men.

Between the years 1570 and 1580, the rapier began to make its appearance, and being much more practical for individual fighting than the clumsy old-fashioned sword, never complete as a weapon without the buckler, the latter rapidly went out of fashion. But the foreign weapon was not admitted, and the old one discarded, without the usual murmurs and regrets.

Fig. 10.—Sword and Buckler in Elizabethan days. From Grassi.

"Sword and buckler fight begins to grow out of use," says a sturdy Briton, in "The Two Angry Women of Abingdon,"[1] "I am sorry for it, I shall never see good manhood again; if it be once gone, this poking fight of rapier and dagger will come up; then a tall man, that is a courageous man, and a good sword and buckler man, will be spitted like a cat or a rabbit."

Stow's "Annals"[2] contain a passage describing the fashion of sword and buckler fights and its disappearance soon after the importation of the foreign custom of wearing rapiers :—

"And whereas until the twelfth or thirteenth yeare of Queene Elizabeth, the auncient English fight of Sword and Buckler was only in use, the buckler being but a foot, with a pike of four or five inches long; then they beganne to make them full half an ell broad with sharp pikes ten or twelve inches long, wherewith they meant either to breake the swordes of their enemies, if it hitte upon the pike, or els sodainly to runne within them and stabbe and thrust their bucklers with the pike into the face, arme, or body of their adversary. But this continued not long, every haberdasher then sold bucklers. For,

---

[1] A comedy of Henry Porter, written in 1599.
[2] "Annals," continued by Edmund Howes.

shortly after, began long Tuckes and long Rapiers, and hee was helde the greetest gallant that had the deepest ruff and longest Rapier. The offence to the eye of the one, and the hurt that came unto the life of the subject by the other caused Her Majesty to make proclamation against them both, and to place selected grave citizens at every gate, to cut the Ruffes and breake the Rapier's poynts of all passengers that exceeded a yeard in length of their Rapier, and a nayle of a yard in depth of their ruffes."

Judging by these and other passages taken from various annals and like sources of information on that period, it appears certain that although " tucks " and the practice of " foyning " had been in favour some forty years on the Continent, they only became common in England during the first quarter of Elizabeth's reign. Stow is not the only authority who fixes this date. Camden,[1] speaking also of the introduction of rapier fights into this country, attributes it to Rowland Yorke's exploits with that weapon :— " Yorcus ille Londinensis, homo distincto ingenio et præcipiti audacia, suo tempore inter sicarios celebris, quod feralem illam rationem in duellis punctim petendi, summa cum audaciæ admiratione, primus in Angliam intulerit, cum Angli latioribus cæsim depugnarent, et vel punctim, vel infra cingulum ferire minime virile existimarent."

This statement is corroborated by Abraham Darcie,[2] who recounts how " Rowland Yorke, a desperado who betrayed Devanter to the Spaniards in 1587, was the first who brought into England that wicked and pernicious fashion to fight with a Rapier called a Tucke, only fit for the thrust."

" Rapier " was the name given at that time to the Spanish weapon. A Frenchman called his arm, " espée ; " an Englishman, " sword." Both, when they talked of the Spaniard's sword, called it a rapier.

In France, the word " Rapière " soon became a contemptuous term, signifying a sword of disproportionate length,—in fact, the weapon of a bully.

Not so, however, in England, where the word has always meant, since its introduction into the language, a sword especially convenient for thrusting, and adorned with a more or less elaborate guard. As the Spaniards who frequented Mary's court had worn such weapons, many of which were brought over in the following reign as warlike trophies, it naturally enough followed that the word " rapier," meaning the " Spanishe sworde," [3] should have been applied to all swords used for thrusting in the Spanish style.

The principles of this novel system of fencing seem to have been taught for the first time by disciples of the great Carranza. Many

---

[1] " Annals." [2] " Annals of Elizabeth."
[3] Gile du Guez (Dewes), " Introductorie for to lerne to rede, to pronounce and to speke French trewly." London, 1530.

travelled Englishmen, on their return from Spain, recounted the fame that this " father of the science of arms " had acquired in his own country, and caused a general thirst for instruction in this new and deadly science. Spanish teachers came over the seas, and laid the foundation of the new fashion in arms, which was soon to relegate the comparatively barbarous sword and buckler to the Scottish Highlands, where it developed independently into what formed the basis of our English broadsword play.

It may, therefore, be inferred that the science of fence with the " foyning " rapier first came into this country from Spain ; but, on the other hand, the word " tuck "—tucke, stuck, or stock—applied to this new weapon, is distinctly of French origin, being merely the English phonetic for " estoc." [1]

In the Middle Ages, the estoc was carried on horseback, attached to the right side of the saddle. It was a long narrow sword, with a blade generally more and less quadrangular, and was devised specially for thrusting in the event of the lance being lost or broken. The sword proper was carried on the horseman's girdle.

The name estoc, or estocade, was applied later to that kind of weapon which, as we have seen above, was universally called rapier in England, namely, a straight sword, used for cut and thrust.

So, after all, it is somewhat difficult to say with any kind of certainty whence the new fashion primarily came.

Be it as it may, the practice of " foyning " had developed to a high degree on the Continent before the time when it was first heard of in England. It is not to be wondered at that the fashion having once taken a footing on our soil, should have spread with great rapidity, first among gentlemen and courtiers, and after a short time among all swordsmen. Proficiency with rapier and dagger was eagerly cultivated, as the fashionable weapons were admitted in most schools of arms throughout England.

In London especially, Italian and Spanish teachers were the rage, much to the disgust of the old-established English masters of defence. The names, and to a certain extent the biographies, of three of the most celebrated foreign teachers were handed down to posterity by a certain George Silver, gentleman, in a little book, now exceedingly rare, intituled " Paradoxe of Defence " (1599).

In this very curious opuscule, which shall be quoted at length further on, Silver assumes the position of champion to the old English masters of fence, against the popular infatuation for foreign teachers.

From his general tone of bitter vituperation it seems clear that the

---

[1] An old French word, from the Frankish " stock," a pointed straight weapon.

monopoly of the corporation chartered by Henry VIII. had lapsed. Had it been still in vigour, no difficulty could have been experienced in keeping foreigners out of competition by means of the simplest agreement and co-operation among English masters.

It is well known, and a sad fact, that in no profession is jealousy displayed with more bitterness than among fencing-masters, and this spirit is most quaintly displayed on almost every page of the " Paradoxe of Defence," especially in the " Briefe sketche of three Italian teachers of Offence," which concludes the little volume :

" I write this, not to disgrace the dead, but to shew their impudent boldnesse and insufficiency in performance of their profession when they were living : that from henceforth this briefe note may be a remembrance and warning of what I wist.

" There were three Italian teachers of Offence in my time. The first was Signior Rocko : the second was Jeronimo, that was Signior Rocko his boy, that taught gentlemen in the Blacke-Fryers, as usher to his maister insteed of a man. The third was Vincentio.

" This Signior Rocko came into England about some thirteen yeares past : he taught the Noblemen and Gentlemen of the Court; he caused some of them to weare leaden soales in their shoes, the better to bring them to nimblenesse of feet in their fight. He disbursed a great summe of money for the lease of a faire house in Warwick Lane, which he called his Colledge, for he thought it great disgrace for him to keepe a Fence ' Schoole,' he being then thought to be the onely famous Maister of the Art of Armes in the whole world. He caused to be fairely drawne and set round about the schoole all the Noblemens and Gentlemens Armes that were his schollers, and, hanging right under their Armes, their Rapiers, Daggers, Gloves of Male and Gantlets. Also he had benches and stooles, the roome being verie large, for Gentlemen to sit about his Schoole to behold his teaching.

" He taught none commonly under twentie, fortie, fifty, or an hundred pounds. And because all things should be verie necessary for the Noblemen and Gentlemen, he had in his schoole a large square table, with a greene carpet, done round with a verie brode rich fringe of gold, alwaies standing upon it a verie faire standish covered with crimson velvet, with inke, pens, pen-dust and sealing waxe, and quiers of verie excellent fine paper, gilded, readie for the Noblemen and Gentlemen (upon occasion) to write their letters, being then desirous to follow their fight, to send their men to dispatch their businesse.

" And to know how the time passed he had in one corner of his Schoole, a Clocke, with a verie faire large diall; he had within that Schoole a roome the which he called his privie schoole, with manie weapons therein, where he did teach his schollers his secret fight, after he had perfectly taught them their rules. He was verie much loved in the Court.

" There was one Austen Bagger, a verie tall Gentleman of his handes, not standing much upon his skill, but carrying the valiant hart of an Englishman, upon a time, being merrie amongst his friendes, said he would go and fight with Signior Rocco; presently went to Signior Rocco his house in the Blackefriers and called to him in this manner:

" Signior Rocco, thou that art thought to be the onelye cunning man in the world with thy weapon, thou that takest upon thee to hit anie Englishman with a thrust upon anie button,[1] thou that takest upon thee to come over the seas to teach the valiant Noblemen and Gentlemen of England to fight, thou cowardly fellow, come out of thy house, if thou dare for thy life. I am come to fight with thee.

" Signior Rocco, looking out at a window, perceiving him in the street to stand readie with his Sword and Buckler; with his two hand Sword drawne, with all speed ran into the street, and manfully let flie at Austen Bagger, who most bravelye defended himselfe, and presently closed with him, and stroke up his heeles, and cut him over the breech, and trode upon him, and most grievously hurt him under his feet: yet in the end Austen of his good nature (!) gave him his life and then left him.

" This was the first and last fight that ever Signior Rocco made, saving once at Queene Hithe, he drew his Rapier upon a waterman, when he was thoroughly beaten with Oares and Stretchers: but the odds of their weapons were as great against his Rapier, as was his two hand sword against Austen Bagger's Sword and Buckler, therefore in that fray he was to be excused.

" Then came in Vincentio and Jeronimo. They taught Rapier-fight at the Court, at London and in the Countrey, by the space of seven or eight yeares or thereabouts.

" These two Italian Fencers, especially Vincentio, said that Englishmen were strong men but had no cunning, and they would go backe too much in their fight, which was a great disgrace unto them. Upon these words of disgrace my brother Toby Silver and my selfe, made challange against them both to play with them at the single Rapier, Rapier and Dagger, the single Dagger, the single Sword, the Sword and Target, the Sword and Buckler, and two hand Sword, the Staffe, battell Axe, and Morris Pike, to be played at the Bell Savage upon the Scaffold, when he that went in his fight faster backe than he ought, shold be in danger to breake his necke off the Scaffold. We caused to that effect five or sixe score bils of challenge to be printed, and set up from Southwarke to the Tower, and from thence through London unto Westminster, we were at the place with all these weapons at the time appointed,

---

[1] " . . . the very butcher of a silk button."—" Romeo and Juliet."

within a bow shot of their Fence-Schoole : manie gentlemen of good accompt carried manie of the bils of challenge unto them, telling them that now the Silvers were at the place appointed, with all their weapons, looking for them, and a multitude of people there to beholde the fight, saying unto them : now come and go with us (you shall take no wrong), or else you are shamed for ever.

" Do the gentlemen what they could, these gallants would not come to the place of triall.

" I verily thinke their cowardly feare to answere this challenge had utterly shamed them indeede, had not the Maisters of defence of London, within two or three daies after, bene drinking of bottel ale, hard by Vincentio's Schoole ; and as they were comming by, the Maisters of defence did praye them to drinke with them ; but the Italians, being verie cowardly were afraide, and presently drew their rapiers.

" There was a pretie wench standing by that loved the Italians. She ran with outcrie into the street, helpe, helpe, the Italians are like to be slaine : the people with all speede came running into the house, and with their cappes, and such things as they could get, parted the fraie ; for the English Maisters of Defence meant nothing lesse than to soile their handes upon these faint hearted fellowes.

" The next morning after, all the Court was filled that the Italian teachers of Fence had beaten all the Maisters of Defence in London who set upon them in a house together. This wan the Italian Fencers credit againe who therby got much, still continuing their false teaching to the end of their lives.

" This Vincentio proved himself a stout man not long before he died, that it might be seene in his life time he had bene a gallant, and therefore no marvaile, he tooke upon him so highly to teach Englishmen to fight, and to set forth bookes of the feates of Armes. Upon a time at Wels, in Somer-setshire, as he was in great braverie amongst manie gentlemen of good accompt, with great boldnesse he gaue out speeches that he had bene thus manie yeares in England, and since the time of his first comming, there was not yet one Englishman that could once touch him at the Single Rapier, or Rapier and Dagger.

" A valiant gentleman being there amongst the rest, his English hart did rise, to heare this proude boaster, and secretly sent a messenger to one Bartholomew Bramble, a friend of his, a very tall man both of his hand and person, who kept a schoole of Defence in that town.

" The messenger by the way made the Maister of Defence acquainted with the mind of the gentleman that sent for him, and of all that Vincentio had said.

" This maister of defence presently came, and amongst all the gentlemen, with his cap off, prayed Maister Vincentio that he would be pleased to take a quart of wine of him.

" Vincentio, verie scornefully looking upon him, said unto him ; Wherefore should you give me a quart of wine ?

" Marie, Sır, said he, because I heare you are a famous man at your weapon.

" Then presently said the gentleman that sent for the Maister of Defence :

" Maister Vincentio, I pray you bid him welcome, he is a man of your profession.   My profession ? said Vincentio, what is my profession ?

" Then said the gentleman, he is a Maister of the noble Science of Defence.

" Why, said Maister Vincentio, God made him a good man.   But the Maister of Defence wold not thus leaue him, but prayed him again he wold be pleased to take a quart of wine with him.   Then said Vincentio, I haue no need of thy wine ; then said the Maister of Defence : Sir, I haue a schoole of Defence in this towne, will it please you to go thither ?   Thy schoole, said Maister Vincentio ?   what shall I do at thy schoole ?   Play with me, (said the Maister) at the Rapier and Dagger, if it please you.   Play with thee, said Maister Vincentio ?   if I play with thee, I will hit thee 1. 2. 3. 4 thrusts in the eie together.   Then, said the Maister of Defence, if you can, do so, it is the better for you, and the worse for me, but surely I can hardly beleeve that you can hit me : but yet once againe I hartily pray you, good Sir, that you will go to my Schoole and play with me.   Play with thee, said Maister Vincentio (verie scornefully) by God me scorne to play with thee.

" With that word scorne, the Maister of Defence was verie much moved, and up with his great English fist and stroke Maister Vincentio such a boxe on the eare that he fell over and over, his legges just against a Butterie hatch, whereon stood a great blacke Jacke : the Maister of Defence, fearing the worst against Vincentio his rising, catcht the blacke Jacke into his hand, being more than halfe full of beere.   Vincentio lustily start up, laying his hand upon his dagger, and with the other hand pointed with his finger, saying, Verie well : I will cause thee to lie in the gaile for this yeare 1. 2. 3. 4 yeares.   And, well, said the Maister of Defence, since you will drinke no wine, will you pledge me in Beere ?   I drinke to all the cowardlie knaves in England, and I thinke thee to be the veriest coward of them all ; with that he cast all the Beere upon him.

" Notwithstanding Vincentio having nothing but his guilt Rapier and Dagger about him, and the other for his defence the blacke Jacke, would not at that time fight it out.   But the next day he met with the Maister of Defence in the streete and said unto him, You remember how misused a me yesterday, you were to blame, me be an excellent man, me teach you how to thrust two foote further than anie Englishman, but first come you with me : then he brought him to a Mercers shop, and said to the Mercer, let me see your best silken pointes, the Mercer did presently shew him some of seaven groats a dozen, then he payeth fourteene groats for two dozens and said to the Maister of Defence, there is one dozen for you, and here is another for me.

" This was one of the valiantest fencers that came over the seas, to teach Englishmen to fight, and this was one of the manliest frayes that I haue heard of that ever he made in England, wherin he shewed himselfe a farre better man in his life than in his profession he was.

" He set forth in print a booke for the use of the Rapier and Dagger, the which he called his practise, I haue read it over, and because I finde therein no true rule for the perfect teaching of true fact, neither sence or reason for due proofe thereof . . . . ."

Here Silver proceeds to run down the book in question with all the animosity of a competitor in an overcrowded field against a successful member of the profession.

The notice concludes with an anecdote about Jeronimo, son of the unfortunate Rocco.

" Jeronimo this gallant was valiant, and would fight indeed, and did, as you shall heare. He being in a Coch with a wench that he loved well, there was one Cheefe, a verie tall man in his fight naturall English, for he fought with his Sword and Dagger, and in Rapier fight had no skill at all. This Cheefe having a quarrell to Jeronimo, overtooke him upon the way : himselfe being on horse backe, did call to Jeronimo, and bad him come forth out of the Coch or he would fetch him, for he was come to fight with him.

" Jeronimo presently went forth of the Coch and drew his Rapier and Dagger, put himselfe into his best ward or ' Stocata,' which ward was taught by himselfe and Vincentio, and by them best allowed of, to be the best ward to stand upon in fight for life, either to assault the enemie, or stand and watch his comming, which ward, it would seeme, he ventured his life upon ; but however, with all the fine Italienated skill Jeronimo had, the Cheefe with his Sword, within two thrustes ran him through the bodie and slue him. Yet the Italian teachers will say that an Englishman cannot thrust straight with a sword, because the hilt will not suffer him to put the forefinger over the Crosse, nor to put the thumbe upon the blade, nor to hold the pummell in the hand, whereby we are of necessitie to hold fast the handle in the hand : by reason whereof we are driven to thrust both com- passe and short, whereas with the Rapier they can thrust both straight and much further than we can with the Sword, because of the hilt, and these be the reasons they make against the Sword."

Fencing schools under Elizabeth, whether kept by foreigners or

Englishmen, evidently bore a far better character than in the preceding ages. Masters of note were greatly patronized by the nobility, and some of them, as has been seen, were set up on a very grand footing.

Yet they seem to have retained in the estimation of most people something of their old-established evil repute, as may be noticed in Fleetwood's —the Recorder's—letter to Burghley,[1] and in the violent attack on the fencing schools in Gosson's " School of Abuse."

One may likewise quote on this subject a few lines of Dekker's " A Knight's Conjuring," written in 1607 :—

" . . . . hee—' the devil '—was the first who kept a fence school, when Cayn was alive, and taught him that imbroccado by which he kild his brother; since which time he has made ten thousand free schollers as cunning as Cayn. At Sword and Buckler little Davy was nobody to him, and as for Rapier and Dagger the Germane[2] may be his journeyman."

Fig. 11.—Sword and Hand Buckler. Fourteenth century. From a MS. in Royal Library of Munich.

There are many reasons to believe that the art of fencing made very little progress in the right direction until about the middle of the sixteenth century ; but, in any case, investigation is baffled by the absence of any books relating to the subject. The oldest work extant however—that of Lebkommer[3]—describes very fairly the usual methods of fighting current during the fifteenth century ; wrestling and leaping were, according to it, important elements of the fencing of those days.

Nevertheless, the mere existence at any period of a definite pattern of sword in common use throughout a country, supposes a definite system of fencing, and, therefore, schools must have existed long before the appearance of the first treatises on the art.

Indeed, at all times and in all countries, some institution of the kind

---

[1] 1577.

[2] Little Davy was evidently an English Master of Fence ; the " Germane " may refer to Meyer (see Biblio. 1570) or some foreign teacher established in London.

[3] See Biblio., 1529 (German). The works of Pons, Torre, Moncio, and Roman, do not seem to be extant.

must have arisen as soon as it became possible for classes who had not to look upon fighting as their usual occupation, to exist in communities.

As Germany can boast of the oldest existing book on the subject, it will be best to commence by noticing the ancient Teutonic " Fechtschulen," and to leave England for the moment.

No doubt all " fighting schools " on the Continent developed in a manner similar to the old English schools of arms, but their connection with regular corporations is of much older date.

The oldest of these corporations is undoubtedly the " Bürgerschaft von St. Marcus von Lowenberg."

In the course of the fourteenth century some enterprising and redoubtable " fighting-masters " seem to have clubbed together and monopolized the right of teaching this art.   They apparently succeeded in maintaining this monopoly, for anyone attempting to teach fencing in Germany was sooner or later confronted by the heads of this " Fechter-Gilde "—one captain and five masters—and offered the alternative of fighting them in turns or together, with the undoubted result of being cut to pieces,—or of entering the association under their rule.   The result of this policy was that the Fraternity of St. Mark, or Marxbrüder, became the rage, and their headquarters, in Frankfurt-am-Main, a sort of university where numerous aspiring swordsmen came to earn their degrees in arms.   By-and-by, as their reputation extended throughout Germany, all those who wished to set up a school of arms came of their own accord to Frankfort during the autumn fairs, and offered themselves as candidates for the " Brüderschaft."

The ordeal was invested with a certain amount of solemnity.   The captain, and as many of the Marxbrüder as were present in Frankfort, fought with the applicant on a scaffold erected in the market-place.   If the latter sustained the test creditably, the captain, with much pomp, struck him crosswise on the hips with the sword of ceremony, and the new member, after placing two golden florins on the broad blade of the sword, as a fee for his reception, was entitled to learn the various secrets of the brotherhood concerning the management of the sword and other weapons.

The master who had thus graduated henceforth enjoyed the privilege of bearing the heraldic golden lion of the " Marxbrüder," and of teaching the art of fence throughout Germany.

The fraternity had long enjoyed by prescription many privileges which were recognized by letters patent by the Emperor Frederick at Nürnberg in 1480, and renewed in 1512 at Cologne by Maximilian I., in 1566 at Augsburg by Maximilian II., and in 1579 at Prague by Rudolf II.

Fencing being thus imperially honoured, its practice spread with greater and greater rapidity throughout Germany, and, notwithstanding the old-established monopoly of the " Marxbrüder," new associations of fencers formed themselves.

The most famous of these societies, and the only one which ever rivalled the " Marxbrüder," was that of the " Federfechter,"[1] who were the first to adopt the Spanish and Italian sword-play, and to make a free use of the point.

The " Federfechter," while taking care to be proficient in the use of the two-handed " Schwerdt," looked upon the " Feder " as their distinctive weapon, and challenged the " Marxbrüder," wherever they met them, " to fight honourably with them, cut *and thrust.*"

Fig. 12 —From Meyer, 1570. A Marxbruder instructing a Pupil.
This guard is similar to the fourth of Viggiani (see fig. 37).

The usual issue of a combat between the ponderous old-fashioned schwerdt and the swift-thrusting rapier could not have been otherwise than favourable to the latter, which gradually came to be universally adopted even by the " Marxbrüder." About the year 1590 there was no longer any observable difference between the modes of fighting of either society.

The Association of " Federfechter " was first founded in Mecklenburg, from whose duke it received its cognizance, a griffin sable, and its charter as the Guild of " Freyfechter von der Feder zum Greifenfels."

The two great guilds ended by sharing alike the monopoly of the

[1] They derived their name from the " Feder," a slang word for the " Rapier "—the fashion of which began to spread about 1570.

fencing art, their only distinction being, that the head-quarters of the former remained at Frankfort, whilst that of the latter was established at Prague. The "Oberhauptmänner" of both remained at the Imperial Court as their representatives and advocates. They were accounted persons of very great importance and "ex officio" arbiters on all matters of honour and questions of fighting.

The same customs and principles were followed by Marxbrüder and Federfechter, and they displayed an equal observance of honour and discipline. Indeed, any member of the guild who transgressed the law, or acted against the honourable customs of the corporation, or brought dishonour on himself and discredit on the guild, was proclaimed unfit to be a master, publicly deprived of his sword, and struck out of the rolls of " an admirable community."

All the most celebrated masters of the art arose from either of these communities. There are notices, however, of another society, " Lux Brüder,"—the Fraternity of St. Luke,—but little is known about it. It was one of those associations which never gathered sufficient strength to compete against the Marxbrüder. The Luxbrüder are not heard of later than the fifteenth century, but it is believed that from them are descended the so-called "Klopffechter." These were a species of gladiators who, until as late as the beginning of the seventeenth century, wandered from fair to fair and displayed their skill in prize fights, a purpose for which they were often engaged by great lords on festive occasions.

Thus, on the main points, the history of the Teutonic fencing communities bears much resemblance to that of the English sword-men of the same period.

Societies similar to that of the " Marxbrüder " in their heyday, holding by prescription or by charter a monopoly of the right to teach the science of arms, existed also in Spain and in Italy.

The gladiatorial institutions—which survive to a certain extent in the national pastime of bull fighting—held a firmer footing in Spain after the fall of the Roman Empire than in any other province. The schools of fence so scientifically conducted by the " Lanistæ " in the old days of Rome, remained in Spain under altered conditions through the numerous barbarian invasions, and were congenial enough to the customs of the Moors to live through their reign.

The management of spear and shield, of sword and buckler, of axe and poniard, of short sword or braquemars, of falchion, and of all the varieties of hastate weapons, were taught by well-known masters. The schools of arms of Leon, Toledo, and Valladolid are mentioned by ancient authors as being much frequented, but the name of no teachers previous to Pons of Perpignan and Pedro de Torre, whom that great oracle on the science of

arms, Don Luis Pacheco de Narvaez, mentions as having taught during the
latter part of the fifteenth century, and printed in 1474 books which
unfortunately have long since disappeared.

Notwithstanding the want of exact data on the subject, the numerous
incidental references found in copious writers, such as Narvaez, Marcelli, and
Pallavicini, make it clear that the profession of fencing-master in Spain
during the fifteenth and sixteenth centuries was one which required serious
preparation and unusual physical qualifications, and that a society of such
masters exercised the monopoly of teaching and admitting candidates.

Among some legal records still to be found in the Hotel de Ville at
Perpignan, there exists an account—in the shape of an official document
testifying to the proficiency of some aspirant to the degree of master of arms
—of the ordeal which had to be undergone before it could be conferred.
The document of course was written in days when Perpignan was Spanish
territory, and may be taken as a fair example of the customs in force in the
early part of the sixteenth century.

The carefully definite Latin terms which are used show that the institution was of old standing and well recognized.

The art of fence is described as " Ars Palestrinæ ; " the beginner, the
"tyro" or student, the undergraduate in short, is called " Lusor in Arte
Palestrinæ."   After a given period and an examination in the use of a variety
of weapons—five or seven in number—the " lusor " proceeded to the degree
of " licentiatus in arte et usu Palestrinæ," which corresponds to that of
bachelor in the universities, or of "provost" in schools of arms.   Lastly,
when he had acquired the use, theoretically and practically, of all weapons,
the " licentiatus " assumed the dignity of " Master of Arms," or as the Latin
document has it, " Lanista, seu magister in usu Palestrinæ."

The fully-privileged master was a very great person indeed, on all
accounts, and very full of his importance, if any judgment as to his character
can be formed from the ponderous books he subsequently indited.

There was certainly some justification for his conceit, considering the
ordeal he had gone through, having had to fight the whole board of his
examiners, first separately, " ingeniose et subtiliter," and then all together,
" simul et semel."

A certain moral value was attached to the ceremony of installing a
master ; he was expected to swear "super signo sanctæ crucis facto de
pluribus ensibus" never to use his skill for any but the most laudable
purposes—a chivalrous undertaking, it must be said, as much honoured in the
breach as in the observance.

It will be seen that in Italy the oath administered on such occasions
was restricted to the more practical limits of never using the skill about to be
imparted against the teacher himself.

Beyond the fact that there were regular and well-known schools of arms in Spain during the fifteenth century, and the fact that Spanish bands—the best trained in the use of arms of all European troops at that period—over-ran Italy and the Low Countries during the sixteenth century, and therefore may have diffused the Spanish methods of fencing in those parts, there are no reasons, notwithstanding the current opinion to that effect, to ascribe to Spain the birthplace of the art.

The subdivision of Italy into a great number of independent states, constantly at war with each other, fostered too much jealousy between different provinces ever to admit of any widespread associations of masters. Every town had its school, and each school followed a particular fashion according to the taste of the owner thereof. Nothing could be less conducive to improvement, and accordingly, until Marozzo's days, when Italy took the lead on matters of fencing, the Italian schools could not boast of any great superiority. Towards the year 1530, however, a kind of privileged association undoubtedly existed, which had its headquarters in Bologna, and Achille Marozzo for chief.

It is somewhat curious that in France, fencing schools of any kind are not heard of previous to the sixteenth century; and even, during the latter part of the same century, the most important ones were kept by Italians.

It will therefore be better to begin by analyzing the works of the four leading Italian authors of the sixteenth century, namely, Marozzo, Agrippa, Grassi, and Viggiani, and then examine the work of Carranza, "the father of the science of arms" in Spain, and notice their followers, Henri de Sainct Didier in France, Meyer in Germany, and Saviolo in England.

CHAPTER II.

MANCIOLINO and Marozzo, who may be taken as typical of the masters of that period, afford a curious insight into the notions of swordsmanship prevalent in Europe during the fifteenth and the beginning of the sixteenth century. It seems impossible to discern a general leading principle or settled method in the works of that period : each individual master taught merely a collection of tricks that he had found, in the course of an eventful life, to be generally successful in personal encounters, and had practised until the ease and quickness acquired in their execution made them very dangerous to an unscientific opponent.

All these tricks—for any other word can hardly be applied to modes of attack and defence so utterly contrary to all our principles—were dubbed with quaint, and even fanciful names.

Manciolino's text is so much filled up by wise dissertations on the rules of honour and way of picking and deciding quarrels in a gentlemanly manner, that very little actual " fencing " has found its way into his little work. Of the four guards therein described, the only one recognizable as being intended for any definite purpose, is a " high guard " somewhat similar to the modern head parry.

The other three bear a very distant resemblance to " quinte," " tierce," and " octave." All that can be gathered concerning the attacks " ferite " is, that they were delivered on the march. No distinction seemed to be made between cut and thrust, the great aim was merely to place oneself in such a position relative to the adversary that either mode of striking was possible.

Marozzo's book, however, published five years later, fixes in a more precise manner the systems in favour before the superiority of the thrust over the cut became a matter of principle.

Marozzo is generally looked upon as the first writer of note on the art of fencing. It would be perhaps wiser to consider him as the greatest teacher of the old school,[1] the rough and undisciplined swordsmanship of which depended as much on dash and violence and sudden inspiration as on carefully cultivated skill.

Marozzo was a Bolognese, but he kept his school in Venice.[2] His reputation was very great, to judge from the numerous editions of his works, five of which were published between 1536 and 1615.

No master of fence is likely to have written a book until he had acquired a widespread reputation as a teacher, and therefore it may be supposed that it was late in life that he undertook his " Opera Nova," the second edition of which appeared in 1550, and the third in 1568. It is presumable that he died between those dates, as the dedication of the third edition—by the painter Giulio Fontana, to Don Giovanni Manriche—speaks of Marozzo as one who " was, as the world knows, a most perfect master in this most noble of arts," who " had trained an immense number of valiant disciples, and lastly written this work for the benefit of the public."

What was said of Manciolino can be repeated of Marozzo, with this difference, that the latter has much more to say on the subject.

Notwithstanding the little value of his teaching from our modern point of view, his work is remarkably in advance of any other at that period, and foreshadows the superiority of the Italian schools.

The " Opera Nova, Chiamata Duello overo fiore dell' Armi, &c., composta per Achille Marozzo, Gladiatore, Bolognese," follows on the whole a pretty rational " progression."

After an invocation to the Holy Virgin and the " Cavaliere San Giorgio," the " Maestro " places a sword into the " Disepolo's " hand and explains the various ways of holding it, and likewise the advantage of passing one or two fingers over the quillons in order to obtain easier mastery over the movements of the blade.[3]

He then proceeds to explain the different uses of the " falso filo " and " dritto filo,"[4] a distinction which was much more important with the double-edged weapon of those days than it is now. Guards were then distinguished by the relative position of the edges. What is now called a guard in the inside line—such as carte, for instance—was distinguished as being in " dritto filo," or right edge ; *vice versâ*, one in the outside line—

---

[1] Towards the later years of his life he was elected "Maestro generale de l'arte de l'armi," a title corresponding to the " Hauptman " of the " Marxbruder."

[2] Most of the treatises that appeared in Italy during the sixteenth century were printed in Venice.

[3] It must be remembered that in all the plates of Marozzo's book, although the sword is represented with a plain hilt, the actual sword worn in his days had pas d'anes and counterguards for the protection of the fingers—see also the last chapter.

[4] False edge and right edge.

like sixte—was a guard in " falso filo," or false edge.   This on the whole
was a fair classification, well adapted to a double-edged weapon mainly used
for cutting.

The master then draws on the wall a diagram illustrating all the cuts,
from the right and left sides—" mandritti" and "roversi."   All cuts
delivered from the right, consequently on the adversary's left side, and with
the right edge, were called " mandritti."[1]   A mandritta could be either—

Mandritto " tondo " or circular, delivered horizontally.
　　,,　　　" fendente " or vertical, downwards.
　　,,　　　" montante " or vertical, upwards.
　　,,　　　" sgualembrato " or oblique, downwards.

All cuts delivered from the left with the right edge—that is, on the
adversary's right side—were called " roversi," and could be, in a similar
manner, " tondo," " sgualembrato," " fendente," or " montante."

Frequent use was also made of the false edge for cuts, generally
directed to the wrists and knees, which were called " falso dritto " or " falso
manco " according as they were delivered from the right or left.   The
pupil practised these cuts in front of the figure.   Marozzo does not speak
of this exercise as an innovation of his; in fact, it was but an improvement
on the old-fashioned " pel."

From this elaborate nomenclature it is obvious that the manner of
using the edge *for offensive action* was well understood, and that little
progress has been made since then in that department of fencing.   This
fact is quite in accordance with the favourite theory then prevalent that a
sword was made chiefly for cutting and slicing, and that the safest way of
fighting was to try and anticipate the enemy in the attack.

When the pupil, who, it seems, generally took his first lessons in
private, was proficient in the variety of cuts, he proceeded to learn his
guards, no special attention being paid to the thrust.

A curious point about all books of fence written during the sixteenth
century, is that although the word " parry " is continually used, not a single
parry is ever defined.   The principle on which the masters of that period
founded their practice, was evidently that all attacks, if they could not be
warded off by a buckler, a cloak, or a dagger, were to be met by a counter
attack, or avoided by a displacement of the body.   Even without stepping
aside, it was believed that a similar cut to that of the assailant, dexterously
delivered so as to obtain mastery over his " faible," could always be counted
upon to act as a parry as well as an attack.   This notion was evidently a
relic of the ideas impressed on generations of men by the habit of never
looking to their sword for any but offensive action.

[1] From " mano dritta," right hand.

Marozzo's guards carry but little of the meaning which is now attached to the word.

They are merely a collection of attitudes, each of which is merely the preliminary to one or two attacks. They are connected in a series in the same way as cuts and thrusts are concatenated in any sword exercise, and so arranged in pairs that in going through the whole series the fencer finds himself alternately right and left foot forward. All the guards and cuts can therefore be gone through with alternate steps forward or backwards.

The attack was delivered by stepping forward or sideways, and the parry—if it may be so called—or counter attack, by stepping back or sideways on the opposite side.

It is impossible to understand the meaning not only of Marozzo's guards, but those of all the authors previous to the seventeenth century, unless it be remembered that a guard was only the first stage of a *given set of* "*botte*," [1] and was in no way supposed to cover any part of the body. These attitudes, which, for some reasons, by no means obvious, had been found suitable, bore curious names, strongly savouring of slang, [2] and were devised either by Marozzo himself, or by his master Antonio de Lucha, likewise a Bolognese, "whose school produced more warriors than ever came out of the horse of Troy." He speaks of them, however, as if they were perfectly well-known and required no explanation.

Before proceeding to the description of the set guards, the author, with the moral authority due to his position as " Maestro Generale," sketches the general plan that the master ought to follow in his teaching.

" I wish thee to make thy scholar practise these things "—the cuts and parries in the form of counter attacks—" during four or five days with thee. As soon as he knows them well, I wish thee to begin and examine him in every guard, but especially in those of Porta di ferro larga, stretta, o alta, also in Coda lunga e stretta. This thou shalt do as in a combat with sword and target or shield or buckler, or with sword alone. Let this indicate to thee that in teaching a scholar to play with any of the above weapons, thou must make him understand all these guards, one by one, step by step, with their attacks and parries and everything pro and contra. Thou shalt see in these writings, and in the figures therein to be found—and therefore do not

[1] The word " botta " means, in a broad sense, what is called in French " coup ; " it comprises the action of the attack from its beginning to its completion.

[2] These names of guards are difficult to translate. *Porta di ferro* probably means a given way of holding the sword (*ferro* having the same signification as the Latin *ferrum*), qualified as *larga* (open or wide), *stretta* (strait or close), or by such words as *cinghiara* (girth or waist). *Coda* no doubt refers to the point, and is likewise qualified as *longa* (long or advanced), *alta* (high), &c. *Becca* (beak), qualified as *possa* or *cesa*, is still more puzzling; it may perhaps carry the meaning of *sustained* in the former case and *drooping* in the latter. The meaning, however, of such guards as *di intrare*, *di faccia*, *di testa*, is obvious.

fail to succeed in teaching the same—that I make no difference in the
guards on account of the weapons.   But, in order not to cover too much
space and to avoid repetition, I explain them merely in connection with the
sword alone, or with the sword and buckler.

"And so follow me in the name of the *all-powerful God.*

"GUARDIA DI CODA LUNGA E STRETTA.

"Let thy scholar stand with the right leg foremost, with the sword and
the target well out, and see that his right hand be well outside his right knee
with the thumb turned downwards as may be seen in the fig.

Fig. 13.—"Coda lunga e stretta" and "Cinghiara porta di ferro."—Marozzo.

"This is called *coda lunga e stretta,* and is meant for striking and parrying. The scholar being in this guard, thou wilt show him how many attacks
he can make therefrom being *agente,*[1] and how many parries with the shield
he can perform as *patiente,*[2] from above and from below, and likewise
their variations one from the other.   Thou wilt also show him the parries
against his own attacks.

"Then make thy scholar deliver a mandritto squalembrato, and cross
over sideways, with the left leg a little in front of his right, and inform him
that his sword is held on the guard of

"CINGHIARA PORTA DI FERRO.

"Thou shalt give thy scholar to understand that whenever he forms this

---

[1] Agente, that is, active, or on the attack.   [2] Patiente, passive, on the defensive.

guard, he must needs be *patiente*, because all low guards are rather for the purpose of parrying than of striking. However, should he want to attack, thou knowest that this can only be done with the point, or the false edge; therefore thou wilt show the said scholar, being on that guard, if anyone deliver an attack of any kind, in what way he must parry and then strike, advising him rather to strike with false edge, since thou knowest that the false edge can wound and parry at the same time.

"After this thou wilt make him pass his right leg forward, and lift his sword hand up; this new position is called

"GUARDIA ALTA.

"Thy scholar being placed on that guard, thou wilt show him how many cuts are derived therefrom, carefully remarking that this guard is meant

Fig. 14.—" Coda lunga e alta," and " Porta di ferro stretta overo larga."—Marozzo.

chiefly for the attack. Then show him the parries in a similar way, and make him pass his foot either forward or back, according to the occasion.

"Then thou wilt make him carry his left leg forward and lower his sword to about half his height; this guard is called

"GUARDIA DI CODA LUNGA E ALTA.

"I wish thee to know that, when remaining *patiente*, this is a good guard, and most useful, and accordingly advise thee to tell thy pupil that he had better assume this guard on the defensive, and make him understand all that can be done on it, pro and contra. . . .

" After some practice in this, thou wilt make thy scholar deliver a man-dritta fendente, and pass with the right leg foremost, and he will thus come down to the guard of

" PORTA DI FERRO STRETTA OVERO LARGA."

All the "botte" that could be delivered in cinghiara porta di ferro, especially with the false edge, were possible from this guard.

The passage to the next was thus :—

" Thou must cause thy pupil to remain with his left leg forward and lower his sword. He shall thus come to the guard of

" GUARDIA DI CODA LUNGA E DISTESA.

Fig. 15.—Guardia di testa—Guardia di intrare.—Marozzo.

" Being on this guard, thou wilt cause him to be *agente*, especially with dritti falsi, or with the point, with roversi, and such other attacks as can be derived from the said guard. Thou must also teach him the parries thereto, since the art of striking is but little in comparison with a knowledge of the parries, which is a fine and more useful thing. After giving him good practice in all the said parries and strokes, running from guard to guard, and from step to step, and always questioning him on the names of said guards, thou wilt cause him to pass his right leg forward in front of the left, and hold his sword-point lifted in the air; with his arm extended straight toward his adversary, as thou seest in the fig.

" This is called—

" GUARDIA DI TESTA.

" In this head guard one can be both *agente* and *patiente*, but I shall first speak of the defence.

" If any one should cut at him with a mandritto fendente or sgualembrato, or a tramazone,[1] thou wilt make him parry in head guard, and then from this guard pass to the attack ; he can do so with a thrust from the right over the hand, or a mandritto fendente, or tondo, or sgualembrato, or a falso dritto. From this head guard, thou wilt make him proceed with a thrust from the left[2] in his adversary's face, and advance his left leg in front of the right, rather sideways to the left, and point his sword straight in his adversary's face.

" He will thus find himself in the

" GUARDIA DI INTRARE.

" On this guard one must be *patiente*, as few attacks can be made from it. . . . Thou wilt make thy pupil lead off with roverso, and follow up the stroke by passing his right leg foremost, drawing back the arm at the same time, and extending his fist toward the ground ; thou wilt then inform him that he is on the guard of

" CODA LUNGA E LARGA.

" Take notice that on this guard thou canst both assault and defend, for it is possible to use the false edge from the left, and to cut tramazone with both right or false edge, or tramazone roverso, or false filo tondo, and roverso sgualembrato, by turning the sword to its proper place. Likewise thou canst deliver thrusts from the right or left, with or without feints, and all the roversi that belong to them, &c. . . . .

" After this thou wilt make thy scholar move his left foot forward and drop his sword-point towards the ground, turning the pummel upwards, and thou wilt see that he extend his arm and turn his thumb under and towards the point of the sword.

" This done, thou wilt inform him that he is on the guard

" GUARDIA DI BECCA POSSA.

" Having thus examined thy scholar in every guard, I am of opinion that on his assuming the becca possa, thou shouldst advise him to oppose it to his adversary whenever the latter assumes that of porta di ferro larga, or stretta, or alta, and to follow him step by step, and from guard to guard. That is,

---

[1] The tramazone, or stramazone, here mentioned for the first time, was a cut delivered from the wrist with the extreme edge of the sword.

[2] Punta roversa.

if the adversary goes in coda lunga e distesa, he must go into becca cesa ; against coda lunga e larga, make him oppose coda lunga e stretta; against becca cesa, cinghiara porta di ferro alta ; against guardia di intrare, guardia alta.

" Let him now advance the right leg forward and turn his point towards his adversary's face, thumb upwards, arm fully extended, and then tell him he thus finds himself on the

" Guardia di faccia.

" Having made him assume this guardia de faccia, inform him that in this he can both assault and defend at the same time.   On his adversary's cutting mandritto tondo, or fendente dritto, he should thrust at the same time at his face."

Fig. 16.—Coda lunga e larga.—Becca possa.—Marozzo.

The great art in the fencer was to pass with rapidity from one of these guards to the other.

By thus changing the guard, and consequently changing the probable attack, the quicker fencer of the two forced his adversary into new attitudes in order to deliver the necessary counter attacks, which held the place of parries proper.

One thing must be remembered in considering the very imperfect theories current at the time concerning the art of single combat, namely, that the sword then in common use, although devised for cutting almost to the exclusion of the thrust, was eminently ill-constructed for the purpose ; very heavy in proportion to its breadth, it had not yet become divested of the characteristics necessary for its employment against armour—stiffness and heavy weight.[1]

The target or buckler was held on guard in two positions: either at arm's length straight in front of the body, or close to the chest or the face, with the elbow square. Cuts were parried at an obtuse angle, so as to make the blow slide outwards, right or left; thrusts were beaten sideways with the flat.

Practice in "passing" was facilitated in the schools by means of lines traced on the ground. Marozzo considered that fencers should go through their exercises with stiff and sharp blades, "in order to make them good parriers and strong in the arm."

It is, therefore, no wonder that he insists on the necessity of never allowing beginners to play loose, and later on of only allowing pupils to fence

Fig. 17.—Guardia di faccia. Becca cesa.—Marozzo.

with "proficient swordsmen of pleasant dispositions." He even advises young men "on such occasions to make a collation together, for the promotion of good feeling."

The masters of the sixteenth century had already found out the truth of a principle which is not sufficiently regarded in our days, namely, that to become a proficient swordsman, a fencer should not attach too much importance to hits received in practice, and never show temper, but rather take his mishap as a lesson, and learn to prevent its recurrence in good style. For the better preservation of the equanimity requisite for sound

---

[1] The point was rarely used, but, when employed, the thrusts were generally aimed at the face. This habit was probably due to the fashion of wearing shirts of mail.

fencing, a rule was enforced in the schools that no comparisons should be made between, and no remarks passed on, the fencers at play.

Pupils only met for practice, the lessons were generally given in private, and even with the utmost secrecy on those occasions when the masters condescended to teach their favourite "botte" to a privileged scholar.[1]

There was a great deal of pomp and circumstance displayed on the installation of a new pupil. From our point of view, considering the rudimentary state of the art at that period, masters had little else to give to their pupils than the opportunity of practising with a man who was well used to all kinds of fighting. They had no system which could compare for a moment with the most elementary course of fencing in our days. But a knowledge of the use of weapons was then of such paramount importance, that naturally great swordsmen and recognized masters tried to enhance the glamour of their profession by keeping up the belief in the "botta segreta," and surrounding their lessons with no little amount of secrecy. Such has always been the case with sciences before their establishment on the basis of indisputable principles.

Marozzo accordingly binds his scholars upon a cross hilt, "as it were God's Holy Cross, never to take part against the master, and also never to teach any other person without his permission the secrets he is about to impart."

Most of the old books of fence dwelt as long on the use of military weapons as on that of the sword, for purposes of single combats or duels.

Marozzo's work is typical in that respect, and is divided into five books : the first two deal with the sword alone, or accompanied by the buckler, target, brochiero, imbracciatura, dagger, or cloak.[2]

The third with the use of spadone,[3] to which the same principles and the same guards are applied.

The fourth is devoted to the hastate weapons : pike, partisan, voulge (roncha) and poleaxe, alone or with the buckler.

The fifth deals with those matters which generally suffuse and involve the text of most fencing books of that time, namely, the application of philosophical principles to the art of fighting, and the resolution of knotty points in honourable difficulties arising under the laws of the duello.

Marozzo's work is very complete and carefully written, but it shows no tendency towards the reduction of the art to definite principles. Indeed, it does not profess to advocate any innovation. The popularity of the book was

---

[1] Brantôme, " Discours sur les duels et rhodomontades."

[2] The sword during the sixteenth century was rarely used alone. The buckler (rotella) covered the whole forearm, to which it was attached by two straps. The target and "brochiero" were varieties of the hand buckler. The imbracciatura was a long shield, somewhat similar to the Roman scutum or the pavois of the Middle Ages.

[3] Two-handed sword.

very great, however,—three editions appeared after his death, at long intervals, —and it was evidently still in great request among some old-fashioned fencers in the early years of the seventeenth century, when such great masters as Fabris, Capo Ferro, and Giganti were keeping their flourishing schools.

Seventeen years after the first appearance in print of Marozzo's system of fencing, the printer Antonio Blado published in Rome, " con privilegio di N. Signore Papa Giulio III.," a remarkable work on swordsmanship, which advocated some very bold and new principles : it was the " Treatise on the Science of Arms with a philosophical dialogue " of Camillo Agrippa, a Milanese.

Agrippa is better known to biography as architect, mathematician, and engineer, in which capacities he wrote sundry books. He is especially celebrated for having brought to a successful issue the operation of raising the needle in the middle of the Piazza di San Pietro.[1]

But, like many of his contemporaries, and especially his friend Michelangelo, who did not find his stupendous works sufficient to quench his superabundant energy, Agrippa devoted much of his time to practice in the schools of fence.

Not being a teacher, he was not shackled by any conventionalities, and accordingly his book is original, and much in advance of the popular notions of his days. As an engineer he studied the link movements performed by the various parts of the human anatomy in the actions of thrusting and cutting, and his mathematical mind revelled in geometrical figures and optical diagrams devised for their explanation. No doubt his " philosophical dialogue " on that subject is very tedious, but "theory" led him to the useful practical result of discarding, on most occasions, the cut in favour of the thrust.

Most weapons suggest at first a " round " hit ; even in mere pugilism an untutored man will strike in that way, and uses his fist as a club. A straight hit along the shortest way, and with the body's weight in its direct prolongation, is the result of both theory and practice. The cut is the more natural, that is, the easiest action ; the thrust is the result of a complicated and carefully regulated combination of movements. This fact alone shows why the thrust belongs to a more advanced stage of the art.

The practical value of his theory must have made itself patent to Agrippa during many a personal encounter in the dark winding Roman streets, if his mode of life was, and there is little doubt of it, as obstreperous as that of the immortal Buonarotti.

Agrippa was an educated man, who had taken up swordsmanship with a scientific interest, and naturally detected the fundamental errors of the popular modes of fencing, and devised a much simpler system.

---

[1] The account of this undertaking is given in his "Trattato di trasportar la guglia in su la piazza di San Pietro."—B. M.

One of the most obvious errors was the number of different guards, connected with each other by the most artificial ties, and each of which afforded opportunities for only a limited number of strokes, whereas every possible kind of hit can be delivered from any one position in which the sword is held in front of the body and menacing the adversary.

Another was the little use made of the point, notwithstanding the fact that less exertion and less time is requisite for the thrust, which is also more

Fig. 18.—Prima Guardia.—Agrippa.   Fig. 19.—Prima Guardia, on a pass.—Agrippa.

difficult to parry. A third was the unnecessary amount of exposure afforded by any guard where the left foot is kept foremost, whilst the sword is held in the right hand.

Accordingly, discarding all the old-fashioned fantastical titles, he reduced the number of useful guards to four, giving them plain numerical names, "prima, seconda, terza, quarta."

It so happens that, as far as the position of the hand is concerned, those guards have some kind of relation to our prime, seconde, tierce, and carte.

As a practical man, the author wisely considered the first guard to be assumed in the act of drawing the sword: men did not then stand on much punctilio in matters of fighting, and, in a quarrel, to draw and to be on guard had to be one action.

A long "rapier" could not be whipped out as deftly as a court sword;

before the point had left the scabbard the hand was above the head. Accordingly, the position of a man who had just drawn and turned his point to his adversary's face, was Agrippa's first guard. Both feet were on the same line, the body slightly bent.

The second only differed from the first in that the arm was lowered to the level of the shoulder.

In the other guards the feet were kept apart; in the third the hand was just above and outside the right knee, whilst in the fourth it was held more to the left.

Translated into modern technical terms, and with reference only to the position of the right hand,—

Fig 20.—Quarta Guardia.—Agrippa.   Fig. 21.—Seconda Guardia, on a pass.—Agrippa.

Prima guardia is somewhat similar to prime.
Seconda   „   „   „   to a high seconde or tierce.
Terza   „   „   „   to low tierce.
Quarta   „   „   „   to a low carte.

These were the fundamental guards, but there were also others, differing therefrom only by the greater or lesser extension of the arm, so as to suit the act of "passing" and "timing."

The thrust was delivered by fully extending the arm, bringing the right shoulder forward, so as to be better covered, and slipping the left foot back. The face was even often turned away on the delivery of an attack. It was usually aimed at the face or breast.

One would think that this series of positions might have suggested to his analytical mind some better kind of "lunge" as a complement. However, the invention of the "development" was reserved for a later period.

Like everyone else, Agrippa used " passing "[1] both in attack and defence. Neither did these guards, which are so suggestive of parries, lead him to devise anything better than " effacements," passes, or counter thrusts, as means of avoiding or meeting an attack.

On these principles he explained the best methods of fighting, chiefly with sword and dagger—those being weapons that every gentleman always wore; with two swords, which was a rather clumsy extension of the same; with sword and buckler, and sword and cloak.

Fig. 22.—Sword and Buckler.   A thrust from the " quarta guardia," by a slip to the right.—Agrippa.

He likewise mentions the use of the halbert, the two-handed sword, and has some words of advice to give on the subject of fighting on foot against a mounted adversary; also on the best course to adopt in a mélee.

Many of the plates in the original edition of Agrippa are attributed to Michelangelo.[2]   One of them illustrates the immense popularity enjoyed by Agrippa as an adept of the art, by representing him as surrounded by

[1] " Passing," in contradistinction to " lunging," consists in the action of carrying one leg in front of the other, instead of preserving the relative position of the feet and merely increasing their separation.

[2] See Biblio.   Certain masters, Pallavicini, Marcelli, and others, pretend that Agrippa wrote his treatise in 1536, without however giving any reason for their statements.   But still less likely is the presumption of the compilers of the Della Crusca dictionary, that the figures for his work were designed by Leonardo da Vinci.   Leonardo died in 1519.

friends, Venetians and Romans, recognizable by their costumes. The former are dragging him away, while the latter are striving to retain him in Rome.

It is probable, however, that the Venetians carried the day, and succeeded in attracting him, since two editions of his treatise appeared later in Venice, the first of which was brought out by the painter Giulio Fontana at the same time as that of Marozzo.

In 1570 appeared the " Ragioni di adoprar sicuramente l'arme " of Giacomo di Grassi,[1] a work which obtained a great reputation and had the honour of being " Englished, by a gentleman," of forming the basis of the more elaborate work of Henri de Sainct Didier, and of being imitated in Germany by Meyer and Sutor.

Grassi introduced a few important improvements in the *theory* of the art, and taught a very much simpler method than that of Marozzo. Typical instances of his system will be found in Sainct Didier and Saviolo's works.[2]

Grassi seems to have been the first to define the different parts of the blade with reference to their properties for defence or offence, and to have had an inkling of what is now termed " centre of percussion." In his preliminary remarks he divides the blade into four parts, the first two—nearest to the hilt—he explains should be used in parrying; the third, about the centre of percussion, in cutting ; and the part nearest the point, for thrusting.

He strenuously insists on the superiority of the point over the cut for direct attacks, and speaks of the " tocchi di spada " and a sense of touch with the blade in a manner which is remarkable, as blades were so rarely engaged in rapier-play. He also mentions explicitly the necessity of parrying with the *right* edge, deeming parries with the *false* edge dangerously weak.

All his attacks are delivered by means of " passes ; " in this respect his teaching is retrograde. Agrippa had long before clearly explained the advantage of keeping the right foot forward in most cases.

Although in favour of the thrusts, Grassi goes into careful details concerning cuts, which he classifies according as they are given from the shoulder, from the elbow, or from the wrist, and explains on what occasions the cut is a quicker return or counter attack than the thrust.

Considering the rapid changes in the relative distance of the combatants which was the consequence of " passes," it is obvious that on many occasions the measure was too small to admit of thrusting, although cuts might be still available.

Grassi settles the question of distance by carefully defining the length and direction of paces.

These were " passo recto," used only to close the measure, " passo obliquo," and " mezzo passo obliquo o circolare."

Grassi is the first author who takes into consideration the question of

---

[1] See Biblio.   [2] See Chapter V.

"lines," which he divides into inside, outside, high, and low: "On all occasions the sword is held either in low line (di sotto), in high line (di sopra), inside (di dentro), outside (di fuora)." But although admitting four lines of attack he only teaches three guards, subject to slight modifications: high, low, outside—guardia alta, bassa, largha.

Fig. 23 shows the first two, right and left hand. The third is assumed with the elbow square with the shoulder, hand in tierce, point menacing the adversary's chest. All these guards are very imperfect; indeed, in all the passages relating to the subject of defence, nothing but most uncertain "dodges" are mentioned as ways of avoiding destruction.

The greater part of the treatise is naturally devoted to the practice with sword and dagger, brochiero, or cloak. This more practical portion is expounded very clearly. In the introduction, "Della spada et pugnale," the author remarks, "It seems proper, passing from the simple to the complex, to speak now of those arms which are most generally used nowadays; we mean the sword

Fig. 23.—The Two Swords, the "case of rapiers" of English masters.—Grassi.

accompanied by the poniard: these are, of course, much more valuable for offence as well as for defence. It must, therefore, be declared that with these can be practised the desirable art of parrying and striking at the same time, which is impossible with the sword alone. . . . These two arms being of different size and weight, such a part must be ascribed to each, in the offence and the defence, as it is capable of performing, that is, to the poniard, being short, that of guarding the left side as low as the knee, and to the sword, that of defending the whole of the right side and the left below the knee. It must not seem strange that the poniard should be expected to protect all the parts on the left, for it can do so with the greatest ease if it goes and meets the sword about the first and second part. But it cannot do it with any kind of safety if it meet the sword about the third and fourth part, as the force of the blow there is too great."[1]

Grassi is not of opinion that the prevailing method of parrying a cut

---

[1] The dagger was usually grasped in the same manner as the sword. Sometimes the thumb was held flat against the heel of the blade, sometimes even the forefinger and thumb were crossed over the guard. But in fencing the dagger was never held with the thumb nearest to the pummel, as it is so often pictured nowadays.

with the sword and dagger crossed is recommendable, on the ground that it is impossible to return the hit without loss of time and giving up the advantage of the double weapon, namely, that of countering.

He believes so much in the value of the dagger when used in the way described, that he maintains that it can hold its own alone against most other weapons.

The guards with the dagger are the same as those with the sword. When both weapons are used together, different guards, such as largha and alta, or bassa, are assumed with either, so as to multiply the difficulty of attack and to facilitate countering in a different line from that of attack.

" To proceed with the consideration of those arms which men most usually carry with them, we must, after the dagger, consider the cloak."

When the cloak (capa) was resorted to for protection, it was seized by the " capuccio," and turned twice round the left forearm, so as to leave a part hanging loose.

The loose part of the capa, "owing to its flexibility," was deemed capable of stopping cuts, and of sufficiently entangling the point as to be a protection against thrusts, provided that the fencer took care " always to carry the foot differently from the arm, and not to rush into peril by having the forward leg on the same side as the cloak, for the cloak is no protection if it have a solid part behind it."

" The buckler being a very commodious arm and of much use," Grassi also considers its management. " With the intention of making the brochiero, notwithstanding its small size, cover the whole of the body, it is necessary to hold it as far forward as possible, and always to move the arm and the buckler of a piece, as if there were no joints, always turning the whole face of the buckler towards the enemy ; in this manner the whole of the arm is covered. All cuts are parried in this way on the second and third parts of the blade, and likewise the thrusts."

The use of the two swords together,—the case of swords, as it was called in England,—of which Grassi speaks with great enthusiasm, was evidently a mere reproduction of the sword and dagger play, the only difference being that more offensive action was possible to the left hand armed with a sword, than with the shorter dagger. Agrippa and Marozzo had already taught this mode of fencing, which never could have been of much practical use.

Whether the hand buckler, the dagger, the cloak, or a second sword was held in the left hand, the combat was conducted in a manner very similar to a pugilistic encounter in modern days ; one hand was employed in stopping the adversary's attacks, whilst the other delivered counters, or " led off " in the various lines. Both combatants edged off to the right, or " slipped " to the left, trying to place themselves in a position of vantage.

Grassi, on the whole, introduced but few *practical* improvements in the science of arms, but he reasoned very clearly on the current theories of his time.   Most distinctly he remains inferior to Agrippa.   The latter had made some approach to the invention of the " lunge "—if we are to judge from his plates, although his text offers no explanation on the subject—but Grassi merely pursued the tradition of Marozzo's school, merely reducing the number of fundamental guards, and giving the preference to the point over the edge.   Still it is to be remembered that Marozzo's system embodied the perfection of the " vieille escrime " mentioned by Rabelais, and his principles were still sufficiently recognized to justify a reproduction of his treatise as late as 1615.[1]

Grassi's[1] work expounds the application of the old theories to the freer employment of the point, and in it may be recognized the system most commonly followed in Europe during the latter part of the sixteenth century.

[1] And that of his contemporary Agocchie.   See Biblio., 1572.

CHAPTER III.

Fig. 24.—Estocade. From Lacombe's "Armes et Armures."

IT has been already mentioned[1] that no regular fencing schools appear to have existed in France previous to the sixteenth century. The first institutions of that kind were kept by Italian masters, some of whose names have come down to posterity under a Frenchified form : Caize, the same who taught the much maligned De Jarnac the famous "falsomanco" by which he disabled that bully La Chastaigneraie ; Pompee and Silvie, who taught at the Court of Charles IX. The latter is celebrated as having taught the Duc d'Anjou, who became later Henri III., and who, unaccountably enough, considering his effeminate character, obtained the reputation of a " fine lame," and even passed for one of the best swordsmen of his age.

During the early part of the century, the German mercenaries in the pay of the French kings were generally resorted to for instruction in the art of fighting, as most of them had had some kind of regular training in the use of arms, and they probably included a few Marx- or Luxbrüder among their officers. It is not astonishing, therefore, that the first book published in French, indeed one of the first ever printed, should have borne a close resemblance in its teaching to that of the old German schools.

[1] Chapter I.

The anonymous author of " La noble science des joueurs d'espée " was probably a captain of Reîtres or Lansquenets, who reproduced into French some of the tricks used by " Marxbrüder." Indeed, the text of the book and its plates have a strong likeness to Lebkommer's " Der Altenn Fechter an fenglicke Kunst." [1]

The title itself seems but a translation of the usual elaborate titles of the old German Fechtbücher :

Fig. 25.—Braquemars and Anelace.

" The noble science of fence, containing the chivalrous art of sword-play with the two-handed and such like swords, as well as braquemars (anelace) and all short cutlasses which are used with one hand."

Like all the books of that period, it only professes to describe a collection of tricks apparently unconnected by any kind of principle.

Fig. 26 has been selected as showing something like " fencing " action, most of the others are merely " rough and tumble " encounters, in which wrestling and tripping play the most prominent part.

Fig. 26.—Braquemars.—" La noble science des joueurs d'espée."

The following short passage, which is reproduced in its quaint old French, gives an example in point :—

" Comment on le tiendra à terre, Quant il est jectté à terre, si tombez sur lui au costé dextre avecq le genoul droict entre ses jambes, et avec la main senestre tombez devant à son col, lui prendant sa defence, puis besoingnez à vostre plaisir." (!)

With the exception of this little work, which by the way contains nothing on the subject of rapier fight, the only book in the French language at that epoch is the " Traicté contenant les secrets du premier livre sur l'espée seule, mère de toutes les armes, par Henri de Sainct Didier, gentilhomme Provençal." [2]

This book is looked upon by the French as the first treatise on an art

[1] See Biblio., Germany, 1529.   [2] See Biblio., 1573.

which they consider as essentially their own. It was, however, nothing of the kind, but merely a collection of illustrations, with explanatory notices, of the system followed by Italian masters of the school of Marozzo—such as Pagano, Grassi, Agocchie—improved perhaps by a few notions derived from Agrippa's work.

Although the Provençal gentleman does not openly own the first source of his knowledge, it is evident that he took advantage of the proximity of his native place to the Italian schools, to go across the border and learn the science which he came later to teach in Paris under the thin disguise of Gallicized terms.

Any book of fence, bad or good, would have met with success in Paris at that epoch. The old chivalrous French notion that it was unworthy of a gentleman to learn the cunning of fence,[1] had died away in those days of civil strife, in consequence of the too obvious disadvantage accruing therefrom in daily encounters. Indeed, in the early part of the century, although gentlemen shunned the reputation of " bon escrimeur," it was nevertheless the custom to go to Italy, surreptitiously to learn the practice of arms in the Bolognese and Venetian schools, and also when possible a few tricks of the trade in the shape of some infallible secret thrust purchased for fabulous sums from some redoubtable " spadacino."

These arts they brought back to France and practised on their un-sophisticated countrymen, with a confidence in the " botte sècrete apprise en lointain pays " which was not always justified by the result.[2]

Brantôme is very full of this subject in his " Discours sur les duels et rhodomontades," and gives a vivid description of the foolhardy manner in which men exposed their lives on trivial occasions. Long before Brantôme the French had already acquired the worldwide reputation of being the most quarrelsome as well as frivolous of nations ; [3] but the latter half of the sixteenth century saw, with the disuse of the judicial duels, the rise of that extraordinary mania for private duelling which cost France in 180 years the useless loss of 40,000 valiant gentlemen, killed in single combats which arose generally on the most futile grounds.

About the time when Sainct Didier's book appeared, the exasperation by political circumstances of that factious spirit which made of " Fair France "

---

[1] "Dans mon enfance la noblesse fuyait la reputation de bon escrimeur et se derobait pour l'apprendre, comme mestier de subtilité dérogeant à la vraye et naive vertu."—Montaigne, " Essays."

[2] " Nous allons en Italie apprendre à escrimer et l'exerçons aux depens de nos vies avant de le scavoir."—Ibid.

[3] "Indiscrète nation ! Nous ne nous contentons pas de faire scavoir nos vices et folies au monde par reputation, nous allons aux nations étrangères pour les leur faire voir en presence. Mettez trois Francois aux deserts de Lybie, il ne seront pas un mois ensemble sans se harceler et s'esgratigner."—Ibid.

one vast "champs clos," where Papist and Huguenot, Royalist and Ligueur, met daily to try conclusions with that worst of arguments, the sword, naturally put the art of fence at a premium.

It was the time when a woman's power of fascination was reckoned by the number of duels, and consequently of deaths, she had caused, and when the quarrel of two men involved the participation of all those of their friends who were at hand.

Anyone who reads Brantôme will recognize that Mercutio's rebuke of Benvolio did not go one jot beyond the mark in describing the quarrelsome habits of empty-headed young men of those days.[1]

" Thou ! why thou wilt quarrel with a man that hath a hair more or a hair less in his beard than thou hast.   Thou wilt quarrel with a man for cracking nuts, having no other reason than because thou hast hazel eyes; what eye but such an eye would spy out such a quarrel ? Thy head is as full of quarrels as an egg is full of meat ; and yet thy head has been beaten as addle as an egg, for quarrelling.   Thou has quarrelled with a man for coughing in the street, because he hath wakened thy dog that hath lain asleep in the sun." Such a description might well have applied to a courtier of Charles IX.

It is not to be wondered at, therefore, that the first appearance of a treatise on the secrets of the sword should have met with such wonderful success—notwithstanding its comparative worthlessness—especially as it was accepted by and dedicated to a king who, with the weakest of frames and the weakest of minds, nevertheless interested himself greatly in all questions of arms and sport.

Were it not for the fact that the " gentilhomme Provençal " is looked upon as the father of the national science of arms by the French, his book might be merely noticed for the sake of the historical anecdotes it contains,[2] and as a remarkable bibliographical curiosity.

Sainct Didier is the first who adopted the convenient method of referring to two typical persons in order to explain their respective actions.   Beyond this improvement, and the introduction of numerous figures arranged in series so as to show the progressive stages of the antagonistic actions, it will be seen to be a mere rearrangement of that part of Grassi's method which treats of the sword alone.

Sainct Didier teaches three guards : the first is low, being in fact Grassi's third guard.[3]   The second is as high as the shoulder, the point of the sword being directed to the adversary's left eye.   The third is very high,—Grassi's first guard,—the point of the sword is directed from above downward to the enemy's face.

---

[1] " Romeo and Juliet," Act iii., Sc. 1.
[2] Such as the account of Sainct Didier's assault with the Duc de Guise, in presence and by order of the king.   [3] See Fig. 23.

The position of the left arm constantly varies, the hand being held forward, or back, high or low, according to the ever-shifting relative position of the adversaries.

It is somewhat remarkable that the left hand, when unarmed with the dagger, should not at all times have been kept behind the back, considering that his system included at least as many cuts as thrusts, and that the elevation of the left arm, when "passing" was the only mode of progression employed, had no obvious use for purposes of equilibrium.

Sainct Didier calls "Démarches" the various systems of steps by which the adversaries close or retire. Unscientific and dangerous as they were, he attempts to classify them and adapt them to every kind of attack or defence.

The footprints indicated in the woodcuts show the irregularity and complication of the movements supposed to be a necessary preliminary to the different kinds of attacks.

Following the prevalent fashion of Gallicizing all foreign as well as Latin words that were wanting in common speech, Sainct Didier classifies all possible hits under three heads : maindraicts, renvers, and estocs.

The original of the first two are obviously the Italian mandritti and rinversi. Estoc, though akin to stoccata, is a legitimate French word, meaning a thrust. He ignores the distinction between stoccata and imbroccata.

The Italian authors spoke of "parate" and "riparare" in a general way, without ever defining a single parry. Sainct Didier is on the whole nearer the truth when speaking of the universal method of meeting a cut or a thrust by a counter, either cut or thrust, he calls the action "croiser l'épée."

The science which the author professes to impart is illustrated by a series of combats between two personages, the Lieutenant who acts the part of the master, and the Prevost, who is to be taught. See Fig. 27.

Fig. 27.—"Tenue et garde du premier coup pour executer et faire le quatriangle, pour le Lieutenant et le Prevost."

"Si après sera monstré un fort bon coup pour le Lieutenant assaillant et pour le Prevost deffendant, en maniere de quatriangle et tout ce qui y est requis scavoir par lesdits Lieutenens et Prevosts, et par consequent aux autres supposts."

"Premier coup et suite du quatriangle pour le Lieutenant et Prevost."

The Lieutenant passes his right foot from the triangle to the "quatriangle," placing it on the footprint marked 2, and delivers a " raide estoc d'hault," [1] nails upward. (Fig. 28.)

On his side the Prevost draws his foot back from 1 to 3 on the triangle, and "crossing" his adversary's thrust, fort on faible, nails up, offers a thrust at his left eye.

Fig. 28.—" Voila ce que doit faire ledit Prevost pour soy deffendre dudit quatriangle tiré par ledit Lieutenant assaillant."

Seeing that the Prevost has " shown himself clever and not ignorant, since he defended himself well," the Lieutenant passes his sword under that of the Prevost, and carries his foot to the further corner of the quatriangle, delivering a " maindraiçt " at the same time, and drawing his body slightly back in so doing.

This is again parried by the Prevost, who crosses his opponent's sword by offering an estoc to his face, nails down.— " Voila ce que doit faire ledit Prevost pour se garder de cest dite opposite qu'a tiré le Lieutenant jusques icy." (Fig. 29.)

The Lieutenant then brings his left foot from 2 to 3, passes (desrobe) his sword under that of his adversary, and delivers either a " maindraiçt " or an " estoc," which the Prevost again " crosses " either with a cut upwards or a thrust at the face, nails up ; and this is " La fin

Fig. 29.—" Première opposite et suite du quatriangle."

dudit quatriangle pour ledit Prevost."   (Fig. 30.)

" After treating," says Sainçt Didier towards the end of his book, " of the art, order, and praçtice of the sword alone, and having defined all that is requisite therein, I have felt willing to teach and demonstrate four good and subtile ways of seizing your enemy's sword, which may be found of avail as well in the attack as the defence."

---

[1] Literally, " a stiff thrust above."   An Italian would have called it " imbroccata."

One of these examples is reproduced here, as it results in the adversaries exchanging swords, an incident which often occurred in rapier-play.[1]

The Lieutenant, who came on guard left foot foremost, delivers an estoc at the Prevost by passing his right foot forward. The Prevost draws his left foot back, crosses his opponent's sword, fort on faible, nails up, and, suddenly bringing his left foot again to the front, seizes the Lieutenant's sword. He keeps his own point menacing his adversary's face, and tries to wrench the sword away. (Fig. 31.)

" Voicy la fin de la première prinse presque executée par ledit Prevost deffendeur contre ledit Lieutenant."

Fig. 30.—" S'ensuit le parachevement dudit quatriangle, qui est sur un maindroit ou estoc d'hault, tiré par ledit Lieutenant contre le Prevost."

The Lieutenant thus finding himself in jeopardy, bends his body to the right and brings up his left foot, seizing at the same time the Prevost's hilt round the quillons. (Fig. 32.)

Either party, by twisting the quillons of his adversary's sword, obtains the advantage of leverage over the sword hand. The shortest plan at this juncture is evidently for either to abandon his own sword and continue the fight with that of his opponent, as is shown by figure 33, where the fencers are seen in the act of falling back and passing their rapier from the left hand to the right.

Sainct Didier's exercises are

Fig. 31.—" Premier coup tiré sur le maindroit ou estoc d'hault, pour la première prinse par le Lieutenant et presque executée par le Prevost, comme icy est monstré."

illustrated by a succession of sixty-four woodcuts. The set reproduced in this book is chosen as representing the most complicated systems of steps in the whole of Sainct Didier's work. These woodcuts, although quite correct as regards the costumes, represent the actors armed with an

[1] Shakespeare shows himself as well acquainted with the art of fence as with most other subjects in his stage direction concerning the fencers in the last act of " Hamlet."

utterly conventional weapon. It is needless to remark that the swords used in personal combat at that period were never so heavy and clumsy as they are therein shown. Even the weighty "estocade," the favourite arm of the French,—to which, by the way, Sainct Didier seems exclusively to devote his attention,—was incomparably slenderer.

Fig. 32.—" A prinse faut faire contre prinse comme est icy monstré par ce Lieutenant au Prevost."

It seems at first remarkable that when Sainct Didier went to Italy to seek the principles of a science then considered so essentially Italian, he should not have adopted those of the most " pronounced " masters, who advocated the almost exclusive use of the point and the " spada lungha." [1] But it is probable that the old-fashioned prejudice in favour of hard knocks existed in France as it did in England at the same period, and that the mass of fencers only reluctantly admitted the superiority of a puncturing play. Consequently Grassi's and Agocchie's system, applying as it did to the French " estocade," was adopted as more suitable to the general taste.

But there is no doubt that the rapier-play after the manner of Cavalcabo and Fabris was also in high favour among the " raffinés " —the insatiable duellists of the Courts of Charles IX. and Henri III.

Fig. 33.—" Voila la fin de la contreprinse exécutée par le Lieutenant contre le Prevost."

Sainct Didier himself was well acquainted with the new method, although he did not acknowledge its superiority. He gives, at the end of his book, the account of a discussion he had on theoretical grounds with two masters of that school—one of which is the " Napolitain Fabrice," who may have been connected with Salvator Fabris, as the profession of arms ran more in families then than now. The chief point of the discussion was

---

[1] Viggiani in Venice, Fabris in Padua, Patenostrier in Rome, Cavalcabo in Bologna.

whether it was possible to classify thrusts into various categories and make
a more frequent use of them than was advocated by the French master,
a theory which the latter flatters himself to have proved false on every
point.

At the conclusion of the work a parallel is introduced between the
fencing art and the game of tennis,[1] in which the author applies the

Fig. 34.—Prima guardia difensiva imperfetta formata dal cingersi la spada al
manco lato, da cui nasce il rouescio
ascendente.—Viggiani.

Fig. 35.—Seconda guardia alta offensiva
perfetta ; formata dal rouescio ascendente,
da cui nasce la punta sopramano offensiva ;
ò intiera ; ò non intiera.—Viggiani.

expressions " renvers " and " maindraicts " to the different ways of taking
the ball, although he acknowledges the necessity of stopping the simile short
of " estoc," " veu que raquette n'a poins de pointe."

Although the art of fence was nowhere of greater use than in France,
we must return to Italy to watch its development.   Two other Italian books
are extant, both printed in Venice about the same period.

" The three books of Fence " of Giovanni dell' Agocchie[2] need not be
considered after Grassi ; but Viggiani's work[3] is worthy of attention as it
professes to be original, and indeed contains some indications of the new
school, namely, that in which " passing " tends to be replaced by the " lunge."

---

[1] Jeu de paume.   [2] See Biblio., 1572.   [3] See Biblio., 1575.

Agrippa had already foreshadowed the theoretical advantage of that mode of progression, but his system was not sufficiently well defined to upset the apparently more natural habit of passing right and left. Unfortunately for his glory as a fence-master, Viggiani was not bold enough in his innovations to apply the principles of his celebrated "punta sopramano" to

Fig. 36.—Terza guardia, alta, offensiva, imperfetta ; formata dal rouescio ascendente, da cui nasce un mandritto, descendente, ò intiero o mezo.—Viggiani.

Fig. 37.—Quarta guardia larga, diffensiva, imperfetta ; formata dalla punta intiera sopramano, da cui nasce il rouescio ritondo.—Viggiani.

all attacks, so that after all he remains one of the followers of Marozzo, instead of being the founder of the modern school—an honour which was reserved for Giganti and Capo Ferro.

Although the first edition bears the date of 1575, it is known that in deference to the author's wish his book appeared long after his death, and that it was finished in 1560. His teaching was then contemporary with Agrippa's, perhaps with Marozzo's. His principles were in a great measure similar to those of the former, but, in point of theory, he went very much further.

In his treatise Viggiani professes to expose a new and peculiar mode of fencing, and as there is internal evidence that his method was carried into Germany and practised and published by Meyer—the best authority on matters of fence in that country at the time—this book is of high interest, notwithstanding that the writer did not create a distinct school in Italy.

" Lo Schermo d'Angelo Viggiani " is divided into three parts, the first of which treats of the inevitable comparison between literature and the

Fig. 38.—Quinta guardia stretta, difensiva, perfetta ; nata dalla meza punta sopramano, offensiva, da cui nasce un mezo rouescio tondo.—Viggiani.

Fig. 39.—Sesta guardia larga, offensiva imperfetta ; partorita dal rouescio intiero difensivo, da cui nascerà il rassettarsi in guardia alta offensiva ; perfetta.—Viggiani.

science of arms, the second of offence and defence.   A few of the headings of this part will suffice to show in what a tough matrix of nonsense these preposterous philosophic masters of the sixteenth century imbedded their precious principles : " Difesa negli animali, nelle piante," " Prudenza della pantera et dell' elefante," " Perche nô si possa per la difesa prendere argumento dal cielo," " Perche si movesse il serpente ad ingannare l'huomo," and so on for some forty pages.

Happily, however, the third part treats pretty exclusively of fencing, and therein is to be learned that Viggiani taught seven guards.   Most of them have resemblance to Marozzo's, as far as the position of the arm is concerned, but they are divested of their fanciful names and only bear distinguishing numbers. They are widely different also in this respect, that the right foot is always in front and at the same distance—about thirty inches—from the left.

Viggiani teaches the same "mandritte" and "rinversi" as all the other masters of his day, but gives the preference to the latter as being more quickly delivered and possessed of greater power. He pays, however, special

Fig. 40.—Settima guardia stretta offensiva, perfetta, partorita dal mezo rouescio difensivo ; da cui nascer potrà il rassettarsi in guardia alta offensiva perfetta.—Viggiani.

attention to the thrust, which he considers vastly superior to the cut, and whereas all his predecessors only recognized one sort of thrust in a general way, Viggiani classifies minutely the different positions in which the point may be used.

Punta dritta, delivered from the right.   (Hand in pronation.)

Punta rovescia, delivered from the left.   (Hand in supination.)

Each of these is further subdivided into ascending, descending, or straight thrusts.

Punta dritta (o rovescia) ascendente.

    ,,   ,,   ,,   descendente.

    ,,   ,,   ,,   ferma.

His seven guards are shown in the figures.

Viggiani calls a guard perfect when it admits of the delivery of a thrust ; imperfect, that which does not ; a distinction in accordance with his predilection for the use of the point, in the cut and thrust fencing of his day, *e.g.* the second, fifth, and seventh guards are " perfect."

He calls " strait," a guard in which the point is held in line with the

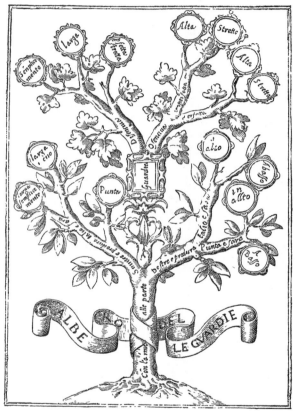

Fig. 41.—Classification of the Guards.—Viggiani.

adversary, and " open," one in which the point is held away ; " offensive," when the sword is held on the right side ; " defensive," when it is held on the left. This terminology suggests the usual mode of parrying an attack by a counter. As, in his estimation, the quickest and most powerful cuts are the " rovesci," he naturally calls a position favourable to the delivery of a " rovescio " a " defensive " guard. Indeed, he looks upon a " rovescio tondo " as an almost universal parry, which may even break the adversary's blade, and which he considers "perfe&t" if it be immediately followed by a "punta sopramano."

This famous "punta sopramano," which contains the first perfe&tly clear indication of a "lunge," is a favourite "botta" with Viggiani, who performs it from all those guards he calls "perfe&t."

"When thou shalt have a mind to deliver a 'punta sopramano,' see that the right foot advance one great step, and immediately let thy left arm fall, and let the right shoulder at the same time press the arm forwards, dropping the point slightly downwards from above, and aiming the while at my chest, without in any way turning the hand. Push thy point as far as ever thou canst."

All these particulars, as well as many others of interest to philosophers alone, are imparted under the form of a dialogue between the "most illustrious Signor Luigi Gonzaga, called 'Rodomonte,'" and the "excellent Messer Lodovico Boccadiferro, philosopher."

In the third part the "Conte d'Agomonte" is introduced to give his opinion of knotty points of discussion.

Thirteen years later a new edition of Viggiani's work was produced by Zacharia Cavalcabo, in Bologna. Here the author's name is spelt "Vizani," in deference probably to the habit of hearing it so pronounced by the soft-mouthed Venetians, his pupils.

CHAPTER IV.

Fig. 42.—Spanish Sword. Early sixteenth century. From Lacombe's " Armes et Armures." [2]

T is a remarkable fact that in Spain, the supposed birthplace of systematic swordsmanship, so little progress should have been made towards what may be called the more *practical* use of the sword. Whilst the Italians, and, after their example, the French, Germans, and English, gradually discovered that simplification led to perfection, the Spanish masters, on the contrary, seemed to aim at making fencing a more and more mysterious science, requiring for its practice a knowledge of geometry and natural philosophy, and whose principles were only explainable on metaphysical grounds.

Carranza's is the first of the long series of ponderous Spanish treatises on the " raison démonstrative," in which the ruling principle, after the Aristotelian method, is the " conocimiento de la cosa por su causa," and the purpose, to demonstrate that a perfect theoretical knowledge must infallibly lead to victory, notwithstanding grievous physical disadvantage.[1] This arrogant theory, which applied no better to the long rapier than to any other weapon, was unfortunately so plausibly expounded by the early masters as to ruin any prospect of improve-

[1] " The book of Jeronimo de Carranza treating of the philosophy of arms and the dexterous mastery thereof, as well as of Christian attack and defence." See Biblio., 1582.

[2] This figure, which represents imperfectly the celebrated sword of Gonzalvo de Cordova, now in the *Armería Real* of Madrid, shows an early shape of pas d'âne hilt.

ment in the Spanish schools, where it was never discarded.   The French foil
fencing has now all but absolutely driven away the Spanish rapier-play from
the Peninsula.

Carranza informs his reader that his book was finished in 1569, when a
few copies were printed by command of the Duke of Medina Sidonia, but
it was only issued for circulation in 1582, and appeared simultaneously at
San Luca de Barrameda and at Lisbon.

As the title leads one to anticipate, there is as much of the author's
ethical and theological theories in this celebrated work as of swordsmanship
proper.   Its production, joined to Carranza's reputation as " esgrimidor,"
certainly entitled him to the name of " inventor of the science of arms," of

Fig. 43.—Gaining the advantage by traversing (ganando los grados
al perfil).   The two groups represent the two stages of the action.
Adapted from Girard Thibaust.

that Spanish science at least that based its principles on the mathematical
relation of angles to their subtending arcs, of tangents and chords to their
circle, and all that pompous nonsense which Quevedo, a century later, ridicules
so finely[1] when he describes a scientific " espadachin " put into a corner by
an uninitiated but resolute antagonist, notwithstanding the fact that the former
had " ganado los grados al perfil," the infallible result of which operation
should have been complete mastery.

A second edition of Carranza's book was published in 1600, in all
respects similar to the former, together with the first of that long series

[1] " Vida del Gran Tacaño."

of works, either by Don Luis Pacheco de Narvaez, or about him, which forms nearly the whole literature of fencing in Spain during the seventeenth century.

As Narvaez's first production embodies all the principles of Carranza, it will be better to analyze summarily his " Book of the Grandeur of the Sword, in which are expounded many secrets of the works composed by the Commander G. de Carranza, and with which everyone will be able to teach himself and learn without the necessity of a master to direct him." "Composed by Don Luis Pacheco de Narvaez, native of the town of Sevilla, &c., &c., and dedicated to Don Philip III., King of All the Spains, and of the greater Part of the World, our Master."

Don Luis Pacheco de Narvaez, as a pupil of Carranza, reproduces in every detail the characteristic method of the "primer inventor de la ciencia," and introduces for its explanation curious little diagrams, in which the adversaries' bodies are represented by a small circle, and the relative positions of the blades at the final moment are figured by two conventional swords crossed at various angles, either piercing or tangent to the small circles according as the blow is thrust or cut.

After an immense amount of grave disquisition on the necessity of self-defence imposed on man by laws human and divine, and on the praiseworthy occupation of perfecting oneself in the art of arms for the confusion of heretics and the protection of Church and King " from the tyrants who persecute them," supported by the most logical arguments in the world, the author at last begins to mix some questions of swordsmanship to his discourse. Then we are able to find out that the guard advocated at the middle of the sixteenth century was in all essentials the same as that represented by Angelo as the Spanish guard at the end of the eighteenth.

" The body erect, but in such manner that the heart be not directly opposite the adversary's sword ; the right arm extended straight, the feet not too much open. . . . . Three advantages derive from these principles, the point of the sword is carried nearer to the adversary, the sword itself is held with greater force, and there is no danger of a wound on the elbow." There is no question of " engaging " swords. The adversaries are to fall on guard out of measure, and, in order to systematize the general notions of correct distance, Carranza and his illustrator Narvaez imagine a circle drawn on the ground—" circonferencia imaginata entre los cuerpos contrarios."

The opponents on guard are to be at opposite ends of the diameter, whose length is regulated by the effective length of the arm, with the sword extended horizontally as explained before. Tangent to the circle, and at the opposite ends of the diameter, are imagined two parallel lines, which are called infinite—" lineas infinitas "—for the simple reason that both adversaries might travel for ever along these lines together without altering for any practical purpose their relative positions. On the other hand, either combatant who crosses the space between these parallels, that is, who travels along any chord of the imaginary circle, immediately comes " within measure ; " since the longest chord of a circle is its diameter, as soon as the opponents are separated by any other, they are within striking distance. The result of any step taken by one of the fencers may be of three kinds : either his opponent takes a corresponding one along the circumference of the circle, so that they remain at the extremity of a diameter and nothing is altered, or he may strike him as he passes, or be struck himself should he miss his " time." These two latter cases may also be modified by the possibility of parrying the blow by a counter. But as the chief object of " passing " is to place your adversary in a disadvantageous position for parrying, he who succeeds in " passing " within striking distance of his adversary without being " timed," has the obvious advantage. This danger of being stopped by a time thrust is methodically graduated in Narvaez's book according to the angle along which the pace is made, for it is obvious that a pace of a given length would bring a man nearer to his adversary, posted at its opposite extremity, than the same pace along any other chord.[1]

His " Llave y gobierno de la destreza " is merely a technical expression of the instinct which prompts two boxers to walk round each other when not actually striking, and which is illustrated even by the actions of animals, as anyone knows who has watched two dogs or two cocks about to fight. These side movements remained obviously necessary in fencing as long as no improved method of " engaging " swords had been recognized.

Anything approaching to a lunge seems to have been altogether unknown. The most approved method was to advance with short steps at an obtuse angle with the diameter—always menacing the adversary with the point— and to avoid all violent movements.

The various " compasses " are: " pasada," or a step of about twenty-four inches ; " pasada simple," about thirty inches ; and " pasada doble," consisting of two " pasadas " stepped with alternate feet.

With regard to the combatants taken separately, various propositions of Euclid are employed to map out the space occupied by the human body; some of the disquisitions are very quaint, if not of much concern to the practical swordsman.

" But you should know," says the father of the science of arms, " that the body of man, besides being spherical, as we have explained before, also offers to our consideration two lines : one joins the head to the feet and is called, according to Euclid, perpendicular, and, according to astronomers, vertical ; another, when the arms are held open, joins one to the other. We

---

[1] " Por la linea del diametro no se puede caminar sin peligro " was looked upon as an irrefutable axiom among " diestros."

call it, still according to Euclid, ' linea de contingencia,' or tangent line, and, according to astronomers, ' horizontal.' "

The space measured by the dimensions of these two lines is that in which effectual strokes can be made.

Carranza devotes most attention to the cut, and, although using the thrust very freely, he gives exact definitions of the former, but none of the latter. Narvaez, however, has a good deal more to say about the thrust, but again without any definition of the manner in which it is delivered. It was evidently given like a stab with a jerk, the most natural way, after all, of striking on a " pass."

The cuts are clearly divided into: arrebatar (which means to cut with the whole arm from the shoulder); mediotajo (a cut from the elbow—"doblando la coyuntura del codo "); mandoble (a cut from the wrist, a flip of the point—the Italian " stramazzone," in fact).

The same expressions are applied to the parries, showing once more, what is implied without explanation by all authors of that period, that parries were always made by means of counter attacks.

With these premises, it was the scholar's part to learn and practise a number of passes applicable to as many forms of attack as possible. Both Carranza and Pacheco de Narvaez take a vast number of cases, and explain what is to be done on every movement of the adversary, varying the complication of the passes according as his action is " violenta, natural, remissa, de reduccion, extraño o accidental," and according as his stature and habit be tall or short, muscular or nervous, choleric or phlegmatic, &c.

It seems incredible, at first sight, that fencing taught on such very artificial principles could ever have been found of much practical use. But, as a matter of fact, Spaniards enjoyed during the whole of the sixteenth and seventeenth centuries the reputation of being very dangerous duellists, a fact which may be explained by the habit of coolness developed by those methodical notions, and the necessity of constant and careful practice for the acquisition of even a rudimentary " destreza," starting from such principles.

Long habit in wielding a sword, even with imperfect method, is of course of immense material use, and the more so with a heavy weapon requiring great strength for its management.

Twelve years after the publication of his great work, Narvaez issued an appendix to it, and in 1625 printed a kind of *handbook* of fencing.[1]

Although these books appeared quite outside the period which is now being described, they may be noticed among the early treatises of fencing, for no material improvement on Carranza's method—beyond a freer use of the point—was introduced into the Spanish school. The greater part of the

[1] See Biblio., Spain, 1612, 1625. " New and easy method of self-examination in the art of fencing, for the use of masters, explaining its hundred conclusions or points of knowledge."

book is devoted to the exposition of those principles here briefly noticed, and to their illustration in the shape of dialogues on special cases. At the end, however, is found a description of the order in which instruction is to be imparted to the pupil.

"It imports first to inform the scholar of all the simple and complex movements which the arm can perform, as well as those which belong to the sword. . . .

"Also the six 'rectitudines'—whether simple or compound : how, for instance, a right angle is that which most shortens the distance from your adversary, and is the most favourable to the defence ; . . . to make him acquainted with the lines, collateral and diagonal, which can be considered in the body, and how strokes are made therein. . . . To this ought to succeed a description of the paces, whether simple or compound, which foot ought to take them, and what paces are common to both. . . . Then a description of the circle which is imagined between the two combatants, with its chords and its lines of infinity ; and how, within this, are the passes to be performed. . . .

"The master should pay great attention to the angles resulting from the meeting of the blades, and show the scholar how, whether in delivering the attack or making what is called "ganancia,"[1] the angles must needs be four in number, and either all four right angles, or two obtuse and two acute ; he should impress on him that angles formed by the swords meeting at the middle of their length are the most favourable for the defence, whereas acute and obtuse angles are better suited to defence and offence combined. . . .

"He should tell him that there are only two modes of performing strokes in fencing, one being the result of the position of the sword, and the other being by 'ganando los grados al perfil.'[2] . . . That in fencing there are only five strokes : cut, reverse, thrust, half cut, and half reverse,[3] and explain to him how to perform the various movements composing each stroke, whether the sword be free or engaged. . . . To show him how the sword is to be held in the hand, and how important to hold it firmly in order that the force communicated by the body through the arm may be received by the blade, and its movements be strong and rapid. . . . That we should always come on guard at right angles, with the arm straight and without allowing the hand to waver high or low, or to either side. . . . That the body should be held profile-wise, equally poised on both feet, one

[1] This is the "guadagnare di spada" of the Italians—covering oneself on the march by forcibly engaging the adversary's blade. The "ganancia," however, was a notion unknown to Carranza.

[2] Literally, "gaining the degrees to the profile," i.e. gaining the advantage by successive steps round the adversary.

[3] "Tajo, reves, estocada, medio tajo y medio reves." *Half* cuts or reverse were more or less *flipping* cuts, from the right or the left respectively.

heel being in front of the other, but at no greater distance than half a foot, in such a way that if the left foot turned on its heel, its point would just touch the heel of the right. . . . He should teach him the four general strokes, and on what occasions each has the advantage. . . . It would be better that the pupil should never ' play loose '—' batallar '—at the beginning, nor even draw the sword except with the master himself, until he be thoroughly instructed, as well in the practice as in the theory."

All the points of theory that really bear on fencing have been touched in this sketch; but there are a great many more which the author explains, with the utmost gravity, as being of importance to a thorough understanding of this difficult science; such as, for instance, a knowledge of the exact number of different angles that the various parts of the human body can form between themselves. It appears, from his calculation, that this number is eighty-three.

It was only natural that teachers of a system so elaborately worked out in all its aspects should believe in the absolute infallibility of well-performed passes, at least on the supposition that the opponent acted according to the rules of this complicated game. The following naïve passage is picked from a dialogue between master and disciple.

" Disciple.—In all strokes which can be done perfect in ' matter, form, and execution,' there must be one person who acts and another who suffers thereby. The first can do no more than, nor even can he help that the latter should suffer bodily by receiving the stroke.

" Master.—That point I must needs concede, for I cannot deny it."

Carranza seems to have done for Spain what Marozzo did for Italy, namely, to have collected the most approved tricks of swordsmanship in favour among the various teachers of his day—whether " diestros " and members of the corporation of fencing-masters, or mere " espadachinos " and adventurers full of experience—and to have reduced them to a system. But, unlike Marozzo, he spoilt the practical value of his book by his insupportable prolixity.

Carranza and Don Luis Pacheco were household names in England about the end of the sixteenth century, if their frequent occurrence in the works of the dramatists of that period is any criterion.[1]

" They had their time and we can say they were, so had Carranza, so has Don Lewis. . . . Don Lewis of Madrid is the sole master now of the world." [2]

The Germans, as we have seen, were always great fencers; with the

---

[1] Ben Jonson especially, *passim, e g.,* "Every Man in his Humour," where Captain Bobadil, the Paul's man, is so full of the great Carranza.
[2] Id., " The New Inn."

Fig. 44.—Rapier-play in German Schools about 1570.—Meyer.

"Düsack" and the "Schwerdt"—national weapons in Germany, as were the sword and buckler in England—they were, no doubt, second to none.

Fig.45.—A German Guard, Oberhut zur rechten, with the "Rappir."—J. Sutor.

But those were forms of the sword which were destined to disappear before the more elegant and even more practical "Feder." In this respect, notwithstanding the renown of her fencing schools, Germany was in the same position as France and England, and had to follow the lead of Italian masters. But although Germans originated little or nothing in the rapier-play, they practised it with a remarkable vigour, and were always more or less independent of foreign teachers, contenting themselves with translating and assimilating their works. It will be seen that at most times German treatises were, as far as the rapier and small sword are concerned, either translations or imitations of French or Italian books. Lebkommer, however, who dealt with the national weapons only, was original, and even had imitators out of Germany.

Fig. 46.—Meyer's Fencing School. The master teaching the "punta sopramano" of Viggiani. The radii drawn on the target indicate the direction of the cuts, which are the same as those taught by Marozzo. The footprints indicate the previous position of the feet during a pass or lunge.

Meyer's celebrated work, which appeared in 1570, contains in a more systematic shape an equally complete account of the use of the popular weapons, "Düsack," "Schwerdt," "Helleparten," and "Pflegel" (halbert and flail), together with a thorough system of the rapier, imitated from that of Grassi and Vigviani. Although a "Marxbruder" withal, the "Freifechter" of Strasburg had not been above going to Italy in search of the latest information concerning the new fashion in sword-play. Indeed, it may be said that he pushed the practice of this outlandish weapon to a high state of perfection.

Fig. 47.—A German Guard with Sword and Dagger. This is obviously Agrippa's fourth guard.

Fig. 46 shows Meyer instructing a pupil in

that imperfect lunge that was apparently invented by Viggiani,[1] and fig. 12 represents him in the act of teaching the Italian master's fourth guard, whilst fig. 47 is an energetic reproduction of one of Agrippa's attitudes with sword and dagger. The old-fashioned " Schwerdt " and " Düsack " were still practised in Germany long after the use of similar weapons—the

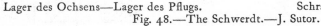

Lager des Ochsens—Lager des Pflugs.   Schranckhut—Hangetort.[2]

Fig. 48.—The Schwerdt.—J. Sutor.

claymore, the " spadone " and the " montanto "—had been discarded by other countries. Nearly all the early Italian authors, also, describe incidentally the practice of the " spadone," but as that weapon could, at any time, have but the remotest influence on the development of rapier-play, it need not be noticed here otherwise than superficially.

The chief requisite for the two-handed sword was great muscular strength combined with suppleness of the wrists. The point was rarely used, and the cuts were nearly the same, and bore the same names, as those of the sword and " Düsack;" the only difference was that they were all *sweeping*. The object aimed at in practice was a combined and opposite action of the two hands on the grip round an imaginary fulcrum. The sword being held with the left hand near or on the pummel, and the right near the quillons, in all cuts delivered from the right the left hand was drawn backwards and the right pressed forward, and in all cuts delivered from the left the action was the same, but the arms were crossed. On the blade of the " Zweyhänder " and the " spadone "

Fig. 49.—Practice at the Target with the Düsack.—J. Sutorium.

---

[1] Viggiani's book, written towards the end of the master's life, was only printed many years after his death. His school flourished in Venice between 1555 and 1563.

[2] The ox, the plough, the cross guard, the hanging guard.

there were generally a pair of hornlike projections situated about a foot below the guard ; these acted as a second guard [1] when it was found necessary to shift the pummel hand, either on account of the impossibility on certain

Fig. 50.—The Düsack.—Countering a cut.

occasions of crossing the arms, or when it was necessary to shorten the weapon in the assault. In such a case, the hand which was previously

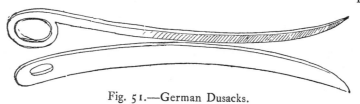

Fig. 51.—German Dusacks.

nearer the pummel was carried below the guard and grasped the blade— which was blunted at that point—under the protection of the horns. The parries were likewise similar to those practised with the sword, namely, counter-ing blows across the adversary's line of attack, with the purpose either of breaking his guard and striking him at one and the same time, or, by throwing his weapon out of line, to make room for a second cut in time. Precisely the same principles were applied to the use of the "Düsack."

Fig. 52.—The Rappier.—J. Sutor.

Forty years later, the work of another "Marxbruder" appeared in Frankfurt and achieved a great reputation in Germany, notwithstanding the fact that it was but a feeble imitation of Meyer. Although Jacob Sutor belonged to the flourishing epoch of Fabris, Giganti, and Capo Ferro's teaching, the rapier-play he describes shows even less perfection than that of Meyer.

[1] This second guard is *not* shown in Sutor's figures.

The Germans seem to have followed the example of Marozzo and Agocchie in the fanciful names of their guards.

The most usual were :—

Oberhut, Underhut, zur rechten oder zur linken (upper and under guards, to the right and to the left), being, in fact, the *becca cesa* and the *coda lunga e larga* of Marozzo.

Eisenport, similar to *cinghiara porta di ferro.*

Rechte oder linke Ochs, which recalls the *guardia d'alicorno*, the unicorn guard of Agocchie.

Langort, similar in meaning to *coda lunga e distesa.*

There were many other attitudes preliminary to such strokes as *Schedelhau oder Oberhau* (skull or top-cut) ; *Schielhau* (skew or cross-cut) ; *Hufft-hau* (hip-cut) ; *Halsshau* (neck-cut) ; *Handhau, Fusshau, Mittelhau, Doppelhau* (hand, foot, middle, and double-cuts) ; *Rundtstreich, Doppelrundtstreich* (round and double round strokes), &c.; also *Dempffhau*, probably from *dàmpfen*, to quell—an "extinguisher," in fact.

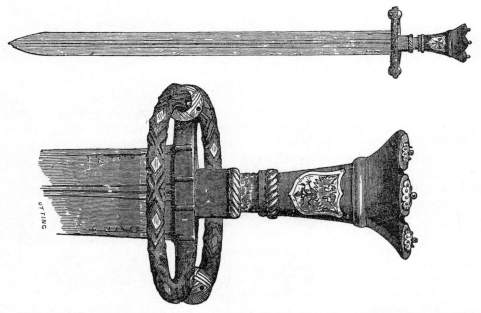

Fig. 53.—Lansquenette or *Landsknecht's* sword. Showing the chief characteristics of the broadsword commonly worn by German foot-men in the sixteenth century. Its practice in fencing was essentially the same as that of the Dusack—length of blade about two feet. (The above sword was found on the north bank of the Thames near Westminster ; it is described in the Journal of the Archæological Institute, vol. xxxiii., p. 92, from which the illustration is taken.)

CHAPTER V.

HE only English treatise on the rapier-play of the sixteenth century, besides a translation of Grassi's work,[1] is " Vincentio Saviolo, his Practise, in two bookes, the first intreating of the use of the Rapier and Dagger, the second of Honor and Honorable quarrels."

This work, which seems to have excited much jealousy among his confrères, is dedicated " as a new yeares gift" " To the Right Honorable, my singular good Lord, Robert, Earle of Essex and Ewe, Viscount Hereford, Lord Ferrers of Chartley, Bourchier and Louain, Master of the Queene's Majesties horse, Knight of the most noble order of the Garter and one of her Highnesse's most honorable privie councell."

Saviolo, though to a smaller extent than his brother swordsmen of Italy and Spain, cannot refrain in his introduction from giving his opinion about letters and arms in general and their respective position and merit, and introducing Minerva with other myths and present entities, whilst he agreeably discusses whether the art and exercise of the rapier and dagger " is not much more rare and excellent than anie other, considering that a man, having the perfect knowledge and practice of this art, although of small stature and weaker strength, may, with a little removing of his foot, a sodaine turning of his hand, a slight declining of his body, subdue and overcome the fierce braving pride of tall and strong bodyes."

This popular teacher was a master of his art, to judge from the report of fame and from the inherent qualities of his treatise. His progression, as moderns would call the systematic arrangement of his passes, is very cleverly devised, and as far as can be seen he was acquainted with both Spanish and Italian fashions. Indeed, he boasted that " he had changed five or six sundrie manners of plaies, taught by divers masters, and reduced unto one by no little labour and paine."

If, however, he made no great advance towards a more effectual system of fencing, he had the merit of having been able to demonstrate the most

[1] See Biblio. True art of defence, 1594.

usual practices without the mysterious tracing of diagrams, circles, chords, and tangents, so dear to authors of the continental schools.

The lessons take the form of dialogues between master, Vincentio, and scholar, Luke, sometimes philosophical, sometimes practical, always very wise indeed, and dogmatic on the master's side, but candid and naïfs on the scholar's.

" *Luke.*—You have with so many reasons and proofes shewed the necessitie of this worthie art, that in truth I greatly esteem and honor it. But, I pray you of freenship, tell me how there can be such disagreement, since all that art consisteth of downe right or crosse blowes, thrustes, foynes, or overthwart prickes." This the master explains by the diversity of methods and weapons in use, and expounds the fact, which was found out by the earliest teachers, and is to this day insisted upon by all fencing-masters, " that the true foundation from whence you may learne all things belonging to this art is the Rapier alone. Moreover, all men of valour and quality have a Rapier, with a point and two edges, by their sides."

Saviolo, separating from the Spanish school, is not of opinion that the rapier should be held with the two first fingers under the cup or guard.

" *Vincent.*—For your Rapier, holde it as you shall thinke fit and commodious for you : but I might advise you should not holde it after this fashion, and especially with the second finger in the hilte. For holding it in that sorte, you cannot reach so far, either to strike direct or crosse blows, or give a foyne or thruste.

" I would have you put your thumb on the hilte "—Saviolo means the quillons—" and the next finger toward the edge of the Rapier."

Nevertheless, not the faintest attempt in the figures accompanying the text is made to represent either the hilt then in fashion, or the manner of holding the rapier ; the weapon shown is of the most conventional type.

Next comes the question of guards, of which indeed, at the time, as Saviolo confesses, there were a "diversitie."

" *Vincent.*—I come therefore to the point and say : that when the teacher will enter his scholler, he shall cause him to stand upon his ward ; so the teacher shall deliver the Rapier into his hand and shall cause him to stand with his right foote formost, with his knee somewhat bowing : but that his bodye rest more upon his left legge, not steadfast and firm, as some stand, which seem to be nailed to the place, but with a readinesse and nimblenesse ; as though he were to perform some feate of activitie.

" And in this sort let them stand, both to strike and to defend themselves. Now when the Maister hath placed his scholler in this sorte, and the scholler hath received his Rapier in his hand, let him make his hand free and at liberty, not by force of the arme, but by the nimble and ready moving of the joint of the wriste of the hand, so that his hand be free and at liberty from his body and that the ward of his hand be directlye against his right knee. And let the teacher also put himselfe in the same ward and holde his Rapier against the midst of his schollers Rapier, so that the pointe be directlye against the face of his scholler, and likewise his scholler's against his. And let their feete be right one against another. Then shall the Maister begin to teach him, moving his right foote somewhat on the right side in circle wise, putting his Rapier under his scholler's Rapier and giving him a thruste in the bellye.

"*Luke.*—And what then must the scholler do?"—L. is evidently somewhat alarmed.

Fig. 54.—Saviolo's Guard with the Rapier alone.

"*Vincent.*—At the self same time the scholler must remove, with like measure or counter time, with his right foote, a little aside, and let the left foote follow the right, turning a little his bodye on the right side, thrusting with the point of his Rapier at the bellye of his teacher, turning redily his hand, that the fingers be inward toward the body, and the joint of the wriste be outward. In this sorte the saide scholler shall learne to strike and not be stricken. And I alwaies advise noblemen and gentlemen that, if they cannot hit and hurt their enemy, that they learne to defend themselves that they be not hurt."

Continuing the lesson, Saviolo shows his scholar how he beats away the thrust, and recovering, delivers a "crosse blowe"—mandritta—at his opponent's head. At this instant the scholar is to pass forward with his left foot and deliver a foyne, an *imbroccata*, lifting his guard to meet the blow. This new thrust the teacher avoids by caving his body; very little caving obviously would suffice in this case.

Thus the bouts succeed each other, master and scholar passing right and left, thrusting imbroccatas and stoccatas, and parrying them either with the left hand, or by escaping backwards or sideways; returning with mandrittas or downright cuts, which in their turn are stopped by counter thrusts delivered with a high opposition.

Saviolo has already volunteered the information that he teaches the cream of many schools; hitherto his practice has been essentially Italian, after the method of Grassi. The following bout, however, is essentially Spanish :—

"*Vinc.*—At the same time that the Maister shall give the said mandritta, the scholler shall doo nothing else but turne the point of his foote toward the bodye of his Maister and let the middest of his left foote directlye respect the heele of his right : and let him turn his bodye upon the right side, but let it reste and staye upon the lefte and in the same time let him turn his Rapier hand outward in the stoccata or thrust, that the point may be toward the bellye of his Maister, and let him lift up his hande and take good heede that he come not forward in delivering the saide stoccata. This is half incartata."

When the scholar has become familiar with the art of passing sideways and " with great readiness thrusting his Rapier into his Maisters belly," he is introduced to passes backwards, accompanied by riversas at the head of his assailant on the delivery of a stoccata.

The foils used by our great grandsires were certainly a severe enough sort of implement, eliciting vague ideas of pokers and crowbars, but then the art they practised was of a most systematic and elegant character ; any man who hit his adversary anywhere but on his fencing jacket committed an act of clumsiness not to be tolerated too often. But what the process of teaching and being taught the cut and thrust fencing of the sixteenth century must have cost in bruises and disfiguration is a difficult thing to realize. Although the word " foil" is used constantly by authors of that period, there are no reasons to believe that they were anything less severe than blunt or rebated swords. In a system, however, which consisted of deliberate thrusts at the face and belly at very close quarters, and of cuts not only from the wrist but from the forearm, the practice in the school was probably of a very conventional type.

In an encounter with sharps, the wounds on both sides were numerous.

Measure and time are of course of great importance in Vincentio's eyes, but, notwithstanding his sententious disquisition on the subject, his good scholar seems to remain somewhat sceptical on the score of " theory."

" *Luke.*—What, I pray you, cannot everyone of himself without teaching, give a mandritta ?"—and thereupon the patient master explains at length what ought, even in our days, to be explained to our young officers when they are put through the course of rhythmical flourishes with round sticks called sword exercise, " that everye man hath not the skill to strike and make it cutte " without exposing himself, or falling forward if the cut be avoided.

Notwithstanding his numerous dissertations on the cuts, mandritti, riversi, stramazoni, and caricadi, which he only taught apparently to meet the natural love of Englishmen for that mode of fight, it is plain that Saviolo believes implicitly in the " point " as meeting all the requirements of personal combat.

" I would not advise any friend of mine, if he were to fighte for his credite and life, to strike neither riversi, nor mandrittaes, because he puts himselfe in danger of his life : for to use the poynt is much more redye and spends not the like time."

Like all the masters of his day, especially in Spain, and singularly at variance with our modern simplified notions, he strongly urges his pupils never to advance in a straight line on their adversary. " I saie that in my judgment it is not goode to use the right line : whereas in removing"—passing—"in circular wise you are more safe from your enemy and you have his weapon at commandment."

The master of fence, especially one of renown, was by common consent, and so to speak ex officio, arbiter on matters of punctilio, honour, and deportment, and looked upon as a kind of master of the ceremonies in all difficulties arising therefrom. Indeed, the bulk of most Italian and Spanish treatises on the art seems to be devoted to the exposition of the art of quarrelling in a gentlemanly manner, quite as much as to the means of utilizing the " honourable weapon " to the greatest advantage.

Accordingly Saviolo, in his position of fashionable master, never loses an opportunity of delivering himself of wise precepts, although he reserves his full consideration on nice points of honour for his " second booke," in which they are all methodically discussed.

After recommending his pupil never to fight without good cause, but if he meet any man sword in hand, to do his best "lest he should be hurt out of his good nature," he goes on to consider general principles, and proceeds at first to explain the use of the left hand.

" *Luke :* But, I praye you, is it not better to breake with the sworde than with the hand ? For, me thinketh, it should be dangerous for hurting the hand."

Vincentio. " I will tell you, this weapon must be used with a glove, but if a man should be without a glove, it were better to hazard a little hurt of the hand thereby to become maister of his enemie's sworde."

Considering the weight and length of the swords still worn at that time, there can be no doubt that very little parrying could be done with the sword itself, except by a countering hit, with anything like safety and rapidity, and therefore the left hand necessarily came into action in order to limit the motion of the sword hand to that of attack.

As Vincentio does not begin by defining the various thrusts and cuts that he proposes to teach his scholar, before giving a few specimens of bouts with the rapier alone, and with rapier and dagger, a classification of cuts and thrusts as they were taught by the Italian masters will not be out of place.[1]

Of thrusts there were three kinds. The first two were classified according to the point of arrival on the adversary's body : the *imbroccata* reached him over his sword, hand, or dagger, travelling rather in a downward direction, and was delivered evidently with the knuckles up, except in the case of

---

[1] Most Italian fencing terms of that period are to be found in Florio's " First Fruit."

a "volte."[1]   It evidently corresponded pretty closely with our thrust in "prime" or "high tierce."

The *stoccata* reached the enemy under the sword, hand, or dagger, and might be delivered with the hand in pronation or any other position.

The third kind of thrust was delivered *from* the left side, and called "punta riversa," and might be directed to any part, high or low.

This classification, which seems somewhat specious now, was practical considering that the rapier, being generally used for offence only, was not necessarily kept in front of the body, and consequently most hits were delivered from a somewhat wide guard on the right.   Hence a thrust from the left side (after passing to the right of the adversary, for instance) was looked upon as belonging to a distinct category.

It was called "riversa" from its analogy with the rinversa, as opposed to mandritta.

Saviolo classifies cuts after the manner of Marozzo.[2]

The passata was the chief means of closing the measure, as well as escaping a hit in a way which allowed of a counter attack at the same time.

Passes were made to the right or left with the right foot followed rapidly by the left; also to the front, provided the opponent's blade had been beaten aside with the left hand or dagger.   To the rear, for the purpose of getting out of measure, or countering with an "imbroccata," a low thrust or a cut at the knee.

The *incartata* corresponded practically to the "volte" as practised till the end of the last century.   The half incartata in a like manner to "demi-volte."

"*Vincent.*   As soon as your rapier is drawne, put yourselfe presentlye on guard, seeking the advantage, and goe not leaping, but while you change from one ward to another, be sure to be out of distance, by retiring a little, because if your enemy is skilfull, he may offend you in the same instant.   And note this well also, that to seke to offend, being out of measure, and not in due time, is very dangerous.   Wherefore, as I tolde you before, having put yourselfe on guard, and charging your adversarie, take heed how you go about, and that your right foot be formost, stealing the advantage little by little, carrying your left legge behinde, with your poynte within the poynte of your enemie's sworde; and so, finding the advantage in time and measure, make a stoccata to the bellye or face of your adversarye, &c."   And now concerning "time."   "When your enemie will charge in advancing the foote, and when he offereth a direct stoccata, then is the time.[3]

"But if he will make a 'punta riversa' within measure, passe forward with your lefte foote and turne your poynte withall, and that is the time.

---

[1] "Incartata."   [2] See page 36.

[3] Saviolo gives no definition of "time" in the abstract, but explains the notion by means of practical examples.

" If he put an imbroccata into you, answer him with a stoccata in the face, turning a little your bodye toward the right side accompanyed with your poynte.

" If he strike a thruste at your legge, carry the same a little circular wise and thrust a stoccata to his face, and that is your right time.

" And if he offer you a stramazone to the head, you must beare it with your swoorde, passing forward with your lefte legge, and turning wel your hand that your poynte may go in, in manner of an ' imbroccata.' "

It is somewhat remarkable that Saviolo so rarely should speak of thrusts in the breast, but rather in the belly or face. By the belly is meant all the part of the body below the ribs. The explanation is probably that in such a place a much slighter puncture would suffice to cause a serious wound. The same would apply to the face, not only on account of its unprotected state, but also of the distressing action of blood in the eyes and mouth.

The rest of the first part of the " Practise " treating of the sword alone, is occupied by directions concerning passing and retiring, time and measure, and beating with the left hand, upon typical attacks.

On rare occasions, especially on the adversary's passes to the right, Saviolo admits of a " beat" with the sword, followed by a stoccata under the arm.

Changing the rapier from the right to the left hand was, it seems, regularly taught and practised with success.

The rapier alone (spada sola) was looked upon in the best fencing schools as the foundation of the science of arms, but as the intervention of the left hand was absolutely necessary for the complete action, at once offensive and defensive, rapier and dagger always went together.

Twenty years before Saviolo wrote his treatise, a small hand buckler or target was the usual complement of the sword in the costume of a gentleman walking abroad,[1] but when the foyning play came in fashion, it was discarded in favour of the dagger, which was at once more elegant and better fitted to ward off a thrust to either side, and cover the enemy's blade.

The second part of the first book " entreats" of the more practical sword and dagger play.

" I will now shewe you how to put yourselfe en garde with your Rapier and Dagger, for if I desire to make a good scholler, I would myself put his Rapier in one hand and his Dagger in the other, and so place his body in the same sorte, that I have before spoken of in the single Rapier, setting his right foote formost with the pointe of his Rapier drawne in short, and the Dagger helde out at length, bending a little his right knee, with the heele of his right foote directlye against the midst of the lefte, causing him to go round toward the lefte side of his adversarye in a good measure, that

---

[1] See Fig. 8.

he may take his advantage; and then I would thrust a stoccata to his bellye beneath his Dagger, removing my right foote a little towards his lefte side.

"*Luke*. And what must the scholler do the whilst?

"*Vincentio*. The scholler must breake it downward with the pointe of his Dagger toward his lefte side, and then put a stoccata to my bellye beneath my Dagger, in which time I, breaking it with the pointe of my Dagger, goe a little aside toward his lefte hand and make an imbroccata above his Dagger; and the scholler shall breake the imbroccata with his Dagger upward, parting circularely with his right foote toward my lefte side, and so thrust unto mee an imbroccata above my Dagger, in which time, with the pointe of my Dagger, I will beate it outward toward my lefte side and answere him with a stoccata in the bellye under his Dagger, parting circularely with my right foote toward his lefte side, stepping toward my lefte side with his right foote; at which time I must moove with my bodye to save my face, and breake his pointe toward my right side, answering him with a riversa to the head, and so retire with my right foote. At this time he must go forward with his lefte foote in the place of my right, and his Dagger high and straite, turning his swoorde hand so that his pointe may go directlye to my bellye, and he must take the riversa on his swoorde and Dagger."

Stoccatas and imbroccatas were generally beaten "outwards" with the dagger, that is, the left side.

Imbroccatas riversas were beaten "inwards," to the right.

The dagger was often used to beat the adversary's point aside, preliminary to making a thrust at the face.

"*Vincent*. Either of you being within distance observing time, the first offerer is in danger to be slain or wounded in the counter time especially if he thrust resolutelye; but if you be skilfull, and not the other, then you may gain time and measure and so hit him saving yourselfe. . . . .

"Some are of opinion that they can hit him that shall hit them first, but such have never fought: or if by chance in one fight they have been so fortunate, let them not think that summer is come because one swallow is seene! . . . .

"If your enemie carry his swoorde short in an open ward, you maie come straight on him and give him a punta riversa, either in the bellye or face, with such readiness that your swoorde be halfe within his Dagger before hee can breake it, turning nimblye your hand toward your lefte side, so that in offering to breake it, he shall make himselfe be hit either in the face, or in the bellye: and forget not to retire an halfe pace with the right foote accompanied with the lefte.

"If the adversary assume a high guard, you may feint a stoccata to his bellye, so causing him to answere you, then pass your bodye to his lefte side; then, on his thrust, bear it to the right, passing your right foote at the same moment to your lefte, at the same time making a riversa above his swoorde." . . . .

Against a low guard—

"You may charge him on the right side, bending you bodye to the lefte, and then, having gotten the advantage, you must suddenly pass with your lefte foote, turning withall your pointe under his swoorde, that it ascend to his bellye, and clap your Dagger as neere as you can to the hiltes of his swoorde : all which, together with the motion of the bodye, must be done at one instant."

Another guard with rapier and dagger was thus :—Right foot foremost, sword hand near the right thigh, point as high as the mouth, dagger hand about the height of left breast, point pointing to adversary's shoulder. In this guard the master will—

"Give a stoccata in the middle of the Rapier, in punta riversa to his scholler, or else betweene the Arme and the Rapier, escaping a little backward with his right foote, accompanied somewhat with his lefte, towards his lefte side.

"*Luke.*—What shall the scholler do in the meane while?

Fig. 55.—Saviolo's Second Guard with Rapier and Dagger.

"*Vincentio.*—While your maister giveth you the thrust you shall not strike it by with your Dagger, but onlie turning your Rapier hand, passe with your lefte foote towards his right side, the pointe of your Rapier, being placed above his and thruste forward, shall enter right into his bellye.

"*Luke.*—And what shall the maister do to save himselfe?

"*Vincentio.*—When hee giveth the thruste and you passe towards his right side, hee shall with great nimbleness recoyle a little backward with his right foote, bearing his bodye backward and searching your Rapier with his Dagger give you a mandritta at the head.

"*Luke.*—Then what remains for me to do?

"*Vincentio.*—You shall come with your right foote to the place where your Maisters right foote was, and shall give him a thruste in the bellye or in the face, receiving the mandritta upon your Rapier and Dagger," &c. &c.

Saviolo attaches great importance to the position of the dagger hand, which he considered should be very steady, and to that of the point, which was to be kept down or up, according as the adversary's attack was delivered upwards or downwards.

Saviolo advocates also a third guard with sword and dagger, which is as follows :—Left foot forward, dagger hand well out in front in line with shoulder, knuckles outwards, sword hand close to right hip, point on a level with that of dagger.

These few extracts will suffice to show, although in no way original, Saviolo so understood his art as to justify his great reputation. Rapier-play, coarse as it may seem to modern fencers, was such an improvement on the older-fashioned sword and buckler fighting, and so much better suited to the requirements of a gentleman, that the first successful teachers of the foreign art were bound to be looked upon with immense favour by the society which flourished under Elizabeth ; the quaintness of the foreign terms they used, and the philosophical digressions on what had hitherto been considered as a most matter-of-fact subject, that of hard knocks, were then thought especially fascinating.

There was something wonderfully novel to sturdy Englishmen in such a description of a pugnacious gallant as the following : " O he's a courageous captain of complements : he fights as you sing prick song, keeps time, distance, and proportion ; rests me his minim rest ; one, two, and the third in your bosom : the very butcher of a silk button ; a gentleman of the very first house, of the first and second cause : ah ! the immortal passado ! the punto riverso, the hay ! " [1]

The " captain of complements," the " first and second cause," and " fencing by the book of arithmetic," [2] were notions evidently gathered in the school of some pupil of Carranza, but the " butcher of a silk button " could only refer to the well-known anecdote which has been given in the " Notice of three Italian masters of fence." [3]

Many references to Vincentio as a fashionable teacher are to be found in authors of that period ; his name was as familiar then, as was that of Angelo some sixty years ago.   The following is rather quaint :—

Oh ! come not within distance Martius speaks
Who ne'er discourseth but of fencing feats,
Of counter time, fincture, sly passataes,
Stramazzone, resolute stoccataes ;
Of the quick change with the wiping mandritta,
The caricado with th' imbroccata.
The honourable fencing mystery
Who does not honour ? Then falls he in again
Jading our ears ; and somewhat must be sain
Of blades, and Rapier hilts, and surest guard,
Of Vincentio and the Burgonian's ward.[4]

---

[1] " Romeo and Juliet."   [2] " Romeo and Juliet," act iii. sc. 1.
[3] See page 23.   [4] Marston's " Scourge of Villany," Sat. xi. Book 3.

There was then a perfect infatuation for the rapier, the scientific play of which naturally delighted the more refined and educated classes. But the foreign fashion always met with much opposition among the bulk of Englishmen, old-fashioned, untravelled, and matter-of-fact.

" Tut, sir," says Shallow, on hearing of the Frenchman's skill in rapier fight, " I could have told you more. In these times you stand on distance, your passes, stoccadoes and I know not what : 'tis the heart, Master Page : 'tis the heart : 'tis here : 'tis here. I have seen the time, with my long sword I would have made you four tall fellows skip like rats." [1]

But it was especially among the old-established masters of fence that the resentment against the influence of foreign teachers ran highest, as was shown in George Silver's malicious biographical sketch of Rocco, Saviolo, and Geronimo.

Not having succeeded in disposing of Saviolo sword in hand, Silver undertook to combat him with the pen, by attacking all the points of Italian fencing in his " Paradoxe of Defence," which, in order to be even with Saviolo, he dedicated :—

" To the Right honorable, my singular good Lord, Robert Earle of Essex and Ewe, &c. &c. &c.

" Fencing (Right honourable) in this new fangled age is like our fashions, resembling the Camelion who altereth himselfe into all colours save white : so fencing changeth into all wards save the right . . . . To seek for a true defence in an untrue weapon is to angle on the earth for fish, and to hunt on the sea for hares. . . . And (Right honourable) if we will have true defence we must seeke it where it is, in short swords, short staves, the half pike, Partisans, Gleves, or such like weapons of perfect length, not in long swords, long rapiers, nor frog pricking poniards. . . . English maisters of defence are profitable members in the commonwealth, if they teach, with ancient English weapons of true defence weight and convenient lengths, within the compasse of the statures and strength of men.

" But the rapier in reason ought not to be, nor suffered to be taught, because it maketh men fearfull and unsafe in single combats and weak and unserviceable in the warres. . . .

" To prove this I have set forth these my paradoxes, different I must confesse from the maine current of our outlandish teachers. . . .

" We, like degenerate sonnes, have forsaken our forefathers vertues with their weapons, and have lusted like men sicke of a strange ague after the strange vices of Italian, French and Spanish fencers, little remembering that their apish toyes could not free Rome from Brennus' sack, nor France from Henrie the fifth his conquest.

---

[1] " Merry Wives," act i. sc. 1.

" These Italian fencers teach us offence not defence.[1]

" They teach men to butcher one another at home in peace, wherewith they cannot hurt their enemies abrode in warre. For your honour well knows that when the battels are joined, and come to the charges, there is no roome for them to drawe their bird spits. And when they have them, what can they do with them ? can they peerce his corslet with the point, can they unlace his helmet, hew under their pikes with a stocata, a riversa, a dritta, a stramason or other such like tempestuous terms ?

" No, the toyes are fit for children not for men, for straggling boyes of the campe to murder poultrie, not for men of honour to try battell with their foes . . . . they kill our friends in peace but cannot hurt our foes in warre."

Claiming to have most perfect experience of all manners of weapons, George Silver advises his countrymen " to beware how they submit themselves into the hands of Italian teachers, but hold to the good ancient weapons. Our ploughmen have mightily prevailed against them, as also against maisters of defence both in schooles and countries that have taken upon them to stand upon schoole trickes and jugling gambalds : whereby it grew a common speech among the countriemen, bring me to a fencer and I will bring him out of his fence trickes with good downright blows, I will make him forget his fence trickes. I speake not against masters of defence, —they are to be honoured,—nor against the science—it is noble and in mine opinion to be preferred next to Divinitie.—And moreover the exercising of weapons putteth away aches, griefes and diseases, it increaseth strength and sharpeneth the wits, it giveth a perfect judgment, it compelleth melancholy choleric and evil conceits, it keepeth a man in breath, perfect health and long life. It is unto him that hath the perfection thereof a most friendly and comfortable companion when he is alone, having but only his weapon about him, it putteth him out of all feare.

" And for as much as this noble and most mightie nation of English-men, of their good nature are always most loving, very credulous and readie to cherish and protect strangers, yet that through their good nature they never more by strangers or false teachers may be deceived once againe, I am most humbly to admonish them that from henceforth, first before they learne of them they cause a sufficient triall of them to be made, whether the excellencie of their skill be such as they professe or no : the trial to be very requisite and reasonable, even such as I myself would be contented withall, if I could take upon me to go into their countrie to teach their nation to fight. And this is the trial : they shall play with such weapons as they profess to teach withall, three bouts apeece with three of the best maisters of defence, and three bouts apeece with three unskilful valient men, and three

---

[1] There was some truth in this statement.

bouts apeece with three resolute men halfe drunke. Then if they can defend themselves against these maisters of defence, and hurt and go free from the rest, they are to be honored, cherished, and allowed for perfect good teachers, what countreymen soever they be ; but if of anie of these they take faile ; then are they imperfect in their profession, their fight is false and they are false teachers, deceivers and murtherers and to be punished accordingly, yet no worse punishment unto them I wish than such as in their triall they shall find.

"There are foure especiall markes to know the Italian fight is imperfect and that the Italian teachers and setters of books of Defence never had the perfection of the true fight.

"The first marke is, they seldome fight in their owne countrie unarmed, commonly in this sort : a paire of gauntlets upon their hands and a good shirt of maile upon their bodyes. The second marke is that, neither the Italians nor any of their best scholers do never fight but they are commonly sore hurt, or one or both of them slaine. The third marke is, they never teach their schollers, nor sett downe in their bookes of defence anie perfect lengthes of their weapons, without the which no man can by nature or art fight safe against the perfect length. For, being too short, their times are too long and spaces too wide for their defence, and being too long, they will be, upon everie crosse [1] that shall happen to be made, whether it be done by skil or chance, in great danger of death because, the Rapier being too long, the crosse cannot be undone in due time, but may be done by going backe with the feete : but that time is always too long to answere the time of the hand, therefore every man ought to have a weapon according to his own stature. . . .

"The fourth marke is, the crosses of their Rapiers for the true defence of their hands are imperfect for the true cariage of the guardant fight without the which all fights are imperfect."

In many respects Silver was greatly in advance of his age with regard to true principles of the art of fighting. He seems to have been the first who clearly explained the necessity of proportioning the length of the weapon to that of the arm, and pointed out that the weight of the sword then in fashion was such as altogether to prevent fencers " to offend and defend in due time, and by these two last causes many valiant men have lost their lives."

"OF THE FALSE RESOLUTIONS AND VAINE OPINIONS OF RAPIER MEN, AND OF THE DANGER OF DEATH THEREBY ENSUING.

"It is a great question and especially among the Rapier-men who hath the vantage, of the thruster or the warder.

---

[1] Crosses = parries, *i.e.* by crossing or countering.

"Now when two happen to fight being both of one mind that the thruster hath the vantage, they make all shift they can who shall give the first thrust: as for example two Captaines at Southampton even as they were going to take shipping upon the key, fel at strife, drew their Rapiers and presentlye, being desperate, hardie and resolute as they call it, with all force and over great speed, ran with their Rapiers one at the other and both were slaine.

"Now when two of the contrarie opinion shall meet and fight, you shall see very peaceable warres betweene them, for they verilye think that he that first thrusteth is in great danger of his life, therefore with all speede do put themselves in ward, or stocata, the surest guard of all others as Vincentio sayth, and thereupon they stand sure saying the one to the other; thrust and then dare; strike or thrust and then dare for thy life sayth the other. These two cunning gentlemen standing long together upon this worthie ward, they both depart in peace, according to the old proverb: it is good sleeping in a whole skin! . . .

"Then thus I conclude, that the truth may appeare for the satisfaction of all men, that there is no advantage absolutely nor disadvantage either in the striker, thruster or warder, but whosoever gaineth the place in true pace, space and time hath the advantage, and this is my resolution."

In Master Silver's opinion, "the cause that so manie are slaine and many sore hurt in fight with long rapiers is not by reason of their dangerous thrustes, nor cunningness of that Italianated fight, but in the length and unwieldiness thereof." Also, that if we consider the two different methods of "running and standing in Rapier fights, the runner hath the advantage."

"OF SPANISH FIGHT WITH THE RAPIER.

"The Spaniard is now thought to be a better man with his rapier than is the Italian, Frenchman, high Almaine, or any other country man whatsoever, because they in their rapier-fight stand upon so many intricate trickes, that in all the course of a man's life it shall be harde to learne them, and if they misse doing the least of them in their fight, they are in danger of death. But the Spaniard in his fight, both safely to defend himselfe and to endanger his enemie, hath but one lying and two wardes to learne, wherein a man with small practise in a verie short time may become perfect.

"This is the manner of Spanish fight: they stand as brave as they can with their bodies straight upright, narrow spaced, with their feet continually moving, as if they were in a dance, holding forth their arms and rapiers verie straight against the face or bodies of their enemies: and this is the only way to accomplish that kind of fight. And this note that as long as any man shall lie in that manner with his arme and point of his rapier straight it shall be impossible for his adversary to hurt him, because whichsoever way the blow shall be made against him, by reason that his Rapier hilt lyeth so farre before him, he hath but verie little way to move to make his ward perfect.   In this manner : if a blow be made at the right side of the head, a verie little moving of the hand with the knuckles upward defendeth that side of the head and bodie, and the point being still greatly endangers the striker ; so likewise if a blow be made at the left side of the head, a verie small turning of the wrist, with the knuckles downward, defendeth that side of the head and body.   And if a thrust be made on them, the wards, by reason of the indirections in moving the feet in manner of dancing as aforesaid, maketh a perfect ward and still withall the point greatly endangereth the other ; and thus is the Spanish fight perfect."

However, Silver has enough sense to see that the chief difficulty is to keep that point straight in the adversary's eyes, by dexterously defeating any attempt to beat it aside.

"ILLUSIONS FOR THE MAINTENANCE OF IMPERFECT WEAPONS, AND FALSE FIGHTS TO FEARE OR DISCOURAGE THE UNSKILFUL OF THEIR WEAPONS, FROM TAKING A TRUE COURSE OR USE, FOR ATTAINING THE PERFECT KNOWLEDGE OF TRUE FIGHT.

"First, for the Rapier (saith the Italian or false teacher) I hold it to be a perfect good weapon, because the crosse hindreth not to hold the handle, to thrust both far and straight and to use all manner of advantages in the wards, or sodainly to cast the same at the adversarie, but with the Sword you are driven with all the strength of the hand to hold fast the handle.   And in the warres I would wish no friend of mine to weare swords with hilts, because when they are sodainly set upon for haste they set their hands upon their hilts instead of their handles : in which time it hapneth many a time before they can draw their sword they are slaine by their enemies.   And for Sword and Buckler fight it is imperfect because the buckler blindeth the sight, neither would I have anie man lie aloft with his hand above his head to strike strong blowes. Strong blowes are naught, especially being set above the head, because therein all the bodie and face is discovered.   Yet I confess, in old time, when blowes were only used with short swords and bucklers, and back sword these kinds of fight were good and most manly, but now in these daies fight is altered. Rapiers are longer for advantage than swords were wont to be when blowes were used ; men were so simple in their fight, that they thought him a coward that wold made a thrust, or strike a blow beneath the girdle.   Againe if their weapons were short, as in times past they were, yet fight is better looked into

in these days than then it was.   Who is it in these dayes seeth not that the
blow compasseth round like a wheele whereby it hath a longer way to go,
but the thrust passeth in a straight line and therefore cometh a nearer way
and is done in a shorter time than is the blow ?   Therefore there is no wise
man that will strike, unlesse he be wearie of his life.   It is certaine that the
point for advantage everie way in fight is to be used, the blow is utterly
naught, and not to be used.   He that fighteth upon the blow, especially with
a short sword, will be sore hurt or slaine.   The Devill can say no more for
the maintenance of errors."

The following are a few of the arguments advanced by Silver on behalf
of the English masters of fence.   Comment as to the fallacy of some of
them, and on the apparently wilful misconception of the Italian system, is
useless :—

"That a blow cometh continually as neare a way as a thrust, and most
commonly nearer, stronger, more swifter, and is sooner done.

" Perfect fight standeth upon both blow and thrust, therefore the thrust
is not onely to be vsed.

"That the blow is more dangerous and deadly in fight, then a thrust, for
proofe thereof to be made according with Art, an Englishman holdeth argument against an Italian.

" *Italian.*—Which is more dangerous or deadly in fight of a blow or a
thrust ?

" *Englishman.*—This question is not propounded according to art, because there is no fight perfect without both blow and thrust.

" *Italian.*—Let it be so, yet opinions are other wise holden, that the
thrust is onely to be vsed, because it commeth a nearer way, and is more dangerous and deadly, for these reasons : first the blow compasseth round like a
wheele, but the thrust passeth in a straight line, therfore the blow by
reason of the compasse, hath a longer way to go than the thrust, and is therefore longer in doing, but the thrust passeth in a straight line, therfore hath
shorter way to go then hath the blow, and is therfore done in a shorter
time, and is therfore much better than the blow, and more dangerous and
deadly, because if a thrust do hit the face or bodie, it indangereth life,
and most commonly death ensueth : but if the blow hit the bodie, it is not so
dangerous.

" *Englishman.*—Let your opinions be what they wil, but that the thrust
commeth a nearer way, and is sooner done than the blow, is not true : and for
proofe thereof reade the twelfth paradox.   And now will I set downe probable
reasons, that the blow is better than the thrust, and more dangerous and
deadly.   First, the blow commeth as neare a way, and most commonly nearer
than doth the thrust, and is therefore done in a shorter time than is the
thrust : therfore in respect of time, wherupon standeth the perfection of fight,

the blow is much better than the thrust.   Againe, the force of the thrust passeth straight, therefore any crosse being indirectly made, the force of a child may put it by : but the force of a blow passeth directly, therefore must be directly warded in the counter-checke of his force : which cannot be done but by the conuenient strength of a man, and with true crosse in true time, or else will not safely defend him : and is therefore much better, and more dangerous than the thrust, and againe, the thrust being made through the hand, arme, or leg, or in many places of the body and face, are not deadly, neither are they maimes, or losse of limmes or life, neither is he much hindred for the time in his fight, as long as the blood is hot : for example.

"I haue knowne a gentleman hurt in Rapier fight, in nine or ten places through the bodie, armes and legges, and yet hath continued in his fight, and afterwards hath slaine the other, and come home and hath bene cured of all his wounds without maime, and is yet living.   But the blow being strongly made, taketh somtimes cleane away the hand from the arme, hath manie times bene seene.   Againe vpon the head or face with a short sharpe sword, is most commonly death.   A full blow vpon the necke, shoulder, arme or legge, indangereth life, cutteth off the veines, muscles, and sinewes, perisheth the bones : these wounds made by the blow, in respect of perfect healing, are the losse of limmes, or maimes incurable for euer.

"And yet more for the blow : a ful blow vpon the head, face, arme, leg or legs, is death, or the partie so wounded in the mercie of him that shall so wound him.   For what man shall be able long in fight to stand vp, either to reuenge, or defend himselfe, hauing the veines, muscles, and sinewes of his hand, arme, or leg cleane cut asunder? or being dismembred by such wound vpon the face or head, but shall be enforced therby, and through the losse of bloud, the other a little dallying with him, to yeeld himself, or leaue his life in his mercie?

"And for plainer deciding this controuersie betweene the blow and the thrust, consider this short note.   The blow commeth manie wayes, the thrust doth not so.   The blow commeth a nearer way than a thrust most commonly, and is therefore sooner done.   The blow requireth the strength of a man to be warded ; but the thrust may be put by, by the force of a child.   A blow vpon the hand, arme, or legge is a maime incurable, but a thrust in the hand, arme, or legge is to be recouered.   The blow hath manie parts to wound, and in euerie of them commandeth the life ; but the thrust hath but a few, as the bodie or face, and not in euerie part of them neither."

CHAPTER VI.

E might pass over Marco Docciolini, who certainly introduced no improvement into the art, but for one passage which illustrates clearly how general was the method of looking on time thrusts as the most perfect attacks, and on " crossing "—what the French call " barrer "—as the best parries, both attacks and parries being performed on a pass sideways.

In a paragraph treating of " tempo, contro tempo," and " mezzo tempo," " It is necessary," say Docciolini, " that in taking a ' time ' thou shouldst remove thy body from ' the line ;' and that thou shouldst seize thy ' time ' whenever thy adversary displaces his point from the line of thy body. So much for ' tempo contra tempo ;' ' mezzo tempo ' is this: *when thine enemy thrusts at thee, break thou his thrust, striking him at the same time.*"

After wading through the meandering discourse of so many philosophical swordsmen, it is refreshing to turn over the leaves of Fabris' " Schermo," and find at last a clear, methodical exposition of the science of arms.

Fabris, if not a great innovator, was at least a man who knew all that was to be known on swordsmanship in his day, and who made a system out of the best methods he could find. The extraordinary work which he published towards the end of a life devoted to his profession, embodies practically the whole of the science of fence as it was understood in the latter part of the sixteenth century.

Fabris was born in Bologna in 1544, and began the profession of arms when Marozzo was still teaching in his old age, when Agrippa yet lived, and when Agocchie and Viggiani, his own fellow-townsmen, taught in Venice, as also did Grassi. Later on he travelled through Spain, France, and Germany. From Sainct Didier and Meyer he probably had nothing to learn, but one may feel sure that in Spain he found means of meeting the great Carranza and studying his method.

Towards 1590 he was attracted to the Danish Court by Christian IV., a great devotee of the science of arms, under whose patronage he published his treatise.

Fabris considered that nothing on earth was so great and good as fencing, and consequently devoted all his time to it ; there is not a word in his 250 folio pages, nor one of his 190 plates, which does not refer to " practical " fencing. It is easy to trace in his exposition of the subject some portion of the methods of most of his predecessors, although he dismisses the treatment of all that refers to the cut—" tagli "—in very few words. Indeed, towards the end of the sixteenth century, the tendency of masters was decidedly to discard cutting almost altogether.

As Fabris' system contains all the principles that had been found most practical in his time, and foreshadows all the refinements and the simplifications that were to take place during the seventeenth century,—moreover, as he is the first author who followed throughout the rational system of defining before applying, and of proceeding from the general to the special,—an analysis of his work will be a fitting conclusion to this sketch of the first epoch in the history of fencing.

Fabris divides his work into two books and six parts. The first book treats thoroughly the question of broad principles and of the more " academic " actions with the rapier, alone or accompanied with dagger or cloak ; it discusses in a very exhaustive manner the relative value of the past and present methods. The second book is one " wherein is demonstrated certain rules with which it will be possible to strike the enemy from the moment the sword is drawn, without halting or waiting any time, principles which have never been treated by any master or writer."

This second book is written on the same plan as, and is merely an elaborate amplification of, the first. It describes a more active way of fighting on the march, applicable to occasions when the conditions of the encounter are not settled beforehand, as they would be in a strictly " single " combat or in the fencing room.

When it is remembered that duels were at that epoch rarely fought without seconds, and that the code of honour never prevented a man who had despatched his adversary from rushing to the help of his friends, the reason is obvious why Fabris attaches such importance to his method of engaging with an opponent without halting in front of him. But as it contains no new principles, a sketch of the introduction to the first part will suffice for the purpose of this book.

The four principal guards of Fabris bear a great resemblance to those of his predecessors in Italy who believed in the superiority of the point—those of Agrippa, Grassi, and the "perfect guards" of Viggiani. He preserves the old meaning of the word " guardia," namely, that of an attitude favourable to the delivery of a certain set of attacks. The notion of defence—

beyond that of being in a position to strike the adversary—was, of course, quite subordinate as long as the theory was held that to parry without attacking at the same time was a mistake.

But in his definition of the "contra postura" or "contra guardia" the beginning of the modern meaning of a guard is to be found.

Fig. 56.—Ferita di seconda, contra una quarta, passata di pie sinistro. A thrust "in seconda," by a pass, timed, on the adversary's pass to the left, by disengaging, from outside.—Fabris.

The four principal guards are thus formed :—

"The *first* is the position assumed when, the sword being just drawn out of the scabbard, its point is turned towards the adversary, for we think it better that all guards should be formed in that manner ; the *second* is when the hand is slightly lowered; the *third,* when it is held naturally without being turned, either to one side or to the other ; the *fourth,* when it is turned towards the inside,"—the left side.

"But besides these four principal, there are three *intermediate* guards, suitable to special occasions."

Fig. 57.—Ferita di quarta, contra una terza. Time thrust taken on the adversary's feint of disengagement.—Fabris.

These definitions refer only to the position of the sword. Any one of them may be assumed with any given "postura," or position of the body. Against any posture assumed by the adversary Fabris considers it wise to oppose a similar one as a "contra postura."

As the author seems to have exercised his ingenuity in representing all the possible postures that can be assumed by human bodies with any given guard, some of the plates do certainly represent the most preposterous attitudes.

The fencers are directed to fall on guard and assume such posture, with that guard, as best suits them. The guard is a position for attack for the hand; the guard and posture combined determine the kind of thrust—the "botta"—that is to be delivered. It is therefore necessary for the defensive side to assume the "contra postura," with the same guard as his opponent.

"Wishing," says Fabris, "to form the 'contra postura,' it is necessary so to place the body and the sword, that without touching the enemy's weapon one should be protected in the straight line which comes from the adversary's point towards the body, and that one should be thus in safety without making any movement whatsoever. In short, that the enemy should not be able to strike the part menaced, but, on the contrary, be obliged—for the purpose of attacking—to carry his sword elsewhere. In so doing he must use more time and afford a better opportunity to the parry. . . .

"But in assuming that position it is also necessary so to hold the sword that it can resist the pressure of the adversary's. This rule holds good against all his postures and changes of guard, whether he also use a poniard, or any other defensive weapon, or only his sword. He who shall display most cleverness in thus maintaining himself in the proper 'contra guardia,' shall have great advantage over his enemy. . . .

"But it often occurs that while you form the 'contra postura,' the adversary assumes another 'postura,' and this often also out of measure, so that when you advance to strike him, he can at the same time that you move your foot assume the advantage over you by means of a new 'contra postura.' It is therefore necessary to be rich in expedients."

Fabris defines the two measures much more closely than any of his predecessors: "misura larga," wide measure, that in which it is possible to strike the enemy by advancing one step; "misura stretta," close measure, that in which this can be done by merely extending the arm without moving the body.

The adversaries assume their "contra posture" out of measure, and, by advancing cautiously on each other, come within "misura larga." They take care never to close to "misura stretta" without either delivering a thrust, or making a feint in order to stay the inevitable time hit. "In all attacks," says Fabris, "be careful not to throw the thrust with too much violence and not to over-reach,"—a precaution of even greater moment with the unwieldy rapier than with light modern swords.

The question whether it was better to adopt the method of making two distinct motions in parrying and returning had been mooted and decided in the negative by nearly all the masters of the age. Fabris expresses himself even more decidedly in favour of the "stesso tempo," single time, against the "dui tempi," double time.

"And now, to come to the subject of the 'dui tempi,' we have to say, that although this method may succeed well enough against certain men, nevertheless, it is impossible to consider it as good as that of parrying and

striking at the same time.   For the correct and only secure way of fighting
is to meet your adversary's body at the same time as it presses forward, otherwise it will immediately retire safe and sound. . . . Our experience has been
that most of those who practise the method of ' dui tempi ' are in the habit
when they meet the adversary's blade, of beating it, so as to go in afterwards
and strike.   This method might succeed generally, but for the danger of
being deceived."

Fabris goes on to explain, in great detail, when it is proper to parry and
when it is a mistake, and to demonstrate that no parry is good that does not
strike the adversary at the same time.   He maintains that a blow may always
be warded by menacing the opponent, on his attack, by a movement which also
covers the body ; in short, by assuming in time the necessary " contra postura."

Fig. 58.—Ferita di quarta contra una seconda.   A counter by
means of a " volte " on the adversary's disengagement, avoiding the
parry attempted by the left hand.—Fabris.

This theory of the " stesso tempo " remained an article of faith among
fencers as long as the length of the blade remained uncurtailed.   It exists
at the present day nearly unchanged in the few old Spanish fencing schools
where the *spada* [1] is still taught, and is perceptible in a modified way in the
modern Neapolitan play.   It was only discarded by the French when, some
eighty years later, they began to reduce the dimensions of their swords to
such an extent that practice blades were used even shorter than the modern
French foil.

The " contra postura" was not complete, when within close measure,
without the engagement of the adverse blade, the " trovare di spada."

After the question of distance naturally comes that of time.

" A ' time ' is a movement that one of the fencers makes within distance
. . . thus a time is an opportunity, either for striking or assuming an advan-

---

[1] In contradistinction to the *florete*.

tage over your enemy. Indeed, that name of time was given to any movement which is made under arms, in order to express that during that time the enemy can do nothing else : and that is the moment to strike him."

The obvious attack against a man well covered in his "contra postura," is the disengagement—the "cavatione"[1] of the sword. Again Fabris is the first master who absolutely defined the rules of engagement and disengagement.

"When the enemy tries to engage your sword, or to beat it aside : without letting him engage or beat it, you must make a cavatione di tempo "— *i.e.* time a disengagement.

" A 'contra cavatione'[2] is that which can be done, during the time that the enemy disengages, by disengaging yourself, so that he shall find himself situated as before. . . .

" A 'ricavatione'[3] is what you may do after the first cavatione, and whilst your adversary makes a 'contra cavatione ;' in other words, making a second disengagement so as to deceive his action. . . .

" We call 'meggia cavatione'[4] one in which the sword does not complete its passage from one side to another, but remains under the opponent's blade."

This passage from a high line to a low one is still called " mezza cavazione " by the Italians.

On the subject of feints, Fabris is very anxious to let his pupils beware of useless, and therefore dangerous ones.

"Some, when making feints, move more with their feet than their swords, stamping as much as they can, trying to frighten the enemy and disturb him before striking him. This may sometimes be effectual, in the schools especially, where the floor being made of boards is consequently highly resonant, but out in the open, in the fields, where the ground is not sonorous, no such effect can be produced. . . . Moreover, should this be done within measure, it is time lost. . . .

" Others make feints of attacks with the body, but without much extending the arm, hoping that the enemy may not meet the sword on his parry, and to strike him when his point is thus displaced by his futile attempt. But although this device may succeed with timid persons, it will be of little avail with one who understands the art, for he would certainly check it with a time thrust. . . .

" There are others again, who feign to carry their point forward, and when the adversary comes to parry, first draw in their sword and then hurl back the thrust. This is even a worse mistake than the others, for then

---

[1] Literally, "drawing away."
[2] Counter disengagement—" contre."
[3] Double disengagement—"doublé."
[4] Literally, half disengagement.

the sword, which ought to go through one motion only, performs three instead."

Then the author proceeds to show that in order to succeed with a feint, it should be pushed sufficiently far to oblige the adversary to take notice of it, and should be directed against such parts only as are obviously uncovered, so as to be really threatening. He explains that the change from the false to the real attack should only take place when the adversary begins to parry the former; "remembering that there is always a danger of being stopped by a time thrust if the 'contra guardia' is not correctly kept"—in other words, if the attacking party uncovers himself during the feint.

Had Fabris taught his pupils the lunge, even as it was practised by his younger contemporaries Giganti and Capo Ferro, nothing would have been wanting in his method to make it as perfect a system of fence as could be

Fig. 59.—Ferita di seconda contra una quarta. A thrust by disengaging and passing, with an opposition of the left hand.— Fabris.

devised for the rapier. But he does not appear to have appreciated the value of the innovation, for he speaks of the " ferire a piede fermo," [1] merely as an expedient to be used on few occasions. This is how he defines the imperfect method of lunging that was becoming a feature in the science :—

" By ' ferire a piede fermo' I mean a way of delivering a thrust by carrying the right foot forward and retiring immediately afterwards, or that of striking by merely moving the body, but without stirring the left foot. Passing, on the other hand, consists in carrying forward both feet alternately."

In both cases he recommends constant practice in bending the body forward so as to increase the reach, and in recovering rapidly in order to avoid the counter.

[1] " Tirer de pied ferme."

Concerning the way of holding the Rapier.

"Many are the ways of holding the sword, and keeping the arm. Some hold their swords at an angle, and their arm a little forward towards the knee.[1] Others draw their arm back, but have their sword so as to form nearly a straight line from the elbow to the point. Others, again, keep their arm and sword in a straight line from the shoulder."[2]

Fabris gives the preference to the last two methods; to the second because he considers it convenient for parrying, and to the third because it keeps the adversary away and is convenient for time thrusts.

After discussing the best attitudes, he explains, very plausibly, why a man should reduce his effective length by doubling himself up, and so obtain

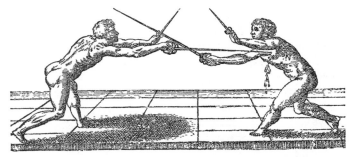

Fig. 60.—A counter, on the adversary's thrust in quarta, which is parried with the dagger.—Fabris.

better cover behind his guard, as well as save time in the attack, " since," as he before demonstrated, "an attack is much more efficacious when the body is well pressed forward." Moreover, as the great desideratum is a variety of postures with each guard, and a fertility of resources in passing from one to the other, it is better, in his opinion, to gymnasticize the body into as many attitudes as possible, so as to minimize the danger of time thrusts by the unforeseen nature of the attack.

These are the broad principles which Fabris applies to his series of one hundred and ninety cases, illustrated by as many plates, ranging from the mere opposition of guards and contra postures, to the most complicated bouts his long experience had acquainted him with.

The science of arms owes to Fabris the elucidation of many hitherto half understood principles : a clear definition of the word "guard," under the name of " contra guardia; " of opposition, which he calls " trovare di spada; "

[1] See Fig. 54.—Saviolo.   [2] See Fig. 43.—The Spanish Guard.

of disengagement; circular parries and their deceptions, which he calls " contra cavatione " and " ricavatione " respectively ; of the nature of feints ; of time, and of distance. He was the first who proved the incontestable superiority of a system of fencing in which rapidity of action in seizing the time is the main object, over one which depends on elaborate preliminaries to the attack.

He has been credited with the invention of the " volte,"—" incartata,"— but without foundation. Saviolo's works stand as one of the proofs that this was a recognized action in the fencing of his time. Among Fabris' favourite " botte " is found one which is still practised in the Neapolitan school of our days under the name of " sbasso " and " passata sotto," and which he called a " ferita di prima." [1]

The last part of the book treats in a very concise manner of the practical application of his principles to irregular fighting, such as dagger against sword, cloak against sword or dagger, or sword against pike or halbert, the use of the pummel in close action, various ways of disarming, &c.

Fabris' work met with such success that no less than five editions, and as many translations or adaptations, appeared during the seventeenth century in Italy and Germany. Bologna, although the mother already of no few celebrated masters of fence, erected a monument to the memory of her valorous son. It has been considered better to analyze Fabris, in preference to his contemporaries, Cavalcabo, Patenostrier, and Giganti, as being more complete than the two former, and more imbued with old theories than the latter, who may be taken as the first of an uninterrupted series of masters who worked up the science to its present state of perfection.

[1] See Fig. 2.

CHAPTER VII.

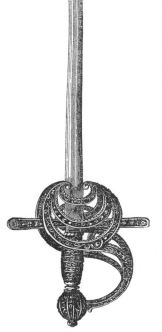

Fig. 61.—Italian Rapier. From Lacombe's "Armes et Armures."

TOWARDS the very end of the sixteenth century, there were in Italy several masters who taught the improved swordsmanship, and professed the principles so clearly expounded by Fabris —without, however, complicating their system by the analysis of all postures *possible* to the human body,—thus opening a fair way to the constant improvement which kept pace with the simplification of body movements.

Hieronimo Cavalcabo of Bologna—probably a son of that Zacharia Cavalcabo who edited Viggiani's work —published, about the last years of the century, a treatise the original of which does not seem to be extant. But when its author was called to the French Court, the book was translated into French,[1] together with an equally undiscoverable opuscule of the great Patenostrier of Rome, touching the " sword alone." These masters, with Giganti, Capo Ferro, and the great " Tappe de Milan," mentioned by Brantôme—who, however, does not seem to have written anything—maintained so highly the supremacy of Italian swordsmanship, that the nobility of all countries—always excepting Spain, who held to her worship of Carranza—found it absolutely necessary to cross the Alps to learn their precious secrets. Cavalcabo later on settled in France, and after him his descendants taught the art of fence in that country until

[1] See Biblio., 1609.

the beginning of Louis XIV.'s reign.   The Germans likewise translated his work, as they did later on those of Fabris, Giganti, and Capo Ferro.[1]

All these masters taught the same guards, four in number;[2] Patenostrier urged the advisability of reducing their number to two (corresponding pretty closely to our " high tierce " and " low carte ") by taking the mean of the two high guards for the first, and that of the two low ones for the second.   The chief feature of Cavalcabo's method is the systematic use of the " beat,"— which in the French translation is called " battre de main,"—to prepare the way for the " cavazione "—the " passer dessous " of Villamont.   Cavalcabo still ascribes some special value to guards on the left side for defensive action, considering those on the right as more suitable to the attack, according to Viggiani's theory.   It is, in fact, very probable that he was Viggiani's pupil.[3]

Patenostrier seems to have been the first to speak of the " filo "—the " coulé d'épée "—a term which he applied to the action of forcibly entering within the adversary's guard by judicious timing and opposition of fort to faible.   The properties of the different parts of the blade were perfectly understood in those days, and of even greater practical interest with the " spada lunga " than they are now.

In this new school the difference of the guard depends only on the position of the sword arm ; the " botta," however, is described not merely by reference to the attacking party's guard, but also and chiefly by reference to the part it is directed against.   Thus, we are beginning to hear of a " thrust inside the arm " as being in " quarta ;" one " outside," or over the arm, as in " terza," in Patenostrier's system of two guards.   This is indeed the commencement of rational fencing: the number of botte will increase, their definition and limitation will become more accurate, and, in presence of the multiplicity of attacks, proper parries will be devised.

To Nicoletto Giganti belongs the honour of having first clearly explained the advantage of the " lunge," and applied it to most attacks.   It is true that Capo Ferro, who was contemporary with him, explained its mechanism still more carefully, but Giganti's work has certainly the priority of date.   The first plate of his " Teatro " represents a man in the act of " tirare una stoccata longha," and whose position does not differ very materially from a correct lunge in our days.

Like Patenostrier, Giganti admits of several guards, but only employs two, corresponding likewise to " quarte " and " tierce."   He combines the principles of the " contra postura " and of the " trovare di spada " in his " contra-guardia," which is a regular " engagement."   This action of covering the body when engaging blades he calls " coprire la spada del nemico,"

---

[1] See Biblio., 1619, 1630, and 1665.
[2] See Figs. 62-3-4: prima, seconda, terza, quarta.
[3] See Biblio., 1588.

and according as it is in "quarte" or "tierce," the action is "stringere di dentro via" or "di fuora via." Thrusts are made by disengaging and lunging; or, on the adversary's disengagement, by taking either a time with an opposition, or a circular parry with the arm extended. They are made in "high" and "low lines" without any difference in their designation. Feints are always simple, as complicated feints with the "spada longa," by no means admitting of a swift motion, would have entailed the risk of time hits.

One of Giganti's plates represents an action which closely resembles the modern "flanconnade"—the "fianconata" of the Italians.

It appears that Giganti published, two years later, a second work, in which he advocates a guard with the left foot foremost, and announces his intention of bringing forth another treatise, " wherein he will show that all actions can be performed with the left foot forward."

This incomprehensible retrogression to faulty principles is not accounted for, neither did the book in question ever make its appearance. In its stead were published French and German translations, as well as fresh editions, of his first work.

Giganti's book was wonderfully perfect and complete in comparison with the mass of those which were written before it; but of all the Italian works on fencing none ever had such a share in fixing the principles of the science as the "Great Simulacrum of the Use of the Sword, by Ridolfo Capo Ferro da Cagli, Master of the most excellent German Nation in the famous City of Sienna." [1] The theories which he enunciated, the system that he followed, and many of his "ferite," were hardly improved on by anyone before the days of Rosaroll and Grisetti. For once the title of the book fully represented its contents.

This small but comprehensive work is divided into introductory chapters full of clear definitions and correct conclusions and a large collection of practical examples.

The first two chapters treat of the science of arms in general.

The third, of the properties of the sword, the divisions of the blade, and the strength and use of its different parts, of the false and the right edges, and the proper length of the sword, which the author considers " should be as long as the arm twice."

The fourth defines the different " measures," which he reckons as the distance between the point of the sword and the adversary's body. The measures are two : " misura larga " when it is only possible to hit the enemy by lunging; " misura stretta " when this can be done by merely pressing the body forward.

The fifth explains the meaning of " time " and its restriction, in fencing parlance, to the period occupied by any single action, either of sword or foot.

[1] See Biblio., 1610.

The sixth treats of the body, and in particular of the head—a consideration of importance, since most of the hits in high line were directed to the face.

The seventh considers the trunk itself, which should be bent forward as much as possible, so as to diminish its apparent surface, and increase the reach of the lunge.

The eighth defines the rôle of the arms, and for the first time is the use

Fig. 62.—Capo Ferro.—A. Prima Guardia ; D. Quarta Guardia.

of the left arm as a counterpoise to the right and a help to the recovery, clearly mentioned in any book. Capo Ferro lays much stress on the necessity of turning the hand in pronation or supination according as the thrust is

Fig. 63.—Capo Ferro.

Seconda Guardia.   Sesta Guardia.

to be made outside or inside the adversary's blade, and disapproves highly of the old-fashioned habit of keeping the sword arm bent.

The ninth analyzes the movements of the thighs, legs, and feet, and describes the various steps used in fencing. For the first time we find a pretty clear definition of the closing step, that is, with the right foot forward, followed by the left. Capo Ferro, although he admits the use of oblique steps on occasion, is very strongly in favour of the straight line. He consequently disapproves of much " volting," of crossing the legs, and all such tricks, which were so much in favour with the ancients. He even looks upon " passing " as a loss of time which might be avoided by closing the measure before lunging, and considers a good recovery as one of the most important points in fencing.

The tenth treats of defence, and in particular of the guard. Capo Ferro goes further than any of his predecessors in his definition of that word.

Fig. 64.—Capo Ferro.—c. Terza Guardia ; e. Quinta Guardia.

" A guard is a posture with the arm and the sword extended in a straight line towards the middle of the attackable parts of the adversary, and with the body well established according to its own pace, so as to keep the adversary at a distance, and to strike him should he approach at his peril." According to his definition he recognizes that " prima " and " seconda "[1] are of little use, " for with these one cannot close the measure without danger, since they are not equally near all parts of the body. The terza is a true guard ; the quarta uncovers too much of the body."

Considering that these two guards had pretty elastic meanings, that they referred only to the inside and outside lines, and that they were opposed to low thrusts as well as high ones, it is obvious that to them can be traced the origin of the four principal guards which are now considered, strictly speaking, sufficient for all purposes of defence, viz., carte, tierce, half circle, seconde.

This restriction reduced the other two, prima and seconda, to the rank of special parries, applicable only to special cases.

[1] See plates.

The eleventh considers the factors of " offensive action," the most important of which consists in seeking the measure. This, according to Capo Ferro, ought to be done with much caution and patience, and without disturbing the body until the moment of striking. " Many, in seeking the measure, disengage and counter disengage, make feints and counter feints, cover themselves from one side to another, travelling in zigzags, twisting their bodies, doubling themselves up, and drawing back in many extravagant ways, contrary to good principles, and calculated only to impress fools.

" However, with my guard, the only precaution necessary is to hold the sword straight in front and cover the ' weak' of the adversary's blade, so as to have power over it without touching it, before the moment of delivering the thrust, either on the inside or the outside, according to the occasion."

The twelfth chapter classifies the modes of striking on various occasions, as when one or the other combatants, or both, are moving, when the thrust is delivered inside or outside, high or low, &c. Capo Ferro disparages the habit of cutting in most cases, except on horseback, as it entails loss of time and necessitates a closer measure.

The last chapter deals shortly with the question of the dagger in conjunction with the sword.

One of the most obvious principles of the new school is that the sword alone is sufficient for defence. The brochiero or target is generally abandoned in Italy, and the dagger, no longer looked upon as of paramount importance, is only considered advantageous for *facilitating* the counter attack.

The introductory chapters expound at length the leading principles of the science. Next come many practical declarations, in which the author admits that there is a wide margin between the art in its theoretical perfection and its practice. He proceeds accordingly to give general recommendations for practical swordsmanship against the world at large.

1. " First of all, when anyone is engaged in fighting, he must keep his eye on his adversary's sword hand, rather than on any other spot, so as to see all its movements, and consequently judge of what he had better do.

2. " A good swordsman, when playing, must never fail, on parrying, to retort with a thrust, nor must he go forward to strike without being sure of parrying the return ; he must not throw himself aside without striking at the same time, and should he parry with the dagger, he must attend to letting his sword strike at the same instant as the dagger moves to parry.

3. " It is to be understood that the sword is the Queen, the foundation of all weapons, and that the practice thereof is all the more useful, that thereby a man learns to parry, strike, and escape, to disengage, counter disengage, and gain on the adversary's weapon in all the guards. In the above-mentioned

movements my advice is to keep the arm well extended, so as to force all the adversary's hits well away from the body.

4. " Shouldst thou have to deal with a brutal adversary, who, heedless of time and measure, attacks thee impetuously, thou canst act in two ways : firstly, by using the 'mezzo tempo,' as I teach in the proper place, thou canst hit him on his attack with a cut on the hand or the sword arm ; or, secondly, thou canst let him strike in vain by retiring backward and then thrust at his face or breast.

5. " Anyone who wishes to become an accomplished swordsman must, beyond taking lessons from a master, strive to play every day, and with different antagonists, and when possible he must select better fencers than himself, so that by playing with so many practical men, he may see wherein dwells perfect merit.

6. " In my book on the art I acknowledge only one good guard, that is, the low guard, called terza, with the sword held straight out horizontally, so that it divide the right side by the middle, and so that the point be always menacing the opponent's body. This guard is much safer than the other, with which there is the danger of being wounded in the leg. . . .

7. " Feints are not good, for they cause loss of time and distance ; in fact, feints must either be made within distance or out of it. If made out of distance, they are useless, as thou needst not answer them. If, on the other hand, the adversary feints within distance : as he feints, strike."

8. Contains a warning against imperfect teachers.

9. " It is no small advantage, and of the greatest elegance, to know how to 'gain' on the adversary's sword in all his guards, and no less so, when the adversary himself has ' gained' on thy sword, to know how to recover the advantage ; thou canst do different things in such cases : first, never disengage and stop, but rather disengage as a parry and then strike ; also by retiring a little, and slightly dropping the body, thou canst lower thy sword, and as the adversary follows on, at the self-same instant that he approaches to 'gain' afresh, strike him under or over his sword, as may be most convenient.

10. " In many ways it is possible to strike in 'contra tempo,' but I only approve of two methods. One is, when thou findest thyself with thy sword in ' quarta,' so that the point is inclined towards thy right, and thy adversary strives to 'gain' on thee, then, at the very instant that he moves his right foot in order to rest his sword on thine, thrust at him in the same position of quarta, ' passing' the left foot forward, or 'lunging' with the right. The other is when thou findest thyself in terza, and he comes to ' gain' on thee from outside, then thou must act similarly.

11. " Many and various are the opinions of masters on the subject of passes sword in hand. I say, according to my judgment, that in passing to

the right of the adversary, as well as to his left, it is advisable always to move the left foot, and accompany its motion by that of the right. If thou shouldst have to pass in a straight line, one foot must drive the other, whether forward or backward.[1] But the true meaning of passing is to walk naturally, always taking care that the right shoulder be kept forward, and that when the left foot goes across, its point be turned to the left.

12. " Thou must know that when thy adversary has his sword point out of line, thou must immediately point thine straight at his hand. By bending the body slightly back thou canst gain the measure in safety, and having gained it, deliver a thrust in ' mezzo tempo ' at his hand by pressing the body forward and bending the right knee.

13. " Having delivered thy thrust with a long step, right foot forward, with sword alone, or with sword and dagger or cloak, thou must retire with a short step, according to the room in rear. If there be little room, thou must only remove back the right leg, and follow with thy sword that of thy adversary. If, on the contrary, there be much room, thou must retire two short steps, so that the last brings thee back on guard. These are the only true ways of retiring, although they do use others in the schools."

Concerning Parries.

" Parries are made sometimes with the right edge, sometimes, though very rarely, with the false ; in a straight line as well as obliquely ; now with the point high, now with the point low; now under, now over, according as the attack is cut or thrust. But it is to be borne in mind that all parries ought to be done with a straight arm, and must be accompanied by the right leg, followed by the left. When the ' dui tempi' are observed, as the parry is made, the left foot must first be brought up against the right, and then, as the attack is returned, the right foot must move forward."

Concerning those who move round their Adversary in Fighting.

This is a piece of advice on the way of meeting those who, according to the old school and the Spanish method, walked round and round their opponent.

" As it might easily occur that thy adversary in moving round and round should ' gain ' inside on thy sword, in such a case thou shouldst disengage and move sideways. On his trying to ' gain ' again, thou shouldst again disengage and thrust in quarta, with a lunge."

---

[1] This action is obviously similar to our way of advancing and retiring, and very different from the true pass, although Capo Ferro devises no special term for the movement.

Beyond the legend of Fig. 65 Capo Ferro gives no explanation of the manner of performing the "botta lunga." The following extract from Giganti's "Teatro" may therefore conveniently be introduced here :—

"To deliver the stoccata lunga, place thyself in a firm attitude, rather collected than otherwise, so as to be capable of further extension. Being thus on guard, extend thy arm and advance the body at the same time, and

Fig. 65.—Capo Ferro, 1610.—"A figure showing the guard, as practised in our art, and the incredible increase of reach due to the 'botta lunga,'[1]—all the limbs moving together in the attack."

"A. The left shoulder, on guard.
B. The left knee, on guard.
C. The sole of the left foot, on guard.
D. The usual pace.
E. The sole of the right foot, on guard.
F. The right knee, on guard.
G. The right hand, on guard.
H. The increase in the reach of the hand due to the 'lunge.'
I. The advanced position of the right knee, equivalent to one pace.
K. The advanced position of the foot.
M. The left knee advanced by half a pace."

bend the right knee as much as possible, so that thy opponent may be hit before he can parry. Wert thou to advance the whole body, thy adversary would perceive it, and, by taking a time, parry and strike thee at the same moment. . . .

"In order to retire, begin the movement with the head, and the body will naturally follow on ; then likewise draw back thy foot ; if thou wert to retire it first, both head and body would remain in danger. . . . "

---

[1] "Botta lunga"—Lunge.

Fig. 66.—Capo Ferro, 1610.—Modo di ferir di fuora, prosupponendo il stringere di dentro et il cavar del tuo aversario di punta per ferire.—Time thrust, by a lunge, on the adversary's disengagement.

" Had the man marked c, however, shown himself skilful in his art, he would merely have disengaged his sword and kept his body well back, and then, as the man marked D confidently came forward to push his thrust he might have parried, either with the false edge and cut a mandritto, or with the right edge and thrust an imbroccata."

Fig. 67.—Alfieri,[1] 1640.—Figura che ferisce di passata mentre che l'aversario cava per ferire.—Time thrust, by a pass, on the adversary's disengagement.

" Had," says the author, " the man marked 14 perceived his opponent's intention, he might have thwarted the counter attack by drawing back his right leg so as to be out of measure, or else he might, by crossing to his left, have delivered an imbroccata at his enemy's breast."

[1] See Biblio. This and many other plates of Alfieri's treatise are exact reproductions— but for the costumes—of some of Capo Ferro's, and are reproduced here for the sake of variety.

Fig. 68.—Capo Ferro.—Figura che ferisce di quarta nella poccia sotto il braccio destro, mentre che l'aversario cava per ferire.—Time thrust in quarta on the adversary's attempt to deliver a riverso.

" On the other hand," continues Capo Ferro, " if the man who is now wounded, instead of turning his hand round to give the riverso, had retired one short step and drawn back his sword, he might have parried the attack by a half mandritto, and cut his opponent's face immediately with a riverso, or give him a thrust in the bosom."

Fig. 69.—Capo Ferro.—Figura che ferisce di scannatura di punta nel fianco destro di passata, mentre l'aversario cava per ferire.—A thrust by a pass, using the left hand to hold the adversary's sword arm, timed on his disengagement.

" A stroke of this kind is said to be di ' scannatura ; ' to perform the same the man here shown on the left of the picture kept himself well covered on the outside, and when his adversary disengaged in order to thrust at his face, he passed forward, left leg in front, and put in his own thrust, using his hand as you observe."

Fig. 70.—Alfieri,[1] 1640.—Figura che ferisce sotto la spada nimica, di contra-tempo, senza parare, solo con l'abassar la vita.—A time thrust, on the adversary's disengagement, by dropping under his point. The swordsman marked 25 has also the choice of a thrust at the face, or a riverso cut at his adversary's knee.

Fig. 71.—Capo Ferro, 1610.—Figura che ferisce di quarta nella gola, solo con afalsar la spada et abassar il pugnale per parata, mentre l'aversario cava di spada e cerca col pugnale per parare.

"If thy adversary be in terza alta, and holding his dagger on a level with the fort of his sword, cover thyself well outside; as he disengages parry with the dagger, low and to the left; at the same time disengage with thy sword under his dagger and thou shalt strike him in the face or any other convenient place."

See note on p. 114.

Fig. 72.—Capo Ferro.—Figura che ferisce di quarta per di sotto il pugnale nel petto, portando in dietro la gamba dritta, e parando col pugnale alto, mentre che l'aversario passa con la sua gamba innanzi per ferire di seconda sopra il pugnale.

"Should thy adversary assume terza bassa, thou shouldst oppose him with terza alta, and hold thy dagger on a level with thy blade. As he passes forward to strike thee over thy dagger, thou canst strike him in quarta by merely drawing back thy right foot, lifting his sword with thy dagger, and disengaging thy sword under his dagger, as he lifts the latter to parry."

Fig. 73.—Capo Ferro.—Figura che ferisce di seconda sopra il pugnale nel petto, mentre che l'aversario passa col pie manco per ferire, solo col ritirare, nel suo venire, la gamba dritta indietro e parando col pugnale sotto il suo braccio destro.

"Should thy adversary place himself in quarta, with his sword drawn back and his dagger high and wide,[1] I advise thee to place thyself in quarta also, but with the arm extended. As he attacks by a pass draw back thy right leg, beat his sword down to the left with thy dagger, and pass thy sword over his dagger. Thou shalt be able to strike him in seconda."

[1] See Fig. 62, p. 108.

Fig. 74.—Capo Ferro.—Figura che ferisce di una punta tra l'arme nel petto, cavandola di sopra il pugnale, mentre che l'aversario stava in guardia larga et lascia arrivare il nimico a misura.—Simple disengagement under the dagger pushed with a lunge.

Fig. 75.—Capo Ferro.—Figura che para il stramazzone riverso con la spada et con il passare in un subito col pie sinistro innanzi, dandoli una pugnalata sotto il braccio destro nella poccia.—A stab with the dagger delivered by a pass and timed on the adversary's cut, which is parried at the same moment by a high quarta.

Fig. 76.—Capo Ferro.—Sword and Cloak. The cloak is turned twice round the forearm ; parries with it are practically the same as with the dagger. Even cuts may be stopped with the cloak, provided they be met on the fort of the blade.

Fig. 77.—Capo Ferro.—Sword and Buckler. Against thrusts the buckler is no better protection than the dagger, as it must necessarily be held sideways so as not to interfere too much with the play.

Capo Ferro concludes his work with an account of a parry which he calls universal, useful in a mêlée or in the dark, but one which, from our point of view, it seems very easy to deceive. It is a sweeping parry, crossing all the lines from tierce to seconde, passing through carte.

Girard Thibaust, d'Anvers.

CHAPTER VIII.

HE existence of the "Académie d'Armes" in Paris, whose origin dates as far back as the reign of Charles IX., and which received its first privileges from Henri III., shows how assiduously the science of arms was cultivated by the French; yet, before the middle of the seventeenth century, we hear of very few masters of note bearing *French* names. Noël Carré, Sainct Didier, Jacques Ferron, Le Flaman, and Petit Jean are the only Frenchmen known to have been teachers of the art of fence to the most quarrelsome society that ever existed. None of them, except Sainct Didier, seem to have left any works behind them, and even the very much overrated " gentilhomme Provençal " did little more than curtail and combine the theories of two contemporary Italians.

Henri IV. and Louis XIII., whilst they vigorously persecuted such scholars as tested the theory practically by duelling, favoured the corporation of masters in a most partial manner ; nevertheless, until the end of the latter king's reign, the Italian masters held their own in France, whether they entered the Academy, or eluded its not yet all-powerful monopoly. It is highly probable, however, that men like the Cavalcabos, being appointed masters to the king, were, *ex officio*, members of the corporation, even if they did not hold some distinguished office therein.

Passages occur in most Spanish treatises of the first half of the seventeenth century, containing descriptions of the French method of fencing which accord most completely with what we know to have been taught by the Cavalcabos, Giganti, Patenostrier, " e tutti quanti." This is a useful indication in the absence of French treatises between Sainct Didier and Le Perche ;[1] it seems naturally to point out that the sound principles of the Bolognese school took root in France and remained long the basis of the art of fence in the " Académie du Roi."

With their aptitude and liking for swordsmanship, the French soon rivalled the Italians in the national art of the latter, until, about the middle of Louis XIII.'s reign, it was so completely assimilated as to have ceased to be looked upon as coming from foreign parts. The courtiers of James and Charles came over to Paris to perfect themselves in the science which they had learnt from the successors of Saviolo and Rocco.

It is, however, surprising that nothing beyond the book of Villamont should have appeared in print on this Franco-Italian art, which was held in such high estimation.

Notwithstanding the universal adoption of the Italian sword-play by the French, there were, no doubt, also a great many Spanish masters who taught the pompous science of Narvaez to the Hispanicized courtiers of Louis XIII. The influence of Spanish fashion had survived the downfall of Spanish preponderance ; the height of " bon ton " in France during the first quarter of the sixteenth century was to imitate, as closely as the difference of races would allow, the gravity not unmixed with affectation, the dignity tempered by the most extraordinary weaknesses, of those conquerors who had once held a footing in most parts of the Continent. The " estilo culto," which took firmer root at the French Court than did euphuism in England, necessitated, for its perfection, a knowledge of the philosophical " destreza " and its decorous bearing.

There can be no doubt, however, that for *practical* swordsmanship the Italian teachers remained masters of the situation. This is borne out by the

---

[1] Villamont's book is only a translation (see Biblio., 1609), and Thibaust's learned treatise an embellished enlargement of Carranza and Narvaez.

fact that the Spanish school had no influence whatsoever on the French system of fence even at its earliest period, and, indeed, did not remain in favour, even as a matter of fashion, much after 1630.

There is only one book known treating of this Hispano-French fencing, but that book is a monument in itself.

" The Academy of the Sword, by Girard Thibaust of Antwerp,[1] wherein are set forth by mathematical rules, on the basis of a mysterious circle, the true and heretofore unknown secrets of the use of weapons on foot and on horseback," can be reckoned, without exception, the most elaborate treatise on swordsmanship, and probably one of the most marvellous printed works extant, from a typographic and artistic point of view.

If the handsome man whose intelligent and keen countenance is depicted in the frontispiece over the significant motto, " Gaudet patientia duris," had devoted to the complete illustration of the sound Italian school of his days the immense labour that he bestowed on the Spanish system, he would, without a doubt, have been looked upon as the founder of the science of arms in France.   As it was, the lifetime which he spent on the production of this Academy—the impression of which alone took fifteen years—only resulted in the production of a bibliographic curiosity.   By the time the first part of the book came out, the infatuation for Spanish fashions was already on the wane.   The premature death of the author in 1629,[2] before even having the satisfaction of seeing his first volume in print, prevented the production of the second part of the work treating of equitation.   The expense entailed by this extraordinary work could only have been met with the support of the French king, who was, as everyone knows, a great amateur of fencing; nevertheless Thibaust was not his master, as Henri IV. had appointed César Cavalcabo, son of the great Bolognese, to teach the prince.   Be it as it may, Louis XIII. granted his privilege to the author ten years before the completion of the book, for which nine reigning princes of Germany likewise subscribed.

Anyone looking at the huge folio, with its forty-six superb double-page plates signed by the best engravers of the age, and the unique typographical magnificence of the text, must at first wonder how the author who was in a position to bring out such a work never had the smallest influence on the development of the science of arms in any country, and that so few of the principles which he spent a lifetime and a fortune in expounding remain a part of modern theories.   The fact is, that in the elaborate plates, each often containing upwards of fifteen pairs of fencers gravely passing on each other in all the plans of a vast perspective of marble halls, nothing is represented but an artistic illustration of the Spanish system set forth at such length by Don Luis P. de Narvaez ; in the text, on the other hand,

[1] See Biblio., 1628.
[2] Although bearing the date 1628, the book was only published in 1630.   See Biblio.

methodical and highly corrected as it is, we find nothing but the complication and subtilization, so to speak, of that already sufficiently artificial science.

Girard Thibaust never acknowledges the source of his information, nor

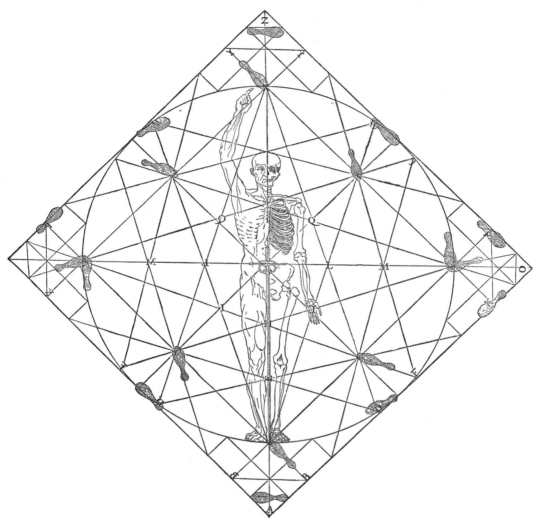

Fig. 78.—Thibaust's mysterious Circle.

does he mention the name of any master, but it is merely necessary to turn to the first plate to recognize the illustration of Narvaez's peculiar principles, complicated, however, by the introduction of even more irrelevant geometrical and mechanical theorems. Thibaust's treatise is indeed " filosofia de las armas," with a vengeance.

The diameter of the mysterious circle which, in his opinion, is the foundation of the science of arms, divides the length of a kind of anatomical preparation in two parts, one of which is skeleton and the other still adorned with its flesh. The extremities of this diameter rest against the ends of this figure's extended hand and between its heels; the length of the human body, so disposed, represents the first dimension of the mystic diagram.

It appears, according to Thibaust, that, in a properly constructed man, the navel divides equally the length of a line joining the heel to the uplifted finger above the head; consequently the horizontal diameter of the circle passes across this spot. Narvaez had mentioned that the length of the sword should be proportional to the man's height, and Capo Ferro and others had fixed this length to twice that of the arm. Thibaust, in order to harmonize the proportions of the sword with both the mystic circle and the first measure of its dimension, requires the sword blade to be equal to the radius, so that when held perpendicularly between the feet the quillons are on a level with the navel.

In the circle are inscribed, first, a square whose diameter is that occupied by the anatomical figure; secondly, a large number of chords. The points of intersection of these chords divide them into lengths bearing a relation—which is explained on the most artificial postulata—to the various proportions of the body, and, consequently, to all its movements. They mark the relative position of all the steps that may be taken by either combatant to obtain physical advantage over certain parts of his adversary's body. A circle such as we have briefly described can be traced roughly on the ground wherever it is wanted, by standing in an upright attitude, heels joined on the spot intended for the centre, and extending the arm, holding a sword of requisite dimensions obliquely down, so that when it just touches the ground, the point, the wrist, and the shoulder are in one straight line. The distance between the sword-point and the heels can then be taken as a radius, and the mysterious circle drawn with all its accompanying chords. Finally, a square is circumscribed to the figure, and the pupils are placed with their left feet at the opposite extremities of this square's diameter, and their right touching the circle.

The operations of every bout are to be performed in the circle, or along the square, by stepping from one to the other of the aforesaid points of intersection.

But before beginning these *strategic* movements the pupils are instructed in the more *tactical* operations of striking and parrying. Just as the Spanish masters, Thibaust practically teaches but one guard, with the body perfectly erect, the knees straight, the feet but a few inches apart and forming an angle of forty-five degrees with each other, the arm extended horizontally and holding the sword on a straight line with the shoulder. But, if there is only one guard, the parries are as numerous as the possible opportunities for them; one condition only, for a proper parry, being that the fort should always be opposed to the faible.

The adversaries assume the guard out of measure, and then begin stabbing at, and inveigling, each other.

This system is most palpably that of Narvaez: the adversaries begin on opposite sides of a certain circle, the diameter of which bears some relation to the length of the blades. Outside that circle are drawn parallel tangent lines—the sides of the circumscribed square—which are no other than the " lineas infinitas " of the Spaniard.

This straight arm guard is the starting point for cuts and thrusts delivered to all parts of the adversary's body, but preferably to his face, as soon as the " passing " operations have brought about a favourable opportunity.

The thrusts are not defined beyond their division into imbroccata, over the arm, and stoccata, under the arm, but they seem to be invariably delivered like stabs, with a jerk, by the arm alone, as the weight of the body must always be kept as well balanced between the feet as possible, in order to allow a rapid performance of the complicated series of steps taught in this science.

As in Narvaez, the cuts are well classified into: shoulder cuts, forearm and wrist cuts, with regard to the attacking party; and as perpendicular, oblique, ascending and descending, with regard to the side operated upon.

Armed with these principles, and imbued with the notion of the infallible virtue of the passes they are about to perform, the scholars face each other with irreproachable dress and grave countenances. The master then proceeds to explain his science and expound its application to the most probable cases. He first demonstrates that the distances between the points of intersection agree " most naïvely " with the natural paces of man, and that a careful choice of such points will determine an infallibly successful " instance," or approach on the enemy. The governing rule touching the choice of "instances" is, that any succession of points approximating to the diameter of the circle is dangerous. This is a double-distilled manner of explaining Carranza's theory that to walk straight on the adversary entails the danger of a time hit. Thibaust goes on to say that the time bears a ratio to the length of the paces, " as can be proved to the curious by mathematical rules," forgetting that to any commonsense person the time employed in delivering a hit is obviously proportional to the number of paces taken in so doing.

One of the pupils is sacrificed for the sake of the demonstrations, whilst the other circumvents him in perfectly correct style.

The points of intersection of the mysterious lines are numbered from A to z. Alexander, the correct pupil and representative of the master's genius, begins at A, and Zacharia, the ingenuous tyro, places his foot on z. Either Alexander or Zacharia begins the attack, and, according to Zacharia's movements, the learned Alexander steps rapidly, and with great deliberation, from A to E or F, avoiding the point or warding it aside, and so on to any letter, until he is in a position of vantage, and can coolly run his wretched opponent through the eye, or hamstring him, according to his fancy.

Narvaez taught his pupils to dodge about, avoid some hits and parry others, so as to try and " gain " on their adversaries ; he gave rules for certain cases calculated to enable the fencer to oppose his fort without difficulty to

Fig. 79.—The disadvantage of not stepping correctly across the mysterious circle.—Thibaust.

his adversary's faible, but Thibaust goes further and maintains that if Alexander only take his paces correctly, Zacharia can *not* help himself and *must* submit to the cruel treatment illustrated in the plates.

Such a system is really incredible. How the Italian and the French masters must have laughed when the gorgeous work appeared, and wished that they but held some of Thibaust's pupils, sword in hand, at the opposite end of the mysterious diameter, with an opportunity of delivering a " stoccata lunga " on the first symptom of such peregrination.

Such as it is, the huge folio is certainly one of the most curious books extant, and shows what power fashion could have over people's intelligence.

It was the fashion in Spain to fight according to artificial rules, France copied Spanish fashions, and enough support was afforded to an eccentric master of fence in Flanders to enable him to bring out this enormous volume of nonsense in the most gorgeous manner that the Leyden Elzevirs could devise.

To the student, however, the "Académie de l'Espée" has one special merit,—it supplies the want of illustration to the Spanish books of that period. Neglecting the text of Thibaust's preposterous assurance that there can be no " imprévu " in fencing, the plates represent very accurately what Spanish fencing remained until the middle of the eighteenth century. Curiously

Fig. 80.—Circles Nos. 1 and 2.

enough, the dogmatic Thibaust, who is loth to admit anything but perfectly definite factors in his calculations, speaks of " le sentiment de l'espée," "sentiment du fer," as moderns would call it, in a way which would indicate that his practice was better than his method.

The description of a few bouts will suffice to illustrate the manner in which these principles were put in action. The explanations of each circle correspond to what modern masters would call " une phrase d'épée."

CIRCLE No. 1.

" At the same instant that Alexander drops his foot on the point marked G, Zacharia steps forward and delivers an ' imbrocade ' at his breast. The adversaries having previously been on guard at the first instance with their swords held straight and parallel, Alexander began to work round in order to master his 'contrary's' blade on the second instance x, on the inner side of the diameter. This doing, at the same moment that he places his right foot on the letter G, and proceeds in a circular manner with the left, Zacharia bears on him, carrying his right foot inside the circle as far as the letter s, on the inner side of the diameter, bending forward on the right foot, and rounding the arm by the same action so as to turn the exterior branch of the sword vertically upwards. Thus he delivers the imbrocade on his adversary's breast, proceeding further by carrying the left foot outside, on the inside of the quadrangle. All this is represented by the figure of the Circle No. 1."

Fig. 81.—The Sword alone against the Sword and Dagger. The learned Alexander, armed with the sword alone, defeats Zacharia and his double weapon by menacing an " estocade " as is shown here, and as his opponent comes to parry with his dagger, *passing* to his right and striking him over his dagger hand.

This operation is only explained here to demonstrate with greater evidence the intention that Zacharia hopes to carry out, in order that it may be easier to comprehend the operations of Alexander represented by the following circle.

CIRCLE No. 2.

" Alexander foreseeing the imbrocade that his contrary is about to deliver, at that moment surprises the adverse blade, turning round with his left side outwards, and presenting the point to his eyes.

" As, therefore, the above-said operations of Alexander and Zacharia are begun and continued until the moment that Zacharia begins to advance his foot, round his arm, conduct and turn the exterior branch of his sword inwards on a level with his shoulder in order to drive his imbrocade into his adversary's breast, Alexander is made clearly aware of his adversary's approach by the ' sentiment of the sword ' as well as the sense of sight.   He therefore, at the right moment, stiffens his arm, and turns the interior branch of his sword vertically outside as high as the top of his head.   In this wise he seizes the adverse blade from under, forces it upwards, turning away at the same time the left side of his body (where the blow had been aimed) by the judicious movement of his feet, and offering his point straight to his adversary's eye, but holding it withal by courtesy.   In this manner Zacharia cannot advance further without wounding himself.   So it is depicted in the figure."

CHAPTER IX.

AFTER such masters as Capo Ferro and Giganti it would be use-less to dwell long on their successors in Italy during the seven-teenth century, who all adopted their methods, without materially improving them.

Indeed, Torquato [1] and his precepts are, if anything, retro-grade; and of Quintino's [2] work it will be sufficient to give the title, the quaintness of which recalls the phraseology of the early sixteenth century :—

Fig. 82.—Time thrust, delivered as the adversary moves his hand to cut at the head. Instead of the thrust at the face, a "mezzo-dritto" on the wrist, or a "rovescio" outside the knee might be used.—Alfieri, 1640.

" Jewel of wisdom, in which are contained marvellous secrets and most necessary precautions concerning the art of defence against men and various

---

[1] "Precetti sulla Scherma," Roma, 1609.   [2] See Biblio., 1613.

animals, newly given to the light by me, Antonio Quintino, for the use of all noble spirits "—which marvellous secrets consist merely of his favourite tricks, unsupported by any method.

Gaiani expounds various exercises applicable to the sword on foot and on horseback, but introduces no theoretical innovation of any kind.

Alfieri's [1] work is, in all important points, produced on the lines of Capo Ferro's. The plates, which are extremely artistic in the original, are more numerous than those of his model. The few here reproduced show how little the principles of the art had been altered since the beginning of the century. The dimensions of the sword, however, had been reduced by a few inches, and its weight by many ounces.

Fig. 83.—A thrust timed on the adversary's cut at the knee, which is avoided by drawing back the leg. A *fendente* on the head, or a mezzo-dritto on the wrist, could also be used in such a case.— Alfieri.

It was between 1560 and 1570 that the French began to develop a school of their own, distinct from that of the Italian masters. While Le Perche, Besnard, and La Tousche were laying the fundamental principles of what was to become the small-sword play, it may be well to consider briefly the works of contemporary Italians.

In 1660 there appeared " A treatise on the true management of the

---

[1] See Biblio., 1640. Alfieri is also the author of works on the management of the pike and the two-handed sword (spadone), and of a very curious one on the effective display and flying of banners.

sword," by the "Bolognese gentleman," Alexander Senese,[1] dedicated in curious Latin to Charles Ferdinand of Austria, and accompanied by many other proofs of classical knowledge. It contained, however, no real innovations. A cursory view of its contents will suffice to show the adaptation of the old principles to the somewhat lighter rapier of those days.

The treatise touched on the various kinds of play, which were called :—

"Giuoco lungo,"[2]—fencing at long distance. "Giuoco perfetto,"—so termed when, by rapid management of the feints, the thrust was delivered without meeting the adversary's blade. (This result, only obtainable from a light weapon, was considered perfection, and accordingly very difficult to acquire. It is curious that this point, which is claimed by the French as a

Fig. 84.—Sword and Cloak. Paralyzing the adversary's sword-arm by throwing the cloak over his blade. The choice of attacks lies between a thrust at the breast or the face, and a rovescio on the arm.—Alfieri, 1640.

characteristic of their school, should have been so clearly stated by an early Italian master.) "Giuoco corto,"—or fencing within measure, which the author disapproved of " as being uncertain."

We may also notice the expressions :—

"Il peso,"—the balance,—supposed to be perfect if the weight of the body bore on the left leg when on guard, and on the right when attacking.

"Tempo indivisibile,"—which is taken when the repost results from the parry without any pause.

---

[1] See Biblio.

[2] The "development" of Capo Ferro and Giganti was then universally used.

"Linea perfetta e linea retta,"—keeping the line with the sword's point always directly menacing the adversary.

"Trovata di spada,"—engaging the adverse blade,—which ought always to be preliminary to feints and binding.

Senese taught the same guards as Fabris and Giganti, and one besides, in which the left knee is bent and the right kept straight. "With this," he declared, "one can make parries which, in the street, are worth a treasure, and which cover a man absolutely"—a fact which we may presume to doubt.

Like Capo Ferro and Giganti he extolled one universal parry, capable, in his opinion, of meeting any blow whatsoever. This seems to have been a heavy sweep in seconde from a high quarte at arm's length. It is difficult to see, however, what virtue could be attached to that rather than to any other sweeping parry.

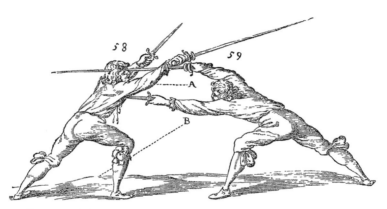

Fig. 85.—Time thrust by a *pass* under the adversary's blade, as the latter lunges with the hand high.—Alfieri, 1640.

Ten years later appeared "La Scherma illustrata" of Morsicato Pallavicini,[1] a pupil of the great Matteo Gallici, who wrote nothing himself, but shone in the work of his pupil.

The book is elaborate, but its chief interest lies in the various pieces of information it contains on contemporary and historical matters concerning fencing and fencing-masters. It seems that Morsicato Pallavicini travelled all over Europe, and from him we learn that the corporation of fencing-masters which had existed in Spain since the Middle Ages, still enjoyed their old monopoly in his days, and that no man could teach fencing who was not recognized by the General Examiner residing in Madrid. This may explain the stationary character of Spanish swordsmanship.

[1] See Biblio., 1670.

It also appears, according to his researches, that a similar institution existed in Italy until about the time of Marozzo.

The author professes to have had intercourse with swordsmen of all countries—Spanish, French, and Roman—and stoutly maintains that the school of the latter is the best :—

"From whose principles the Spaniards have derived their play; a fact confirmed by Narvaez, a pupil of the great Carranza, who had discovered the true value of our principles." [1]

All the treatises on the art of arms refer to the sword proper, naturally enough, and the illustrations invariably represent the complete success of some " botta " or other, so that it is with pleasure that we come across some indication of the kind of instrument that was used *in practice.*

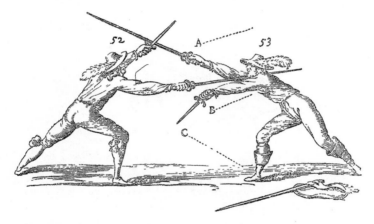

Fig. 86.—A Counter.　Stopping the adversary's attack with the dagger, and deceiving his parry by a *cavazione* over his left hand.— Alfieri, 1640.

Pallavicini says that in his days they used in assaults swords provided with a button, " which, when wrapped in leather, was about the size of a musket ball." He also mentions cardboard plastrons as worn by fencers, but does not refer to masks of any kind.

His points of theory differ but little from those of his predecessors, so we need only notice the expression " tirare in moto "—thrusting on the adversary's feint—as a definite method of taking a " time." This seems to have been done without necessarily engaging and disengaging or binding, and shows, independently of what we know of the sword of that period, how very

---

[1] This is, however, an equivocation : Carranza traced the origin of Spanish swordsmanship to the " armatura " of the Romans, not to the Roman " schools of fence."

much lighter they must have been to allow of such quick motion. Cuts were still resorted to with the Italian rapier, and in consequence of its lessened length were possible in even greater number than those detailed by Marozzo and his contemporaries.

Among the cuts most frequently used may be mentioned the " mezzo rovescio," delivered from the elbow at the adversary's left side ; the " stramazoncello," a tearing cut from the extreme point ; the " mandabolo " and the " montante sotto mano," both ascending cuts with the false edge, such as are still practised with the featherweight Italian sabre.

In the same year that Wernesson de Liancour [1] was publishing in Paris the great work which was to serve as a model to literary fencers in France and England, a celebrated Roman master—Marcelli [2]—expounded the

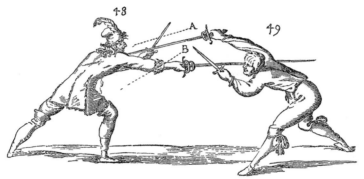

Fig. 87.—Parrying inwards, *passing*, and disengaging under the adversary's dagger.—Alfieri.

" Rules of Fencing," in a thick volume illustrated, indifferently it must be confessed, by drawings of his own. These " Regole de la Scherma " were taught by his father in Rome, and by his uncle in those Neapolitan schools which were then beginning to compete with the Bolognese.

Amongst others of a similar style, the following announcement to the reader occurs in the introduction :—

" Read then, but with judgment ; learn, but fruitfully ; correct thyself, but on good grounds ; and bear in mind that if thou canst discover any fault with these principles of fencing, thou must indeed be a great man, unique in this world, for until now no other man has been able so to do."

Marcelli taught three guards : " prima," corresponding to the modern Italian carte ; " seconda " and " terza," corresponding to the two ways of taking the modern tierce in " giuoco Napolitano " and " giuoco misto "

[1] See Biblio., 1686, France. [2] See Biblio., 1686, Italy.

(that is, his " seconda " was taken with the arm extended, hand in tierce, and his " terza " with the arm bent and the point elevated).

These guards could be modified, in the same way as Capo Ferro's " quarta " and " terza," to meet low thrusts. The position of the legs is the same as that recommended by Senese for proper balance or " peso," namely, the left knee is bent when on guard, so that the weight of the body bears principally on the left foot, whilst the right leg is kept nearly straight. This we may remark was also the guard adopted by the French masters of the period, and is shown in the figures taken from Liancour.

The attack is formed—and this is the first time that such an exact description of the Italian lunge is to be met with—" by first extending the arm, taking the right foot forward, bending the right knee, and straightening the left, at the same time the left arm—which on guard is kept bent, so that the hand is as high as the shoulder—is thrown back and extended *in line with the right arm*."

The disengagements are the same as Capo Ferro's and Fabris', namely, " mezza cavazione "—disengagement from above downwards, in either line ; —" cavazione "—disengagement from inside outside, or *vice versâ;* " contracavazione" and " ricavazione," our " contre " and " deception of the contre."

Marcelli passes for the inventor of the " botta " called " passata sotto," although it seems difficult to see on what grounds, since many bouts are explained by Fabris, Giganti, and Capo Ferro, which are similar to his " sotto botta." But, as far as can be ascertained, he is the first to explain the " intrecciata." This is a favourite action of the Italians, facilitated by their straight guard, consisting of a " froissement,"—" striccio,"—followed either by disengagement, or a binding as in " fianconata."

On the subject of " tempo," Marcelli improves on the notion of " tempo " proper by explaining clearly that when the repost cannot be given *on the parry*, —" culpo d'incontrazione,"—it is better to deliver the attack *on the adversary's recovery*. He gives an indication of a parry which has disappeared from modern Italian practice, and which is similar to our sixte or carte outside, when he recommends that thrusts delivered on the inside line be parried with the true, and those on the outside *with the false edge*.

" L'Exercice des armes ou le maniement du fleuret," published in 1635 by Jean Baptiste Le Perche du Coudray, a pupil of the great Pater, the most famous *French* teacher of fence in Louis XIII.'s days, was the first of that long series of treatises brought out by masters of the " Académie Royale d'Armes."

In Italy, as we have seen, fencing had but little progressed, in *theory* at least, since the early days of the century. But in France, owing probably to the greater variety of movements due to the lighter weight of the rapier there in fashion, more advance was made towards a methodical classification of strokes and parries.

This improvement is clearly set forth in Besnard's [1] " Theory of the art and practice of the sword alone or the foil," a book which embodies all the progress made in sword-play since the days of H. Cavalcabo.

There were still four guards, similar to those of Fabris and Giganti. But whilst the Italians had practically discarded the two high ones to make their *quarta* and *terza* suffice for the whole work of parrying, the French, by improving the prima and seconda, that is, by modifying them so as to make it possible to thrust from those guards with a certain amount of security, had obtained a more varied play, and a greater choice of attacks.

And so we gather from Besnard's work, that not only did they use the four natural guards, but that their respective " bottes " were perfectly well defined.

" The thrust in prime," he explains, " is given from above downwards, the wrist being held higher than the head. It is the thrust that one delivers just after drawing the sword. It is, however, a dangerous one, as it uncovers the body too much." This is the first mention of a thrust in " prime " proper.

Remembering that the old masters made *quarta* and *terza* parry in a high as well as in a low line, Besnard's definition of seconde will appear less strange to modern fencers. " The thrust in seconde is delivered in two ways, ' tierce en seconde ' (nails down), and ' quarte en seconde ' (nails up)." Both are on the inside of the sword.

" The thrust in tierce is pushed on the outside and over the sword, nails down ; whilst the thrust in quarte is given inside the adversary's blade in this wise : at one and the same time you will push your thrust, turn the left side of the body as you throw out the arm, drop back the left arm on the hip, and extend the body in such a way that the right shoulder, right knee, and the toes of the right foot find themselves in the same perpendicular line."

This is a fair definition of the lunge in quarte, but no great improvement thus far on the Italians. The French often made use of this "development," but not by any means in most cases, as it is generally believed. They lunged chiefly with the thrust in quarte, but used the pass of the left foot whenever the action became at all complicated. In addition to the above four distinct " bottes," Besnard describes the " flanconnade" in a way that shows that, as a botte, it has very little changed. But it was not an invention of his own, as some pretend, for many instances of similar thrusts are found in Fabris and Giganti.

As a consequence of the improvement of the above-mentioned guards,

[1] See Biblio, France, 1653 ; in the same year appeared the second edition of Alfieri's treatise. See Italy, same date.

the " engagement," which in the Italian school was only practical in quarta and terza, became so with all the guards in the French style.

" These four guards," Besnard explains, " bring about four engagements; the four engagements, four openings, and consequently four disengagements.   The four disengagements suggest four feints."

These four disengagements were nothing new.   A disengagement from a low line to a high one is simply the action taught by the old Italian masters as " mezzo (or meggio) cavazione; " but the systematic classification of feints, as derived from the guards themselves, was an innovation, and one in the right direction.

The Italians never classified their feints, which consequently never were refined, and thereby introduced an element of irregularity into their play which only disappeared under the influence of quite modern masters.

The lightening of the sword forcibly brought the old question of " stesso tempo " or " dui tempi " to the front again.   With the long rapier rapid action of the hand was obviously impossible, and offensive power had to be cultivated in the parries; in other words, the parry had to be formed in such a way as to act as a repost.   This resulted in an universal tendency to " time," and caused an amount of uncertainty in the parries which necessarily restricted the play, except when the dagger was adjoined to the sword.

As the fashion in swords became lighter and shorter, the advantage of parrying first and reposting afterwards became more obvious.

Besnard, indeed, lets us see, although he does not expressly state it, that it was the rule among French masters to fence " en deux temps," that is, to parry and repost separately.   From his time we begin to hear of parries proper, although they do not actually, as yet, bear the name of their corresponding " botte."

With separated parries and reposts the advantage naturally asserted itself of redoubling any attack which the adversary parried without reposting, and Besnard accordingly explains the action under the name of " reprise," which it has borne to this day.

The sword then in use admitted of effective parries with the false edge —weaker parries which would have been " forced " by the heavy rapier of the previous age.

Besnard describes, but without naming them, parries in the four lines, with the right and false edges, with the hand in pronation and in supination. It is, therefore, probable that seven out of the eight modern parries, " prime, seconde, tierce, quarte, sixte, septime (half-circle), and octave," were practised, after a manner, at the Académie d'Armes in France in the early days of Louis XIV.'s reign.

Besnard seems to have been the first to have taught the courteous practice of the "salute," which he calls "révérence." The rapier in favour among the French had not yet dwindled down to the proportions of the small sword, but cutting was considered quite as an obsolete action. The edge of the sword was preserved sharp, but only for the purpose of increasing its penetrating power and to prevent the seizing of the blade, and accordingly Besnard teaches that the use of the left hand for parrying is faulty.

From the day when all cutting action was discarded, no reason remained for the necessity of practising with *flat* blades, and the "fleuret"—the foil as we understand it now, fitted only for the thrust—was devised for the sake of greater lightness.

It is true that "*foils*" are heard of long before that period, but the English word applied to all rebated [1] weapons, whether a sword for practice, a lance, or any other weapon.

About that period the French seemed to have wished to separate their school altogether from the Italian, and a curious result of this piece of "Chauvinisme" showed itself in the shape of the foil they adopted.[2]

Whilst the Italian foil represented a rapier of diminutive weight, with "vette" and "coccia" complete, the French devised an implement the guard of which was composed of a kind of "pas d'ânes," forming a crown at the shoulder of the blade. The grip was square and short, but nevertheless was held like the modern French foil, that is, all the fingers resting on the grip itself, instead of closing round the shoulder of the blade below the guard and through the "pas d'ânes," as had been done previously. This guard had all the complication of that of the rapier without any of its advantages. It was all the more strange that the habit of crossing the fingers over the blade should have been discarded so soon with the French foil, as the arm was still held out very straight when on guard, after the manner of the Italians.[3] This curious foil, which was at first the same length as the sword it represented, became very much shorter towards the latter part of the seventeenth century, but the cumbersome guard never changed until about the middle of the eighteenth.

There is no reason to believe that Besnard was the inventor of the more "subtils" principles set forth in his book, but in the absence of any other treatise during that period, their origin must be dated from his days.

Twelve years later appeared a book [4] the influence of which has been greatly overrated, and which in fact advocated quite retrograde principles.

The "development" which had been so well defined by Besnard is

[1] Foil, a rebated weapon, from the old French "fouler," "refouler," to turn back.
[2] See Fig. 94, in which the old-fashioned French foil is shown. The word fleuret, like the Italian fiorete, was applied to the buttoned foil on account of its resemblance to a flower bud.   [3] See Figs. 89-93.
[4] Philibert de la Tousche. See Biblio.

exaggerated by La Tousche in such a manner as to become quite an acrobatic feat, and to prevent any possibility of smart recovery.

This is how he describes the lunge :—

On any of the five " bottes " (prime, seconde, tierce, quarte, and quinte—a high septime, as it would now be called), the arm being extended, the right foot takes as long a step as is anatomically possible, and the body is thrown forward until it actually rests on the thigh.   The left foot is turned on its side until the left ankle nearly touches the ground ; the head is dropped as low as possible.

With such a lunge the fight could only be carried on by means of " remises," the first attack once parried.   This performance was called an " estocade de pied ferme "—*pied ferme* sounds ironical applied to such an overreach.

Fig. 88.—The " estocades de pied ferme, in prime and tierce," of La Tousche.   From Danet's " Art des Armes."

Another mode of delivering the thrust was of course the " passe." The " estocade de passe " was performed in a similar manner, by passing the left foot in front, bending the body over the thigh till the chin rested on the left knee, and placing the left hand on the ground for the sake of equilibrium.

La Tousche is apparently the first who applied the name disengagement —dégagement—to that passage from one line to another which the Italians called " cavatione," and Besnard had termed " deliement."

He names also a fifth guard, consequently a fifth engagement, and is the first to give to some parries the names of their corresponding " bottes," but, oddly enough, he restricted this application to the first three.

" There are three principal parries answering to the three ways that a thrust can be pushed, namely, inside, over, or under the blade (our quarte) ; inside, over with a high point (our tierce) ; and under with the point low (our seconde)."   Circular parries—the " contra cavazione " of the Italians— were evidently practised by some masters, for La Tousche is very particular to forbid them.

Although an advocate of the " Attaque de pied ferme," he is in favour of retiring, as a rule, on the parry. Voltes and passes are also, in his eyes, as good methods of avoiding a delivery as any.

La Tousche is the first to describe that curious mode of holding the rapier with both hands, which seems to have been in favour in France throughout the second half of the seventeenth century. He gives the name of " La botte du paysan " to one way of so using the sword, which consisted in seizing the blade with the left hand just below the guard, and thus with both hands beating the adversary's sword down or out of line, then passing with the left foot and delivering the point.

On the whole, the theories of La Tousche are far behind those of Besnard, and, indeed, it would appear that they met with much detraction, as he continually brings forth explanations in their defence.

For all that, in his position of teacher to the Queen's household, and that of the Duc d'Orléans, Philibert de la Tousche enjoyed a high position among his " confrères," and was as successful " à la cour " as " à la ville " : one plate of his book represents an assault in which he took part before Louis XIV. in the Palace of Versailles.

Le Perche's " Exercice des armes, ou le maniement du fleuret " [1] contains however far sounder principles than the works of the royally favoured La Tousche.

If he is really to be considered as the first who insisted on the importance of the " riposte," Le Perche can be looked upon as the father of the modern French school—" quand la parade est bien faite," says he, " c'est un coup sur que la riposte." It is a pity that he followed at all the principles of La Tousche and his exaggerated movements.

His attacks are practically the same as those of Besnard and La Tousche, but he does not employ the " botte de prime," and keeps to the seconde and tierce, quarte, low quarte, quarte outside, and the flanconnade.

He advocates three parries, devised to meet attacks inside, outside, and under the arms, which he calls " quarte," " tierce," and " cercle " (our half-circle or septime).

La Tousche taught similar parries under the names " quarte," " seconde pour le dessus," and " seconde pour le dessous," the last of which was devised against all attacks in low lines. Le Perche is consequently the first who applied their modern names to the parries of tierce and circle (half-circle or septime).

Like all other masters of his days, he concerns himself greatly about various ways of disarming.

Although recognizing the possibility of engaging in the four lines, he only actually taught engagements in quarte and tierce.

[1] See Biblio., 1676.

CHAPTER X.

E Maistre d'armes ou l'exercice de l'espée seulle dans sa perfection, par le Sieur de Liancour," notwithstanding its immense reputation, contains nothing very original. But the author must have been a very sound master, and he seems to have eliminated from his teaching most of what was radically wrong in the theories of his predecessors.

This book was obviously used as a model by many French and English masters until the latter part of the eighteenth century.

Liancour recognized the five guards and thrusts, each individually named by some, but not all acknowledged by every one of his predecessors in the Academy, viz., the "prime," "tierce" and "quarte" of Besnard, the "seconde" (pour le dessous) and the "quinte" of La Tousche, and the "septime" (circle) of Le Perche, but he only *advocates* engagements in quarte and tierce, and parries in carte, tierce, seconde, and cercle (septime); the two former being taken with different altitudes of the hand, to meet attacks in low as well as in high line.[1]

Like La Tousche, he forbids all parries in "contre degagement," and likewise discountenances the use of the left hand, and is as highly in favour of a distinct "riposte" as Le Perche. In fine, on matters of principle, he advocates all that was most rational in the French school of his days.

The dislike of French masters for circular parries is explained by the fact that the sword, although much shorter, was still rather heavy in the hand, and a circular parry with such a weapon could not be so certain as a simple one.

The Italians used the "contra cavazione," but only with time thrusts, as

---

[1] Fig. 89 shows the orthodox manner of drawing and coming on guard; 3 and 4 show guards in quarte at two different degrees of altitude.

Les veritables principes de l'Espée seulle

Fig. 89.—1, 2, 3, Drawing and falling on guard; 3, 4, Two elevations of the hand; 5, a " pass."—Liancour.

Parade du fort au dedans des armes. ⟨❧⟩ *Le coup qu'il faut a cette parade.*

Fig 90.—Thrust in quarte, parried quarte.—A thrust in quinte.—Liancour.

in such cases the increase of time entailed was compensated for by simplification of movement. In the French school, which kept parry and riposte separate, the *practical* difficulty of circular parries (contres) with a heavy sword must have been strongly felt.

Besides the five " bottes " already mentioned, Liancour used of course the flanconnade, and taught also the " botte coupée," the " quarte coupée sous les armes," and the " coupé " proper, as we understand it now, but without appearing to attach much value to this last important action, which was destined to become a distinguishing feature of the French school as separate from the Italian.

He insisted on the proper performance of the lunge, which he considered as one of the fundamental principles of the art ; his development is essentially the same as ours, the left foot being kept flat on the ground, the right knee square over the instep, and the body well sustained.

Although recognizing the general superiority of the lunge as a means of delivering the " bottes," he still made use of passes and voltes.

Liancour recommended the use of several different kinds of foils : " The master's foil," he explains, in his last chapter, " ought to be lighter than the scholar's, so that his arm may not be too easily tired by long successive lessons. The foil used by the scholar in the lesson must be heavier than that employed in the assault, and, moreover, should have no guard, in order that he may learn to parry with his fort, and never rely upon his guard to displace the adversary's blade ; it must also be shorter than the master's, so that he may better beware of time thrusts, and proceed with decision in his attacks." All this shows how the old Italian principles still lingered in the French schools, since the masters had to have recourse to such artifices in order to make their pupils put their theories in practice and learn to avoid time hits.

It is somewhat curious that after such academic teaching Liancour should have still thought of mentioning a universal parry, consisting in a circular sweep covering rapidly the four lines.

He published his book very soon after starting independently on his career. His principles are those, he tells us, of his master, of whom he speaks with the utmost gratitude.

Liancour practised in Paris during forty-six years after the publication of his book, differing in this respect from other great masters, who generally only wrote towards the end of a busy life ; it is therefore no wonder that, having commenced under such auspices, he should have acquired that widespread reputation which made him one of the foremost figures in the annals of the " Escrime Française."

It was during the reign of Louis XIV. that the " Académie d'Armes " reached the summit of its importance. Having originated in an association of celebrated masters during the last years of Charles IX.'s reign, and been

Parade du fort au dehors des armes. ❧ *Le coup a ceux qui parent en esleuant leur espee.*

Fig. 91.—Thrust in tierce, parried tierce.—A thrust in seconde.—Liancour.

Parade de la pointe au dedans des armes. ❧ *Le coup qu'il faut a cette parade*

Fig. 92 —Thrust in quinte parried "cercle"—A thrust in quarte.—Liancour.

recognized, privileged, and dubbed royal by Henri III., Henri IV., and Louis XIII.—all three kings remarkable for their delight in swordsmanship —it obtained still more substantial proofs of royal favour in 1656 from Louis XIV., who conferred on this company, by letters patent, the absolute monopoly of the right to teach fencing in France.

Thus far, however, its privileges were no greater than those enjoyed by many older associations of the same kind, such as the corporations of Masters of Defence in Madrid and in London, the Marxbrüder in Frankfort, and similar associations in Italy during the sixteenth century.

Parade de la pointe au dehors des armes. ⟨⟩ Le coup qu'il faut a cette parade.

Fig. 93 —Thrust in tierce parried quarte (outside).—Disengagement in quarte.—Liancour.

But the " roi soleil " did more for his academy. Besides conferring on it a coat of arms,[1] he called the five-and-twenty masters into his presence and bade them nominate six of their body, to whom he granted letters of nobility to be enjoyed by them and their descendants, further promising that the eldest master of the corporation should in future receive the same mark

---

[1] " Champs d'azur à deux épées mises en sautoir, les pointes hautes, les pommeaux poignées, croisés d'or, accompagnés de quatre fleurs de lys, avec timbre au dessus de l'écusson et trophées d'armes autour."

of favour on the demise of one of the ennobled six, provided he had professed the science of arms for at least twenty years.

The corporation was at the same time reduced to twenty *masters.*

No one was to be allowed to teach anywhere in the kingdom who had not been " prévot " under some master of the Academy in Paris.

The degree of " Maistre en fait d'armes " was only conferred after six years of apprenticeship under some member of the corporation, and a public trial of skill with three other masters.

When Strasburg was annexed by Louis XIV., the old Marxbrüder school —once conducted by Joachim Meyer, and since then one of the most flourishing fencing grounds in Germany—was Frenchified as much as possible, and received the name of " Académie de Strasbourg."

Brussels was also the seat of an academy which owed its origin to a flourishing school of fence established by the Spanish during their domination in the Low Countries, and the importance of which was kept up by periodical fencing tournaments conducted after the manner of the public examination for a fencing degree in Spain,[1] or for the " master's prize " in London in the days of Elizabeth. The prizes contended for in these tournaments were richly decorated arms, solemnly awarded to the winners in the " Broodt Huys " in Brussels.

The origin of the " Académie d'Armes du Languedoc," better known as the " Académie de Toulouse," was in all probability the same as that of the foregoing. That part of the country remained long under the influence of Spanish fashions, and most likely followed the example of Spanish schools of arms in the Roussillon, by holding periodical meetings of swordsmen. Annual competitions of the kind formed part of the " jeux floraux."

A most celebrated family of masters, the Labats, taught at Toulouse from the end of the sixteenth century until the middle of the eighteenth.

Notwithstanding the ambitious title of Academy assumed by these associations, there is no reason to believe that they ever possessed any special rights or privileges ; whatever influence they laid claim to was the result of the personal merits of their principal master. Indeed, in France during the eighteenth century many flourishing schools took the name of " Académie," much as nowadays institutions of the most different types adopt similar ambitious names in England.

Besides regular schools, there were various societies or " gildes," bound together, some by brotherly ties, others by charters or letters patent which limited their numbers and entitled them to honorific distinctions.

The most celebrated of these, and one of the very few which survive to this day, for most royally privileged bodies were broken up during the French

[1] See page 32

Revolution, is the Confrérie Royale et Chevalière de Saint-Michel at Ghent. It originated during the very first years of the seventeenth century in a private association of gentlemen and burgesses devoted to the pursuit of arms. In 1603 the society received the distinction of the Golden Fleece, the collar being worn by their syndic on solemn occasions, in recognition, it seems, of valuable military services performed at the siege of Ostend. In 1613, under Albert and Isabella, it was recognized as royal and knightly. From about that time it seems to have become very exclusive. The number of members was reduced to one hundred, and none but reigning personages, or the noblest names of the Low Countries, were admitted into the Confrérie.

Fig. 94.—Thrust and parry in quarte, with opposition of the left hand.—Labat.

The old Draper's Hall at Ghent, which has been the seat of the society ever since 1611, contains the portraits of all the syndics who have presided over this association of fencers since the first days of its existence. Under its auspices periodical fencing tournaments were held, the results of which were registered in a " livre d'or."

The archives of the Confrérie de Saint-Michel would no doubt have proved a mine of information on the subject of fencing ; [1] they were unfortunately destroyed during the Revolution. This old institution is now a fencing club, of which the great Duke of Wellington was once a member.

The art taught towards the end of the seventeenth century under the sanction of the " Académies du Roy," had ceased to be that of the rapier, to become that of the small sword. The change in the use of the sword corresponds to that observable in its form.

[1] They might, perhaps, have settled the question as to whether the Spanish or German (*i.e.* Italian) school was most in favour in the Low Countries during the seventeenth century.

As soon as *all* cutting action was discarded in sword-play, light triangular fluted blades were almost universally adopted.[1]

From that time dates the origin of small-sword fencing.

Fig. 95.—Thrust and parry in tierce.—Labat.

Rapier-play (that is, sword-play chiefly with the point, but not altogether to the exclusion of the cut) was, however, cultivated to a much later period in Spain, Italy, and in some German schools.

Fig 96.—Thrust in tierce parried by yielding the faible.—Labat.

By thus divesting itself so early of most of the traditions connected with the rapier, the French school took the lead in the art of wielding the weapon destined to become universally adopted in Europe.

[1] Flat (*i.e.* cutting) blades are necessarily rather heavy, especially at the point ; indeed, a fair amount of weight about the centre of percussion is one of the requisites of a cutting weapon. But when the play is strictly limited to thrusting, lightness is the chief desideratum.

The long traditions of the " Académie," an institution unique of its kind, at least during the seventeenth and eighteenth centuries, necessarily favoured the development of a very perfect system.   Benefited by a long

Fig. 97.—Thrust in tierce by yielding the faible, with opposition of the left hand —Labat.

series of masters, each imbued at the outset of his career with sound principles, it was but natural that constant improvement should take place.   This improvement in the art of elegantly despatching a neighbour to the next world

Fig. 98.—Thrust and parry in seconde.—Labat.

consisted rather in the clearer definition and restriction of particular movements, and the elimination of imperfect or uncertain actions, than in the discovery of fresh modes of attack and defence.

The tendency of good masters, in fact, was rather to make success depend on closeness and accuracy than on a variety of tricks or mere agility of body. These are still the principles of the French school.

But the old notions, such as for instance the use of the left hand in

Fig. 99.—Thrust in quarte under the wrist (quinte.)—Labat.

parrying, which satisfied the instinctive tendency in fighting to counter and parry at the same time, or the advantages which volting, lowering the body, and traversing seem to give to the young and active, were too deeply

Fig. 100.— Thrust in low quarte (quinte), parried by the circle (septime).—Labat.

engrained on the minds of the fencing community to be altogether abandoned.

Accordingly, we see that although all good teachers disapproved of such unacademic actions, they were nevertheless obliged to admit the same, endeavouring, under protest, to systematize and improve them.

A work published in the last years of the century by Le Sieur Labat,[1] one of that celebrated family of fencing-masters already mentioned in connection with the Académie de Toulouse, may be noticed here as a good typical example in case.

Fig. 101.—Flanconnade.—Labat.

On many points the art taught by Labat does not materially differ from the most generally received notions of modern fencing.

His guard, his lunge, his methods of advancing and retiring, many of his bottes, parries in the four lines, simple feints, beats, bindings, and coupés

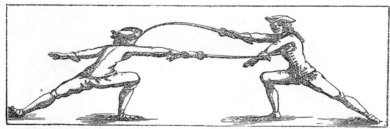

Fig. 102.—Flanconnade parried by the opposition of the left hand.—Labat.

are, to any but hypercritical adepts, practically the same as those now taught in our schools.

But side by side with these sound principles of simplicity he likewise taught the old-fashioned parry with the left hand, to allow of countering,

[1] See Biblio., 1696.

and the opposition of the same after a parry proper, in order to prevent the following thrust and to make room for the repost.

He taught passing as well as lunging on all attacks, and similarly countering low thrusts by volting, and high ones by lowering the body—

Fig. 103.—A pass in quarte, parried in quarte.—Labat.

these tricks were remnants of the old rapier-play, but lost all utility when the sword was worn so light as to be moved far more rapidly than the body.

One of the reasons, presumably, why body movements of no advantage

Fig. 104.—A " time," taken on a pass by lowering the body.—Labat.

in small-sword play were cultivated in those days, and even to the end of the eighteenth century, was that fencing was practised not only with a view to duelling, but also against the contingency of a sudden encounter, when a gentleman's object was rather to disarm his adversary than to wound or kill. Such disarming, or seizing of the sword, was generally done by means of voltes or passes. As long as the sword remained part of a private gentleman's dress, the frequency of such promiscuous fencing kept up the necessity of tricks later on to be banished from all fencing schools.

Fig. 105.—Time, taken on a pass in seconde, by volting.—Labat.

Volting, passing, &c., being thus thought admissible in some special cases, were naturally resorted to as alternatives to lunging and to parrying.

Fig. 106.—Seizing the hilt by turning the body sideways, on a pass in tierce.—Labat. "In the case of a pass in tierce, you must parry with your feet firm and seize his guard, drawing back the right foot, and presenting your point."

Labat does not advocate circular parries, "parades en contre dégageant." It seems difficult to understand why so many French masters should have objected to that action which has now become so typical of their play.

On the other hand, he insists on the value of parries by yielding as opposed to binding—a mode of attack often resorted to against the straight guard which seems to have been much in favour, especially with flat blades.

Fig. 107.—Disarming by a heavy parry.—Labat.

A curious point to be noticed in Labat's tuition is the stress he lays on the advantage of accentuating feints with a slight movement of the foot,[1]

Fig. 108.—Stepping forward with the left foot and seizing the blade, after displacing the adversary's point by a beat outward.—Labat.

(similar to our "appel," or single attack). Six years later he published a small handbook of fencing[2] for the use of his pupils.

[1] This habit has been preserved in some Italian schools, where all offensive movements of the sword are accompanied by a stamp of the foot.

[2] See Biblio., 1701.

Labat's two works, although of unpretending dimensions, rank among the soundest treatises on practical fencing.

Indeed, from the days of Liancour and Labat till quite the latter part of the eighteenth century, all the books written by the followers of the French school are more or less close imitations of their works.

This was most palpably the case with De Brye's [1] "L'Art de tirer des Armes" and "Le Maistre d'Armes" of Le Sieur Martin [2] of the Strasbourg Academy. The latter work contains a curious proof of the influence of the Paris Academy on matters of fence in the shape of an approbation of the professed and privileged "maistres en fait d'armes" of that corporation.

A retired naval officer, Le Sieur Girard, brought out in 1730 the most splendid work on fencing, with the exception of Angelo's, that ever appeared since Thibaust's ponderous folio.

The "Nouveau traité de la perfection sur le fait des Armes, dédié au Roi," [3] contains 116 copper plates representing the various attitudes of the French school and the way of successfully opposing them to the Italian, German, and Spanish guards; the latter, by the way, is represented in a most ridiculous light, without however being professedly a caricature. The infatuation of the Spaniard for the true, *i.e.*, the old "destreza," and his well-known partiality for long blades, were considered sufficient grounds for asserting that he was in the habit of wearing swords some eight feet long.

Being the work of an officer and not that of an academic "maistre d'armes," Girard's treatise is devoted in great part to the practical side of sword-play, and to the opposition of the small sword to all other fencing weapons, such as broadsword, pike, spontoon, &c. It even deals in an excursive manner with the use of the hand grenade, the musket, and the flail.

Besides its historical value to the military antiquarian, Girard's work is important among fencing works as registering some innovations introduced into the theory of the small sword during the last forty years.

It would seem that there were five distinct "bottes" taught in his days, namely, high and low quarte, tierce, seconde, and flanconnade. There were eight parries :—

Quarte, for high inside.

Tierce, for high outside.

"Cercle les ongles en dessus," for low inside (our half-circle or septime).

"Cercle les ongles en dessous," for low outside (our seconde, but with the hand kept high).

A fifth parry closing the low outside line, hand in supination (our octave), which was called quinte.

Prime, which he thus defines: "hand very high, nails turned downwards, arm extended, point low."

---

[1] See Biblio.   [2] See Biblio.   [3] See Biblio.

He seems to have been the first to give its modern name to this *parry*.

"Contre de tierce" and "contre de quarte," which are spoken of as excellent, showing that the French Academy had apparently overcome its prejudice to circular parries.

It is true that the sword in fashion under the "Régence" was light enough to compare with our modern duelling sword.

Opposition of the left hand was still as much in fashion as ever, not as a parry proper, but as a means of stopping a redoublement and keeping a clear way for the repost. Feints, which in the days of Liancour and Labat were generally simple, and never more than double, were then it seems often trebled.

It is evident that fencing was rapidly approaching that state of completeness and elegance which was to shine forth in the works of Danet and Angelo.

CHAPTER XI.

GIRARD'S work is a mine of information, inasmuch as it displays in its elaborate plates the many sides of the art, and the possibility of successfully opposing the "queen of weapons" to all others; on the one hand its rough and ready use in an unexpected fight, and on the other the elegance and precision of small-sword play in a courteous bout, or in a duel between gentlemen.

Fig. 109.—Coming on Guard, and First motion of the Salute.

As a matter of fact, however, during the eighteenth century fencing in most places except the German universities was looked upon *chiefly* as a refined accomplishment, and the schools of arms, in Paris especially, were as much schools of deportment as of fighting. The effeminate "petit maître" left the academy after fencing a few bouts in his high-heeled shoes and cocked hat without having disturbed his wig or his ruffles much more than if he had paced a minuet.

This change in the manners of the school seems to date from the early days of Louis XIV.'s reign, when, as we have seen, the salute under the name of "révérence" is heard of for the first time. In every school of any standing a code of rules regulating the assault was enforced by custom. On such occasions an accomplished fencer was expected to display the utmost regularity, avoid time hits, only repost as his adversary recovered, so as to avoid wounding his face, &c.—in fact, style had come to be far more considered than vigour.

Full masks with wired openings for the eyes seem indeed to have been worn in some salle d'armes about the middle of this century, but they were generally proscribed in fashionable schools as unnecessary to good players, who were always supposed to *place* their hits on their adversary's breast.

Fig. 110.—The Salute, second and third motions.

Such fencing must, in truth, have been most "academical," though, at the same time, very artificial.

The fear of wounding an adversary in the school, which would have disgraced a fencer for life, could not act otherwise than detrimentally on his velocity of movement, however it might tend to keep up his *form*. How different a "salle d'armes" in Paris or London in those days from the old Italian schools of Queen Bess and Henri III., which men never left but covered with bruises, perchance minus an eye or a few teeth!

During the thirty years which separate the dates of Girard's work and that of the great Danet, there appeared the following books :[1] another edition of Le Perche's "Exercice des Armes;" the "Principes et quintessence des Armes" of G. Gordine, "capitaine et maitre en fait d'armes" at

[1] See Biblio. from 1740 to 1766.

Liège, who attempted—and failed—to remodel the theory of fencing ; " L'Escrime pratique " of Daniel O'Sullivan, of the Académie du Roi, 1765, a most orthodox master, but whose work calls for no especial notice beyond the fact that he is the first author to give the modern names of " demi-cercle " and octave to the two parries in low lines with the hand in supination.

The Encyclopédie of Diderot and D'Alembert, in the volume which appeared in 1756, contained, however, already, under the head " Escrime," a pretty complete " résumé " of the principles followed by the Academy—the same, in fact, as those expounded by O'Sullivan.

About this time the first Angelo (Malevolti) was directing his flourishing and aristocratic school in London and preparing that marvellous typographic production, " L'Ecole des Armes," the appearance of which so

Fig. 111.—High carte parried carte (First degree and " prime des modernes" of Danet).

sorely enraged the amour propre of the French maîtres d'armes, and especially that of their syndic, Guillaume Danet, who was then thinking of bringing out his *magnum opus*, " L'Art des Armes."

The choice made by the compilers of the Encyclopédie, who acknowledged that they could find no sounder treatise to reproduce in their volume of plates (1765), and inserted under the head " Fencing " Angelo's work *in toto*, merely reducing his plates, did not tend to allay the irritation.

But whatever trouble the work of " l'auteur de Londres "—for no other title will he vouchsafe to Angelo—caused Danet, his own book was destined to be the source of much greater tribulation. Its appearance created so much jealousy, and ultimately such undisguised ill-feeling among the members of the " Compagnie," that Danet at last sent in his resignation of the office of syndic, which he had filled for so many years.

It would seem that about that time especially, the Academy of Arms was not a very closely united fraternity, and that a great deal of petty squabbling took place among its members, if a certain " Mémoire pour le Sieur Menessiez, Maître en fait d'armes, etc., contre la Communauté des Maîtres en fait d'armes," [1] exposes the facts such as they were.

At all events, the animosity displayed by Danet's colleagues soon after the appearance of his book is not easily understood, as he merely exposed the incorrectness of some terms used as household words by all fencing-masters, advocating a general revision of the nomenclature as well as a more systematic classification.

Assuming that his position of eminence in his profession gave him a

Fig. 112.—Carte parried carte outside.—First degree ; " prime moderne dessus les armes " of Danet.

certain right to dogmatize, he set forth an improved arrangement of bottes and parades on the numerical system, according to which numerical names were made to tally with their natural order, so as to have really some meaning in relation to *small-sword* play.

Before analyzing Danet's work, a short digression will be necessary.

It must often seem strange to beginners that the thrusts and parries which are the first to be taught in a course of fencing should be dubbed fourth and third—such being the meaning of carte and tierce—whilst the one most rarely used should be called prime, or the first.

The truth is, that notwithstanding Danet's solitary effort we still use

[1] Paris, 1763.

a nomenclature which was partly devised for, and only applicable to *rapier-play*, and partly at a later period for the small sword and the foil.[1]

Remembering the unwieldy nature of the cut-and-thrust rapier and the imperfection of its practice, we know that the most natural attack was a high thrust in pronation, or a cut over the head.

This being the case, the first guard of the majority of early masters [2]—prima, or prime, in fact—was one that could meet such an attack.

This high guard or parry uncovered the body, and others were devised with different elevations of the hand. In two of these the hand was kept

Fig. 113.—Prime parried prime.—First degree; " piime ancienne " of Danet.

more or less in pronation, that being decidedly the strongest position for meeting attacks in the outside line—they were the second and third (or tierce). In the fourth, which was opposed to attacks on the inside, the hand was held in supination or in the medium position.

---

[1] That such is the case will be obvious to anyone who gives their proper names to the only guards used in cut-and-thrust play, such as that with sabres or sticks : Prime, seconde, tierce, and carte being approximately the guards used in the early fashion of rapier practice, when the cut was much resorted to.

　To wit—Prime, covering the head and left side of body, high and low.

　　　　Seconde, covering the lower part of the right side.

　　　　Tierce, covering the upper part of the right side.

　　　　Carte, covering the upper part of the left side.

[2] Viggiani and some others specialized their first guard still further, considering it to be assumed when the hand was round the grip, ready to draw.

Different masters taught a different number of guards, but most of them recognized four principal ones, as above described, qualifying some of them as high or low. Such is the origin of prime, seconde, tierce, and carte. The reason why seconde and tierce, as now understood, have exchanged their relative position, is this: when prime was given up as an engaging guard in favour of quarte, fencers only looked upon prime and seconde as parries, the first for a high, the second for a low line, distinguishing ultimately the latter as high or low seconde. High second finally took and retained the name of third or tierce.

Fig. 114.—Tierce parried tierce.—Second degree; " seconde moderne " of Danet.

If the reader will refer to Figs. 62-3-4, representing the six guards of Capo Ferro, he will find instances of these assertions: prima, seconda, and terza only differ by the altitude of the hand, and defend the outer line; quarta defends the inner line; quinta and sesta are only low terza and quarta.

The early French masters classified seconde as *seconde pour le dessus* (our tierce) and *seconde pour le dessous* (proper seconde); the name of tierce applied to the former only appears for the first time in Le Perche (1676).

In Italy, however, and in all countries which followed the Italian method, quarta and terza always retained their relative meaning.

Although there are only four fundamental lines to close, and consequently four ways essentially different of reaching the adversary in relation to his sword hand, there are, with a light weapon at least, many more ways of effecting parries and delivering attacks.

This was discovered early in the transition days of the rapier into the small sword, and each master who wrote a system attempted to give each botte or parry a numerical name suited to what-seemed its natural order. These varied considerably with different authors.

For instance, the name of quinte, which was applied finally by La Boëssière (1818) to a low carte with the hand somewhat in pronation, was first given to what is now called septime (half-circle), and later on to what is now octave. Our half-circle, on the other hand, was first practised under the name of low carte, then under that of circle, and finally of septime. The parry in supination high outside only obtained its present name of sixte from La Boëssière, having previously been denominated as a *qualified* carte or tierce.

Fig. 115.—Carte parried low tierce.—Third degree ; " tierce basse moderne " of Danet.

This inadequacy of fencing terms and the classification based thereon inspired Danet with the ambition to found the " Art des Armes " on principles which, in his opinion, could not fail to appear obvious and acceptable to all, and which would consequently carry his name down to posterity as the father of the modern science of arms.

Guard (see Fig. 109).

Danet only admits one guard, similar to our engagement in carte, but with the weight of the body thrown back more on the left leg. He maintains, rightly, that it is applicable to all occasions, and can be made the starting point of all attacks and parries.

Advancing and retiring he teaches on the same principles as are now followed. He also approves of a leap backward on both feet in cases where the adversary would have a chance of seizing the sword.

Attacks. Danet considers that in fencing there are five *degrees* of height for the hand, and nine different *positions* of the arm and wrist whilst delivering a botte.

The degrees are determined, from above downwards, by the height of the hand *at the moment that the thrust is delivered;* the position of the hand is the result of the combination of the height with the turn of the wrist, either in pronation or supination.

Three bottes are delivered in the first degree, viz., prime, quarte, quarte outside.

One in the second, viz., tierce.

Fig. 116.—Seconde parried seconde.—Third degree ; " tierce moderne " of Danet.

Two in the third, viz., seconde and quarte coupée (low carte, cut over the point).

Two in the fourth, viz., low carte and flanconnade.

One in the fifth, viz., quinte.

With these premises Danet would call a high carte *Prime des modernes,* and carte outside *Prime dessus les armes des modernes;* prime he would call *Prime ancienne.* Similarly, tierce would become *Seconde des modernes,* seconde *Tierce des modernes.* Quarte and quinte would retain their old position.

Thus it would appear that Danet advocated a very high hand, since he found three different ways of " pushing carte," which he called his prime, quarte, and quinte.[1]

---

[1] Quinte is really nothing more than a low carte.

He happily did not devise improved names for all his simple parries, of which, by the way, he professed to teach eighteen. Only those which could in a certain measure be looked upon as corresponding with the bottes that had been re-christened, were classified in the same manner.

Thus he has the parries—

>Prime moderne (high carte) ;
>Prime moderne dessus les armes (carte outside) ;
>Seconde moderne (tierce) ;
>Tierce moderne (seconde) ;
>Quarte moderne (carte).

Fig. 117.—Carte parried half-circle.—Third degree ; " quarte ancienne "
of Danet.

Also tierce basse ; demi-cercle ; octave; two parades de flanconnade—one by turning the hand from supination to pronation and extending the arm to the position of " tierce moderne," and the other by yielding; " parade de pointe volante "—a parry in carte (carte outside generally) taken by cutting over ; three circular parries, viz., contre de quarte, contre de tierce, and cercle.[1]

Danet describes at length, and insists on the advantages of the exercise called in French schools " tirer au mur," consisting of a series of disengagements in all the lines performed with as much style as possible, which the

---

[1] Hitherto such parries had been called contre-dégagements.

adversary either parried with equal precision and deliberation, or allowed to be placed on his plastron for the sake of practice.

On the subject of the " coupé " (cutting over the point), Danet is of opinion that it is a dangerous mode of attack, often resulting in interchanged thrusts (coup fourrés), and that it should be restricted to the riposte.

It seems that a freer use of the appel (usually called in England " single attack ") was then made than now, and that it was accompanied by a close beat of the blade.

Similarly, the name of double appel, as it was always accompanied by a double stamp of the foot (our " double attack "), was then given to what is now called " double engagement."

Fig. 118.—Carte coupée parried octave.—Third degree ; " quarte ancienne " of Danet.

He also mentions the " coulé " as an effective preliminary to a simple thrust or a feint. English masters called this action " glizade."

Curiously enough, the academical Danet admits in his tuition a parry which was merely an adaptation to the light small sword of that breaking sweep with the rapier advocated in olden days by Italian masters as a universal parry " in extremis," and which he calls " parade de cercle." Although admitting that it might tend to disorder the play, he explains the advantage it might offer to a man who felt himself hard pressed, as it checks all feints and half thrusts, and meets all possible " bottes."

" For the proper performance of the cercle," says the author, " hold your hand in supination as high as your mouth, keeping your point low, and, by a swift movement of the wrist, cause your sword to describe the figure of a cone . . . . having met the adversary's sword, send your riposte in carte."

This circle was also performed in prime and in seconde in a similar manner, with a riposte in those lines.

The last part of Danet's first volume is devoted to what he calls " decisive play,"—that is to say, *with sharps*,—and deals with various approved methods of disarming, either by using the left hand, or by " crossing," binding, or whipping the adverse blade with the sword alone.

He explains the nature of voltes, half voltes, and passes, which it seems were still practised in many schools, but strongly disapproves of them all the

Fig. 119.—Low carte parried low carte.—Fourth degree ; " quarte moderne " of Danet.

while, and deals in the same way with what was then called " dessous,"—the " sbasso " of the Italians,[1]—time thrusts delivered on the adversary's attack or feint *in a high line*, by lowering the head and body.

Danet's principles were, on the whole, those received at the Académie d'Armes, but his special hobby was the " modern " classification of the nine ways of delivering a thrust, and a belief in the existence of eighteen, no more nor less, " simple " parries to the same. On one tenet, however, he disagreed with some of the dogmas. He *could not* see any material difference between what masters called " demi-contres " and " contres " proper.

This seems to have particularly aggravated Monsieur de la Boëssière,

[1] See Fig. 2.

one of the most eminent members of the Compagnie, especially celebrated as having been one of the masters of the Chevalier de Saint George, and as the inventor of wire masks.[1]

La Boëssière published in the same year a pamphlet intituled : " Observations sur le ' Traité de l'Art des Armes,' pour servir de defense à la verité des principes enseignés par les Maîtres d'armes de Paris.   Par M. * * * Maître d'Armes des Académies du Roy, au nom de sa Compagnie," in which he rated Danet in bitter terms, sneered at his classification, his " simple " parries, and especially his ignorance of the nicety of the " demi-contre."

This distinction of " demi-contre," as intermediate between simple and

Fig. 120.—Flanconnade, with opposition of the left hand.—
Fourth degree of Danet.

circular parries, is, it must be said, mere hair-splitting, and it is not much considered now.

Nothing abashed by the reception of his first volume, Danet in the course of the next year brought out the second, with a refutation of the criticisms which, having been made in the name of the Company, he was bound to take notice of.   In this volume he sets forth his arguments at full length, basing them, however, on a very incomplete sketch of the history of fencing, and considers foreign swordsmanship as compared with the French, much, it is needless to add, to the disadvantage of the former.

---

[1] These masks which he tried to bring in fashion about 1750 were similar in shape to the old English pattern of fencing masks, but were tied on the head with strings. This kind of mask is seen is some of Rowlandson's drawings.

Danet, however, was really too sound a master, and too well known, to suffer long from his difference with the Company of which he had been syndic.

Indeed, ten years later we hear of him as director of the "Ecole

Fig. 121.—Quinte parried quinte.—Fifth degree ; " quinte ancienne et moderne " of Danet.

Fig. 122.—Parade de pointe volante.

Royale d'Armes." On the occasion of his appointment he published a second edition of his work, in which is to be found an " approbation " of the masters of that school, highly commending Danet's theories, and declaring them acceptable to the Academy ; " wherefore," it goes on to say, " we cannot better express our gratitude than by offering this our approbation, without heeding the ill-founded criticisms which were passed on them."

Among the signatures affixed to that document occurs that of Teillagory, celebrated in the annals of fencing as the first master of Angelo, and of those celebrated figures of Angelo's old school, the Chevalier (or Chevalière) d'Eon, the Maréchal de Saxe, and the Chevalier de St. George, that "admirable Crichton" of the eighteenth century.

With Danet we conclude our sketchy analysis of French works on fencing. His "modern" nomenclature was not adopted; it went against too old associations, but his principles remained those of the Académie until the last days of its existence, and indeed they may be looked upon as the foundation on which, during this century, La Boëssière fils, Lafaugère, Jean-Louis, Gomard, Grisier, Cordelois, and so many others wove in all the niceties of the present French school of foil fencing.

One of Danet's most celebrated pupils was J. de Saint-Martin, who, during the last few years of the eighteenth century, established an aristocratic and very celebrated school in Vienna, where he taught, during the first quarter of this century, the science of arms as approved of by the old French Academy.

The famous "Compagnie des Maîtres en fait d'Armes des Académies du Roi en la Ville et Faubourg de Paris," after a flourishing existence of nearly two hundred years, was dissolved during the Revolution. Augustin Rousseau, its last syndic, whose father and grandfather had taught Louis XV. and Louis XIV., was guillotined in '93, probably for the mere fact that he had been, as the act of accusation termed it, "maître d'armes des enfants de Capet."

Coat granted to the *Académie d'Armes de Paris* by Louis XIV. in 1656, registered *en Parlement*, Sept. 3, 1664. The usual sign over the entrance of a fencing school was an arm brandishing a sword.

CHAPTER XII.

EFORE continuing our sketch of the history of the fencing art and of the characteristics of fencing schools in this country from the days of Saviolo to those of the Angelos, it may be well to notice some points of interest touching the swordsmanship of Spain, Italy, and Germany during the same period, and thus dismiss the subject.

FENCING IN SPAIN DURING THE SEVENTEENTH AND THE EIGHTEENTH CENTURIES.

The *verdadera destreza*—the true art of fence, at least in the opinion of the Spaniards—had found its complete exposition in the ponderous works of Don Luis Pacheco de Narvaez, that typical figure of Spanish solemnity, the acknowledged arbiter on all questions of import to a true cavalier. During the greater part of the seventeenth century the literature of the sword consisted practically of his writings or of others supporting or illustrating his principles. Indeed, as long as there existed a purely Spanish system of swordsmanship, it was based on the lines so carefully traced in the " Libro de las Grandezas de la Espada," and reiterated with only unimportant variations in Narvaez's numerous later works. His authority on the subject was assured by his position as master to the " King of all Spains and of the greater portion of the world." [1]

Indeed, Carranza and Narvaez always remained the fountain-head of knowledge, and with reference to their successors retained the same position as Giganti and Capo Ferro in Italy at the beginning of the seventeenth century, and Liancour and Labat in France at the end of it.

Knowing the broad principles of the " verdadera destreza," which are

---

[1] See in B blio. the various dedications.

explained in the chapters relating to Carranza and to Thibaust, the reader will find the magnificently sonorous titles of the twenty-eight different treatises on the philosophy of arms and their dexterous use detailed in the Bibliography quite sufficient to complete his impression of this school.

The fact that a great number of these were written in defence of Narvaez's doctrines would tend to show that there must have been many attempts to introduce foreign notions of swordsmanship—attempts which were, however, strenuously opposed by the masters of the Corporation of which Narvaez was apparently the head. As long as this association lasted—and it seems to have only begun to lose its influence about the last years of the seventeenth century—the unaltered tenets of the old cut-and-thrust rapier-play, with its passes and complicated preliminary operations, were alone recognized and cultivated. The works of Ettenhard y Abarca,[1] one of the most popular masters of the reign of Carlos II., may be referred to as an example in point, being typical of all Spanish treatises of that period, prefacing their instruction with an account of principles of geometry " indispensable to whosoever would wield his sword with true dexterity ; " settling once for all the angles at which blades should be crossed in all possible actions—" oposicion de angulos y de movimientos ;" minutely defining paces and passes, and encompassing all their figures within intricate diagrams of circles in all planes, of chords, and of tangents.

As a consequence of this infatuation for obsolete principles, the sword underwent less change in size and shape than in any other country. As late as the middle of the eighteenth century the *Espada* most in favour among Spaniards was practically the rapier of the early seventeenth century, with its cutting edges, its cup guard, and its long quillons.

The eighteenth century, however, seems to have produced very few masters of note, and, in the rare works[2] that we are able to meet with, we no longer find that uncompromising assertion of the indisputable perfection of their peculiar and old-fashioned notions.

The swaggering and pugnacious " diestros," "matamoros," "valentones," " guapos "—those picturesque brawlers so vividly depicted by Quevedo Villegas, Velez de Guevara and his imitator Lesage, and all the picaresque writers of the seventeenth century—in other words, the ragged but haughty adventurers so well personified in Don Cesar de Bazan, whose very existence depended on their consummate skill in the management of their prodigious rapiers, are types which likewise seem to have become extinct during the

---

[1] See Biblio., 1675, and 1697. These two books are to be found in the Brit. Mus. Library.

[2] There are only five Spanish works on fencing at present known as belonging to that age, and they make a very poor display as compared with the pompous productions of the previous century.

eighteenth century.[1]   At that time, also, the wearing of the sword, which hitherto every Spaniard had assumed as a right since the days of Charles V., was a privilege which fashion as well as oft-repeated police ordinances began to restrict to gentlemen only,—although, as every independent Spaniard is "hidalgo" in his own opinion, this restriction had a less sweeping effect in that country than in any other.

Among the commoner devotees of the art of fence superiority began to be sought in the management of the dagger, when the monopoly of the sword was assumed by their betters.

To this we may ascribe the origin of the art of wielding the *navaja*— the long Spanish knife—which, when practised with the capa, was based on the principles of ancient sword-and-cloak play, and when alone, on those of the single rapier according to Carranza's teaching.   In the first instance, the left arm, protected by two turns of the cloak, was used for parrying, the left foot when on guard being kept forward—the dagger was held in the right hand, thumb flat on the blade.   In the second case, as there could be but little parrying except by seizing the wrist, true dexterity consisted in tempting the adversary into making some movement which might afford an opportunity for a time hit.   On every occasion the stab was delivered by a pass.

Much decision was required for this play, and perhaps even more real love of fighting than in the mathematical and philosophical rapier fence.   Seville was reputed a great resort of proficients in the art of the dagger fight.

These principles seem to have been handed down without much alteration to modern amateurs of the "cuchillo."

As the prestige of the ancient Corporation gradually waned, foreign teachers of fencing obtained a little influence in Spain, but, in presence of the rooted infatuation for the national style, they were reduced to forming a mixed system of Italian or French and Spanish schools, with however, as might be expected, poor results and few followers.   Accordingly, we find that all foreign authors who have noticed the Spanish play in their treatises, such as Liancour, Girard, Danet, and Angelo, invariably represent the Spaniard as fencing in accordance with the principles laid down by Narvaez. Fig. 123, which it is needless to remark is ludicrously exaggerated, is in all essentials similar to illustrations of the Spanish guard to be found in the above-mentioned authors, and tallies closely with G. Silver's description of the Spanish fight with the rapier written in 1599.

Towards the middle of the eighteenth century appeared at last a book treating of the foil and the sabre as belonging to different plays.   This shows

[1] Also in most relations of travels through Spain of the seventeenth century.   See A. de Sommerdyck ("Voyage d'Espagne," 1665) and Madame d'Aulnoy ("Relation du Voyage d'Espagne," 1629), *passim.*

that the rapier had begun to lose the character of a cut-and-thrust implement and to assimilate itself to the small sword—the *Espadin*.

The author, D. Juan Nicolas Perinat,[1] fencing-master to the Academy of Guardias Marinas in Cadiz, prided himself on being the first who adopted that new art. His treatise seems to be the last book of any importance on the subject of fence published in the Peninsula during that century. It may be said to have foreshadowed the gradual adoption of French and Italian, and the extinction of the genuine Spanish schools, which may be considered as completely effected now. In the absence of any book of importance dating from the last years of the eighteenth century, it is difficult to say whether the following account, given by Angelo in his later edition (1787), of the Spanish system of fencing, tallied with facts in his own days, or whether he

Fig. 123.—The Spanish Guard, according to Danet, "Art des Armes," 1766.

took the notion out of Girard's work, which he seems indeed to have imitated on many points :—

" The Spaniards have in fencing a different method to all other nations; they are fond often to give a cut on the head, and immediately after deliver a thrust between the eyes and the throat. Their guard is almost straight, their longe very small; when they come in distance they bend the right knee and straighten the left, and carry the body forward ; when they retire they bend the left knee and straighten the right ; they throw the body back well, in a straight line with that of the antagonist, and parry with the left hand, or slip the right foot behind the left.

" Their swords are near five feet long from hilt to point, and cut with both edges ; the shell is very large, and behind it is crossed with a small bar, which comes out about two inches on each side ; they make use of this to wrench the sword out of the adversary's hand, by binding or crossing his

[1] See Biblio., 1758.

blade with it, especially when they fight against a long sword ; but it would be very difficult for them to execute this against a short sword. Their ordinary guard is with their wrist in tierce, and the point in a line with the face. They make appels or attacks of the foot, and also half thrusts to the face, keep their bodies back, and form a circle with the point of their swords to the left, and straightening their arm, they advance their body to give the blow on the head, and recover instantly to their guard, quite straight, with their point in a direct line to their adversary's face."

If this account was correct in 1787, short as it is it shows that the " destreza " never altered its principles, but to its last days remained essentially what Narvaez had made it.

FENCING IN ITALY DURING THE SEVENTEENTH AND THE EIGHTEENTH CENTURIES.

There can be little doubt that during the eighteenth century at least, the masters of the " Académies du Roy " placed the French school in a position of indisputable supremacy, a fact plainly displayed by the invasion of French teachers of fence in England, in Germany, as far as Russia, and even, though on rare occasions, in Italy and Spain.

The Italians do not seem to have been able to transform their old system of swordsmanship sufficiently to make it quite suitable to short and light blades such as were used in France and in England. They modified some details of the old rapier fence taught by their redoubtable masters of the seventeenth century, but retained the fundamental principles of the *stesso tempo*—the single time, the parry and counter attack combined—that had been the very soul and life of a fight with lengthy and ponderous rapiers, but became more and more uncertain and dangerous as greater rapidity in the management of the point was possible. It may be safely asserted that from the day when the sword grew light enough to admit of *double* feints and active wrist play, the " single time " principle, applied to all occasions, became decidedly vicious. The complication that could be introduced in the attack necessitated a greater variety of parries than could possibly be combined with a repost in " stesso tempo."

The art of fence, which had been in the previous age one of the great specialities of the Italians, seems to have been comparatively neglected during the eighteenth century, if the small number of treatises known to exist may be considered a criterion—five against thirty-one belonging to the seventeenth century. In any case, it is evident they did not keep up their old supremacy.

To enter into details concerning the works of Calarone, A. di Marco,

Mangano, Lovino, and Micheli[1] would be merely to weary the reader. Suffice it to say that during the eighteenth century Italian fencing assumed the character so vividly set forth in the treatise "of the two friends Rosaroll and Grisetti," the last which figures for Italy in the bibliographical list. Although it contains some very old-fashioned notions of swordsmanship, it was long looked upon by the majority of Italian masters, and is even now by some Neapolitans, as the standard work on sword-play.

The usual guard in favour among the Italians was very much more like that shown in Fig. 1 than Danet's representation (see Fig. 124). Danet was not as careful in his dealings with foreign plays as with his own; he seems to have contented himself with imitating this plate from one of Girard's.

Fig. 124.—The Italian Guard opposed to the French, according to Danet. To suit this play the Italian should be represented with a cup-hilted sword as in Fig. 1.

Although the movements executed by the sword itself were comparatively simple, especially among good fencers, active body movements played a great part in their system. They made much use of attacks on the march, accentuating all their feints either with a short step or a call of the foot.

The principle of the single time was not then *absolutely* adhered to, but time thrusts, especially on the adversary's feints, were as much a feature of the Italian school as the well-defined parry and riposte of the French. When properly executed, especially on a feint, they were by no means so faulty or uncertain as it pleased French masters to assert, for as the Italians kept their sword arm invariably straight, very close parries, fort on faible, were, without ceasing to menace him with the point, sufficient to remove the adversary's blade from the body. The shape of their sword also, that of a reduced cup-hilted rapier, was eminently favourable to this sort of play.

[1] See Biblio., Italy, 1714 to 1798.

The whole art of delivering time thrusts with certainty depends on the power of keeping the " opposition " in whatever line it is menaced by the adversary, and this practice of "keeping the line " as they called it was carefully cultivated as quite the ruling principle of fencing.

In presence of this recognized system of timing, no very elongated lunge was much resorted to, but rather a series of short attacks in various lines, attempting to gain on the adversary so as to oblige him to make his parries wider, or to force an entrance by binding his blade. The left hand was kept level with the breast, in readiness to stop those time thrusts which were delivered on a feint, but when lunging it was generally thrown back in line with the sword arm for the sake of balance. Time thrusts delivered on the adversary's attack, by lowering the body (when the attack was in a high line), by volting (when it came in an inside line), or by passing to the left (when it came outside), were still looked upon as quite academical. These actions were called respectively *sbasso*,[1] *inquarto*, and *intagliata*.

The Italians used four guards, and although the most common engagement was carte, they also engaged in the three other lines, and as there were only four single parries in common use, guards and parries were in all cases strictly interchangeable terms.

As the arm was kept fully extended,[2] whether in a position of guard, defence, or attack, coming to a parry in a given line was simply to change the guard so as to cover that line.

These parries or guards were :—

For the high inside line, prima (with the hand in pronation, on a level with chin, point menacing the adversary's body) and quarta (see Fig. 1) ; for the high outside line, terza (same as quarta, but hand in pronation) ; for the low inside line, *mezzo cerchio* (which would be shown by Fig. 124 were the Italian's arm extended from the shoulder, and his hand a little lower) ; for the low outside line, seconda (hand in pronation on a level with the waist, point menacing the adversary's hip).

All passages from an inside to an outside line were very simple and very few. The Italians always adhered to the principles of their old rapier-play, and considered that agility and vigour, and discernment in seizing a time, were more useful qualities in earnest sword-play than the most scientific combinations.

It seems somewhat curious that Angelo, who was of Italian origin, should have been so excessively incorrect in his description of the Italian guard, which is here quoted :—

---

[1] See Fig. 2.
[2] Excepting, of course, the case of parries by yielding, or *cedute*, when the arm must be bent—being re-extended, however, immediately on the completion of the parry.

"The Italian guard is commonly very low; they bend equally both knees; carry the body between both legs; they keep the wrist and point of the sword low, and have a contracted arm; they keep the left hand at the breast, to parry with it, and straightway return the thrust.

"Though this guard is natural to them, yet they vary every moment, to perplex their adversaries, in keeping a high wrist and point to the line of the shoulder; in keeping a high wrist and a very low point; and making large gesticulations of the body, and turning round their antagonist, sometimes to the right and sometimes to the left, or by an immediate advance of the left foot to the right; and they thrust straight thrusts at random, or make passes and voltes. They have much dependence on their agility, and the parade of the left hand: for that reason, when two Italians fight together they often are both hit together, which is called a counter thrust: this happens seldom with two good swordsmen, because they know how to find the blade by a counter disengage, or by the circle, and because they have a quick return.

"And yet, nevertheless, I am persuaded that the above Italian method would puzzle a good swordsman, if he did not take the necessary precautions," &c.

The modern system of Neapolitan fencing is based on those old principles of the " spada lunga " play, which have been roughly sketched in this book, but it eschews all unnecessary body movements, as well as parries with the left hand. It is, on the whole, simpler than the French, and although less brilliant for foil play, is perhaps better suited for the *sword* than the latter. But the frequent and excessive turning of the wrist which is the action paramount in a play where the arm is constantly extended, is only practical with swords or foils mounted in the old-fashioned rapier style—that is, with quillons and a cup guard, with or without pas d'âne, so as to allow of closing one or two fingers and the thumb round the base of the blade. This form of the sword is not now much used out of Italy, although it is sometimes to be found in German and Spanish schools.

FENCING IN GERMANY DURING THE SEVENTEENTH AND THE EIGHTEENTH CENTURIES.

It was stated in the chapter on early German fencing schools that the practice of the rapier was popularized in Germany by the society of " Federfechter," and that by the end of the sixteenth century the " Feder " or " Rappier " was adopted in all schools of arms.

As the fashion came from Italy, not only its principles but many of the terms connected therewith were naturally enough closely copied from those in favour among the best known masters of that country, even as we have seen Sainct Didier coining uncouth words in his attempt to assimilate the Italian manner, and the Elizabethan devotee of the rapier discoursing in an outlandish jargon—Italian grafted on Spanish—on the "*stocado*" and "*punto reverso*," "putting a stock," or "counterchecking a montanto."

On points of fashion imitators are naturally somewhat behind-hand at all times, and although Meyer in his first edition (1570) embodied all the best methods known in his days, his system was already obsolete when the second appeared at Augsburg in 1610; and in 1612 Jacob Sutor had not progressed one step beyond the methods of Marozzo, Agocchie, Grassi, and Viggiani, which were then considered quite antiquated in Italy by the followers of the Bolognese school.

In the same year, however, Conrad von Einsidell, fencing-master in Jena, " presented to all lovers of the praiseworthy art of fence " a German reproduction of Villamont's translation of Cavalcabo's work.[1] Five years later the Elzevirs published at Leyden the first German translation of Fabris' " Schermo," many other translations or editions of which were issued from various German presses throughout the seventeenth century and as late as the first quarter of the eighteenth.

In 1619 a translation into French and German of the great Venetian master, Nicoletto Giganti, was published at Frankfort by J. von Zetter,— presumably a *Marxbruder*,—a second edition of which appeared in 1622.

In 1620 Hans Wilhelm Schoffer von Dietz, fencing-master at Marburg, collected in a huge volume, illustrated by 670 copperplates, the teaching of all the most celebrated Italian masters of his days, but especially of Salvator Fabris.

Three editions of a similar work, combining the writings of Fabris and Capo Ferro, but of smaller dimensions, were issued between 1610 and 1630 by Sebastian Heussler, " Kriegsmann und Freyfechter von Nürnberg."

Since all these Italian treatises ran through several editions, and as most other authors, such as Hundt, Koppen, and Garzonius, did not offer any marked difference in their doctrines, it may be safely asserted that the rapier fence in favour throughout Germany during the seventeenth century was purely that of the Italian school, founded on the teaching of the three sturdy swordsmen, Fabris, Giganti, and Capo Ferro. For cut-and-thrust play— " auf Stoss und Hieb "—such as was so much in favour at the universities till

---

[1] See Biblio., German, 1612 ; French, 1609 ; also p. 106.

the beginning of this century, it remained the foundation of the German school.

Towards the last third of the century, however, some German masters, amongst others Daniel Lange, *Fechtmeister* at Heidelberg, and G. Paschen, who seems to have professed in Frankfort, in Halle, and in Leipzig, where he also published several editions of his work, adopted some of the French terms and attitudes; but, notwithstanding the renown of the French, and the comparative lack of great masters in Italy during the eighteenth century, the play of the latter seems to have been more congenial to the Germans till quite modern times.

A great change in the character of the schools themselves—the " Fecht-boden "—took place soon after the sixteenth century; they were more and more abandoned by the citizens, and ended by being almost exclusively patronized by students and officers, the old fighting associations of the bur-gesses having gradually become converted into " Schutzen Kompagnien."

The " Schwerdt " and other heavy weapons so much in favour among the Teutons during the sixteenth century were fast becoming obsolete,[1] whilst, on the other hand, the rapier was considered an exclusively noble arm, only to be worn, and consequently only cultivated by the "high born."

Members of all universities, however, professors and students—the "nobility of knowledge "—assumed the right to wear—and use too—the noble rapier, a right which they preserved by prescription, notwithstanding the well-known prohibition in all the statutes of universities founded during the sixteenth century.

The Thirty Years' War, which threw the country into such hopeless disorder, had an especially demoralizing effect on these bodies.   The amount of bloodshed caused among the pugnacious youth of Germany by the prepos-terous habit of wearing the sword instead of the gown in academic centres was hardly less than that brought about by the incomprehensible duelling mania which raged in France from the days of Henri II. to those of Louis XIV.

At the close of the war another attempt was made to restrict the privilege of wearing arms, but without success; the habit was too deeply engrained, and it was persisted in, in spite of all opposition, by students as well as men of "higher quality," until the end of the eighteenth century.

Although the *Marxbrüder* and *Federfechter* did not preserve their monopoly, most of the university fencing schools were directed by some of their members; and, as students were more often attracted by the renown of the " Fechtmeister " than by that of the other learned *professors*, it gradually

---

[1] Oddly enough, however, a treatise on the " *Schwerdt*" and the " *Dusack*" appeared in Wurzburg during the latter part of the seventeenth century, at a time when these weapons were practically forgotten.   See Biblio., Verolinus, 1699.

came to pass that the best schools were always to be found at the most popular of these institutions.

Kahn [1] is the principal authority on the subject of these university fence schools, and an account of what he calls the " Kreusslerische Schule " is given at some length in his works.

About the year 1618 there came to Frankfort-on-the-Main the son of a Nassau schoolmaster, who, " preferring the noble blade to the ferule," apprenticed himself to the " Marxbrüder," and was eventually admitted to the confraternity. On becoming a privileged master he went to Jena, where during sixty years he initiated many generations of students into the mysteries of the " Feder." He died in 1673. This was the great Kreussler, the founder of that race of famous fencing-masters whose names remained household words in most German universities for so long a time.

His portrait, together with that of the captain of the " Marxbrüder-shaft" who proclaimed him master, is still to be seen in the library of the Jena University, and represents him dressed in black, with a broad white collar, provided with his professional sword and gauntlet. His right shoulder, and indeed his whole right side, is depicted as more powerfully developed than his left, and his *right* eye, especially, as bright as a falcon's,[2] indications of his exclusive devotion to right-hand fencing.

Kahn considered Kreussler as the founder of the art of the " Feder." It would have been more accurate to say that he was one of the first " Marx-brüder " who almost exclusively cultivated and raised to a high pitch of practical perfection in Germany the art of Cavalcabo, Fabris, and Giganti.

Be it as it may, it appears that it was from Jena that this mode of fencing first spread to the other universities.

There are many examples of a family of fencing-masters retaining a high position in their profession for many generations. We have seen the Bolognese Cavalcabos teach in Italy and France for nearly a century ; the Le Perches in Paris and the Labats in Toulouse keep up the prestige of their name from father to son for even a longer period ; we know that the family of Rousseaux taught the art of arms to the last three kings of the Bourbon dynasty before the Revolution, and that the Angelos kept the most popular school in London for more than a century; but none of these can compare with the Kreusslers, who furnished some twenty well-known fence-masters to various universities between the first quarter of the seven-teenth century till the end of the eighteenth.

Wilhelm Kreussler, the founder of this numerous family, had twelve children, most of whom became masters of note.

His eldest, Gottfried, first went to Leipzig, where he must have met

---

[1] See Biblio , 1739.　　　　[2] Ott, " System der Fechtkunst," 1853.

with Triegler, Paschen, and J. Hynitzchen, all literary masters, whose works figure in the Bibliography; the last was an ardent admirer of Fabris, a fresh translation of whose writings he brought out in 1677.[1]

On his father's death Gottfried took the direction of the old " fighting ground" at Jena. He, like his father, made fencing-masters of his numerous sons, most of whom adopted the ancestral profession; among these, the eldest, Johann Wilhelm, also eventually succeeded to his father's post at Jena, whilst another, Heinrich, acquired especial celebrity in various parts of Germany as a redoubtable champion. He is credited with the reputation of having been instrumental in fixing the principles of the true German school, which, about the middle of the eighteenth century, began to be looked upon as the best in Europe for cut-and-thrust play.

Fig. 125.—The German Guard opposed to the French.—Danet. The Germans used more generally a cup-hilted sword similar to the Italian.

The portraits of Gottfried, Johann, and Heinrich Kreussler are also extant in the University Library[2] at Jena. Many of their descendants— one of whom, by the way, was a " Doctor Juris," but returned late in life to the traditional occupation of his family—professed till the beginning of the century at Leipzig, Giessen, and Jena.

Although the Germans never originated much in rapier-play, having adopted, first, the Italian, and, later on, a mixture of Italian and French styles, they were highly considered as practical swordsmen both in France and Italy. During the eighteenth century it was even deemed a necessary

---

[1] See Biblio.   [2] Ott, " System der Fechtkunst," 1853.

part of a French swordsman's practice to be able to oppose his fight to that of the German. Naturally, the French masters of that period expounded, in the most plausible manner, infallible rules for overcoming the Teuton sword in hand; but from all accounts the "Kreusslerische" fencers who came to Paris—it was part of their system to study foreign swordsmanship—generally proved themselves formidable opponents. Indeed, it would seem as if, from the middle of the eighteenth century, fencing was quite the study of paramount importance at the university. At Jena, Halle, Leipzig, Heidelberg, and, later on, Goettingen, Helmstadt, and Giessen, duels were so common and so dangerous—the usual play being what we would call spadroon or cut-and-thrust fencing—that the most peaceable student was never sure of his life for a single day.

As to their small-sword play, it was a slight modification of the Italian, as the following description, taken from Angelo's "Ecole des Armes," printed in 1763, will sufficiently show :—

"In the position of the German guard, the wrist is commonly turned in tierce, the wrist and arm in a line with the shoulder, the point at the adversary's waist, the right hip extremely reversed from the line, the body forward, the right knee bent, and the left exceedingly straight. The Germans seek the sword always in prime or seconde, and often thrust in that position with a drawn-in arm. They keep their left hand to the breast, with an intent to parry with it, and the moment they draw their sword they endeavour to beat fiercely with the edge of their sword on their antagonist's blade, with an intent to disarm them if possible."

Besides this truly German small-sword and the national spadroon or cut-and-thrust play, regular *academical* fencing as it was practised in Paris was likewise taught in a few German schools, generally, however, for the special use of the small Courts, where everything French was curiously imitated.

Among most noteworthy masters whose names have come down to us chiefly through their treatises, the following may be noted: at Nürnberg, Johann Andreas Schmidt and Alexander Doyle (a Germanized Irishman), at Ingoldstadt, J. 'J. de Beaupré (a Frenchman, who taught a mixture of Italian and French play), and the great Friedrich Kahn, who was, as Ott says, "an ornament, first of the Goettingen, then of the Helmstadt universities."

Curiously enough the Kreusslers do not seem to have published any books,[1] but their successors at Jena, the numerous family of Roux, are the authors of several important works published towards the end of the eighteenth century.

About this time there was a marked diminution in the love of duelling,

---

[1] Unless we ascribe to a Kreussler the anonymous work signed B. K. published in Jena in 1798. See Biblio.

and consequently of fencing, one of the signs of which showed itself in a general tendency to abandon the old cut-and-thrust rapier—the thrust being considered too dangerous to be employed in students' encounters—and to replace it almost universally by the "Hiebcoment," the play of which was very similar to the backswording in favour among us about the same period.

The students of Jena, however, as well as those of Halle and Erlangen, insisted on retaining the privilege of being killed or seriously wounded, instead of merely scarified, in their duels, and refused to be parted from their old-fashioned rapier till about the third decade of this century.

As the German university schools lost their importance, the modern French foil play, and the "contre pointe," gradually, but surely, came into favour among German officers and private gentlemen, whilst the system of fencing followed by the *students* became so specialized as to have lost most of the characteristics of what can be called fencing—namely, the art of defending oneself and offending the adversary in the simplest and surest manner.

The students' Schlaeger play is a peculiar one, requiring the use of a very peculiar sword; most natural fencing actions are prohibited, and the conditions so regulated that the precautions which are most elementary, as well as of paramount importance, in natural fighting, can be entirely neglected, the fencer's sole attention being devoted to the one object of lacerating his opponent's face or the top of his head, and of course preventing him, as much as possible, from doing the same.

If this is not fencing, it is, however, a very severe and difficult exercise, and a duel with Schlaegers, although very rarely dangerous, must be considered a very fair test of pluck and endurance.

———

A description of the main features of a *modern* German students' duel, although outside the general scope of this book, may be found of some interest.

The Schlaeger is a basket-hilted sword with a long *pointless*, flat, and rather flexible rapier blade, which, when used for duelling purposes, is sharpened for a length of seven or eight inches from the point on the right edge, and for about two inches on the false. The hilt is much larger than is usual in close-guarded swords, in order to allow a very free action of the wrist. The grip is made very thin near the hilt and somewhat thick at the pummel end, and is provided with a loop, generally of leather, wherein the forefinger can be inserted, so that the Schlaeger may be held in a very easy, and, at the same time, very secure manner—this being the great desideratum in the *flipping* play of which its practice solely consists. In some universities a pair of diminutive quillons provided with *pas d'ânes* are in favour, instead of the loop, for the purpose of securing a firm grip.

The adversaries fall on guard within close measure, holding their

Schlaegers in a position of very high *prime*, with the arm fully extended and the point on a level with the mouth.

The face and head being the only objective of the attack, a very elaborate system of armouring and padding is resorted to in order to protect the wrist, arm, and shoulders, and, in short, all parts of the body liable to receive by accident cuts aimed at the face, and the defence of which does not form part of this curious system of fencing. The eyes are protected by iron " goggles," the branches of which likewise afford some protection to the temples. In some cases even, especially in duels between *freshmen*—" Füchse"—the head is further protected by a cap.

The play is very simple, but so unnatural that it requires much vigour, long practice, and the development of particular muscles of the forearm, for perfection. It consists of flipping cuts delivered from the wrist—not with the centre of percussion, but with the extreme part of the blade, which alone is sharpened—and directed to either side of the adversary's face, and to the top, or even the back of his head. At each blow the point describes nearly the whole circumference of a circle.

From the high prime guard cuts can be delivered in the four lines : in carte, tierce, low carte, and seconde (Quart, Terz, Tiefquart, Sekonde), the last two cuts passing *under* the adversary's point.

Parries are performed by raising the hand as high and as much forward as possible, still keeping the point very low, to meet attacks in high lines, and by shifting the opposition, to meet cuts attempted, under the point or otherwise, in low lines. The chief difficulty in parrying being, not merely to meet the opposite sword in time, but so to meet it as to prevent its point *flipping over*. Very little feinting is resorted to, but cuts are rapidly exchanged, success depending on the *vigour and rapidity* with which they can be returned.

It is needless to remark that encounters " in pads," and with such restrictions, can hardly be called *duels* in the ordinary acceptance of the word, but should rather be looked upon as *matches* in a particular game. As a matter of fact, German students' duels are not necessarily the result of private quarrels, but are as often as not arranged every week by the presidents of the various " fighting corps" of the University. The most usual order of such duels is either the exchange of a given number of cuts, say 24, or to fight during a given number of minutes, usually 14. A duel under these conditions is as much a trial of endurance as of skill, for no wounds on either side, excepting such as may be deemed really dangerous, are allowed to put a stop to the fight.

CHAPTER XIII.

N England during the seventeenth century rapier fencing was an accomplishment only cultivated by *gentlemen*, and to all appearances chiefly by those who brought back Cavalier manners from Spain and Italy. Anglicized Italian or Spanish or even French terms are of frequent occurrence in the literature of the first third of this century, but it seems difficult to find any positive intimation that schools of fence of the kind which enjoyed such popularity in Elizabethan days under Saviolo and other foreigners ever became regular institutions. It is probable that the bitter and persistent opposition of " the profitable members in the commonwealth," the English " Maisters of Defence," succeeded in preventing their permanent intrusion in this country.

Although we hear a great deal of the back and the " sheering " sword— the short sword " of perfect length " so much extolled by Silver on behalf of *English* fencing—very little is ever said concerning the rapier except in connection with foreign topics. Gentlemen must either have studied the art abroad, or have had private masters, usually foreigners or old soldiers, attached to their households, for there can be no doubt that whatever may have been the popular feeling against the " bird spits," [1] the rapier remained the only arm in favour among the upper classes.

People of lesser " quality " had to deal with the common fencing-masters, who, when we first hear of them again as a body, seem to have gone back to that very inferior condition of gladiators which kept them in such bad repute during the Middle Ages.

Whenever we hear of fencing-masters in the seventeenth century, they are also spoken of as prize fighters who made of their stage fights an

---

[1] In this respect there was a marked difference of fashion between Northern and Southern countries, for in Italy, Spain, and even France, no matter what class he belonged to, no man with any pretensions to smartness would be seen abroad without a portentous rapier by his side.

advertisement for their trade as well as a profitable occupation, even as the pugilists of the next century depended chiefly on success in the prize ring for a livelihood. They taught the use of a great number of weapons, according to the tradition of the old masters of the Tudor period, but generally devoted their energies to the back sword, which, since the buckler had become obsolete in England,[1] was quite recognized as the national arm. It was, moreover, very well suited to the popular entertainment of stage fights, as the very gory and dreadful-looking wounds it inflicted satisfied the expectations of the audience, without usually being very dangerous, at least in comparison with those caused by the foyning rapier. The falchion or cutlass was also in great vogue, and its practice was apparently similar to that of the German " Dusack."

However much the elegance of the thrusting play might please the Cavalier, it never suited the bulk of the nation : the character of English pugnacity being rather a delight in hard knocks than a thirst for the adversary's life.

Englishmen had always loved the exhausting sword-and-buckler fight, and when the latter went out of fashion, the endurance and " bottom " displayed in a hot backsword contest was much more congenial to their feelings than the most cunningly conducted rapier bout.

Under the auspices of the Corporation of Masters of Defence public trials of skill in the use of " verie manie weapons " were of frequent occurrence, and in many instances patronized by the presence of royalty, for we hear that " Bluff King Hal," Philip and Mary, and even the " virgin Queen" herself, assisted at, and showed great interest in such entertainments.

The challenge issued by the Silvers to Saviolo,[2] and which the latter wisely declined, shows that on some occasions more serious encounters than the ordinary fencing tournaments were also held in public. Even after the Corporation had crumbled away—it is never heard of after 1593—these exhibitions of hard knocks, which must have been very popular indeed, evidently remained an institution.

Some masters of greater " martial scorn" than the rest started the habit of substituting " sharps" for " blunts," and took to displaying their gladiatorial prowess in theatres and other enclosures where they could gather entrance money. These stage fights were evidently the origin of modern prize fights.

It seems, however, difficult to discover any account of an actual prize fight of this kind previous to the Restoration, and they probably only became very common after the Parliamentary wars.

[1] It remained in favour among the Scotch to a much later period.
[2] See page 24.

But that they were recognized entertainments and savouring in no way of novelty in 1662 is amply shown by the following entry in Mr. Pepys's Diary :—

"June 1.   The Duke having been a-hunting to-day, and so lately come home and gone to bed, we could not see him, and we walked away.   And I with Sir J. Minnes to the Strand May-pole : and there light out of his coach, and walked to the New Theatre, which, since the King's players are gone to the Royal one, is this day begun to be employed by the fencers to play prizes at.   And here I come and saw the first prize I ever saw in my life ; and it was between one Mathews, who did beat at all weapons, and one Westwicke, who was soundly cut several times both in the head and legs, that he was all over blood ; and other deadly blows they did give and take in very good earnest, till Westwicke was in a sad pickle.   They fought at eight weapons, three boutes at each weapon.   This being upon a private quarrel, they did it in good earnest ; and I felt one of the swords, and found it to be very little, if at all blunter on the edge than the common swords are. Strange to see what a deal of money is flung to them both upon the Stage between every bout.   This day I hear at Court of the great plot which was lately discovered in Ireland, made among the Presbyters and others, designing to cry up the Covenant and to secure Dublin Castle," &c., &c.

The following graphic description was published ten years later in " An Account of a Journey to the British Isles,"[1] by a Monsieur Josevin de Rocheford.   It is quoted at full length as it depicts very circumstantially the manner in which stage fights were heralded and conducted.

" We went to see the ' Bergiardin,'[2] where combats are fought by all sorts of animals, and sometimes men, as we once saw.   Commonly, when any fencing-masters are desirous of showing their courage and great skill, they issue mutual challenges, and before they engage parade the town with drums and trumpets sounding, to inform the public there is a challenge between two brave masters of the science of defence, and that the battle will be fought on such a day.

" We went to see such a combat, which was performed on a stage in the middle of an amphitheatre, when, on the flourish of trumpets and the beats of drums, the combatants entered, stripped to their shirts.   On a signal from the drum, they drew their swords and immediately began to fight, skirmishing a long time without wounds.   They were both very skilful and courageous. The tallest had the advantage over the smallest, for, according to the English fashion of fencing, they endeavoured rather to cut than to thrust in the French manner, so that by his height he had the advantage of being able to strike his antagonist on the head, against which the little one was on his guard.   He had in his turn one advantage over the tall man in being able to give him the Jarnac

---

[1] Paris, 1672.   [2] Bear Gardens in Southwark.

stroke, by cutting him on the right ham, which he left in a manner quite un-guarded. So that, all things considered, they were equally matched. Neverthe-less, the tall one struck the little one on the wrist, which he almost cut off, but this did not prevent him from continuing the fight, after he had been dressed, and taken a glass or two of wine to give him courage, when he took ample ven-geance for his wound; for a little afterwards, making a feint at the ham, the tall man stooping in order to parry it, laid his whole head open, when the little one gave him a stroke which took off a slice of his head and almost all his ear. For my part, I think there is a barbarity and inhumanity in permitting men to kill each other for diversion. The surgeons immediately dressed them and bound up their wounds; which being done, they renewed the combat, and both being sensible of their respective disadvantages, they therefore were a long time without receiving or giving a wound, which was the cause that the little one, failing to parry so exactly, being tired with his long battle, received another stroke on his wounded wrist, which, dividing the sinews, he remained vanquished, and the tall conqueror received the applause of the spectators. For my part, I should have had more pleasure in seeing the battle of the bears and dogs which was fought on the next day in the same theatre."

Although we hear of little else than backsword play among the " gladiating " fencing-masters, the thrusting French play in all its integrity was the only one, from all accounts, cultivated by gentlemen.

The most important treatises extant in the English language on the swordsmanship of that period are the various works of Sir William Hope.

This celebrated swordsman was a son of Sir John Hope of Hope-toun by his second marriage with Lady Mary Keith, eldest daughter of William, seventh Earl Marischal ; his eldest brother was the father of the first Earl of Hopetoun. Born in 1660, he was knighted between 1687 and 1692,[1] and created a baronet in 1698. He was first designed of Grantoun, afterwards of Kirkliston, and in 1705 he purchased the land of Balcomie, in Fifeshire. He served some time in the army, and was for many years (previous to 1706) Deputy Governor of the Castle of Edin-burgh. The complete list of his works on sword-play is given in the Bibliography, but he also wrote some treatises on the farriers' art, one of which, " Le Parfait Mareschal, or the Compleat Farrier," he translated from the French of Le Sieur de Solleysell.[2] He died in Edinburgh, 1724, in his sixty-fourth year, of a fever caused by having overheated himself in dancing at an assembly. Dancing, fencing, and swordsmanship were his most ardent pursuits.

[1] See Biblio., 1687, " Scots' Fencing Master," by W. H., *Gentleman ;* and, 1692, " Compleat Fencing Master," by Sir W. Hope, Kt.
[2] Edinburgh, 1696, folio.

The baronetcy became extinct with his grandson, Sir W. Hope, third baronet, who died in the service of the East India Company in 1763.

Nearly every one of Sir William Hope's books was published both in Edinburgh and in London, but at different periods, a fact somewhat confusing to the bibliographer. There can be no doubt, however, that his first production was the "Scots' Fencing Master," which he published in Edinburgh in his twenty-seventh year (1687).

It is "dedicated to the young nobility and gentry of the kingdom of Scotland," and prefaced by an epistle to the reader in commendation of this noble art.

In this encomium the author draws a graphic comparison between "Artists" and "Ignorants," with the object of encouraging his young countrymen to cultivate an art of which they were apparently very ignorant, notwithstanding its "being of so great use to mankind," and urges them to "enquire after fencing-masters, of whom we have very able ones, so that we need not be beholden to our neighbouring nations for the perfecting of our youth."

"Although," says Hope, "it be not taught with so good a grace as abroad, yet, I say, if a man should be forced to make use of Sharps, our Scots-play is farr before any I ever saw abroad, as for security; and the reason why I think so is, because all French play runneth upon Falsifying (feinting) and taking of time, which appeareth to the eyes of the Spectatours to be a farr neatter and gentiler way of playing than ours; but no man that understands what secure fencing is will ever call this kind of play sure play, because when a man maketh use of such kind of play, he can never so secure himself but that his adversary may contre-temps him every thrust.

" Now, our Scots-play is quite another thing, for it runneth all upon binding and securing of your adversaries sword before that you offer to thrust, which maketh both your thrust sure and your Adversarie incapable of giving you a contre-temps."

This Scots' play is explained in 162 pages of small print, and with the help of twelve amazingly naïves and grotesque plates, by a dialogue between master and scholar, the quaintness of which is generally most refreshing.

" *The Art of Defence and Pursuit, with the Small Sword. Described in a Dialogue between a Scholar and a Master of that Art.*

" *Scholar.* Good morrow, Sir; I am glad that I have once found you at home, for I have called several times for you, and till now could never have the good fortune to meet you.

"*Master.* I am sorry, Sir, that you should have been at that trouble; but now, seeing we have met, what service have you to command me with?

"*Scholar.* Sir, I hear you profess the Art of Fencing, and the great love and desire I have of that noble art made me desirous to be acquainted with you, that I might be instructed in it.

"*Master.* Sir, seeing your enquiring for me is for that end, I shall with all diligence and plainness explain and demonstrate to you the principal grounds requisite to be exactly understood by any who intend either to profess or understand this useful art of defending oneself with the single rapier from their Enemy.

"*Scholar.* I pray you do so, and you shall be well rewarded for your pains.

"*Master.* Sir, I do not in the least doubt that.

"*Scholar.* Which is the first thing, then, you will shew me?

"*Master.* The first thing I intend to shew you is the division of the sword.

"*Scholar.* I pray you let me hear it.

"*Master.* A Rapier, then, is generally divided into two parts, viz., the Hilt and the Blade," &c., &c.

The sword represented in the plates, and shown in especial detail in the first, is a *transition* rapier of the Flamberg type,[1] with a quadrangular blade, and a hilt in all respects, except the absent knuckle-bow, similar to the modern Italian duelling sword. Hope, however, follows the *French* method of seizing the grip, and consequently recommends that the finger should not be passed through the "pas d'âne."

Among the various technical terms which the master next proceeds to explain, we need only notice the following :—

"In quart" and "in terce," to denominate the positions of pronation and supination respectively.

"Within the sword" and "without the sword," to indicate inside and outside lines.

"Breaking the measure;" and its "contrary :" "gathering up the left foot" for the "redoubling of thrusts."

The words, to "elonge," to "respost;" the expressions, "caveating," "falsifying," and "slipping," generally used instead of disengaging, feinting, and deceiving.

"Beating" and "battery," "the difference between the two being that *battery* is the striking with the edge and feeble of your sword upon the edge and feeble of your adversarie, whereas *beating* is done with the fort of your

---

[1] See group the Third, plate III., especially the last two specimens.

sword on the feeble of your adversaries, and therefore secureth his sword a great deal better than battery doth."

" Contretemps," used to express, not a time thrust, but a double thrust or exchanged hits (the "coup fourré" of the French).

" Quarting *upon* the streight line," or " ecarting," to indicate the precaution of sustaining the body and keeping the head well back, to avoid a " contretemps " in the face.

" Quarting *off* the streight line," or " quarting " simply, which corresponds to the French *volte* (from the old Italian *incartata*, or modern *in quarto*); the word " volting " itself being restricted to " the leaping by your adversary's left side, quite out of his measure."

The guards taught by Hope, and of which he speaks as being commonly practised in all schools, are, but for their names, those of the French masters of that period.

" *Scholar.* How many guards are there ?

" *Master.* There are generally but two guards, viz., the Quart-guard and the Terce-guard, but they are subdivided into the *Quart with the streight point*, and the *Quart with the sloping point near to the ground*. The Terce is likewise subdivided into the *Terce with the point higher than the hilt* and *Terce with the point lower than the hilt*.[1]

" There is likewise another kind of guard, but I have not a proper name to it, in which you are to hold your sword with both your hands."[2]

With all these guards the scholar is recommended "to keep a thin body" and turn his right toes well out, which points were much insisted on by French masters.[3] Hope, however, is of opinion that it would be an improvement to turn out the left foot in the same manner, and to bend the knees much more than do the French.

The " parades" are five in number, four of which are represented by the four above-mentioned guards, the fifth being " Terce with the point sloping towards the left side of your adversaries thigh " (prime).

" *Scholar.* You have no other parades than those you have named, have you ?

" *Master.* Yes, I have yet another, which, although it ends always in one of the four former parades, yet there is a great difference betwixt the doing of them and the doing of it, and I can give no other name to this parade but the *counter-caveating* parade."

This is the circular parry applicable to every line which was then called in France " parade en contre dégageant," and in Italy "contra-cavazione." (Caveating evidently was derived from the *cavare* and *cavazione* of the old Anglo-Italian teachers.)

---

[1] " Tierce pour le dessus, tierce pour le dessous " of the French.
[2] See p. 141.
[3] See Fig. 89.

The author speaks enthusiastically of this counter-cavation, " as it crosseth and confoundeth all feints ; yea, not only feints, but in a manner all *lessons*[1] which can be played with the small sword, for that certainly it is by farr the best and safest parade, and therefore I would advise you, when you can make use of it, never (unless it be very seldom) to make use of another." This was, it will be observed, singularly at variance with the principle of the old French school. Hope, however, explains the mechanism of the lunge, and the methods of closing and increasing the measure, on precisely the same system as Liancour. He has a picturesque simile, when insisting on the necessity of having the arm fully extended before the foot begins to move, " a thrust that is right given," says he, " may be compared to the shot of a gun, for he that is wounded with the shot receiveth his wound before he hears the report, so he that is wounded with the sword receiveth his wound before he hears his adversary's right foot touch the ground."

The attacks are delivered by caveating in all the lines, by falsifying singly or doubly, by battery or by binding. Hope's most favourite " lessons " are :—

Feint at the face and thrust in any line uncovered by the parry, and its converse, the *low feint* and thrust in some high line. Both these feints can be doubled so as to " slip " certain parries.

Battery, a plain beat-and-lunge, or beat-and-disengage, in every line.

Volt-coupe, which is described as a feint in a given line, followed by a thrust in the most directly opposite one, such as feint high carte and thrust low tierce. The meaning of the word is, however, incomprehensible, but perhaps it was a phonetical approach to the " botte coupée " of the French.

Flancanade and Under-counter, the latter, he explains, " is almost played like *Flancanade*, only whereas in it (that is, in flanconnade), after you have overlapped your adversaries sword, in this you must go quite *under* his sword, turning your hand in Terce, and bring up his sword, giving him the thrust, as you give it when you play the *Single Feint at the head*."

He likewise recommends binding in many other cases, and for such fencers who perversely keep their point low, in a position unfavourable to bindings, he describes a method of forcibly lifting it with the sword, which he calls " gathering up your adversarie's blade."

Beating, which is to be done on an attack or feint of the adversary, by disengaging, beating and lunging, with the precaution of keeping a strong opposition.

Hope also describes the pass as an alternative to the lunge, but applies it chiefly to various ways of " enclosing " and " commanding " (closing in,

---

[1] This word is often applied to a definite attack, or " botte."

and seizing the adversary's sword), which are in all essentials similar to those we have described under Labat.[1]

All these modes of attack have their " *contraries*," either parades and resports, according to the French school, or " slips " and counter-thrusts by quarting or volting, according to the Italian.

The left hand is kept in readiness to oppose " contretemps," and every feint is to be accentuated by a well-marked stamp of the foot, in order to give them a greater appearance of direct attack, although Hope admits that this usual trick of the school could have but little effect on a " true Artist."

A chapter of the "Scots' Fencing Master " is devoted to the art of fighting on horseback, with pistols and the shearing sword, and recommends that the latter, after the pistols have been discharged, should be brought to a " low terce" guard, that the horseman should endeavour to prevent his enemy closing with him on his left or near side, and also that none but very simple feints should ever be attempted.

It is explained in a succeeding chapter how the small sword can be made to overpower either the broad or the shearing swords, after the first blow has been parried or " slipped," by judicious timing and " enclosing ; " a guard, " with your sword quite cross before your body and your hand in terce," is recommended for the purpose.

A year later Hope published a very small octavo, which he called " The Swordman's Vade-mecum," and dedicated " to all true Artists, or such as have a real respect for and take delight in the art of fencing."

In the preface he explains that in his first book, the " Scots' Fencing Master," he " gave only a bare description of the rules, without any of the reasons subjoined to them," and " as it was designed for the use both of Artists and Ignorants, so this Abstract is only for Artists, there being only contained in it the very marrow and quintessence of fencing."

This quintessence consists of eight golden rules, dependent on an equally golden trinity of qualities ; their explanation and exemplification form the bulk of the book, but it will be quite sufficient to enunciate them in their original quaintness.

" RULE I.

" Whatever you do, let it always (if possible) be done Calmly, and without Passion, and Precipitation, but still with all Vigour, and Briskness imaginable, your Judgement not failing to Direct, Order and Govern you as to both.

[1] See Figs. 106-7-8.

" Rule II.

" With Calmness, Vigour, and Judgement, put your self into as close, thinn, and convenient a Guard, as the Agility of your Body will permit, your Heels being still as near other as possible.

" Rule III.

" With Calmness, Vigour, and Judgement, make use (for your Defence) of the most Excellent, and not to be parrallelled Contre-Caveating Parrade, and that generally upon the outside of your Sword, your left hand always assisting you if in any wayes doubtful of the Parrade ; and that you may with the more certainty defend your self, look always to your Adversary's Sword-Hand.

" Rule IIII.

" With Calmness, Vigour, and Judgement, endeavour to Offend your Adversary, by binding or securing his Sword, and that for the most part also upon the outside, giving in a single plain thrust upon the back of it, or if you please make a Feint upon the back of your binding, your left Hand making always a kind of Parrade, at the giving in of every Thrust, the better to save you from a Contre-temps ; and by no means rest upon your Thrust, but instantly after the performing of it, whether you hitt or not, recover to your Defensive Posture again : This is the true play for a Man's Life : but if you be so far Master of your Adversary, and so merciful to him that you desire not his Life, but only to disable him : Then

" Rule V.

" With Calmness, Vigour, and Judgement, Thrust at his Sword-hand, Wrest, or Arm, or at his nearest advanced Thigh, the wounding of any of which, once, or twice, will seldom fail to disable him.

" Rule VI.

" If your Adversary be Hasty, Passionate, and pursue Furiously, and Irregularly, then with Calmness, Vigour, and Judgement, Cross, Stop, and Oppose his Fury ; but upon the contrary, if Careless, Lax, Slow, or perhaps Timerous, then also Calmly, Vigourously, and with Judgement pursue him.

" Rule VII.

" With Calmness, Vigour, and Judgement, prevent your Receiving one Thrust for the giving another, called (after that dangerous Word, the Artists Bugbear) a Contre-temps, and for that end, the using your left Hand for a Defence upon your Pursute, as I have before told you, will not be found amiss.

" Rule VIII.

" Now to put a Close to my Rules, let them all be done within distance as much as possible, and with little or no Elonge, or stretch of any part of the Body, save only that of the Wrest & Arm (called a Spring) and as I desired you to begin, so I expect you will continue and end all your Actions with that most Excellent Fundamental, and Golden Rule of Three, to wit.   Calmness . . . . Vigour. . . . and Judgement. And then, no doubt, you will procure by the foregoing Rules, advantage proportionable to the Art you have acquired to put them in practice.

" But that my Reduction may yet better answer my Design (which was to be short and compendious) and be more easily kept in your Memory, I have brought it into a narrower Compass, by, as it were, Epitomizing it as followeth.

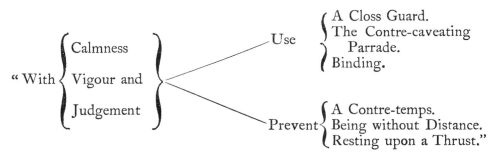

This curious little tome is prefaced by a most flattering letter to the author from William Machrie, " Fencing Master, Judge and Arbitrator of all who make any publick trial of Skill in this noble art of the sword within the Kingdom of Scotland," and is concluded by a few " remarks and observations " on fencing and the schools in general, refuting the assertion that a determined " Ignorant " had as much chance of success in an *earnest* encounter as an " Artist," a comforting theory which seems to have been then very popular, as the author refers to it so often in his works.

" And the Reason why an *Artist* may receive one Thrust for another, from an *Ignorant*, is that when People Assault it is commonly with *Blunts*, and when an *Ignorant*, who undervalueth the *Art* of the *Sword*, and trusteth all to his own Forwardness, is desired by an *Artist* to shew his Natural play, he very well considering that he can receive no prejudice by his being hitt with a blunt *Fleuret*, Rusheth and Rambleth still forewards (let him receive never so many Thrusts) until he either hitteth the *Artist* with one of his Rambling Thrusts, or other wayes cometh so closs, that the *Artist* must enclose with him, and he thinketh, if he hath given the *Artist* but one Thrust (although he himself should receive three or four in the time they are playing) that he hath carried the Day, and quite run down the Art of *Fencing ;* whereas, if they were either to play with Real *Sharps*, or with *Fleurets* having a quarter of an Inch of a point beyond the button, I make not the least doubt but their Rambling would be a little slower, and they would take better notice to what they did, it being Natural even with the most Foreward and Boldest of Men, to endeavour to save themselves by putting a little stop to their Pursute, when they perceive a Sharp point opposite to, and ready to wound, them, and without which stop or pause, they are sensible they might run the Risk, if not of losing their Life, yet at least of being hurt and so smarting for their rash Forwardness : so this is the Reason why *Artists* may receive one Thrust for another from *Ignorants*, to wit, Their *Assaulting commonly with* Blunts ; Therefore, to prevent this inconveniency, if I were to play with an *Ignorant* for a Wager, I would play alwayes with pointed *Fleurets*, and then in GOD's Name, let him Ramble his Belly full ; For in that case I would know a way to come at him which might perhaps cause him repent his Forwardness."

This suggestion might be carried out with advantage in our own days, for the benefit of those uncourteous fencers who make a practice of not acknowledging hits.

In 1692, "The Scots' Fencing Master" was republished in London under the less *local* title of " The Compleat Fencing Master," and two years later the " Vade-Mecum " was likewise reproduced in that city. In both these second editions the author's name appears as *Sir* William Hope, Kt.

When Sir William Hope published his *magnum opus*, the " New Short and Easy Method of Fencing, or the Art of the Broad and Small-Sword, rectified and compendiz'd," &c., he had evidently studied his favourite pursuit in France, or at least carefully digested the leading French works of the period, if we may judge by his more correct quotation of French terms, and the introduction in his nomenclature of the names of guards and " bottes " practised by Le Perche and Liancour.

He seems likewise to have devoted much of his time to the broadsword, as he endeavours to create what he deems an entirely new system, applicable indifferently to both small and broad sword.

He begins by giving an abstract of the art of the small sword, which is practically the same as that contained in his first work, save for the correct technical French terms he employs. He advocates, however, the constant use of a hanging guard in seconde suitable to the back sword, shearing sword, and small sword.

This guard, which had universal advantages in the author's estimation, is remarkably like that in favour among the Germans at the same period. As it was never much used with the small sword, appertaining in fact to the spadroon, it need not here be noticed any further.

In one of the last chapters Sir William Hope gives a full description and insists on the great utility of the practice of " Parieing and Thrusting a Plain Thrust," which is practically the same as the French " tirer au mur." [1] Indeed, the author remarks that it " hath been a very old but bad custom in the fencing schools to fix in a manner the Person who is to Parie, with his back, or at least his left shoulder, near to a wall, so that he may not absolutely break his adversaries measure by the too much bending back of his body." Instead of which it seems that it was then the habit to cause " the defender to pitch himself to his guard or posture of defence with all possible ease, and then to chalk or otherwise mark the floor or pavement at the toe of his right and at the side of his hinder foot, that so he may not, without being observed, move them out of their place in parieing, and thereby, in place of fairly parieing, cunningly evite the thrust."

It is in this book that we find for the first time any mention of the " Society of Sword-men in Scotland," which it seems had been in existence during the last fifteen years.

" In the Year 1692," says Hope, " several Noblemen and Gentlemen, whereof I was one, entered by Contract into a Society for the greater Encouragement of this Art, wherein, besides the Regulations, laid down by us for our more ordinary Meetings, wherein we are to take Trial of, and admit into the Society such Honorable Persons, as should apply to us to be admitted

Fig. 126.—Badge of the " Society of Sword-men " in Scotland.

into it; We had also our more solemn *Anniversary* or yearly *Meetings* appointed, upon which days we were to wear a certain Badge, which amongst other *De-*

---

[1] See p. 168.

vices, carried the designation of the person to whom it belonged, as well as that of the *Society;* which we named *The Society of Swordsmen in Scotland.* But this Society being only Erected by ourselves as private Persons, we were of Opinion, That it would be of far greater Esteem, and serve better the Ends for which we chiefly designed it (and which I shall immediately give an Account of) if we could procure the Civil Sanction to it, and have it Erected into a *Royal Society of Swordsmen:* For which End, about four Years thereafter, we made Application to the then Secretary of State, who assured us, that he would use his Endeavours with King William (of Glorious Memory) to grant us a *Signator* under the *Great Seal* for it; but the Parliament being about that time to meet, which was in Anno 1696, to which the Earl of Tullibardin (now Duke of Athol) was Commissioner; we judged that it would be still more Honorable for our Society, and give it greater Weight and Force, if we could procure an Act of Parliament for it in our Favours.

"Accordingly upon the 16 of September in the above mentioned year, there was a Draught of an Act offered by one of our Society, who was then a Member of Parliament: which after *first Reading* was remitted to the *then Committee for Contraverted Elections,* and upon the 28th of the same Month approved of by them; But the Parliament being very shortly thereafter *Adjourned,* it was not Reported that Session; and so from that time it lay over till this last Session of the Duke of Queensberry's Parliament, Anno 1707, when at one of our meetings it was proposed, that the Design should be again insisted upon, and another New *Overture* or *Act* with some few Alterations and Amendments offer'd; which was agreed to by the Society: and accordingly there was one drawn, whereof, for the Reader's greater Satisfaction, and that he may the more readily understand our most Generous and Gentlemanly Design in it, the Tenor follows."

The document is too lengthy to be inserted here. It will be sufficient to state that this Act, had it been passed, would have constituted the Society into a body corporate, composed of a "preses," a treasurer, clerks and officers, and ordinary members; new members only to be admitted thereafter if, upon trial, they were found qualified. It was to have given this Corporation the power "to Project, Reason, Conclude upon and Enact such Methods and Regulations, alwise consisting with our Laws and Acts of Parliament, as they (the members) shall find convenient for promoting the Art of the Sword; and particularly with full power to them to cognoice upon and determine all differences betwixt parties upon Points of Honour, for the more effectual preventing of duels."

The Society was further to have the right of granting licenses to such fencing-masters as it deemed competent to teach this noble art, and full powers were to be granted to it by her Majesty to call any person whatsoever professing or teaching the said art to a trial and examination therein, and " seize and imprison " all such masters as should refuse to submit to its authority.

The draught was again delivered to a member of Parliament, but time could not be found to bring it before the House, which was then taken up with affairs of the greatest consequence, particularly that of the union of the two kingdoms.

The scheme, moreover, never seems to have obtained the desired sanction—although the Society, in its private capacity, long remained a flourishing one—for it again forms an important topic of the " True and Solid Art of Fighting, &c.," published in 1714, as well as of Sir W. Hope's last work, " A Vindication of the True Art of Self Defence, with a proposal to the Honourable Members of Parliament for erecting a Court of Honour in Great-Britain, to which is Annexed a Short but very useful Memorial for Sword-Men." This book, written only a few months before his death, was suggested by the perusal of Dr. Cockburn's " History and Examination of Duelling," which seems to have induced him to bring once more under public notice the proposal which had emanated from the " Society of Sword-men " in 1707.

The " Vindication " was reproduced in London five years later (1729), presumably on account of the " Memorial to Sword-men," the only part of the book which could have been of interest to the reader at that time.

Sir W. Hope is also the author of two other works : the " Fencing Master's Advice to his Scholar," and " Observations on the Gladiator's Stage-Fighting,"[1] which, however, it has not been our good luck to meet with. The latter, especially, must be of interest, as the " Stage-Fight," which was such an important feature in the life of the fencing community until the middle of the eighteenth century, was considered a particularly attractive spectacle in the days of William III., Anne, and the first George, when the spirit of duelling was so prevalent.

The stage-fight of the eighteenth century, although the outcome of those " prizes " *played* in public by the old " Maisters of Defence " or their scholars, was a prize-fight in another sense. Its object was to win, not merely glory, but likewise the stakes deposited on the wager, as well as the gate-money, which became the property of the gladiator who " kept the stage to the last."

The tenor of the challenges, nevertheless, as regards pomposity and braggadocio, was not much altered since the days of G. Silver, as the

---

[1] All we know about these two books is, that the former was published in Edinburgh between 1692 and 1707, and the latter in London about the year 1716.

following specimens of the usual methods of advertising a coming fight will show :—[1]

> " At the Bear Garden in Hockley in the Hole.

" A Tryal of Skill to be Performed between two Profound Masters of the Noble Science of Defence on Wednesday next, being this 13th of the instant July, 1709, at Two of the Clock precisely.

" I, George Gray, born in the City of Norwich, who has Fought in most Parts of the West Indies, viz., Jamaica, Barbadoes, and several other Parts of the World; in all Twenty-five times, upon a Stage, and was never yet Worsted, and now lately come to London; do invite James Harris, to meet and Exercise at these following Weapons, viz. :—

Back Sword,		Single Falchon,
Sword and Dagger,	} {	and
Sword and Buckler,		Case of Falchons.

" I, James Harris, Master of the said Noble Science of Defence, who formerly rid in the Horse guards, and hath Fought a Hundred and Ten Prizes, and never left a Stage to any Man : will not fail (God Willing) to meet this brave and bold Inviter at the Time and Place appointed, desiring Sharp Swords, and from him no Favour.

" Note. No person to be upon the Stage but the Seconds. Vivat Regina."

Here is another of the same kind :—

> " At the Bear Garden in Hockley in the Hole.

" A Tryal of Skill to be Performed between these two following Masters of the Noble Science of Defence, on Wednesday, the Fifth of April, 1710, at Three of the Clock precisely.

" I, John Parkes, from Coventry, Master of the Noble Science of Defence, do Invite you, Thomas Hesgate, to meet me, and Exercise at these following weapons, viz. :—

Back Sword,		Single Falchon,
Sword and Dagger,	} {	Case of Falchons,
Sword and Buckler,		And Quarterstaff.

" I, Thomas Hesgate, a Barkshire Man, Master of the said Science, will not fail (God Willing) to meet this brave and bold Inviter, at the Time and Place appointed; desiring Sharp Swords, and from him no Favour.

[1] Harleian MSS., 5,931, 50, and 5,931, 277.

" Note. No person to be upon the Stage but the Seconds. Vivat Regina."

Advertisements were generally inserted a few days beforehand in news-papers, which, on rare occasions, gave accounts of some remarkable fights.

The following fragment is due to the pen of Steele, and appeared in the " Spectator " on July 21, 1712 (No. 436) :—

" The Combatants met in the Middle of the Stage, and shaking Hands, as removing all malice, they retired with much Grace to the Extremities of it ; from whence they immediately faced about, and approached each other, Miller with a Heart full of Resolution, Buck with a watchful untroubled Countenance ; Buck regarding principally his own Defence, Miller chiefly thoughtful of annoying his Opponent. It is not easie to describe the many Escapes and imperceptible Defences between Two Men of quick Eyes, and ready Limbs : but Miller's Heat laid him open to the Rebuke of the calm Buck, by a large Cut on the Forehead. Much Effusion of Blood covered his Eyes in a moment, and the Huzzas of the Crowd undoubtedly quickened his Anguish. The Assembly was divided into Parties upon their different ways of Fighting : while a poor Nymph in one of the Galleries apparently suffered for Miller, and burst into a Flood of Tears. As soon as his Wound was wrapped up, he came on again in a little Rage, which still disabled him further. But what brave Man can be wounded with more Patience and Caution ? The next was a warm eager Onset, which ended in a decisive Stroke on the Left Leg of Miller. The Lady in the Gallery, during the second Strife, covered her face ; and for my part, I could not keep my thoughts from being mostly employed on the Consideration of her unhappy Circumstance that Moment, hearing the Clash of Swords, and apprehending Life or Victory concerned her Lover in every Blow, but not daring to satisfie herself on whom they fell. The Wound was exposed to the view of all who could delight in it, and sowed up on the Stage. The surly Second of Miller declared at this Time that he would that Day Fort-night fight Mr Buck at the Same Weapons, declaring himself the Master of the renowned Gorman ; but Buck denied him the Honour of that Courageous Disciple, and asserting that he himself had taught that Cham-pion accepted the Challenge."

It is difficult to understand how men could pass through many such ordeals, and yet remain physically fit to handle a sword with vigour and dex-terity. But such was evidently the case, showing how little dangerous, after · all, mere cutting of muscles is to strong and healthy men—a single puncture with a *small sword* through the lungs or abdomen would probably have settled these sturdy gladiators for life.

The most renowned master of the sword during the first part of the eighteenth century was the renowned Fig, who is, however, still more celebrated in the annals of pugilism as having been the first "champion" (1719-1734). In his day *boxing* began to be generally included in the programme of stage fights.

Mr. Downes Miles, in his "Pugilistica," reproduces a specimen of the bills which advertised such entertainments :—

"At Fig's great tiled Booth, on the Bowling green, Southwark, during the time of the Fair (which begins on Saturday, the 18th of September), the Town will be entertained with the Manly Arts of *Foil Play, Back-Sword, Cudgelling and Boxing.*

"The noted PARKS, from Coventry, and the celebrated Gentleman prize-fighter Mr. MILLAR will display their skill in a tilting-bout, showing the advantages of Time and Measure: also, MR. JOHNSON,[1] the great swordsman, superior to any man in the world for his unrivalled display of the *hanging guard*, in a grand attack of Self Defence, against the all powerful arm of the renowned SUTTON.

"DELFORCE, the finished Cudgeller, will likewise exhibit his uncommon feats with the single-stick ; and who challenges any man in the kingdom to enter the lists with him *for a broken head or a bellyfull.*

"BUCKHORSE and several other Pugilists will show the Art of Boxing.

"To conclude with a *grand parade* by the valiant FIG, who will exhibit his knowledge in various combats, with the Foil, Back-Sword, Cudgel and Fist. Vivat Rex."

The name of Fig as a scientific teacher of all manner of fights recurs constantly in the "Tatler" and the "Guardian," and is mentioned with great enthusiasm in the "Characters of the Masters" which Captain Godfrey gives us, in his "Treatise upon the Useful Science of Defence, Connecting the Small and Back Sword, and shewing the Affinity between them,"[2] and in which also we hear again of Buck, Miller, and Parkes of Coventry. Part of this account seems worth reproducing here for the sake of its curious encomiastical style.

"TIMOTHY BUCK was a most solid Master, it was apparent in his Performances even when grown decrepid, and his old Age could not hide his uncommon Judgement. He was the Pillar of the Art, and all his Followers, who excelled, built upon him.

"MR. MILLER [3] was the palpable Gentleman through the Prize-Fighter.

---

[1] Averred to have been uncle to Dr. Samuel Johnson.

[2] This work is said to have been first published about 1735, but the edition most commonly met with is dated 1747. Its chief interest consists in the details on back-sword play it contains. Another work of the same kind is the "Expert Sword-man's Companion ; or the True Art of Self-Defence," &c., by Donald McBane, Glasgow, 1728.

[3] This *Mr.* Miller in the reign of Queen Anne was a sergeant in a foot regiment. Later on he seems to have gradually established his position as that of a gentleman, and received a

He was a most beautiful Picture on the Stage, taking in all his Attitudes and vastly engaging in his Demeanor. There was such an easy Action in him, unconcerned Behaviour and agreeable Smile in the midst of Fighting that one could not help being prejudiced in his Favour."

"FIG was the Atlas of the Sword, and may he remain the gladiating Statue! In him, Strength, Resolution, and unparallell'd Judgement, conspired to form a Matchless Master. There was a Majesty shone in his Countenance, and blazed in all his Actions, beyond all I ever saw. His right Leg, bold and firm, and his left which could hardly ever be disturbed, gave him the surprizing Advantage already proved, and struck his Adversary with Despair and Panic. He had that peculiar way of stepping in, I spoke of, in a *Parry;* he knew his Arm, and its just time of moving, put a firm Faith in that, and never let his Adversary escape his *Parry.* He was just as much a greater MASTER than any other I ever saw, as he was a greater Judge of *Time* and *Measure.*"

Fig had been the principal master of Captain Godfrey, who informs us that he "followed chiefly the practice of the *Back Sword,* because Conceit cannot so readily be cured with the file (the Foil) in the Small, as with the Stick in that: for the *Argumentum Bastinandi* is very strong and convincing; and though a Man may dispute the full Hit of a File, yet if he is knocked down with a Stick, he will hardly get up again and say, it just brushed him."

"I chose to go mostly to FIG, and exercise with him; partly as I knew him to be the ablest Master, and partly, as he was of a rugged Temper, and would spare no Man, high or low, who took up a Stick against him."

"JOHN PARKS of *Coventry* was a thorough Swords-Man, and an Excellent Judge of all its Parts. He was a convincing Proof of what I advanced about the natural Suppleness of some Men's Joints. No man bid fairer for an acquired Spring than he; but notwithstanding the vast Exercise through such numbers of Battles fought for twenty years,[1] he never could arrive to it. He still remained heavy, slow, and inactive, and had no friend to help him but his staunch Judgement."[2]

captaincy from George II. There is little doubt that the album of fencing plates published in 1738 was brought out under his care. See Bibliography. He is said to have greatly distinguished himself "in '45," under the Duke of Cumberland.

[1] John Parks, who died in 1733, had fought no less than 350 stage-fights.

[2] We may also here mention the following as having been well-known prize-fighters in the heyday of back-sword stage-fighting: John Terrewest, John Stokes, William Gill, Perkins and Butler (both Irishmen), Sutton, Mr. Johnson, Mr. Sherlock, and John Delforce, "a rival to Fig's memory," says Godfrey, "though he fought with the Cudgell only." There was also a Piedmontese called Besson, "who taught the use of the Italian Spadroon." The most popular of these men had amphitheatres of their own, the others were "to be heard of" at the taverns in the neighbourhood of Southwark, and especially Hockley-in-the-Hole, at the Bear Gardens, in Smithfield, and in "Alsatia."

James Figg

Master of y Noble Science of Defence
on y right hand in Oxford Road
near Adam & Eve court. teaches Gentle
- men y use of y small. backsword. &
Quarterstaff at home & abroad

Fig's Business Card, showing the stage, the pit, and the gallery
of an "amphitheatre." Drawn by Hogarth.

The use of the back sword for the purpose of stage-fighting seems to have been on the wane among gladiators during the first part of George II.'s reign, when it gradually gave way before the increasingly popular sport of "Boxing." But to those now-forgotten exhibitions of skill and valour we owe the superiority of what may be called our *national* swordsmanship, that of the broadsword, and even of its imperfect representative, "the single-stick." [1]

Before, however, pursuing this subject, it may be well to take a cursory notice of the works on the small sword which appeared in England before Angelo's, and of which a detailed examination will be unnecessary, as our small-sword play was, as a rule, closely copied from that of the French Academies.

"The Gentleman's Tutor of the Small-Sword," by Henry Blackwell, two editions of which appeared at twenty-five years' interval. [2]

"The English Master of Defence, or the Gentleman's Al-a-mode accomplishment," published at York by one Zach. Wylde.

A very uninteresting work by a Monsieur Valdin, dedicated in 1729 to the Duke of Montague. [3]

The magnificent album of fencing plates published by Captain Miller in 1730.

And lastly, Andrew Mahon's translation of Labat's "Art en fait d'Armes," [4] which appeared first in Dublin, 1734, and the next year in London.

Besides the regular French play, many English masters, however, advocated, in view of a sudden attack or encounter in the dark or in a crowd, the practice of a very much simplified system, with that hanging guard in seconde so much panegyrized in Hope's "New Method of Fencing." Some less nice method of using the sword, especially applicable to midnight scuffles, was deemed requisite in those times against the contingency of a brawl in a

---

[1] The Italians and the Germans had, it is true, a *cutting* play of their own, and from them we took our so-called "Spadroon" or cut-and-thrust play, but it was practised with weapons extremely light in comparison with our English back sword. The practice of the Dusack in Germany, and of the Schiavona or other basket-hilted swords in Italy, does not seem to have been much cultivated after the first years of the seventeenth century.

[2] See Biblio., 1705 and 1730. To the second edition is sometimes annexed, in addition to the six woodcuts in the text, a curious collection of folding plates, most of which are faithful reproductions of Capo Ferro's and Giganti's *attitudes*, in which, however, the figures are *dressed* in the fashion of Queen Anne's reign, with large periwigs, lace ruffles, high-heeled square-toed shoes, &c.

[3] In this book the author announces his intention to bring out a very elaborate and comprehensive treatise "after the manner of Salvator Fabris." This great work, however, does not seem to have yet been discovered.

[4] See p. 152. We may likewise mention here the names of the most popular teachers of the *small* sword—many of whom were evidently Frenchmen—during the reigns of Anne and George I.: Tente, Bergerreau, Martin, Dubois, Morin, Campbell, Brent, Barney Hill, Low, and Tully (this last is mentioned as his principal master by Andrew Mahon).

tavern or a bagnio ; unpleasant encounters were also generally to be expected with the " Muns," the " Hectors," the " Scourers," the " Mohocks " or " Hawkubites," " Bold Bucks" or " Hell Fires,"—whatever may have been the name adopted at the time by the rowdies, fashionable or otherwise, who made the streets unsafe to anyone whom they deemed incapable of requiting their cowardly bullying with a taste of cold steel.

Fig. 127.—The Guard in " Back-swording."

But, to return to the back-sword play, it was an art requiring not so much science and agility as coolness and muscular vigour, and therefore it was very popular among all classes of Englishmen, although it was only much practised by those whose social position did not admit of their wearing " the sword " (*i.e.* the small sword).

The back sword was usually basket-hilted—very much in the same style as what is conventionally called the claymore —with a straight blade some thirty-two inches in length, with only the right edge sharpened, and the point more or less rounded off. It was generally held with all the fingers closed round the grip, but some of the

Fig. 128.—Flip at the head.

best masters, like Fig and Godfrey, pointed out, at a late period, the advantage of extending the thumb along the back of the grip, in order to ensure on all occasions a cut with the true edge. Previous to Fig the guard had apparently always been a hanging one in a kind of high seconde, but at a later period a low tierce, imitated from the small-sword play, was the most in favour.

The old notion, prevalent among the " Swashbucklers" of the sixteenth century, that it was unmanly to strike beneath the girdle,[1] was evidently very obsolete in the eighteenth, for we find that cuts are impartially aimed at all parts of the adversary's body, from his advanced foot, and his wrist, to

---

[1] " This manner of fight he (Rowland York) first brought into England . . . . when the use was with little bucklers and with broadswords, it being accounted unmanly to strike beneath the girdle."—Carleton's " Thankful Remembrances of God's Mercy," 1625.

his head. The play was by no means complicated, none but the simplest feints being accounted practical; parries were always taken in pronation. On all accounts it seems, in fact, to have been in every respect but that the point was not used, similar to our modern play, not with the single-stick, but with the practice sabre.

For practice, cudgels with stout wickerwork baskets were used, but no mention is ever made of any kind of protection for head or body. " I have purchased my knowledge in the BACK SWORD," says Captain Godfrey, " with many a broken Head and Bruise in every part of me."

We find many allusions in Elizabethan literature to " wasters," [1] used with or without the buckler, as a substitute for the sword, and among

Fig. 129.—Cut at the left side parried.

apprentices and such people in the sixteenth and early seventeenth centuries "wasters" seem to have been as popular a sport as " single-sticks " in later days.

Under the Georges, especially the First and the Second, " backswording " with sticks, in imitation of the gladiators' fight, was a never-failing entertainment at all popular gatherings, not only in London, but also in remote provinces. Long after the sanguinary back-sword fights had gone out of fashion, cudgelling or single-stick play for prizes remained a national amusement, especially among country people, and in some parts of England proficiency with the stick was an accomplishment as much admired and cultivated as that of wrestling.

Fig. 130.—A return to the left cheek, over the elbow.

The art of cudgelling, however, as a substitute for swordsmanship, soon acquired a singularly specialized character, being, in fact, as much restricted as the German students' Schlaeger fights.

The manner in which this so-called " backswording " was played during

---

[1] A " waster " was a wooden sword used for practice by the common people. " Thou wouldst be loth to play half-a-dozen venies (bouts) at wasters with a good fellow for a broken head."—Beaumont and Fletcher's " Philaster."

the latter part of the eighteenth century, and in some old-fashioned parts of England as late as the first quarter of this, was usually as follows:[1]—

The combatants, each armed with a basket-hilted stick, somewhat stouter and shorter than our modern single-stick, faced each other within very close measure—somewhat like the German students—holding their weapon in a high hanging guard, with the basket a little higher than the head, the point about on a level with the shoulders.   The left arm was used

to screen the left side of the head, elbow upwards as high as the crown, and as much brought forward as a handkerchief or a belt passed under the left thigh, and grasped in the left hand, would allow. With such an attitude all consideration of *distance* had to be abandoned, and the player's sole attention was directed to that of *time* and *guard*.[2]

The object of the play was to draw blood from the opponent's head, victory being achieved as soon as at least an inch of it appeared anywhere on his head or

Fig. 131.—A successful flip at the head, timed on the adversary's cut at the body.

face.   This was called a "broken" head. Thus the only decisive blows were those that reached the head, but they were also addressed to the arms, the shoulders—in fact, anywhere above the girdle where the result of a blow might be to effect a temporary opening to the head.

The requisites for this very peculiar play were chiefly strength and suppleness of the wrist, from which all the cuts were delivered with great swiftness, and so as to disturb the guard as little and for as short a time as possible; a quick perception of " time"—most successful hits being delivered either on the adversary's feint or on his attempt to bring down the protecting left arm by a cut on the left flank; lastly, great caution and a certain amount of endurance, to enable the player to seize the right time for a flip at his opponent's head without exposing his own, heedless of many smart raps on the elbow or across the ribs.[3]

[1] The only work, apparently, in which the rules of this now obsolete single-stick play are set forth systematically is one called " Defensive Exercises, comprising Wrestling, &c., Boxing, &c., &c., with one hundred illustrations.   By Donald Walker." London : Thomas Hurst, 1840.   8vo.

[2] See Introduction, p. 8.

[3] For a graphic description of the single-stick play as it was practised in our grandfathers' days we may refer the reader to the second chapter of that well-known and delightful book, " Tom Brown's School-Days."

As to the process by which all these peculiar restrictions came to be imposed on this game, so evidently derived from the old waster play, we can only offer the following surmises.

In a contest with cudgels, however telling and painful might be blows received on any part of the body, the only one looked upon as *decisive* was "a broken head," and in a *prize* contest a streak of blood thereon naturally was looked upon as a conclusive sign of defeat. We know that the left hand was always kept in readiness, in rapier and small-sword play, to ward off attacks addressed to the left side of the body,[1] and although such a device could not be resorted to against a *sharp back sword*, there was no reason, in the eyes of unscientific but hardy cudgellers, why a few blows of a *round stick* should not willingly be taken on the left arm or shoulder, if thereby the victorious cut at the opponent's head could be secured.

Later on, we may presume, the rules of the game were made more regular, so as to prevent, among other things, the possibility of seizing the adverse stick, and it became the habit to fix the position of the left hand by grasping a belt or a handkerchief passed round the thigh.

[1] See, for examples, Figs. 59, 94, 97, 102, 123-4-5.

CHAPTER XIV.

HE chief work in the English literature of fencing—in the vulgar meaning of the word, viz., small-sword fencing—is undoubtedly Angelo's "Ecole des Armes," of which as many as six different editions or reproductions were published during the second half of the eighteenth century, and a seventh in 1817.

The well-known institution, "Angelo's School of Arms"—the name of which was a household word among men of fashion in the days of our grand-sires—even now, when the art of fence is so much neglected in England, remains, on account of its old associations, one of the most interesting "salles d'armes" in Europe. In this school three generations of Angelos kept up the honour of English fencing in London for the space of a century.[1]

The founder of this celebrated family of masters, Domenico Angelo[2] Malevolti Tremamondo, was the son of a very wealthy Italian merchant, and was born at Leghorn in 1716. As a young man of no profession, but with a liberal allowance from his father, he travelled all over the Continent, and eventually settled some ten years in Paris, where he studied the art of fence with unusual assiduity under various masters of the Académie, but especially under the elder Teillagory. This Teillagory, besides being one of the most celebrated swordsmen of his age, was likewise from all accounts the most scientific horseman in Europe, and occupied as prominent a place in the "Manège Royal" as he did in the Académie d'Armes.

Under his tuition Angelo, who was especially gifted for all physical exercises, became in a short time, like his master, one of the most "elegant riders of the *high horse*."

The following adventure was the indirect cause of his abandoning

---

[1] A partner of the last Angelo, Mr. William McTurk, has been at the head of this establishment since 1866.

[2] His English friends later on persuaded him to abandon this too outlandish patronymic and adopt the simple name of Angelo.

Paris to settle in England, and is related by his son, Henry Angelo, in his
" Reminiscences " :— [1]

" My father inherited from nature a singularly graceful person : this
rare gift was not bestowed in vain ; he cultivated with assiduity every external
accomplishment, and became proverbially one of the most elegant men of the
age ; indeed, it was to his natural and acquired advantages that he owed his
future fortune and his fame.

" A short period before his quitting France, there was a public fencing
match at a celebrated hotel in Paris, at which were present many of the most
renowned professors and amateurs of that science, most of whom entered the
lists. My father, who was honoured with the particular esteem of the Duc
de Nivernois, was persuaded by that nobleman to try his skill. He had long
before acquired the reputation of the first amateur swordsman, and was no
less reputed for his scientific management of the horse.

" No sooner was his name announced than a celebrated English beauty,
Miss Margaret Woffington, the renowned actress, then on a visit at this gay
city, who, having met my father at a party, became suddenly captivated by his
person and superior address, and following him hither, in presence of a crowd
of spectators, she stepped forward and presented him with a small *bouquet* of
roses. The company, as well ladies as gentlemen of rank, surprised at this,
were not less struck by the gallant manner with which he received the gift.
He placed it on his left breast, and addressing the other knights of the sword,
exclaimed, ' This will I protect against all opposers.' The match commenced,
and he fenced with several of the first masters, not one of whom could disturb a single leaf of the *bouquet*."

One of the results of the intimacy which subsequently sprung up between Angelo and the beautiful Peg Woffington was his accompanying her
to England, where he soon found a wider scope for the utilization of his talents.
He was before long launched in the gay world of London, where his foreign
grace, coupled with so many manly and gentlemanly accomplishments, soon
won him a number of friends in many walks of life,[2] whether artistic, political,
literary, or merely fashionable.

During the first part of his stay in England, Angelo devoted himself
solely to " manège " riding ; " a few months after his arrival in London he
became *ecuyer* to Henry Herbert, Earl of Pembroke, who was one of the

---

[1] " Reminiscences of Henry Angelo, with Memoirs of his late Father and Friends, &c."
Dedicated " to His most Gracious Majesty King George the Fourth." 8vo., London, 1828.

[2] The " Reminiscences " are full of anecdotes concerning some of the most interesting
figures of the last century. It appears that the first Angelos counted among their intimates
such men as Garrick, Reynolds, Gainsborough, Fox, Horne Tooke, Wilkes, Peter Pindar,
Bach, and many others. Henry Angelo was a bosom friend of Richard Brinsley
Sheridan.

most accomplished horsemen of his day, and who had a spacious *manège* near his mansion in Whitehall."

Lord Pembroke " became so attached to his society that after Angelo married, at his patron's desire he took a house in the neighbourhood of his lordship's family seat at Wilton."

There, among other duties, he undertook to train the riding instructors of " Elliot's Light Horse," then considered a crack regiment, and of which Lord Pembroke was lieutenant-colonel. One of these instructors was " old Philip Astley, who afterwards became so celebrated for his horsemanship at his own amphitheatre."

Besides the patronage of Lord Pembroke, Angelo enjoyed that of the Duke of Queensberry, which he owed to the affection of the duchess for his wife. The duke himself withal was an assiduous frequenter of the riding school. It is no wonder that with such powerful friends at his back, and after the praise publicly bestowed on him by the king, his success in London should have been so marvellously rapid : after a performance in presence of King George II., his Majesty declared that " Mr. Angelo was the most elegant horseman of his day."[1] Within a year of his setting up his private manège at the back of his house in Carlisle Street, Soho Square—which was then a most fashionable neighbourhood—he made upwards of £2000 by his tuition in horsemanship.

About the year 1758 he seems to have had some reverse of fortune, which induced him to apply himself strenuously to the purpose of making money, and it is then also that he began to take up fencing in a professional manner.

" My father's celebrity in the manège," says Henry Angelo, in his Reminiscences, " was scarcely less spread than the fame of his skill in the management of the sword, though he had only hitherto practised fencing as an amateur.

" On his return to London with his patron and friend, the Earl of Pembroke, he received a card inviting him to a public trial of skill with Dr. Keys, reputed the most expert fencer in Ireland. The challenge being accepted, the Thatched House Tavern was appointed for the scene of action,[2]

---

[1] " It was in consequence of this interview that his Majesty, when the late Mr. West was commissioned to paint the picture of the Battle of the Boyne, persuaded him to make a study of my father for the equestrian figure of King William for that well-known composition, saying, 'Few painters place the figure properly upon the horse, and Angelo is the finest horseman in the world.' Mr. West adopted the suggestion, and my father sat for the figure accordingly, on his own horse Monarch. It may appear a curious coincidence that he also, through a fortuitous circumstance, sat to the sculptor as a model for the equestrian statue of King William subsequently set up in Merrion Square, Dublin."—" Reminiscences " of Henry Angelo.

[2] It appears, from various contemporary accounts, that assaults of arms often took place

where my father attended at the time prescribed, two o'clock, though he had been riding the whole morning at Lord Pembroke's. His lordship, with his accustomed condescension, walked into the apartment arm in arm with his friend and protegé. My father, however, was not prepared for such an assemblage, many ladies of rank and fashion, as well as noblemen and gentlemen, being present, and he, expecting only to meet with gentlemen, was in riding dress and in boots.

" My father, who had never seen his antagonist until this moment, was rather surprised at the doctor's appearance, he being a tall, athletic figure,

Fig. 132.—The Outside Guard.—Roworth.

wearing a huge wig, without his coat and waistcoat, his shirt sleeves tucked up, exposing a pair of brawny arms, sufficient to cope in the ring with Broughton or Slack; and thus equipped, with foil in hand, he was pacing the apartment.

" The spectators being all assembled, after the first salutation from the doctor, which was sufficiently open and frank, previous to the *assault* he took a bumper of *Cogniac*, and offered another to my father, which he politely refused, not being accustomed to so ardent a provocative.

" The doctor having thus spirited himself for the attack, began with that violence and determined method, which soon discovered to those who were

at celebrated taverns during the last century. Some fencing-masters gave regularly entertainments of that kind in coffee houses.

skilled in the science, that in the true sense of the term used by the French, he was no better than a *tirailleur, jeu de soldat*—Anglicized, a poker.

" My father, to indulge him in his mode of assault, for some time solely defended himself against his repeated attacks without receiving one hit ; for, as the brandy operated, a *coup d'hasard* in the doctor's favour would have only encouraged him the more.   Hence, allowing his opponent to exhaust himself, and my father having sufficiently manifested his superior skill in the science by thus acting on the defensive, with all the elegance and grace of attitude for which he was renowned, after having planted a dozen palpable hits on the breast of his enraged antagonist, he made his bow to the ladies, and retired

Fig. 133.—The Inside Guard.—Roworth.

amidst the plaudits of the spectators. . . . . It was soon after this public display of his superior science that the elder Angelo, urged by his friends, first commenced teaching the science of fencing.   Indeed, the splendid offers which were made him were too tempting for a person in his state of dependence to refuse.   His noble patron, though desirous of retaining his valuable services, yet, with that generous spirit which marked all his actions, advised my father to accept the offers that were pressing upon him.   This at once settled his future fortune, and his first scholar was the late Duke of Devonshire."

Angelo's house very soon became a " school of refinement," where young men were sent for a certain time, not only to acquire proficiency in the gentlemanly arts of manège riding and small-sword fencing, but also to obtain indirectly the benefit of consorting with the brilliant company of wits, politicians, and artists which almost daily met round his hospitable board.

Angelo derived positive affluence from his two schools, and is said to have made upwards of £4000 a year by his foil alone, which income " he spent like a gentleman."

In the year 1758, " having been·introduced to the Princess Dowager of Wales, mother of our late venerable sovereign,[1] he was engaged by her royal highness to teach the young princes the use of the small sword." Subsequently he had the honour of teaching King George III. himself, and the Duke of York.

In 1763 Angelo brought out in the most magnificent style his " Ecole des Armes," the immense expense of which was covered by subscriptions among 236 noblemen and gentlemen, his patrons or his pupils. This immense oblong folio contains forty-seven plates, which were drawn by the painter Gwynn, and engraved by Ryland, Grignion, and Hall. Angelo stood for one of the combatants throughout the whole series, and some of his friends, among others Lord Pembroke and the Chevalier d'Eon, for the other.

The text, which reproduces substantially all the principles of small-sword fencing recognized by the French Academy of Arms about the middle of the eighteenth century, when Teillagory and La Boëssière (the elder), O'Sullivan and Danet, flourished in Paris, calls for no remarks after the notice on the two last masters given in Chapter XI.

Indeed, although Danet affects to despise the " Ecole des Armes," the only difference perceptible between his own work and Angelo's—if we neglect Danet's revised nomenclature and his three altitudes of the hand in pushing carte—is that the latter is immensely more artistic, and was from the very first a much greater success than his " Art des Armes."

Two years later appeared a second edition—with a double column of text, English and French—and a third in 1767, similar in every respect to the second.

In 1787, Henry Angelo, son of Malevolti, who was then practically at the head of the school—he had been assiduously studying fencing in Paris during many years after his leaving Eton—reproduced his father's book, but in a smaller form, with the English text only, and smaller plates.[2]

In his memoirs, engrossed as he is in his anecdotes of celebrated characters, Henry Angelo seems very loth to give us much information concerning his school, and indeed any fencing topics, and in most cases abstains with graceful ease from giving any dates. But it appears that in the elder Angelo's time, his fencing rooms were situated at his old house in Carlisle Street; later on he took a " salle d'armes " in the Opera House Buildings, Haymarket, belonging to a French fencing-master called Redas.

---

[1] " Reminiscences," 1827.

[2] These reduced plates are the same as those which appear in the appendix to Diderot and D'Alembert's " Encyclopédie Méthodique." Henry Angelo's master in Paris was Motet, then known all over the Continent as the strongest *pareur* living.

These rooms were destroyed by fire in 1789, and the " Academy " was transferred to Bond Street, where it remained until 1830.

The elder Angelo died in 1802, at the age of eighty-six. A few days before his death he still gave lessons in fencing.

The present rooms at the top of St. James's Street were taken by Henry Angelo's son in 1830; they were originally part of Colonel Nedham's celebrated riding school. They have preserved their characteristic appearance to this day, and still contain many relics of the old school in the shape of pictures, arms, engravings, and autographs.

Fig. 134.—The Hanging Guard.[1]—Roworth.

The following works, published during the last third of the eighteenth century, are not sufficiently important or original to be noticed here otherwise than superficially.

" The Fencer's Guide,[2] being a Series of every branch required to compose a Complete System of Defence, &c., &c.," by A. Lonnergan, " Teacher of the Military Sciences," a very practical treatise, and the most truly *English* of the eighteenth century, as the author attaches as much importance to the back sword as to the small sword, and endeavours as much as possible to avoid foreign jargon—a plausible purpose, but one, unfortunately, which has the effect of somewhat confusing the reader.

" Fencing Familiarised (L'Art des Armes Simplifié),"[3] by M. Olivier, *Elève de l'Académie Royale de Paris*, in French and English.

Olivier, who kept a flourishing school in St. Dunstan's Court, Fleet

---

[1] Often called by masters the " coward " guard, as they considered it a *very safe* one, but also one which was unfavourable to much offensive action.

[2] See Biblio., 1771-2.   [3] See Biblio., 1771-80.

Street, was perhaps, after Angelo, the most popular master of the small sword in London. His work is very sound, and thoroughly justifies its French title, as it contains a simplified system, shorn of all unnecessary and obsolete details. This is one of the books of that period most commonly met with.

"The Army and Navy Gentleman's Companion," by J. McArthur, of the Royal Navy, of which two editions appeared at four years' interval, 1780-84.

We may finish our sketch of the character of English swordsmanship

Fig. 135.—The Spadroon Guard.[1]— Roworth.

Fig. 136.—The St. George's Guard.—Roworth.

with a brief notice of broadsword and spadroon play, as illustrated by Angelo (in Rowlandson's plates[2]), Lonnergan, and Roworth.[3]

The broad or back-sword play practised during the early part of the century was very simple, very safe, and very monotonous, but required, with an eye for distance a good judgment of time and a great amount of strength in the forearm and in the fingers.

As we have seen, some masters advocated a medium hanging guard, but the followers of the great Fig, and later on of Godfrey, preferred a

---

[1] Rarely used, except with very light swords.
[2] See Biblio.　　　[3] See Biblio.

high one, derived from the small sword, either inside or outside, in carte or tierce.

There was a great deal of traversing backwards and forwards. The attacks were delivered, with a *chopping* action,—the back sword being too heavy a weapon to allow of much *flipping*—at all parts of the body. Cuts below the hips were usually avoided by *slipping* rather than parrying. The parries were five in number : high, outside and inside (tierce and quarte); hanging, outside and inside (low prime and seconde); and the head parry, the so-called St. George's guard.[1] High parries were always accompanied by a recovery, drawing back the foot in order to avoid the danger of a cut at the leg in case the threatened attack should prove a feint.

Later on, the creation of numerous light cavalry corps brought into vogue what was called the Austrian system, in which *chopping* action was replaced by the *slicing* peculiar to the showy practice of the light curved Hungarian sabre.

This play, which was no less effective than the old-fashioned hacking, required a smaller expenditure of energy, and at the same time admitted of weaker parries; its adoption introduced a great deal of variety into the sturdy old English back-swording. But although its monotony was relieved by the admixture, it is difficult to say whether its value as a defensive art was really improved.[2]

The most usual guards were : the medium guard, with the arm extended straight out from the shoulder, and the sword nearly perpendicular, point upwards—from this the outside or inside guards could readily be assumed ; the hanging guard, arm extended, hand in pronation as high as the crown, point low—from this derived the " half hangers," or half hanging guard, inside and outside ; the spadroon guard, arm extended horizontally, hand in supination, point low.

The two following, also enumerated by all these authors as *guards*, were only parries, and " not intended to lie under " :—

The St. George's guard (always accompanied by the recovery) ; and the half-circle guard—the former stopping a direct cut at the head, the latter inside cuts just below the wrist.

The cuts were seven in number, six of which were usually practised in

---

[1] So called, not, as many would believe, as having been invented by the celebrated swordsman St. George, "but," says Lonnergan, "from the position that Holy Champion is represented to have held his arm in, in slaying the Dragon."

[2] At the present day we have returned to a much simpler system, almost identical with the old back-sword play, excepting our use of the point and our disuse of traversing. In France, where this elegant but somewhat feeble slicing play is the only one practised at all, the sabre is so much neglected in favour of the foil, that it is difficult to make any comparison between the contrepointe and our single-stick or broadsword play.

a series in front of a diagram or target on the wall, precisely in the same order and manner as was taught by Marozzo two hundred and fifty years before,[1] the only difference being that the pupil was now recommended to deliver them with as close motions as possible and with a " pushing " or " drawing" action, according as the direction of the cut was *towards* the adversary's body or *from* it.

Thrusts in carte, low carte, tierce, and seconde, were also practised, but were never much in favour in broadsword play.

With the spadroon, however—the light, straight, *flat-bladed* sword used for cut and thrust after the German rapier fashion—the play was in the main rather thrusting than cutting, cuts when delivered as attacks being pushed forward like thrusts, and when as reposts, either with a flip, cutting over the point, or with a drawing action in resuming the guard.

Most of the attacks and parries belonging to the small sword were used with the spadroon, excepting circular ones; simple ones performed with a proper opposition being equally effective against both cut and thrust, whereas circular parries can only be of use against the point.

The Angelos, the last member of which noted family of masters is still familiarly recollected by many men, bring us as far as our own times.

Since the last century there have been in England, and there are still, many masters of note, but the art of the sword, in all its branches, is now so generally neglected, that schools purely devoted to fencing are excessively few. Swordsmanship is in most cases looked upon as a corollary to gymnastics, and a comparatively unimportant one.

The common feeling with regard to this fascinating exercise is that it is to a certain point *un-English*, its practice rather a waste of time, and that, even if it were, as in days of old, valuable for the purpose of duelling, too assiduous a devotion to such an art would be looked up as contrary to our usual notions of honour and fair play.

It is true that the use of the thrusting sword—whether it was the " bird-spit and frog-pricking poniard" of the sixteenth century or the "colichemarde" of Queen Anne's days—was at all times best taught by foreigners, and, although formerly a universally requisite accomplishment, may on that score be considered somewhat un-English. But broadsword play was always a national pastime, of greater antiquity even than our

---

[1] See p. 36.

boxing; nevertheless, it is as much neglected as that of the foil, and, among the few who do take it up, more admiration is bestowed on a cheerful receiver and dealer of loud-sounding blows than on a correct and scientific but too cautious champion.

With regard to the alleged uselessness of fencing, it may be adduced that the question of utility is irrelevant in matters of sport. Many men, for instance—to whom the greatest proficiency as *watermen* can never be of any practical use—devote more time and energy to the acquisition of skill in rowing or sculling than would suffice to make them consummate swordsmen, and this is the case in most branches of athletics. Moreover, the very fact that fencing skill could never nowadays enable anyone to hector and bully his neighbour, ought to be sufficient to remove the objection of unfairness.

One of the causes of the decay of the once " noble science of fence " may be sought in the Englishman's passion for open-air exercise, a passion fostered by his school education, and which makes him dislike the idea of this seemingly monotonous exertion *within doors.*

Of course it would be absurd to urge any man ever to sacrifice the green sward and the racket or the bat for the floor of the fencing-room and the foil or the stick, but there are many occasions when the former can only be longed for, whilst the latter are within reach ; and surely a well-filled fencing-room, where many pairs of clicking and glittering blades are at play, is a sufficiently attractive spot.

Fencing is an exercise which well repays anyone who has the perseverance to submit to the drudgery of its early stages. The " Artist "—to use Sir William Hope's quaint expression—finds work for his head as well as for his limbs in every kind of personal combat ; but this is especially the case with fencing, where it is possible for the observant swordsman to utilize all his perceptive faculties in the discrimination of his opponent's characteristics, and, assuming that practice has sufficiently gymnasticized his body, to find intellectual enjoyment in devising different plays for different adversaries.

The early masters usually devoted one chapter of their treatises to the various methods they deemed best to employ against different idiosyncrasies, such as the " Choleric " and the " Phlegmatic," the " Impetuous " and the " Cautious," the " Timid " and the " Valorous," &c. Of course there cannot be such a conflict of passions in a contest " with blunts " as there was " with sharps," but, in a sufficiently prolonged assault, the player's true character always tends to reveal itself.[1]

" In a good fencer the head works as much as the body," say the best

---

[1] The well-known and witty French writer, Ernest Legouvé, who was once a great *escrimeur*, used to say that he never felt he knew a man's character until he had played a few bouts with him !

masters; to become such a " good fencer," however, very long practice is necessary.

Ars longa, vita brevis.   The art of fence is undoubtedly a long one to master; nevertheless, it would be difficult to discover any swordsman of standing who regrets the time he has devoted to it; it is a wonder that comparatively so few men take up swordsmanship in earnest, and that the most athletic nation in Europe does not assume the lead in that as well as in all other sports.

CHAPTER XV.

THE SWORD DURING THE SIXTEENTH, SEVENTEENTH, AND EIGHTEENTH CENTURIES.

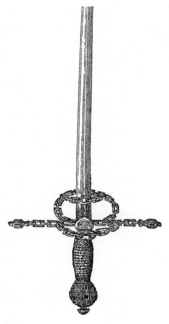

Fig. 137.—German Rapier, early seventeenth century.— From Lacombe's "Armes et Armures."

O doubt the modern small sword presents at first sight very little family likeness to the sword of a knight of old, but, unlike as these weapons are, they are not more so than the men they were devised for.

We can trace in an uninterrupted series the changes which took place in the side arm, not only as far as the time when an iron sword was first constructed, but even to that remote period when its prehistoric ancestor—the club—began to assume some of the characteristics which we are accustomed to associate with the notion of a sword.

It is not our purpose, however, to trace its pedigree so far; such a task would, moreover, require a more learned pen than ours.

Without entering into great detail, we merely intend to give an account sufficient for the purpose of this work, of the manner in which the plain cross-hilted sword of the Middle Ages became converted into the small sword or the military sabre of the last century, according as its purpose was that of duelling or of warfare.

This double transformation took place during the sixteenth, seventeenth, and eighteenth centuries, and consequently an examination of its phases will fitly conclude our retrospective view of the fencing art during the same period, the more so as most of the changes observable resulted from the development of theories touching the management of point and edge.

Any genuine ancient sword, but especially a rapier of the sixteenth century, is invested with a wonderful interest in the eyes of a connoisseur—the more so, of course, if he be a fencer withal. Besides its beauty and picturesqueness, it represents an amount of serious thought and ingenuity which in our days would be considered quite wasted on such an object. But this is merely because, and happily so, the age of the sword belongs to history, and is no longer ours.

We boldly asserted in the Introduction that we have sounder notions concerning the use of the sword now that it is to be looked upon as a pastime, and not as an accomplishment on which our very existence might at any moment depend, and we may pass a similar judgment on the swords which we could produce.

The modern sword cutlers can construct marvellous blades, equal to almost any work, and though it is doubtful whether any modern blade would be actually superior to some of the finest "wolfs" or "Andrea Ferraras," there can be no doubt that equally perfect ones can be manufactured in our days whenever—and such cases are but rare—there is a demand for them.

The sword is now a more or less useless appendage to the military accoutrement, and any decently solid weapon is quite equal to the work which, on very few occasions, it may be required to perform. Only a few of our warriors, who have had practical experience in combats "à l'arme blanche" against Asiatic swordsmen, take any special interest in their side arm, and they often solve the difficulty by inserting an authentic blade some three hundred years old, signed "Sahagum" or "Ferrara," into a modern regulation hilt. The inferiority of modern blades results only from the modern indifference for such objects.

There is undoubtedly a great deal of glamour about an ancient sword : it has been practically tested, and, if it belonged to some ancestor, the blood it has shed was, presumably, shed in an honourable cause ; it was the constant companion and support of its master—a friend always at his side when he walked or rode, who kept watch at the head of his bed at night, and rested behind his chair as he took his meals ; it was never chosen unless it felt in his hand like a part of himself, and was deemed incapable of turning traitor in the most desperate struggle.

It is this fact, that every sword of value was always selected or contrived with the nicest care, and that it was then worth the maker's while to devote the whole of his knowledge and ingenuity to the fashion of any guard, the balance and degree of elasticity of a certain blade, that renders an old rapier of such value and interest to the connoisseur from a sentimental as well as a technical point of view.

In our days the armourer is represented by the gunmaker, who turns all his powers of sagacity and invention to the boring of incredibly resisting gunbarrels and simplified safety locks; there is little or no opening for his talent among the swords, concerning the shapes of which inflexible " regulation" would render his labours purposeless.

Not so in the days of the Rapier; every swordsman, as he gathered experience in the "Steccata," [1] the field, or the fence school, entertained some favourite notions concerning the details of what he considered a good guard, very important in his opinion, and it was the swordmaker's duty to appreciate and carry out these ideas. Thus he had to be swordsman as well as swordmaker, just as his successor the gunsmith has—or ought—to be conversant with the theories of ballistics and explosives, and, if possible, a practical *shot* himself.

Hence the almost infinite variety of rapier guards, based, it is true, on some fundamental principles which varied only as the science of fence changed its own. With certain restrictions we may draw comparisons between the complication of the guard and that of the play, although the one was not the direct necessary result of the other.

At the very earliest time when we hear of sword fencing as an art, the play, which consisted of a very reckless cutting and a good deal of " natural fighting," may be called simple. This was about the first years of the sixteenth century, and we know that the sword was then likewise comparatively simple. The guard in most common use consisted of plain quillons with or without rings or pas d'âne. [2]

During the course of the sixteenth century the science of fence was assiduously cultivated in every country, and about the end of the same century it had become a very intricate one indeed, in which every movement of sword and body was analyzed, and, *pari passu*, during that period the sword guard developed into the complete rapier hilt.

The seventeenth century saw a no less complete change of character, both in the art and in the implement. The cut-and-thrust play became separated, and the fencer, discarding all cutting action from his play as more brutal and less effective than the thrust, gradually reduced the lengthy and heavy rapier to the dimensions of the small sword.

Compared to an Elizabethan rapier the small sword of Queen Anne's days is simplicity itself; the same comparison may be drawn between the evolutions of Carranza's pupils and the sober movements of the eighteenth century swordsman.

---

[1] The Steccata, " which is the place of combat," as Saviolo says in his second book, entreating of honour and honourable quarrels—the Italian term for the French " champs clos," the lists.

[2] See infra, p. 230.

Many puzzling facts have to be encountered, however, as soon as an attempt is made to classify the various forms of the sword according to the dates at which they were most in fashion:—1st, the fashions did not vary at the same rate in different countries;[1] 2nd, they overlapped each other[2] in the same country; 3rd, that the *blades*, and not the hilts, are generally stamped in some way that can elucidate their date, whereas in most cases the *hilt*, and not the blade, is the datum on which we must go to fix the prevalent taste—many good old blades being successively adapted to different hilts in accordance to the dictates of fashion; 4th, with reference to English and French swords especially, the best blades were imported from Spain, in Italy, and in Germany, and mounted according to the fashion of the owner's country.

All this makes it difficult to fix the nationality of a sword, and, within any narrow margin of time, the date when any particular form was actually *worn*, as it may have been affected by some old-fashioned gentleman at a time when his younger contemporaries looked upon it as altogether obsolete.

However, if we allow a sufficient margin for the overlapping of fashions in swords, and if we only consider the question with reference to England and France, who always followed the same style of fencing, it is possible to divide the "modern history" of the sword into four periods.

For want of better terms we may call the first—belonging to the first half of the sixteenth century—as that of the "Sword," such being the word used by G. Silver on behalf of the English Masters of Defence who taught the use of the *Sword*, not that of the outlandish *Rapier*.

The next may be called that of the Rapier; it covers the second half of the sixteenth century and the first quarter of the seventeenth.

It is convenient to define a third period as "Transition," during which the rapier decidedly tended towards simplification, but had not yet assumed the perfectly definite shape which we call that of the *Small Sword*. It may be said to cover the second and third quarters of the seventeenth century.

The last is that of the *Small Sword*, beginning in the reign of Charles II., and ending about the time of the French Revolution.

The character of the sword changed but very little during the Middle Ages; until the end of the fifteenth century its shape remained so simple,

---

[1] For example, Italy and Spain, the latter especially, retained old-fashioned swords very much later than France and England. The modern Italian duelling sword to this day is exactly similar to some types of the transition swords.

[2] As examples, not very conclusive it is true, but interesting, we may point out that many masters represent in their plates a sword of a very much older character than the kind commonly in use at the time when they taught fencing. This is the case with Viggiani, Meyer, Alfieri, Saviolo, and Sainct Didier. Sutor, as well as Agrippa and Marozzo, represent a more or less conventional weapon of mediæval character.

and is so familiar to everyone, that it would be useless to dwell on it.[1]
It consisted, as a rule, of a broad, straight, double-edged blade, broad at its
base and tapering towards its point, a plain grip[2] and cross hilt, and a more
or less flat, disk-shaped pummel. It was essentially strong, stiff, and clumsy,
and, although devised for cut and thrust, ill constructed for either. For its
effective use a strong arm was the chief requisite. Such was the sword
which was to undergo such rapid changes during the sixteenth century.

But before proceeding to analyze them, we may here dismiss with a
cursory description some other varieties of swords used during the Middle
Ages, and which seem to have disappeared almost completely after the
Renascence period.

They had a separate and limited existence of their own, and although
some of their characteristics may have been, from time to time, superadded
to those of the *sword typical* during its various transformations, individually
they never formed part of the chain which we intend to examine link by
link. The variety of these swords is very great, but we need only define
the most commonly recurring names.

The *Estoc* of the Middle Ages[3] was in most cases a two-handed sword
used *only* for the thrust. It had a very long, stiff blade, either three or
four sided, and was the most favourite weapon for combats on foot in the lists.

The *Long Sword*[4] (Claymore, Spadone, Espadon, Zweyhänder, Flamberge, &c.) was two-handed, used on foot and exclusively for cutting.

---

[1] See Figs. 3, 5, 6, 7 (pp. 14 to 17); also Marozzo (Chap. II.); also, Specimen No. 1
(Plate VI.).

[2] A fashion prevailed in the fifteenth century of making the grip exceptionally long, in
which case the sword, when used on foot, was wielded with both hands. This seems to
have been especially the habit in Germany. See Fig. 3 (p. 14).

[3] See also p. 22, and note.

[4] See Figs. 4 (p. 15), 9 (p. 18), 48 (p. 76). The word Schwerdt in Germany was
restricted to the heavier kind of sword, such as was called Long Sword, or the *old-fashioned
sword*, in England. It is needless to remark that *Sword* (or old English Swerd) and *Schwerdt*
come from the same source. The Teutonic type of the word is *Swerda*, "the wounder, that
which wounds," to which is connected the German *Schwer*, painful (Skeat).

Claymore is the English phonetic for two Keltic words, claidheamh-mor, signifying the
Great Sword. The original Claymore was a two-handed sword of the largest type (see Specimen
No. 2, Plate VI.). The basket-hilted sword of Italian origin—of which more will be said
hereafter—which now bears that name, would, in the days of the real claymore, have been
called a Claybeg, *i.e.*, a small sword.

Spadone and Espadon are the augmentatives of *Spada* and *Espada*, the Italian and the
Spanish forms of the Latin Spatha, which was the name given by the Romans to the long and
broad sword of the Gauls. Some etymologists derive the word Spatha from the Keltic *Spad*
(from which comes our word Spade). Similarly, the Spanish for the Small Sword is *Espadin*, a
diminutive of Espada. Zweyhander is of course the equivalent for *two-handed* sword.

Flamberge was, according to Littré, one of the names attributed to Roland's sword.
It seems to have originally been applied, in a slack manner, to any large sword, although more

PLATE I.

SWORDS, EARLY SIXTEENTH CENTURY. (WAREING FAULDER COLL.)

——1. *Sword, first years sixteenth century. Inside view, showing straight quillons and pas d'âne, surmounted by half ring as a counter-guard, the projecting ends of which are seen on the left side. Grooved, double-edged blade, with plain ricasso. From the Simonetti Coll. Probably Italian.*

·——2. *Sword, middle sixteenth century. Chased and inlaid with silver. Outside view, showing slightly counter-curved quillons, with side ring and pas d'âne. Bi-convex blade, with well-marked hollowed ricasso.*

——3. *Sword, same period. Outside view, showing same elements as No. 2, and in addition a ring surmounting the pas d'âne, a knuckle-bow, and a simple counter-guard joining pas d'âne to the latter. Grooved single-edged blade, with "wolf" or "fox" mark.*

——4. *Sword or Rapier, middle sixteenth century. Outside view, showing same elements as No. 1, and, in addition, ring on quillons, knuckle-bow, and connecting counter-guards. Grooved, double-edged blade.*

GERMAN SWORDS, MIDDLE SIXTEENTH CENTURY. (BARON DE COSSON'S COLL.)

5 *and* 6 *are devised for the right hand alone, although the lengthened pummel admits of the use of the left also.* 7 *and* 8, *two-handed swords of moderate dimensions.*

——5. *Outside view, showing same elements as No.* 3, *but without knuckle-bow. Grooved double-edged blade, with plain ricasso.*

——6. *Outside view, showing adaptation of a system of counter-guards belonging to the "Schiavona" type, reaching short of the lengthened pummel so as to allow the occasional use of the left hand. Bevelled double-edged blade, with plain ricasso.*

——7. *Outside view, showing straight quillons like the former, but with ring, pas d'âne, and counter-guard coalescing into an irregular form. Grooved double-edged blade, with plain ricasso.*

——8. *Outside view, showing counter-curved quillons, forming an imperfect knuckle-bow, protecting the forward hand, and coalescing pas d'âne and counter-guard. Flat blade, with strong ricasso.*

N.B. In all these guards the pas d'âne is shown more or less distinctly; with all the lighter kinds of "long swords" some fingers of the forward hand were crossed over the quillons.

RAPIERS. (BARON DE COSSON'S COLL.)

——9. *German Rapier, middle sixteenth century. Outside view, showing quillons slightly counter-curved horizontally, with large ring, pas d'âne surmounted by ring, and two counter-guards joining pas d'âne to quillons. Grooved, double-edged blade, with plain ricasso. On the left side, and not visible, is likewise a thumb ring.*

——10. *German Rapier, middle sixteenth century. False edge view, showing in profile the rings on the quillons and on the pas d'âne, the counter-guards on the left side and the thumb ring; also the increased thickness of ricasso.*

——11. *English Rapier, temp. Elizabeth, inlaid with gold and silver (hatched). Outside view, showing counter-curved quillons (forming knuckle-bow), pas d'âne, and connecting counter-guards coalescing with side ring. Deep grooved double-edged blade, with hollowed ricasso.*

——12. *English Rapier, temp. Elizabeth. (This may be looked upon as a "conventional" type of bar rapier.) Outside view, showing straight quillons and knuckle-bow, large pas d'âne surmounted by ring on right side, and counter guard connecting the extremities of pas d'âne together, and to knuckle-bow (not to the quillons). Deep grooved blade, with hollowed ricasso.*

PLATE I.

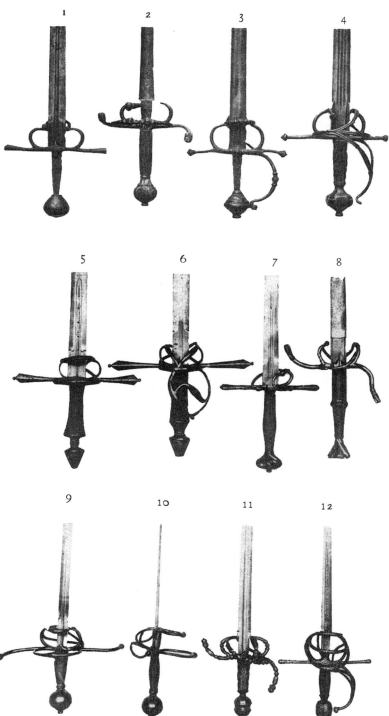

There were two kinds of single-handed *short* swords : the first consisted of those weapons with straight, double-edged blades—diminutives of
swords or augmentatives of daggers—which were somewhat promiscuously
called Braquemars, Malchus, Anelaces, Coustils à croc, Epées de Passot,
Lansquenettes, &c.; the other included all those with more or less curved
blades, after the manner of Eastern weapons, such as Scymitars or Falchions,
Cutlasses or Hangers, or Düsacken. [1]

The complication which the sword guard ultimately attained is so great,

generally restricted to the so-called Swiss flamboyant or undulated swords. Later on, the
term was applied, especially in England, to a peculiar form of the Rapier, of which we shall
speak further on. In France Flamberge soon became a contemptuous term, like that of
Rapière.

[1] The name Braquemar has been applied to many different forms of swords, large or
small, provided they had a broad blade. Du Cange notices the word under Braquemardus and
Bragamardus. As the sword so called was most generally rather short than otherwise, some
would derive its etymology from βραχὺς μάχαιρα, short sword; but this is unlikely. It
probably came from the word *Braquet* (Wallon), meaning a broad sword. We may here
remark that the kind of cutlass which formed part of the accoutrement of the French soldier
during the early years of this century, and was colloquially termed *Briquet*, belongs to that
class of weapon which would have been called a braquemar during the Middle Ages.

Malchus was the name often given to a short, broad, and straight-bladed sword, synony-
mous with Braquemar, in remembrance of Malchus, who had, according to the Gospel, his
ear cut off by St. Peter, presumably with an instrument of this kind. Specimen No. 4 (Plate
VI.) is a Malchus or Braquemar.

The name Anelace was given in England to a species of very broad daggers, similar to
the classical parazonium or pugio—for they can hardly be called swords, their blades being
generally only from eighteen to twenty inches in length—which were called on the Continent
pistos, anelacio, epée de passot. They were often worn behind the back, handle inclining to
the right. See Fig. 25 (p. 54).

The sword specially affected by the German mercenary foot soldiers in the fifteenth and
sixteenth centuries was called Lansquenette, from *Landsknecht*. They had some well-marked
peculiarities. The blade was very broad in comparison with its length, and double-edged.
The hilt consisted generally of two rings, formed by the quillons curved as a figure 8. The
grip was more or less conical, the broad base of the cone forming the pummel. See Fig. 53
(p. 78).

Curved sabres of the Scymitar type were much used during the Middle Ages, after the
Crusades. The Falchion or Fauchon was a smaller type of scymitar in very common use.
The name comes from the Latin Falx, through the Italian *Falcione*, meaning a scymitar, or the
French Fauchon, diminutive of Faux, a scythe. The word Cutlass is derived from the French
Coutel, with the augmentative as, or ace,—*Coutelas* meaning a large knife. Similarly in Italian
there is *coltello, coltellaccio*. Coutelas was rendered in English *Curtleaxe*, and in consequence
its etymology is often supposed to be *Coutel hache*, or *Coutel-axe*, and ultimately *Cutlass*. Florio
gives : "Coltellaccio, a cuttleax, a hanger."

The Düsack is of Hungarian or Bohemian origin, but it soon was adopted throughout
Germany by the middle and lower classes as an excellent weapon, very simple and inexpensive.
It consisted of a single piece of iron, one part of which was fashioned as a cutlass blade, and
another curved into a loop which formed a grip and knuckle-bow combined. The double
curve which resulted from this arrangement was eminently favourable to cutting action. In
Fig. 51 (p. 77) the upper sword is the true Düsack; the lower is an even simpler imitation.

that, in the absence of universally received technical terms, it will be advisable, before proceeding further, to lay down some definitions, which, although they may differ from those sometimes adopted by writers on this subject, will no doubt be found useful in facilitating descriptions throughout this chapter.

To begin with, it seems more natural, as the sword is of greatest interest when in the hand, to refer to the point as its highest, and to the pummel as its lowest part. Accordingly, although the reverse order is usually adopted, we shall always describe the sword as being point uppermost.

The essential parts are the blade, the handle or grip, the guard (whether simple or complex), and the pummel; none of these familiar terms require definitions, but it is otherwise with some *parts* of the guard and blade themselves, many of which have had no absolutely definite technical names attached to them.

The division of the blade into *fort* and *foible*, *point*, *false edge* and *right edge* is sufficiently explicit, but it will be found convenient also, with reference to the guard, to establish some distinction between the *right* and *left* of the hilt, which may be synonymously termed the *outside* and the *inside*. If we consider the sword as held in the right hand, arm extended and thumb uppermost, which is the most natural position, that termed by fencing-masters medium, we may broadly define as the outside (or the right side) of the guard, that part provided for the protection of the back of the hand, and as the inside (or left) of the guard, that provided for the inside of the hand.[1]

Different authors use the words *guard* and *counter-guard*, in a very confusing manner, to distinguish the right and the left portion so defined; others call counter-guard that part which protects the knuckles—the knuckle-bow, in fact.

But the word counter-guard, the meaning of which is so definite among technical terms of fortification, might more fitly be applied, in a similar sense, to those *superadded covering* guards which occur in all complete swords.

As the cross-hilt,[2] accompanied or not by the pas d'âne and a separate

---

[1] Such a distinction of course becomes nugatory in the case of perfectly symmetrical guards, as in some cup-hilted rapiers, flambergs, and small swords, but it is important in the consideration of the numerous unsymmetrical shapes of the sword.

To the fact that the foundation of every hilt is a cross guard may be ascribed the formality of the "recover," although this movement has now lost all meaning. There can be little doubt that this fashion of always bringing the hilt to the lips after drawing the sword originated in the habit of kissing the cross formed by blade and guard whenever the sword had to be unsheathed.

Similarly, it must be supposed that the curious form of salute when " marching past," namely, that of drawing the hilt across the mouth and extending the arm towards the saluting point, is a remnant of the very ancient ceremony of wafting a kiss with the sword hand to the gallery of fair ladies, previously to taking part in the lists or tournaments.

knuckle-bow—of which more presently—is the foundation of any hilt, however complex, and must exist in all cases, however modified its structure, we shall in technical descriptions make the word *guard* apply to these only, reserving that of *counter-guard* to any defensive arrangement occurring over and above them.

As has been seen, the guard of the typical mediæval sword consisted merely of a pair of straight or only slightly curved quillons [1]—quillons being the name given to the branches of the cross hilt.

Such a guard was eminently imperfect, but was considered quite sufficient so long as little or no defensive action was expected from the sword (see p. 13, Chap. I.), and when steel gauntlets offered the necessary protection to the hand. Towards the beginning of the sixteenth century, sword cutlers devised a somewhat improved hilt; that period saw, as we know, the dawn of the modern art of fence. It was found that advantage would be derived from some arrangement which could prevent the adverse blade, when swords were clashed, from reaching the hand over the cross hilt, and thus do away with the paramount necessity of a gauntlet. For this purpose the *side rings* and the *pas d'âne* were invented. The side rings are clearly and typically shown in Fig. 8 (p. 18), and the pas d'âne, in its simplicity, in Fig. 42 (p. 67). The ring very often occurs singly, and in that case on the right side of the sword.

Pas d'âne was the name given in France towards the end of the sixteenth century to a pair of bars, each curved in the form of a loop, added immediately above the cross hilt, on each side of the blade. The meaning of the word is obscure, and unhappily we have no English equivalent. Pas d'âne, according to Littré, is an instrument inserted into the mouth of a horse to keep it open for examination. Such an instrument may bear resemblance to our pair of loop guards, but the question is whether it was so called in the fifteenth century. [2]

A suggestion—which must be taken only for what it is worth—might be made on this subject. This name may have been applied to these loops, placed very close to one another, on account of their resemblance to the close footprints of the ass; such a simile would at least not be more far-fetched than the word "lunette" applied to the French foil guard. It may also have

---

[1] A French word, the diminutive of *quille*, probably from the Latin *caulis*, a stalk; a cogener of our *quill* (Burton).

[2] Although the pas d'âne and the ring, as adjuncts to the hilt, did not come into regular fashion earlier than the sixteenth century, there are several instances to show that they existed as early as the fourteenth century. Demmin mentions a mural painting, dating about the end of the fourteenth century, in the Cathedral of Mondoneda, representing the Massacre of the Innocents, in which some soldiers carry swords with unmistakable pas d'âne hilts. Swords with pas d'âne and rings are shown in some frescoes dating from the end of the fifteenth century in San Gimigniano, near Sienna.

stood for donkey's shoe, smaller than the horseshoe.   Be it as it may, the pas d'âne, once adopted, remained, in conjunction with the quillons, the foundation on which the most complicated as well as eventually the simplest guard was constructed.

The side ring was intended to screen the back of the hand, which it did but imperfectly.   We call it a *ring* for want of a better established term. It had generally the outline of what will be called later a *shell* guard.

Sometimes, instead of adding rings to the cross hilt, the quillons themselves were curved horizontally in the shape of a figure 8, as shown in the Lansquenette, Fig. 53 (p. 78).   Specimen No. 3 (Plate VI.) is likewise one of these kind.

The pas d'âne acted differently from the ring in checking the adverse blade some distance above the quillons, with the similar result of safeguarding the hand, but it had also another and more important purpose.

We see in our early authors,[1] and in old pictures,[2] what a constant habit it was among swordsmen to pass a finger or two over the quillons, in order to strengthen their hold of the sword.   It is just probable that the pas d'âne

Fig. 138.—German Sword, early sixteenth century, with
finger loop.

was specially devised as a protection to these encroaching fingers.[3]   In the specimen here adjoined it was decidedly the case, as a single loop such as this would have been inefficacious for safeguarding the hand, and consequently could not have been constructed for that purpose.

The side ring, if it be possible to make any general rule, was rather a Teutonic invention, and the pas d'âne an Italian, but as both so very soon became combined in all swords and in all countries, they lost all character of nationality.

The value of the pas d'âne as a guard was very soon enhanced by the adjunction of a smaller ring joining the extremities of the branches of the same.   This counter-guard (for all such adjuncts come under our definition

---

[1] See Fig. 10 (p. 30), and Figs. 13 to 17 (pp. 38 to 43).

[2] Instances, for example, are shown where the finger is passed over the quillons as early as the fourteenth century, *e.g.*, Campo Santo, Pisa, in the scene from the life of Saint Ephysius (painted in 1380-90); also in the naval combat painted by Spinello Aretino, Palazzo Publico, Bologna.

[3] See Figs. 19 (p. 46), 20 (p. 47), 22 (p. 48).

PLATE II.

———1. *Italian Rapier, third quarter sixteenth century. Outside view, showing counter-curved quillons and knuckle-bow, pas d'âne surmounted by two rings solidified into shells, and connected with knuckle-bow by counter-guards. Double-edged blade, grooved at base, with slightly hollowed ricasso, inscribed* Antonio Pichinio.

———2. *German Rapier, third quarter sixteenth century. Outside view, showing counter-curved quillons, knuckle-bow, and combined shell and bar hilt. Grooved, double-edged blade.*

———3. *English Rapier, Elizabethan. Straight quillons, same type as No. 2. Grooved blade, with obtuse edges and strong ricasso.*

———4. *English Rapier, Elizabethan. Same type as No. 2. Grooved double-edged blade by* Andrea Ferrara.

RAPIERS. (*WAREING FAULDER COLL.*)

———5. *English Rapiers, last quarter sixteenth century. Outside view, showing straight quillons, knuckle-bow, pas d'âne surmounted by symmetrical shells and joined to knuckle-bow by connecting counter-guards. Double-edged blade, with squared ricasso.*

———6. *English Rapier, Elizabethan, with openwork cup hilt, straight quillons, and knuckle-bow. Diamond sectioned blade.*

———7. *English Rapier of the same type as No. 6, but with counter-curved quillons. Bi-convex blade, grooved at the base. Inscribed on the inside:* For my Christ resolved to dy ; *on the outside,* Vho haves me let him wareme (haves, *engraver's mistake for* hates).

———8. *Italian Rapier, close of sixteenth century, with deep cup hilt, the edge open-worked and coalescing with knuckle-bow, straight quillons (one broken off, the other bent). Grooved blade.*

BASKET-HILTED BROADSWORDS. (*WAREING FAULDER COLL.*)

———9. *Venetian Broadsword, middle sixteenth century. Outside view, showing quillons slightly incurved on the blade, pas d'âne, and knuckle-bow ; all these parts joined together by elaborate counter-guards on both sides. Bi-convex blade, with strong ricasso. This is an early specimen of the type* " Schiavona."

———10. *Spanish basket-hilted Broadsword, middle sixteenth century. Outside view, showing another combination of guards and counter-guards. Pas d'âne on right edge side only, separated from the blade and coalescing with counter-guards. Bi-convex blade, grooved at base. Inscribed* Sahagom (*Alonzo de Sahagom, Toledo*).

———11. *Italian basket-hilted Broadsword, last quarter sixteenth century, of the type commonly known as* " Claymore," *showing the full development of basket hilt, the stunted quillons expanding into a sort of plate, the diminished pas d'âne diverted from its original purpose, and the counter-guards tastefully and fantastically interlaced. Bevelled blade, inscribed* Andrea Ferrara *between eight crowned heads.*

———12. *Italian basket-hilted Broadsword, last quarter sixteenth century, with exceptionally large counter-guards for protection of the wrist, and a remarkably broad blade, grooved, double-edged, marked in Gothic letters* AIL. *The blade is probably much anterior in date to the hilt.*

N.B. All these basket-hilted swords were originally devised chiefly for the use of horsemen.

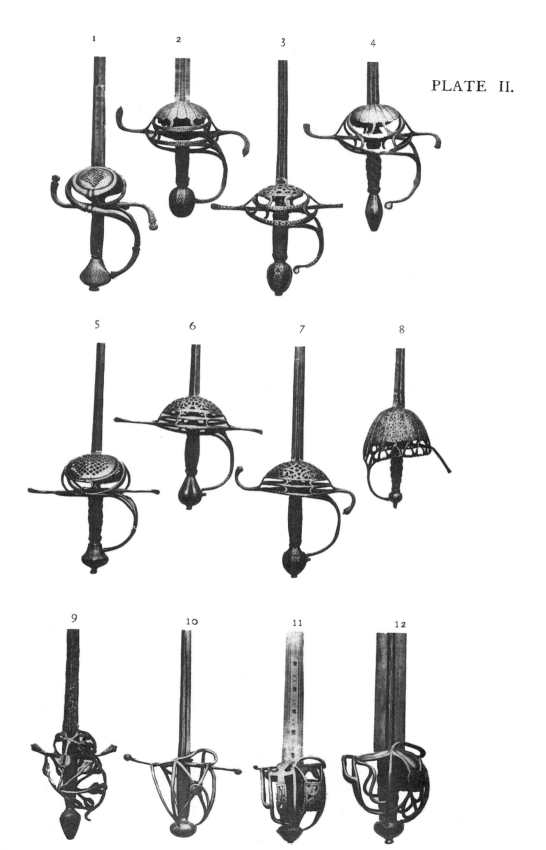

PLATE II.

of counter-guards) is well depicted in the sword worn by Girard Thibaust (p. 120), also in Specimens Nos. 2 and 3 (Plate I.).

When a ring occurs, on both sides of the sword, in conjunction with the quillons, similar ones, or one encompassing the blade, are often placed between the extremities of the pas d'âne. See Zacharia's sword, Fig. 81 (p. 128).

With regard to the quillons, it was obvious that with slight alteration they might be made to protect the hand very much more than they did in their straight condition. Accordingly, one branch was soon curved towards the pummel so as to protect the knuckles, and in such a case, for the sake of symmetry, the other branch was turned similarly towards the point.[1] So that we may add to any of the three simplest systems of defence the *Knuckle-bow*, approximating more or less to the pummel. It may be well to remark here that it is only at a comparatively late period that this guard was made to *unite* with the pummel.

Now it will be found, on inspection of any carefully arranged collection of swords, that the shape of the hilt at all periods since the fifteenth century has depended on the modification of these elements, their connection by more or less complicated systems of bars and counter-guards, and their partial solidification into shells or cups.

In early days, as we have said, the point was but little used, and most cuts were delivered in pronation, so that, as the back of the hand was most exposed, the simplest form of guard commonly used, which consisted generally of a ring on the outside (right side) and pas d'âne, was fairly sufficient protection, especially when a branch of the quillons was contrived so as to form a knuckle-bow.

But as the fencing art became developed, upward cuts, and thrusts in supination came into common practice, and, accordingly, the sword cutlers devised some further protection for the inside of the hand and of the wrist so exposed; the extremities of the pas d'âne were connected on the inside to the extremity of the knuckle guard by means of curved bars, more or less complicated and graceful, according to the good taste or fancy of the owner. For the sake of additional protection, similar bars were likewise added to the outside.

Against a thrusting play the value of lengthened straight quillons was very soon appreciated, but the curved branch being equally valuable as a knuckle-bow, the latter was often retained in this capacity, new quillons of very much increased length being superadded to the differentiated ones.

This stage of complication having been reached, we have one type of the most usual rapier guards.

The habit of crossing the fingers round the base of the blade—through

---

[1] This is shown in Saviolo's plates, although Saviolo instructed his pupils in the use of a very much more complicated sword.

the pas d'âne, over the quillons—soon suggested the advantage of screening the hand as much as possible under the counter-guard.　Accordingly, in a great number of rapiers, especially those of the latter Elizabethan period, the grip is reduced to very diminutive dimensions, being devised, in fact, to rest against the palm, and only held by the third and fourth fingers, the sword being firmly secured in the hand by the quillons.

Before examining the character of the cup and shell hilts, it may be well to recapitulate the parts which composed what may be called the " conventional " hilt of the sixteenth century rapier.

Guards : quillons, pas d'âne, knuckle-bow—the latter, however, is not so universal as the two former.

Counter-guards : ring on the quillons (on each side or only on the right, or outside of the sword), smaller rings on the pas d'âne (again on one side or on both), connecting bars, joining the various parts (similarly on one or both sides).

So much fantasy was displayed in the invention of ornamental hilts of this type that it would be impossible to attempt a classification of their different varieties.　But the foundation of such guards will generally be found to be that which has just been sketched, if we remember that in such a system, with so many factors, and with the possibility of doubling or trebling the number of connecting bars, and interlacing them, the result of their permutations and combinations must necessarily be the production of an almost infinite variety of shapes.

German swordsmen seem to have had a particular fancy for using the thumb, instead of the index, for the purpose of securing the sword,[1] and although the pas d'âne occurs in their swords, a special thumb ring is very often added below the quillons ; it is possible, however, that they used both thumb ring and pas d'âne at once.

From the immense variety of shape and position in which these thumb rings are found, we are to judge that in most cases the sword was " built " under the immediate supervision of its intended owner.

The change in the character of the blade is much more easily explained than that of the guard.　During the transformation of the Sword into the Rapier,[2] improvement was always sought in alterations which would facilitate the delivery of time hits and add greater efficacy to the thrust, without, however, preventing the use of the cut.　With these objects in view the blade

---

[1] See, for instance, Fig. 12 (p. 30).

[2] See pp. 19 to 22.　The etymology of the word Rapier is obscure.　Some derive it from the German *rappen*, or *raffen*, to tear out.　Others connect it, through *raspière*, to the Spanish *raspar*, to scrape or scratch.　Mercutio, stabbed with a rapier, exclaims about " a cat, a dog, a rat, to *scratch* a man to death."　Others, again, will see in it a derivation of ῥαπίς, a rod.

was gradually made to assume slenderer proportions and ultimately increased also enormously in length. Nos. 7 and 9, Plate VI., show to what an extent this increase could be pushed, if we compare the length of the blade to that of No. 1, which belongs to the early part of the century, or even to that of the huge Zweyhänder, No. 5.[1]

The rigidity of such lengthened blades was preserved and their weight diminished by grooving and flutings. They often were even pierced with open work, as is shown by many fine old Spanish blades ; this fluting never extended higher than the third quarter of the blade, nearest the point, where it had to be preserved flat for the purpose of retaining trenchant power.

The part enclosed between the pas d'âne is usually blunted and often squared, or hollowed (in the case of broad blades), for the purpose, in some cases of strengthening the base, in others, of facilitating the closing of the fingers through the loops or under the cup guard.

We have adopted the French word pas d'âne, and we may as well likewise, for want of a better, adopt the Italian word "ricasso," used to designate that part of the blade between the cup guard and the quillons of the Italian foils and duelling swords.

This hollowing out and squaring of the blade at its base—the "ricasso," in fact—is well shown in Fig. 24 (p. 53).

The ricasso is an almost constant feature of the rapier blade, although in such swords, where the blade was particularly narrow, such a contrivance was of course not resorted to.

We saw that towards the very end of the sixteenth century the best masters, although professing the cut-and-thrust play, were strongly prejudiced in favour of the thrust alone. Accordingly, some swordsmen preferred excessively slender blades all but devoid of cutting edges, with a lozenge-shaped section and often nearly square ; the length of such blades could also be immensely increased without detriment to their rigidity or too great an increase of weight.

These swords, which were called Verduns in France, from the town in which they were mostly made, were only used for duelling purposes ; they were generally owned in pairs, with daggers to match. They were so inconveniently long that the swaggering duellists had them carried by a footman behind them.

Later on, the outrageous dimensions of such swords were much reduced. We have seen with what disfavour these " tucks," fit only for the thrust,

---

[1] This excessive length, which modern fencers would deem most disadvantageous, was not then considered a drawback, as the movements of the sword were by no means rapid, being supplemented by a great many displacements of the body. Fabris' system is typical of this style of fencing.

were looked upon in England.[1] Those swordsmen who indulged in the double rapier-play generally carried twin swords in the same scabbard; each sword was flattened on the inside, but as they were held in the right and left hands they were naturally provided with *outside* guards. A set of this kind was termed a case of rapiers.

The prismatic shape of the blade was retained in many duelling swords until towards the middle of the seventeenth century, when it was gradually abandoned in favour of the still more deadly and lighter three-cornered fluted blade. The most usual blade, however, remained until the middle of the seventeenth century one of the double-edged type.

We may now consider the development of *cup* and *shell* hilts. No doubt cup hilts, especially in Italy and Spain, were contemporary with complicated bar guards, and about the end of the sixteenth century it was merely a matter of taste whether to adopt a plain cup hilt of the usual Spanish type, or some picturesque arrangement of bars, of which there was such unlimited choice; but the earliest cup hilt is posterior to the first sword that was improved by the addition of a counter-guard.

We may briefly define the usual cup hilt as consisting of quillons, with or without knuckle-guards, pas d'âne, and, as a covering counter-guard, a cup, either hemispherical or approximating to that shape.

We have seen how commonly the small target—" brochiero " or " broquel "—was used, especially during the first half of the sixteenth century; the idea may have easily occurred to some ingenious maker to adapt a cup over the quillons which would act as a small brochiero in the right hand, whilst the left could then remain free to use the dagger. If we remember that the broquel or target was always held at arm's length, the idea that the cup hilt might perform a similar office was very plausible. The earliest cup-hilted rapier seems to have come from Spain. In Spain, also, the idea of adapting a similar arrangement on to the dagger was first originated. On the latter, however, this modified broquel[2] was so adapted as still to act as target when held in the correct manner. (See daggers in Group I., Plate III.)

It is just possible, also, that the invention of this particular form of " main gauche " was suggested by someone who had attempted to hold both a dagger and target together in his left hand, and conceived the practical notion of combining the two, or it may be a modification of the Moorish Adarga—the spear and hand buckler combined. All these are, of course, mere theories.

---

[1] It seems difficult to explain how the meaning of the word Estoc, or rather " Estocade," as it was called in Sainct Didier's time, should have been so much altered. When the sword was specified as "Estocade," it meant that it was specially for *cut* and thrust, and not a weapon of the Verdun type.　　　　[2] See Specimens, Plate III. and Plate VI.

PLATE III.

SHELL-GUARD RAPIERS. (BARON DE COSSON'S COLL.)

——1. *English Rapier (hatched), last quarter sixteenth century. Outside view, showing counter-curved quillons and knuckle-bow, pas d'âne and symmetrical shells connected by counter-guards to knuckle-bow. Grooved blade, double-edged, with slightly hollowed ricasso.*

——2. *Italian Rapier, close of sixteenth century. Outside view, showing shell hilt of the type conventionally called "ringed guard," in outline that of a deep cup hilt, but formed of numerous and, so to speak, concentric rings, usually seven in number, the last of which is joined to the knuckle-bow. Grooved, double-edged blade, with strong ricasso.*

——3. *Rapier, close of sixteenth century. Inside view, showing counter-curved quillons, knuckle-bow, and pas d'âne surmounted by rings and a shell, connected by counter-guards to the knuckle-bow. Double-edged blade, with hollowed ricasso.*

——4. *German Rapier, early seventeenth century. Inside view, showing counter-curved quillons, knuckle-bow, pas d'âne and shells connected by fantastic counter-guards to knuckle-bow. Grooved blade, with plain ricasso.*

——5. *German Rapier. Inside view, showing counter-curved quillons and knuckle-bow, pas d'âne and large shell (the opposite shell, not visible, is much smaller) connected to knuckle-bow by slender counter-guards. Double-edged blade.*

N.B. This form is unusual; as a rule, the larger shell occurs on the right or outside of the sword; possibly this may have been devised for the left hand.

RAPIERS AND SWORD. (WAREING FAULDER COLL.)

——6. *Spanish Rapier, close of sixteenth century. Outside view, showing long straight quillons, knuckle-bow, and pas d'âne, covered by two large symmetrical shells, connected to knuckle-bow by counter-guards. Double-edged blade by* Juan Martin, Toledo.

——7. *Spanish Rapier, early seventeenth century. Outside view, showing same elements as No. 6. Grooved blade by* Tomas Ayala *of Toledo.*

——8. *German Rapier, early seventeenth century. Outside view, showing counter-curved quillons and large shell covering pas d'âne (shell inscription,* Melrois*), and knuckle-bow. Flamboyant blade inscribed* Clemens Kirschbaum in Sohlingen.

——9. *Spanish Rapier, early seventeenth century. Outside view, showing straight quillons, pas d'âne and plain cup. Knuckle-bow, starting from the cup edge instead of from the quillons, is unusual. Slender, diamond-sectioned blade, of Verdun type.*

——10. *English Musketeer's Sword, early seventeenth century. Outside view, showing counter-curved quillons, on branch forming a knuckle-bow, and side ring. This specimen is here introduced to show how some very early forms of guards remained in use whenever simplicity was a requisite.*

FLAMBERG. (WAREING FAULDER COLL.)

——11. *German Rapier of Flamberg type, close of sixteenth century, showing incurved quillons, pas d'âne, and shells only. Long grooved blade with ricasso, inscribed* Clemes Meigen.

——12. *German Flamberg, early seventeenth century. Long quillons, wide pas d'âne, large flat shells. Grooved blade with ricasso, inscribed* Clemens Potter ihn Scolingen.

——13. *German Flamberg, middle seventeenth century. Same elements as in No. 12, but of smaller and more elegant dimensions. Grooved blade, inscribed* Peter Wundes ihn Solingen.

——14. *Flamberg, middle seventeenth century, showing pas d'âne and shell, without quillons. Bevelled blade, inscribed* Sahagum.

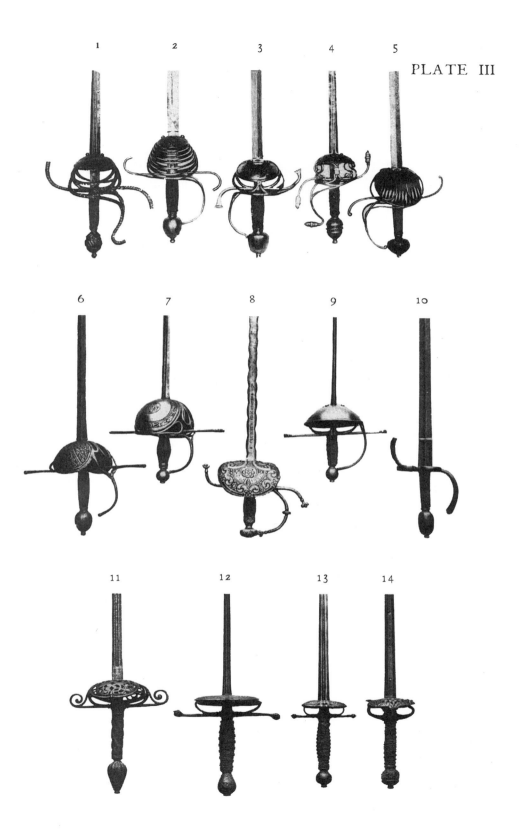

PLATE III

The cup hilt, which is undoubtedly a more perfect form of guard for a thrusting sword, may also have been gradually suggested by the "solidification," so to speak, of various parts of the counter-guard, such as the substitution of shell-shaped solid pieces to the original rings.

Indeed, there are numerous specimens in which, for instance, the rings which were originally added to the extremities of the pas d'âne are partly or wholly replaced by shells. When these shells assume sufficient dimensions, so as to constitute the principal part of the counter-guard, we may call the sword a *shell*-guard rapier.

Complete cup hilts are pretty uniform in their character, but there is an immense variety of hilts consisting partly of a cup or of shells and partly of bars. Some specimens which have the *outline* of a cup hilt are so pierced and hollowed out as to appear to be made up of bars; others consist of very large shells connected by slender additional counter-guards.

A hilt consisting of both shells and bars could obviously be much simplified by the substitution of a simple cup to the whole. This may also be the origin of the cup hilt.

A cup hilt is undoubtedly, in the opinion of modern swordsmen, a more perfect fencing implement than the most elaborate bar hilt, which must necessarily often have entangled the adversary's sword in an unforeseen manner. Many sixteenth century swordsmen, however, preferred them, relying probably, in such cases, on superior strength for mastering the adverse blade; but unless they succeeded in snapping it, they, as well as their adversaries, must necessarily have been deprived as well of offensive power. Then, no doubt, the dagger came into action.[1]

The acme of complication in the hilt and of exaggerated length in the blade seems to have been reached in the last years of the sixteenth century. From that time until now the tendency of all swordmakers has been rather to reduce the dimensions and simplify the guard of the rapier.

About that time there came in fashion a very much simpler rapier, which, in most collections, is classed under the head Flamberg. The special character of this so-called Flamberg is the comparative simplicity of the hilt, which consists merely of quillons without knuckle-bow or pas d'âne, covered by a very shallow cup of moderate dimensions; the blade is usually slenderer than the ordinary rapier of the same period. This kind of sword, which, by the way, could be readily passed from the right to the left hand, according to the teaching of some masters, when the sword alone was used, came gradually into great favour among expert fencers of the seventeenth century

---

[1] With our method of fencing such an entanglement would occur constantly, but we know that the rapier fence was by no means a close one, and the object of these hilts was rather to screen the hand from an accidental cut than from a thrust.

on account of its comparative lightness. We may look upon the Flamberg as the first step in the transition of the Rapier to the Small Sword.

The etymology of the word is as obscure as that of Rapier. The name Flamberg was originally applied to all swords with the fanciful wavy blade, although by some writers it is restricted to the flamboyant Spadone or Zweyhander.

In French the word flamberge, which at first was a common synonym for sword,[1] very soon became, like that of rapier, a more or less contemptuous term. This species of sword, however obscure the origin of its name, is perfectly definite (see Plate III., Group III.).

The Flamberg was probably at first most commonly used in Germany, where the art of fencing with either hand, when the rapier was used alone, seems to have been more actively cultivated than elsewhere, and where rapiers without knuckle-bows are of commoner occurrence than in other countries. But the Flamberg type very soon spread abroad, especially in France and in England.

The seventeenth century—during the first half of which was accentuated the distinction between the military weapon, or sabre, and the walking sword, rapier, or small sword—is essentially the age of transition.

The simplification of the rapier consisted in the almost universal adoption of the cup or shell hilt, the gradual reduction of its dimensions, and the elimination of complicated counter-guards. It is observable that about the middle of the century the cup hilt becomes very shallow, and in the shell hilt the shells open out more and more. The simplest form of the transition rapier may be described as consisting of quillons, knuckle-bow, and pas d'âne, surmounted by either a shallow cup or two plain shells. In fact, there is very little to distinguish it from the small-sword guard except its larger dimensions. The length of the blade varies between thirty-two and forty inches, although there are still examples of excessively long blades belonging to such hilts. When this type of simplicity is reached, the only difference between the flamberg and the *transition rapier* thus described is the absence of knuckle-bow in the former.

About the period of the Restoration the triangular fluted blade came into fashion in England, having apparently been first adopted by the French between the years 1650 and 1660.[2]

The French were, as we know, the first to absolutely discard all cutting from their rapier fencing, and were, in consequence, the first to adopt the lightest form of blade as the best suited for purely thrusting play.[3]

---

[1] " Mettre Flamberge au vent" was a usual expression for drawing the sword.

[2] Of course triangular blades had been known and used long before that date, but their *general* adoption can hardly be admitted as previous to 1650.

[3] It is difficult to find out from Liancour whether he always dealt with a three-cornered blade, but Labat and his successors undoubtedly did.

It is a *triangular* blade united to a very simple hilt which constitutes the *Small Sword*, that is, one which can only be used for thrusting and whose superiority depends on its lightness. In Spain and Italy, and to a lesser degree in Germany, the old-fashioned cup or shell hilt and the flat double-edged blade were retained for more than a century later.

The small sword was essentially a French weapon, and wherever it was worn small-sword fencing was taught by French masters. We have observed what an objection they offered to the utilization of the pas d'âne for the purpose of securing the sword in the Italian and Spanish style, but nevertheless, in all French flambergs, flat-bladed "transition" rapiers, or three-cornered small swords, the pas d'âne are retained in all their integrity.

In Germany, however, the old Italian habit of passing the forefinger through the loop was adhered to until a much later period, and likewise apparently in England, for we find Sir William Hope inveighing most strenuously against this practice.

The conventional shape of the small-sword hilt remained essentially the same from the days of the Restoration until its disappearance towards the end of the eighteenth century, and always consisted of quillons and knuckle-bow, pas d'âne and a double shell (or, more rarely, a single plate); but during the course of the eighteenth century, and as the original use of the loops fell more into oblivion, the pas d'âne was flattened more and more, until, in some late specimens, they became quite rudimentary. As this change occurred, the sword itself was gradually attenuated, until it became the feather-weight weapon of which our modern Court-sword is a fair representative. This excessive reduction in the weight of the triangular blade seems to have taken place in two stages. The blade of the small sword worn during the last part of the seventeenth century, although very much lighter than the double-edged rapier blade, was still comparatively heavy about the point. Between the years 1680 and 1690 came into fashion, at first in France, and then in Germany and England, the type of blade known as " *Colichemarde* "—a very bad phonetic rendering, coined by the French, of Konigsmark, the name of the Swedish Count who passes for its inventor.[1]

The characteristic of the Colichemarde blade is the very great breadth of the fort, as compared with that of the faible. The change is very abrupt; the blade, which is stiff and broad in the portion nearer the hilt, suddenly becoming excessively slender about the region of the half weak. (This shape is particularly well shown in Specimen 23, Plate VI.)

This pronounced difference facilitated the rapid management of the

---

[1] A celebrated soldier of fortune, who served with distinction in Germany and in France (Louis XIV. made him Marshal of France). Königsmark came in 1661 to the English Court as ambassador from Sweden to Charles II. He died in 1686, in the service of the Republic of Venice.

point to an extraordinary extent, without weakening the sword at the fort, with which all parries are made ; so that practically the blade remained as strong as ever.   This form of blade was eminently favourable to methodical fencing, and this is one of the rare instances in which the form of the weapon was not the result of the development of the theory, but one in which the invention of a new shape ultimately altered the whole system.

Soon after its coming into general use we begin to hear of the free use of the " cut over the point," of multiple feints, and of what especially constituted the essence of small-sword or French fencing, in contradistinction to rapier-play, namely, circular parries (contre-dégagements) in the four lines.

This highly perfect form of blade was used between the years 1685 and 1720, and then seems very suddenly to have gone out of fashion, being replaced again by one which tapered very uniformly from the base to the point.

But the advantages of an exceedingly light point were too important to be neglected, and accordingly the *whole* blade was made very slender.   Its character has hardly varied since.

When the French masters began to discourage the habit of holding the sword through the loop of the pas d'âne, they soon perceived the advantage of " setting the blade in quarte,"[1] and in most books of fence rules for performing this operation are given among those for " choosing and mounting a blade."

About the time when the characteristics of what we call a rapier began to assert themselves, the sword, for warlike purposes, became also differentiated in another branch.

Although the narrow-bladed rapier was often used for military purposes, it was more generally worn as a " walking " sword—an attendant companion in case of the emergency either of a duel or of a sudden affray.   As a military weapon the *broad* sword was retained in common use, and from the very first years of the sixteenth century—when, as we saw, the gentleman's sword began to show a tendency to assume the rapier type—the military sword had its guard improved by a system of counter-guards from which was very soon evolved the conventional " basket " hilt.   The Italian basket-hilted broadsword assumed very early the shape retained until now by such weapons.   One feels, however, inclined at first to ascribe quite a modern date to many swords of a model hardly distinguishable from our modern military claymore, which were used by horsemen in Italy and Germany as early as the middle of the sixteenth century.

---

[1] The reason why this slight inclination of the blade to the left is hardly ever noticeable in small swords belonging to collections is that it was probably taken for an accidental defect by their owners, and in consequence rectified.

PLATE IV.

DAGGERS. (BARON DE COSSON'S COLL.)

1, 2, *Early sixteenth century;* 3, *Forked;* 4, 5, 13, 15, 16, *Cross-hilted, sixteenth century ;* 8, 10, 14, *Seventeenth century ;* 9, *Anelace ;* 6, 12, 7, 11, *Shell Daggers, outside and inside views.*

BROADSWORDS, SEVENTEENTH CENTURY. (WAREING FAULDER COLL.)

——17. *Italian Broadsword, first years seventeenth century. Outside view, showing counter-curved quillons, knuckle-bow, large shell on the quillons connected with the knuckle-bow. The pas d'âne are more or less obliterated and useless, except as a kind of counter-guard. On the left side is a thumb ring, not visible here. Grooved flat blade, double-edged, with strong ricasso.*

——18. *Spanish Broadsword, early seventeenth century. Outside view, showing counter-curved quillons and knuckle-bow, pas d'âne surmounted by unequal shells (larger one shown). Bevelled blade, with hollowed ricasso.*

——19. *Cavalry Sword, temp. Commonwealth. (Swords of this type are often called " Mortuary," as a number of them were made in memory of Charles I., and bear his likeness upon the hilt.) Outside view, showing later shape of basket hilt, in which the quillons have expanded into a sort of plate and coalesced with the knuckle-bow, being connected on both sides by means of counter-guards with the bow itself and the pummel. Bevelled blade,* by Andrea Ferrara.

——20 and 21. *Swords of the same type as No. 3, showing same elements differently connected; 4 has a single-edged grooved blade inscribed* Solinger *; 5 has a double-edged blade, remarkable for bearing an English inscription (a rare occurrence),* Ioannes Hoppie Fecit, Grenewich.

——22. *German Broadsword, middle seventeenth century. Outside view, showing counter-curved quillons, knuckle-bow, outside shell on the quillons surrounded by other counter-guards connecting quillons to knuckle-bow. Thumb-ring, not visible, on the inside.*

TRANSITION RAPIERS. (WAREING FAULDER COLL.)

——23. *German Rapier, second quarter seventeenth century. Outside view, showing counter-curved quillons and knuckle-bow, pas d'âne, surmounted by shallow cup, connected by counter-guards to knuckle-bow. Double-edged blade, with blunted ricasso, inscribed* Peter Keisser.

——24. *Italian Rapier, middle seventeenth century. Outside view, showing incurved quillons and knuckle-bow supporting a shallow cup, which coalesces with counter-guards and knuckle-bow. Double-edged grooved blade, with strong ricasso.*

——25. *Transition Rapier, middle seventeenth century. Outside view, showing quillons and knuckle-bow coalesced, and wide pas d'âne supporting symmetrical flattened shells. Long grooved blunt-edged Spanish blade, with squared ricasso, inscribed* Tomas Ayala en Toledo.

——26. *French Rapier, middle seventeenth century. Outside view, showing counter-curved quillons and knuckle-bow, pas d'âne and shallow shells, side ring, and small connecting counter-guard. Grooved blade, with hollowed ricasso, inscribed* En Toledo.

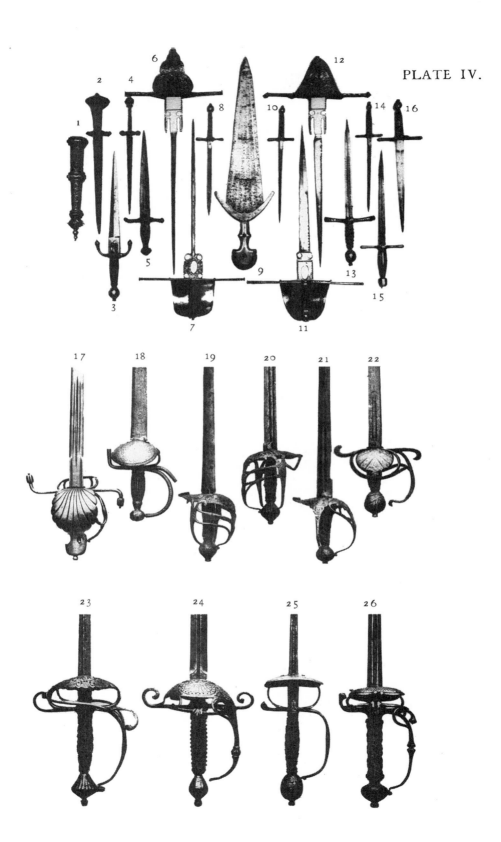

PLATE IV.

A critical examination of the earliest obtainable specimens of such swords warrants the assertion that the basket shape was produced by the same kind of process as the complicated rapier hilt, namely, by the addition of counter-guard to the original cross hilt and pas d'âne.

There are two distinct forms of basket hilt : the Schiavona type and the Claymore type, since we must use that inappropriate name. (In Plate VI., Specimens Nos. 13 to 16 belong to the former, and Nos. 18 and 20 to the latter.) The Schiavona is certainly an earlier type than the Claymore, although at a later period they were used contemporaneously. It is easy to imagine how much simpler it must have been to devise a guard for the hand in the case of a military weapon, where a certain amount of clumsiness was a very small drawback in comparison with the increased value resulting from a strong guard. For a " walking " sword a great many factors had to be taken into consideration which could be neglected in the horseman's weapon.

The earliest specimens of Schiavone show most distinctly quillons, pas d'âne, and superadded counter-guards. (See Specimen, No. 9, Plate II.) As the purpose of the sword was for hacking, there was no necessity for limiting the number of counter-guards in order to allow a free play of the wrist, and accordingly, from the very first, we see connecting bars joining the pas d'âne to the pummel, not only along the knuckle-bow, but to the right and left of the sword, leaving an opening only sufficiently large to allow the insertion of the hand. These bars are likewise connected with each other in many different and artistic fashions, and thus the basket hilt is constituted.

" Cup " and " basket " hilts are often used by different authors as interchangeable terms; it is necessary, however, to restrict the meaning of each, and the distinction is very simple : the *cup* hilt has its opening towards the pummel, and belongs to the rapier class; the *basket* hilt opens at the side, and belongs to that of the broadsword.

As very little thrusting was ever performed with these basket-hilted swords, the utility of the quillons and the pas d'âne was not very obvious; and accordingly, in later specimens, they first of all diminished greatly in importance, then the pas d'âne, having first separated themselves from the blade, still clinging to portions of their connecting counter-guards, ultimately lost almost all their original character. (See Plate II., Group III.)

The ear-like projections which remain on the right edge side of the basket-hilted modern claymore show the last of their existence. They were retained, and even now form part of the regulation claymore, on account of their utility in stopping the adverse blade from slipping on to the arm.

Most basket hilts were provided with a thumb ring which helped, instead of the obliterated pas d'âne, to secure a firm hold of the grip. The quillons ultimately broadened into the solid plate which forms the principal guard of a broadsword.

The Schiavona was essentially the arm of the " Schiavoni," who formed the body-guard of the Doges, but swords of similar form were also affected by many other troops, especially by German " Reiters." The Schiavona, however elegant its shape, was not the best kind of basket-hilted sword, and the " claymore" hilt was soon after invented. There are also many shapes intermediate between the two.

Such swords were generally used by horsemen, but often also as broadswords on foot.

Marozzo's system of fencing, dealing as it did so much with the cut and so little with the point, was well suited for this weapon.[1]

The most common forms belong to the " shearing" or double-edged straight type, but many specimens are found single-edged, or " back sword" blades, generally straight, but sometimes very slightly curved. We must not forget that a very good blade may have been inserted into many different kinds of hilts. This explains the apparently very early date of some swords of this kind, in which we may presume the blade is very much older than the hilt.

The basket hilt seems only to have become common in this country during the very last years of the sixteenth century. It was first adopted in Scotland as a convenient guard for the broadsword, and very soon became so popular that it was almost exclusively used for all single-handed weapons, and the basket-hilted broadsword has remained ever since the national arm of the Scots. The fierce charges of the Highlanders in many bloody battles during the Middle Ages had made the English well acquainted with the word " claymore." When the mighty two-handed claymore went out of use, being gradually superseded by the basket-hilted weapon, the old name, as conveying the idea of the Highlander's sword, was preserved, owing to long habit, notwithstanding its inappropriateness.

In England, for all kinds of broadswords a simpler form of guard was long adhered to, composed merely of quillons and rings, but about the middle of the seventeenth century the Scotch basket hilt was very extensively used, especially by horsemen. Oliver Cromwell's own sword was one of that description.

But another shape remained contemporaneously in favour, in which the side rings, with part of the cross hilt, were solidified into solid shells, the knuckle-bow being retained, and a thumb ring added under the guard, by which the sword could be firmly gripped in the absence of pas d'âne. This form was much affected by the Roundheads.

[1] The sword shown in Viggiani's " prima guardia," Fig. 34, is one approximating to the Schiavona type.

There were two kinds of blades used with these hilts, the " shearing," double-edged blade (this was the name then given to a lighter and more flexible form of the traditional double-edged type), and the " back sword " or single-edged blade. The latter was merely a development of the cutlass, as they were of similar shapes, and both connected with the " falchion " and the " scymitar." The curvature of the sword was merely diminished for the sake of better balance. Back and shearing swords were, as we saw, the popular weapons contemporaneously with the rapier.

But the rapier guard, whether consisting of bars, or shells, or a cup, was very often used with a very broad blade. In such cases the " ricasso "[1] was necessarily much hollowed. Such broad-bladed rapiers were almost exclusively used by horsemen until the wars of the rebellion, when they seem to have been very suddenly replaced by basket-hilted swords, such as are shown in Plate IV. (This remained the type of the cavalry sabre in England until the latter part of the eighteenth century.)

The back sword, of which so much is heard in connection with

Fig. 139.—Back Sword, sixteenth century, showing the single-edged blade.

gladiators' stage fights, had a basket hilt similar to that of the claymore, but a very much slenderer blade, deprived of point, like the modern Schlaeger.

A cutting sword of still narrower dimensions, and with a much simpler guard, approximating to that of the small sword, was called " Spadroon " in England ; it was, in fact, similar to the German cut-and-thrust rapier of the eighteenth century, which had been called *Spadone* or *Spadrone* since the disuse of the regular two-handed swords, in the same way as the claymore retained the old name of a very different weapon. The German Spadroon was a regular double-edged sword, but any very light back or shearing sword was so called in England. Its play was essentially that of our modern single-stick, with a free use of the point, and the addition of a few drawing cuts with the false edge.

During the second half of the eighteenth century the Hungarian curved blade came into favour, especially for the use of light horse troops, and was

[1] See p. 235.

first adapted to the ancient basket hilt, and then to a much simpler one, called the " stirrup " hilt, consisting merely of a cross-bar and a knuckle-bow. (The stirrup hilt, adapted to a Spadroon blade, is shown in Figs. 132-6.)

————

The dagger[1] has been at most times, and in all countries, the natural companion of the sword, and for obvious reasons : a reversion to " natural fighting," by closing in and wrestling, was always a likely termination to a more civilized and scientific combat. Indeed, in modern days, the fact that it is necessary to make it a hard and fast rule that the left hand is not to be used, and that pummelling, wrestling, or tripping is an unwarrantable way of deciding a contest with the sword, shows how perfectly instinctive these actions are.

During the Middle Ages the dagger was brought into action, as a last resource, as soon as the combat was thus carried on at such close quarters that the sword became useless. It was also employed in personal combats, judicial or otherwise, to give the *mercy stroke* to a wounded adversary, or to induce him to beg for his life when held helpless on the ground—hence the common name of *misericorde* formerly given to the dagger by the French.

Its systematic use in actual fencing resulted from the ancient habit of always holding it ready drawn in anticipation of the final tussle, which was almost inevitable in early days, when the science consisted of much cautious stalking, followed by very reckless dashes.

It is possible that at first the dagger may have been held point downwards, thumb near or on the pummel, and thus only used for stabbing, but the very earliest books treating of the sword or rapier invariably represent the dagger chiefly as a *defensive* weapon, held in the left hand in very much the same manner as the sword was in the right.

Fig. 140.—The " Misericorde."

Broadly speaking, there are three typical forms of *fencing* daggers.[2]

[1] Dagger, a word of Keltic origin : *dag* or *dager*, a dagger. The words *dag*, for dagger, and *daggen*, to stab, occur in old Dutch.

Poignard, poniard, pugnale, puñal, in French and English, Italian and Spanish, are of course derived from *pugnus*, the fist.

[2] During the sixteenth and early seventeenth centuries, the sword and dagger worn by gentlemen were most usually of a similar pattern. As the typical shape of the latter varied but little, this fact is important, for, in the absence of any very definite criterion, the style of ornamentation and the general character of the blade are of great use in determining the date of a given dagger by comparison with that of the sword then in fashion.

PLATE V.

TRANSITION RAPIERS AND SMALL SWORDS. (WAREING FAULDER COLL.)

N.B. Notice how, in this group and the following, the pas d'âne gradually becomes stunted and unfit for its original purpose, as the sword is of later date.

———1. *English Rapier, middle seventeenth century. Outside view, showing straight quillons, knuckle-bow, and pas d'âne surmounted by shells. Flamboyant blade. But for the quillons, distinct from knuckle-bow, this hilt shows all the characteristics of that of the Small Sword.*

———2. *Transition Rapier, middle seventeenth century. Old-fashioned flat, grooved, and pierced blade of Spanish type, shortened and adapted to conventional small-sword hilt, namely, one formed of quillons and knuckle-bow coalesced, pas d'âne and small shells, the ricasso being overlapped and covered by an extension of the quillons. (In this specimen the knuckle-bow is unfortunately broken.)*

———3. *Transition Rapier, with small-sword hilt. Quadrangular long blade of Verdun type.*

———4 *Colichemarde. The hilt, probably by Liegeber of Nurnberg, is ornamented with small full-length figures. (The ricasso of the blade remains uncovered.)*

———5. *Small Sword, close of seventeenth century. Triangular blade very wide at base, but not of " Colichemarde " pattern, uniformly tapering towards the point.*

———6. *Small Sword, temp. Queen Anne. Slender triangular blade and silver hilt.*

———7. *Small Sword, temp. Queen Anne. Round plate, instead of the usual double shell, and " Colichemarde " blade. The pas d'âne being so attenuated, the quillons are kept separate from the knuckle-bow in order to support the plate.*

———8. *Small Sword of same type as No. 6, but with the blade slender throughout.*

SMALL SWORDS. (WAREING FAULDER COLL.)

———9, 10, 11. *Silver-hilted " Colichemardes," temp. William III.*

———12. *Small Sword, with tapering blade, inscribed* Je vous le sacrifie. *Temp., end of Louis XIV.'s reign.*

———13. *Small Sword, temp. Louis XV., with chased hilt.*

———14, 15. *Small Swords, temp. George II.*

———16. *Small Sword, temp. George III., with cut steel hilt.*

SPANISH SWORDS, SEVENTEENTH AND EIGHTEENTH CENTURIES. (BARON DE COSSON'S COLL.)

———17. *Rapier Espada, early seventeenth century.*

———18. *Broadsword (Bilbao, Montante), early seventeenth century.*

———19. *Cavalry Sword (Sable), late eighteenth century.*

———20. *Small Sword (Espadin), late eighteenth century.*

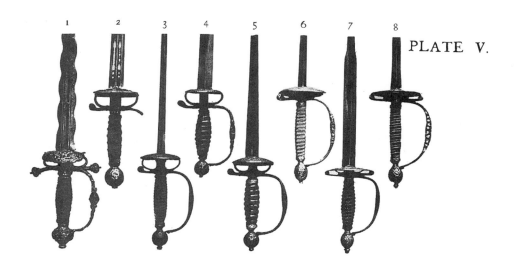

PLATE V.

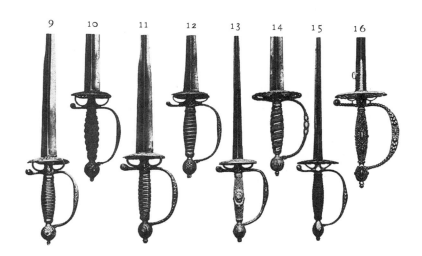

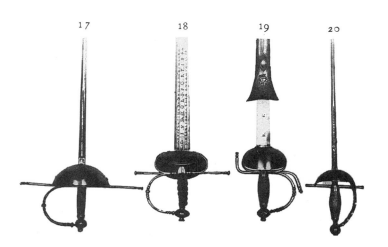

The first is the plain shape—which may be called conventional—with a double-edged blade, some eight or ten inches long, and a simple cross hilt, with or without a side ring.

The second is a great improvement on the first : the quillons are very much curved forward, so as to be capable of engaging the adversary's sword, and even stopping a cut. With such a weapon it was quite possible, after meeting the adverse blade on a parry, to hold it prisoner by a well-timed twist, inside or out, long enough to allow of a deliberate thrust with the sword. The name of "forked" dagger may be given to this shape; it is undoubtedly the one best suited for fencing. In many of these the side ring is replaced by a third quillon, incurving towards the point symmetrically with the other two. On the inside of the blade a well-marked depression or thumb seat is generally hollowed out. The blades of such daggers are usually double-edged, somewhat thick, and varying from eight to twelve inches in length.

These two forms were the most commonly employed, as they were practical for general use as well as mere fencing.

The third form—the Spanish *shell* dagger, the " main gauche "[1] of the French—which is more elaborate, has been already referred to on page 236. It combined the advantages of the target, or " broquel," and the dagger, and was especially convenient with very heavy rapiers, but although some of them have their blades fashioned so as to be able to engage the opponent's sword (see

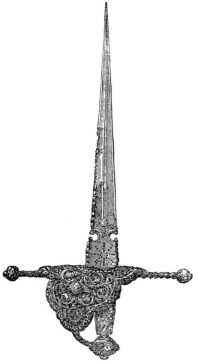

Fig. 141.—Spanish Shell Dagger (main gauche), close of sixteenth century. From Lacombe's " Armes et Armures."

Specimens, Plate IV.), they must have been decidedly inferior to the forked daggers for that purpose. Shell daggers always have very long straight quillons; they were generally used with the long cup-hilted rapier of the Spanish type. All the peculiarities of blade and hilt observable in the

---

[1] The name of " main gauche " is especially applied to this weapon by many writers, apparently because it would be of little use except as a left-hand dagger for fencing. It is needless to remark that the name would apply equally well to fencing daggers of any kind.

sword are reproduced in its companion dagger, as may be seen in the best specimens.

The dagger fell completely into disuse for fencing purposes, even in Spain and Italy, soon after the seventeenth century; in the latter days of its existence it was of a very much reduced type, approximating to that of the " stiletto," and its guard consisting merely of straight quillons with a small ring, the blade as usual reproducing in its slenderness the character of that of the sword.[1]

Mention has been made several times in the course of this book of the various kinds of foils[2] used for practice, which it may be well to recapitulate here.

Until the middle of the seventeenth century, when " fioreti " or " fleurets "[3] were devised, rebated swords were always employed in cut-and-thrust rapier practice. The flexible fleuret could only be used when the play was restricted to the point.

Rebated swords[4] were usually of the same form as the rapier they stood for, but had a simpler guard. During the seventeenth and early eighteenth

[1] The very vicious-looking and somewhat fantastic so-called " Sword-breakers," represented as usual fencing weapons of the " main gauche " class by so many writers on Arms and Armour, never were at any time but the result of individual fantasy. As fencing implements, notwithstanding their elaborateness and forbidding appearance, they are decidedly inferior to any ordinary dagger. If they were ever used at all, it was probably in the right hand and alone, not in conjunction with the rapier. No mention of them is ever made in old books of fence, and their date must be ascribed as *anterior* to the sixteenth century.

[2] See Introduction, p. 7.

[3] See pp. 134, 139, 145.

[4] These rebated swords were formidable implements to practice withal, and from all accounts the acquisition of skill in rapier-play must have been purchased at the cost of much bruising and the risk of serious accidents.

Saviolo informs us that gloves of mail were used on both hands, and there is internal evidence in many works of the same period that shirts of mail or a breastplate and a kind of skull-cap were worn for serious practice, but no protection was devised for the nether limbs.

" I have bruised my shin at rapier and dagger play with a master of fence," says Master Slender, but all devotees of the fence schools were familiar with such slight drawbacks.

Lord Sanquire was hanged in the days of James I. for the revengeful murder of an " Alsatian " master named Turner, who had accidentally put out his eye.

In the seventeenth century the mail gloves were replaced by buff gauntlets, for rapier-play; and with the *small sword*, long soft leather gloves, similar to those still worn in Italian fencing schools, were generally adopted.

Masks (see p. 151 and note on p. 171) were not universally adopted until quite the end of the eighteenth century. The heavy " stick helmet" used in sabre or stick-play seems to have been invented in Germany during the last century.

PLATE VI.

SYNOPSIS OF SOME TYPICAL FORMS OF THE SWORD FROM THE MIDDLE AGES
TO THE EIGHTEENTH CENTURY.

——1. *Sword, early fourteenth century, with plain cross hilt, stiff double-edged blade and disk pummel.*

——2. *Ancient Gothic two-handed Sword (attributed to Wallace).*

——3. *Italian Sword, end of fifteenth century, with square Venetian pummel, quillons horizontally counter-curved, and long flat blade.*

——4. *Braquemar, middle sixteenth century, with short broad blade, incurved quillons, imperfect pas d'âne, and broad side ring.*

——5. *Two Hander, early sixteenth century, with long blade (5′1″) and extraordinarily long quillons. Inscribed* Je pense plus.

——6. *Elizabethan Rapier, close of sixteenth century.*

——7. *Italian Rapier, close of sixteenth century, with ringed guard and blade of prodigious length (5′5″).*

——8. *Elizabethan Rapier (blade 4′2″ long).*

——9. *Rapier with conventional bar hilt. (Blade 5′1″ long.)*

——-10. *German Rapier, close of sixteenth century, showing straight quillons, with side ring, pas d'âne and shells.*

——11. *Rapier, first years seventeenth century, with small hilt, showing an approach to the Transition shape.*

——12. *Italian flamboyant Sword. Hilt without pas d'âne.*

——13. *Venetian Schiavona, with Spanish blade inscribed* Vn Dios una Ley y un Rey. *Date, about* 1570.

——14. *Venetian Schiavona, with Spanish blade inscribed* Viva el Rey de Espana. *Date, about* 1580.

——15. *Venetian Schiavona in its original sheath. Date about* 1580.

——16. *Venetian Schiavona.* 1590.

——17. *Italian basket-hilted Sword, by* ANDREA FERRARA.

——18. *Transition Rapier, early seventeenth century.*

——19. *Broadsword, temp. Charles I. Blade by* ANDREA FERRARA.

——20. *Long Horseman's Sword (Claymore), middle seventeenth century.*

——21. *Rapier or Spadroon without pas d'âne, middle seventeenth century. Blade inscribed* Sahagum.

——22. *Broadsword, latter part of seventeenth century, by* ABRAHAM STAMM, SOLINGEN.

——23. *Colichemarde with silver hilt, temp. Charles II.*

——24. *Small Sword, temp. George I.*

PLATE VI.

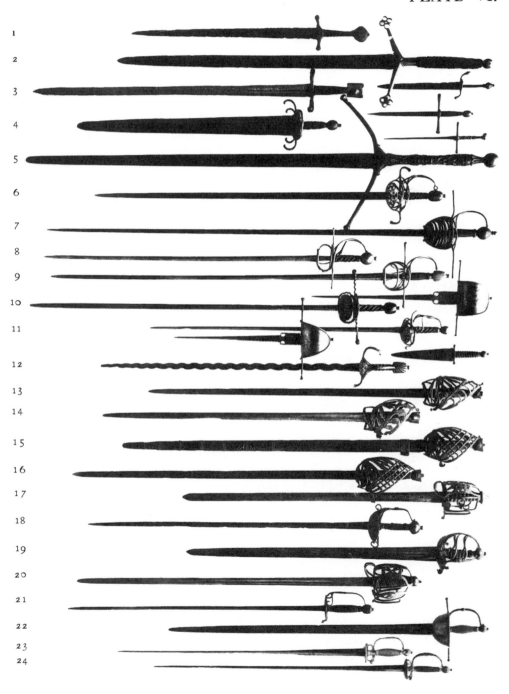

1
2
3
4
5
6
7
8
9
10
11
12
13
14
15
16
17
18
19
20
21
22
23
24

centuries foil blades were likewise mounted in sword hilts of the usual form, except in the case of the conventional French fleuret.[1] Angelo's " Ecole des Armes " shows the foil with a small cup hilt, but without pas d'âne. It was in the last years of the eighteenth century that the French " lunette " guard was devised. This so-called lunette, which may be looked upon as the outline of double-shell, was adopted as being the lightest guard possible.

Practice with cutlass, Düsack, or falchion was carried on with broad curved wooden lathes, provided at one end with a hole for the insertion of the hand,[2] similar in fact to the lower specimen of Düsack represented on p. 77. In England the " waster "—which seems to have been a dummy sword, either with a rounded blade, or one transversely set, so that only the flat could be used—was the " foil " of the back sword during the sixteenth century. Later on, during the early part of the next, wasters are described as cudgels inserted in sword guards.

When the basket hilt came into general use in this country, about the second quarter of the seventeenth century, the cudgel was employed with such a hilt, or sometimes with a wicker-work basket similar to that of the inferior kind of modern single-stick.[3] Later on the basket hilt was universally adopted.

Nowadays the small sword is represented in England by the Court sword, and in France by the " épée de combat; " both have preserved the light triangular blade, but the shells of the latter (the *double-shell* guard is, perhaps, the most common) have resumed larger dimensions since the total abandonment by the French of the pas d'âne, which formerly held them slightly in advance of the guard, and consequently allowed smaller ones to be as effective.

The Italians have preserved the rapier form, with cup, pas d'âne, and quillons, but with a slender quadrangular blade.

Out of France and Italy the duelling sword is but little used; in the

[1] See p. 139.

[2] A mail gauntlet was a necessity with such a rough implement, all but devoid of any protection for the hand.

[3] The word single-stick bears the same relation to the staff, or two-handed stick, as the back sword did to the "long sword" or "two-hander."

The single-stick or the cudgel was, and is, the foil of the back sword, and the staff replaced the long sword in fencing practice. The French use to this day a wooden sword for sabre practice, very similar to the foil of the sixteenth century Düsack.

latter country even, and in Germany, the Spadroon is the most favourite weapon.

In conclusion, it may be remarked—and the wiser portion of the community will probably do so with satisfaction—that duelling of any kind, which in England is a thing of the past, on the Continent is everywhere on the wane, and that the days seem not so very distant when the " Noble Science of Defence," however assiduously pursued in sport, will never need to be put to the test in earnest except on military duty.

BIBLIOGRAPHY.

Sixteenth, Seventeenth, and Eighteenth Centuries.

BIBLIOGRAPHY.

BOOKS relating to the art of fencing are on the whole fairly numerous, since upwards of 400 such works are known to have been published between 1474 and 1884. Nevertheless, as is the case with most special works, *old* books of this kind are excessively difficult to find, owing probably to the fact that most of them were only printed in limited numbers, generally for circulation among the author's pupils. Indeed, in the case of the more important and expensive treatises, the number of copies was practically limited to that of the subscribers.

Besides their small circulation, such treatises are likely to have been much neglected, being of little interest to the merely practical fencer, and offering small attractions to the ordinary bibliophile unless they contained valuable engravings. A good collection of fencing works is consequently a rarity, as the love of old books and a taste for the art of fighting form a combination not often to be found in one and the same man.

It is presumably for the same reason that so little has been written on the *bibliography* of fencing,—the only handy source of information being notices under the head " Fechtkunst " to be found in some German cyclopædias.

A good many years ago a very copious list of books on sword-play was compiled by Mr. W. F. Foster, which, however, being only to be found in some back numbers of " Notes and Queries," has not proved as useful as it might be. Several works mentioned in these pages have been extracted from his list, but it is difficult to believe in the authenticity of some of them, the information concerning which seems to have been somewhat indiscriminately received. Such books are noted with a query after their date.

A want felt by all those interested in the Art of Fence was to a great extent met by Monsieur Vigeant, one of the most eminent of Paris fencing-masters, who brought out in 1882 a fascinating little volume, " La Bibliographie de l'Escrime Ancienne et Moderne."

Besides being a most accomplished master of his art, M. Vigeant is a connoisseur of books and engravings, a very facile writer in the Parisian journalistic style, and the author of several books as artistic in appearance as they are sparkling in tone.

His work, the first of its kind, was greeted with delight by the fencing community ; but, notwithstanding its great value,—chiefly on account of the notes of such a well-known master of the sword,—as it omitted many very important works, it left room for further researches.

The following pages dealing only with authors who lived *before* the beginning of the century, contain no less than fifty-four different books unnoticed in the " Bibliographie de l'Escrime," besides many details concerning others, the titles only of which were registered in that work.

Out of the 230 books here described, fifty-five are to be found in the British Museum, some twenty more existing in the Bodleian and the South Kensington Libraries. The fact has been recorded in each instance among other details concerning the work.

The titles of many old-fashioned books may be often looked upon as a kind of preface, detailing minutely the nature of their contents. Such details, likely to prove interesting when the books themselves are not obtainable, have been fully given whenever it was possible, together with the dedication, the number and nature of plates, the names of the printer and bookseller, &c.

The chronological (instead of the more common alphabetical order) and division into languages have been adopted for the sake of greater facility in referring to any particular period. Among the German will be found all works, including some in French and Latin, printed on German presses. A few books in the French language, printed in England for the use of English fencers, have similarly been ranked with the English. Portuguese and Spanish books have been classed together.

Assuming, for the sake of comparison, that the bibliography given in this book is approximately complete, it seems that Italy brought out, during the sixteenth century, sixteen different printed works or editions, Germany five, Spain four, England and France three each.

During the seventeenth century : Italy thirty-one, Spain twenty-eight, Germany twenty-six, France fourteen, England seven.

During the eighteenth century : England twenty-seven, Germany twenty-five, France twenty-two, Spain seven, Italy six.

Altogether, fifty-six German, fifty-three Italian, thirty-nine Spanish, thirty-nine French, and thirty-seven English.

SPANISH.

——JAYME (Jaume or Jacobus) PONS (or PONA) de Majorca.   Perpiñan.   1474.

——PEDRO DE LA TORRE (or PETRUS DE TURRI).   Same date.
Don Luis Pacheco de Narvaez, Morsicato Pallavicini, and Antonio Marcelli (see 1600, Spain ; and 1670, 1686, Italy) mention in biographical notes these two authors, as having written, in Spanish, on the art of fencing.   Their works, however, have never been discovered.

——FRANCISCO ROMAN. *Tratado de Esgrima.* With plates.   Folio.   Sevilla.   1532.
This, no doubt, is not the true title.   It is given on the authority of Almirante's *Biblio-grafía Militar.*

——JERONIMO DE CARRANZA.   *De la filosofia de las armas, de su destreza y de la agresion y defension Christiana.*   Luciferi Fano (vulgo San Lucar).   4°.   1569.
(See 1582.)

——*Los cinco libros sobre la ley de la lujuria, de palabra o de obra, en que se incluyen las verdaderas resoluciones de la honra, y los medios con que se satisfacen las afrentas, escritos por el Comendador* JERONIMO SANCHEZ DE CARRANZA, *natural de esta ciudad de Sevilla, Caballero del habito de Cristo.*   MS. Pag. 300.   4°.

——*Libro de* JERONIMO DE CARRANZA, *que trata de la filosofia de las armas y de su destreza, y de la agresion y defension Christiana.*   San Lucar de Barrameda.
4°.   Lisbon.   1582.
At the end : *Acabóse este libro de speculation de la destreza año 1569; imprimióse en la ciudad de San Lucar de Barrameda en casa del mismo autor, por mandato del Exemo Señor D. Alonso Perez de Gusman, el Bueno, Duque de Medina Sidonia, &c., &c.*
Portrait of the author.   (See also 1600.)

——The *Bibliotheca Hispana nova. Nicolas Antonio. Madrid.* 1783, mentions the existence of the following MSS. in this wise :
Scripsit F. FRANCISCUS GARÇIA, *Mercenariorum Sodalis* . . . . . etc.: *Verdadera intelligencia de la destreza de las armas del Comendador Geronymo Sanchez Carranza de Barreda* (Barameda ?).
Extat MS. *inter libros qui* . . . . . *nunc sunt excelentissimæ comitissæ.*

——*Scripsit* GUNDISALVUS DE SILVA, *qui se vocat Centurionem (seu Capitaneum, vulgo) : Compendio de la verdadera destreza de las armas. In Villaumbrosana bibliotheca.*   MS.   4°.

——*Anonymus, in bibliotheca Villaumbrosana extans, scripsit: De la destreza de las armas.*

MS. 4°.

——*Anonymus alius scripsit: Libro del Exercicio de las armas. In bibliotheca Escurialensi regia.*

MS.

——The work of JERONIMO DE CARRANÇA (see 1569) was reprinted in Madrid.

4°. 1600.

——*Libro de las grandezas de la Espada, en que se declaran muchos secretos del que compuso el Comendador Geronimo de Carranza. En el cual cada uno se podra liçionar y deprender a solas, sin tener necessitad de maestro que lo enseñe.*
    Dirigido a Don Felipe III., Rey de las Españas y de la mayor parte del Mundo, N.S.
    Compuesto por D. LUYS PACHECO DE NARVAEZ, *natural de la Ciudad de Baeça,* etc., etc.   4°. Madrid. 1599-1600.
    Por los herederos de J. Iniquez de Lequerica. Este libro tiene 8° pliegos, vendese en la Calle de Santiago.
    Portrait of Don Luis, two figures, and 155 diagrams, woodcut, in the text.
    Approbation and royal privilege. In the Brit. Mus.

——*Cien conclusiones, o formas de saber, de la verdadera destreza, fundada en ciencia, y diez y ocho contradicciones a las de la comun, por* D. LUIS PACHECO DE NARVAEZ.
    Apud Lodovicum Sanchez.   Folio. Matriti. 1608.

——*Compendio de la filosofia y destreza de las armas de Geronimo de Carrança, por* DON LUIS PACHECO DE NARVAEZ.   4°. Madrid. 1612.
    A. Don F. de Rojas y Sandoval, segundo duque de Cea. En Madrid por L. Sanchez.
    Woodcuts in the text.

——DON ATANASIO DE AYALA. *El bisoño instruido en la disciplina militar.*

8°. Madrid. 1616.

    This is a military handbook for the instruction of recruits in the use of arms.

——G. S. DE CARRANZA. *Discurso de armas y letras, sobre las palabras del proemio de la instituta del Emperador Justiniano, &c., &c.*   MS. Pag. 28. 4°. Sevilla. 1616.

——DON LUIS PACHECO DE NARVAEZ. *Carta al Duque de Cea, diciendo su parecer acerca del libro de Geronimo de Carrança. De Madrid en quatro de Mayo.*

8°. Madrid. 1618.

——*Apología de la destreza de las armas. Defensa del libro de Carranza sobre ello. Por* D. JUAN FERNANDO PIZARRO.   8°. Trujillo. 1623.

——*Modo facil y nuevo para examinarse los Maestros en la destreza de lars armas y entender sus cien conclusiones, o formas de saber.*
Dirigido al Señor Wolfango Guillermo, Conde Palatino del Rhin, &c., &c.
Por DON LUIS PACHECO DE NARVAEZ, *Maestro del Rey, Nuestro Señor, en la filosofia y destreza de las armas, y mayor en los Reynos de España.*   8°. Madrid. 1625.
Printed by Luis Sanchez. Approbation. In the Brit. Mus.

——*Engaño y desengaño de los errores que se han querido introducir en la destreza de las armas,* *por* DON LUIS PACHECO DE NARVAEZ.   4°. Madrid. 1635.

——*Engaño y desengaño de los errores en la destreza de las armas, por* DON PEDRO MEXIA DE TOBAR.   4°. Madrid. 1636.

——*Advertencias para la enseñanza de la destreza de las armas, asi a pie como a cavallo, por* DON LUIS PACHECO DE NARVAEZ.   4°. Madrid. 1639.

——DIAZ DE VIEDMA. *Epitome de la enseñanza de la filosofia y destreza matematica de las armas.*   8°. Cadiz. 1639.

——*Compendio en defensa de la doctrina y destreza de Carranza, por* LUIS MENDEZ DE CARMONA.   4°. Sevilla. 1640.

——CRISTOBAL DE CALA. *Desengaño de la Espada y Norte de diestros.*   4°. Cadiz. 1642.
In the B. Nacional.

——A second edition of D. LUIS PACHECO DE NARVAEZ's *Modo facil para examinarse . . . . . etc.* (see 1625) was printed *por los herederos de Pedro Lanaja, impressores del Reino de Aragon y de la Universidad* in Zaragoça.   8°. 1658.
With this book is often to be found, as an appendix:
Adicion a la filosofia de las armas. Las diez y ocho contradiciones de la comun destreza, por el mismo autor. Año M.DC.LX. In the Brit. Mus.

——*Defensa de la doctrina y destreza de las armas, por* DON MIGUEL PEREZ DE MENDOZA.   4°. Madrid. 1665.

——*Resumen de la verdadera destreza en el manejo de la Espada, por* D. GOMEZ ARRIAS DE PORRES.   4°. Salamanca. 1667.
Por Melchor Estevez.
In the BB. Nacional y de Fernandez San Roman.

——*Nueva ciencia y filosofia de la destreza de las armas, su teorica y prática.*

A la Magestad de Felipe quarto, Rey, y Senor Nuestro, de las Españas y de la mayor parte de Mundo.

Por DON LUIS PACHECO DE NARVAEZ, *su maestro, y mayor en todos sus Reynos y Señorios.*   8°. Madrid. 1672.

A costa de Manuel de Sossa, assensista de su Magestad, por Melchor Sanchez. Approbation and license.

——DON MIGUEL PEREZ DE MENDOZA Y QUIXADA. *Principios de los cinco sujetos principales de que se compone la filosofia y matematica de las Armas, práctica y especulativa.*
                                                        8°. Pamplona. 1672.

In the BB. de Ingenieros, del Senado, de Fernandez San Roman.

——*Compendio de los fundamentos de la verdadera destreza y filosofia de las armas.*

Dedicado a la Catolica, Sacra y Real Magestad del Rey, Nuestro Señor, Don Carlos Segundo, Monarca de España y de las Indias.

Por DON FRANCISCO ANTONIO ETTENHARD, *Cavallero del Orden de Calatrava.*   4°. Madrid. 1675.

Con Privilegio.   En Madrid por Antonio de Zafra.

Sixteen copperplates.

To the above is generally found joined a smaller work, entitled as follows:

Siguese el papel de Juan Caro, en que impugna la obra con Quince Oiepciones, y la respuesta de el Autor a ellas.

With one copperplate.   In the Brit. Mus.

——*Cornucopia numerosa.*

Alfabeto breve de principios de la verdadera destreza y filosofia de las armas, colegidos de las obras de Luis Pacheco de Narvaez, por D. GASPAR AGOSTIN DE LARA.
                                                        4°. Madrid. 1675.

In the BB. Nacional, de Fernandez San Roman, de Mariátegui.

——*Resumen de la verdadera destreza de las armas, en treinta y ocho asserciones resumidas y advertidas con demonstraciones prácticas, deducidas de las dos obras principales que tiene escritas su autor.*

Por DON MIGUEL PEREZ DE MENDOZA Y QUIXADA, *quien aliciona y enseña la Destreza a su Alteza el Serenissimo Señor D. Baltasar Carlos (que Dios tiene), de la camara de Serenissimo Señor, Don Juan de Austria, y su Maestro de la Destreza, Natural de la ciudad de Logroño.*   4°. Madrid. 1675.

In the BB. de Ingenieros, del Senado, de Fernandez San Roman.

——THOMAS LUIS. *Tratado das lições da Espada preta, e destreza com que hão de usar os jugadores della.*   *29 pag. 8° y 1 lamina.*   Folio. Lisboa. 1685.

——*Resumen de la verdadera destreza para saber los caminos verdaderos de la batalla, por* D. J. ANTONIO ARRIETA, ARANDA Y MORENTIN.   8°. Pamplona. 1688.

——LORENZ DE RADA. *Respuesta filosofica y matematica en la cual se satisfece a los argumentos y proposiciones, que a los profesores de la verdadera destreza y filosofia de las Armas se han propuesto por un papel expedido sin nombre d'autor.*   4°. Madrid. 1695.
  Por Diego Martinez, Abad.
  In the BB. Nacional y de Fernandez San Roman.

——D. DIEGO REJON DE SYLVA. *Definiciones de la Ciencia de las armas.*
                                         8°.· Orihuela. 1697.

——*Diestro Italiano y Español. Explican sus doctrinas con evidencias mathematicas conforme a los preceptos de la verdadera destreza y filosofia de las armas.*
  Dedicado a la Catholica, Sacra y Real Magestad del Rey Nuestro Señor, monarca de España y de las Indias, por DON FRANCISCO ANTONIO DE ETTENHARD Y ABARCA, *Cavallero del Orden de Calatrava, Capitan teniente de la Real Guardia Alemana de su Magestad.*   4°. Madrid. 1697.
  En la imprenta de Manuel Ruiz de Murga. Four copperplates.
  In the BB. de Ingenieros, del Senado, de Fernandez San Roman.   In the Brit. Mus.

——*Las tretas de la vulgar y comun esgrima de Espada sola, y con armas dobles, que aprobo don Luis Pacheco de Narvaez, y las oposiciones que dispusó en verdadera destreza de ella, por* D. MANUEL CRUZADO Y PERALTA.   4°. Zaragoza. 1702.
  In the BB. de Fernandez San Roman y de Mariátegui.

——LORENZ DE RADA. *Nobleza de la Espada, cuyo resplendor se expresa en tres libros, segun Ciencia, Arte y Experiencia.*   Folio. Madrid. 1705.
  Printed at the Royal Printing Press.
  In the BB. Nacional y de Fernandez San Roman.

——*Experiencia del instrumento armigero espada. Por el Maestro de Campo* D. FRANCISCO LORENZ DE RADA.   Folio. Madrid. 1705.
  En Madrid, por Diego Martinez, abad, impresor de libros; vide en la calle de la Gorguera.
  Sixteen copperplates.

——*Ilustracion de la destreza indiana, epistola oficiosa que escribió* SANTOS DE LA PAZ, *al Maestro de campo Don F. Lorenz de Rada, &c., &c., sobre varios discursos publicados por el en la que intituló defensa de la verdadera destreza de las armas.*
  Sacala a luz el Capitan Diego Rodriguez de Guzman, etc., etc.   4°. Lima. 1712.

——D. NICOLAS RODRIGO NOVELI. *Crisol especulativo de la destreza de las armas.*
                                         8°. Madrid. 1731.

——MANUEL MARTINS FIRME. *Espada firme o firme trattado para o jogo de espada preta e branca.*   Folio xxxvi-86. 8º. Evora. 1744.

  In the B. de J. C. de Figaniere.

——*Arte de esgrimir florete y sable, por los principios mas seguros, faciles y intelligibles.*
  Por D. JUAN NICOLAS PERINAT, *Maestro de Esgrima en la Real Academia de Cavalleros Guardias Marinas, primera obra tocante a este Arte.*

            Oblong. 4º. Cadix. 1758.

  At the end : *En la imprenta de la Real Academia de Cavalleros Guardias Marinas.*
Thirty-six copperplates.

——RODRIGUEZ DE CARVALHO. *Resumo breve do Jogo de Florete em dialogo para cualquier curioso se applicar ao serio estudio desta brilhante arte.*
  Traduzido dos melhores Auctores Francéses.   8º. Lisboa. 1804.

——DON MANUEL LOSA. *Nueva ciencia de la destreza de las armas.*

ITALIAN.

——Morsicato Pallavicini and Antonio Marcelli (see 1670 and 1686) mention PIETRO MONCIO as the author of a treatise on fencing printed in 1509. The book does not seem to be extant.

——*Di* ANTONIO MANCIOLINO, *Bolognese, opera nova dove sono tutti li documenti e vantaggi che si ponno havere nel mestier de l'Armi d'ogni sorte, novemente corretta et stampata.*
  Per N. d'Aristotile, detto Zoppino.   16º. Vinegia. 1531.
  A few woodcuts unconnected with the text. In the Brit. Mus.

——*Opera nova di* ACHILLE MAROZZO, *Bolognese, Maestro Generale de l'arte de l'Armi.*
            4º. Mutinæ. 1536.
  At the end is found this notice : *Mutinæ, in ædibus venerabilis D. Antonii Bergola Sacerdotis ac civis Mutin. XXIII Idus Maii.*
  Eighty-two woodcuts. In the Brit. Mus. and South Kens.

——A second edition of ACHILLE MAROZZO's work (see 1536) appeared in Venetia.
                4º. 1550.
  Stampata per Giovane Padouana, Ad instantia de Marchior Sessa.   In the Brit. Mus.

——MARC ANTONIO PAGANO.   *Disciplina dell' Arme.*   4°.   Napoli.   1553.

——*Trattato di Scientia d'Arme, con un dialogo di filosofia, di* CAMILLO AGRIPPA, *Milanese.*
                                       4°.   Roma.   1553.
In Roma per Antonio Blado, stampadore apostolico. Con privilegio de N. Signore Papa Giulio III., per anni dieci.
Portrait of Agrippa, and fifty-five copperplates in the text. Dedicated to Cosimo de Medici. In the Brit. Mus.

——A third edition of ACHILLE MAROZZO's work (see 1536), though bearing no date or printer's name, is presumed to have appeared in 1568.   4°.
This presumption is based on the great similarity of its typographical character with that of the following edition, although the text is slightly, and the plates altogether different.

——*Arte dell Armi de* ACHILLE MAROZZO, *Bolognese, ricorretto et ornato di nuove figure in rame.*   4°.   Venetia.   1568.
Copperplates in the text.
This fourth edition, which contains more matter than the previous ones, was brought out under the care of the painter Giulio Fontana, and printed by A. Pinargenti. In the Brit. Mus.

——*Di* M. CAMILLO AGRIPPA.   *Trattato di scienza d'arme, et un dialogo in detta materia.*
                                      4°.   Venetia.   1568.
Like the preceding book, this edition of Agrippa was printed by A. Pinargenti, and dedicated to Don Giovanni Manriche by the painter Giulio Fontana.
Portrait of the author, and forty-nine copperplates in the text. In the Brit. Mus.

——*Ragione di adoprar sicuramente l'Arme, si da offesa come da difesa; con un trattato dell' inganno, et con un modo di esercitarsi da se stesso, per acquistare forza, giudicio et prestezza.*
Di GIACOMO DI GRASSI, *da Modena.*   4°.   Venetia.   1570.
Appresso Giorgio de' Cavalli.
Some copies bear the indication : *Appresso Giordano Ziletti.*
Portrait of Grassi, and copperplates in the text. In the Brit. Mus. and Bodl.

——*Del Arte di scrimia libri tre di* M. GIOVANNI DALL' AGOCCHIE, *Bolognese. Ne quali brevemente si tratta dell' Arte dello Schermire, della Giostra, dell' ordinar battaglie. Opera necessaria a Capitani, Soldati et a qual si voglia Gentil'huomo.*   4°.   Venetia.   1572.
Appresso G. Tamborino. Con Privilegio.
Dedicated to Conte F. Pepoli. In the Brit. Mus.

——*Lo Schermo d'*ANGELO VIGGIANI, *dal Montone da Bologna. Nel quale, per via di dialogo*

si discorre intorno all' eccelenza dell' Armi et delle lettere, et intorno all offesa et difesa.   Et insegna uno Schermo di Spada sola sicuro e singolare con una tavola copiosissima.   4°. Venetia. 1575.
    Appresso Giorgio Angelieri.
    Nine copperplates in the text.   In the Bodl. and South Kens.

——*Nuovo et breve modo di Schermire di* ALFONSO FALLOPIA, *Lucchese, Alfiere nella Fortezza di Bergamo.*   4°. Bergamo. 1584.
    Appresso Comin Ventura.

——Viggiani's work (see 1575) was reproduced under the care of Zacharia Cavalcabo.
    The author's name was spelt ANGELO VIZANI in accordance with the soft pronunciation of the Venetians, among whom he had so long taught fencing.   4°. Bologna. 1588.
    Per Gio. Rossi—con licenza de Superiori.   All' illustrissimo Signore, il Sig. Conte Pirro Malvezzi.
    The text is slightly altered from the first edition, and a portrait of Viggiani is added to the plates.   In the Brit. Mus. and Bodl.

——MS. *Discorso di* CAMILLO PALLADINI, *Bolognese, sopra l'arte della Scherma; come l'arte della Scherma e necessaria a chi si diletta d'Arme.*   Obl. 4°.   1590 (?)
    Forty-two drawings in red chalk, imitated from the plates in Agrippa's treatise.   In M. Vigeant's collection.

——*Trattato in materia di Scherma di* MARCO DOCCIOLINI, *Fiorentino.   Nel quale si contiene il modo e regolo d'adoperar la spada, cosi sola come accompagnata.*   4°. Firenze. 1601.
    Nella stamperia di Michelangiolo Sermatelli.
    Dedication to Don Giovanni Medici.

——*Essercitio Militare il quale dispone l'huomo a vera cognitione del Scrimire di Spada et dell'ordinare l'Essercito a battaglia, etc., etc.*
    Di GIOVANNI ALBERTO CASSANI, *di Frasinello di Monserrato.*
                                         4°. Napoli. 1603.
    This is rather a general handbook of the military art than a treatise on fencing.   In the Brit. Mus.

——A third edition of CAMILLO AGRIPPA (see 1553) was printed *In Venetia.*
    In the Brit. Mus. and Bodl.   4°.   1604.

——*De lo Schermo, overo scienza d'arme, di* SALVATOR FABRIS, *Capo del Ordine dei sette cuori.*   Folio. Copenhassen. 1606.
    Printed by Henrico Waltkirch.   Frontispiece: Portraits of the King of Denmark, Christian IV., to whom the work is dedicated, and of the author.
    190 copperplates in the text, by A. Halbeek.   In the Brit. Mus.

———*Teatro, nel qual sono rappresentate diverse maniere e mode di parare et di ferire di Spada sola, e di Spada e pugnale; dove ogni studioso potrà essercitarsi e farsi prattico nella proffessione dell' Armi.*
Di NICOLETTO GIGANTI, *Vinitiano.*   Oblong 4°. Venetia. 1606.
Al Sereniss. D. Cosmo di Medici.
Appresso Gio. Antonio et G. de Franceschi.
Frontispiece, with the Medici arms, portrait of the author, and forty-two copperplates out of the text. In the Brit. Mus.

———A second edition of the above appeared *in Venegia.*   Oblong 4°. 1608.

———*Gran simulacro dell'arte e dell uso della Scherma di* RIDOLFO CAPO FERRO *da Cagli, Maestro dell' eccelsa natione alemanna, nell' inclita Città di Siena.*   Oblong 4°. Siena. 1610.
Dedicato al Serenissimo Sig. Don Federigo Feltrio della Rovere, Principe dello stato d'Urbino.
In Siena, al sopportico de Pontani. Appresso Saluestro Marchetti e Camillo Turi, con licentia de' Superiori e con Privilegi.
Portraits of the Duca d'Urbino and of Capo Ferro, and forty-three copperplates engraved by Rafael Schiamirossi. In the South Kens.

———E. TORQUATO. *Precetti sulla Scherma.*   8°. Roma. 1610 (?)

———*Opera intorno alla Prattica e Theorica del ben adoperare tutte le sorti di arme; overo, la Scienza dell' Arme, da* GIOVANNI ANTONIO LOVINO, *Milanese.*   MS. On vellum. 4°.
Mentioned in *Bibliographie Instruttive.* G. F. de Bure, Paris, 1764. *Vol. Jurisprudence et Arts.*

———*Gioielo di sapienza, nel quale si contengono mirabili secreti e necessarii avertimenti per difendersi da gli huomini e da molti animali, &c.*
Nuovamente dato in luce da me ANTONIO QUINTINO *ad instanza d'ogni spirito gentile.*
                                12°. Genova. Milano. 1613.
Stampata in Genova et ristampata in Milano per Pandolfo Malatesta.
Portrait of the author and fifteen woodcuts in the text.

———A fifth edition of ACHILLE MAROZZO's work (see 1568) appeared in Verona.
                                                     4°. 1615.

———*Arte di maneggiar la Spada a piedi, et a cavallo, descritta dall' Alfiero* GIO. BATTISTA GAIANI *e dedicata ai Serenissimi Principi Vittorio Amadeo e Francesco Tomaso di Savoia.*
Opera per le nuove osservationi già desiderata.   4°. Loano. 1619.
Appresso Francesco Castillo. Con licenza de' Superiori.
In the Brit. Mus.

——*Oplomachia di* BONAVENTURA PISTOFILO, *nella quale* . . . . . *etc\, si tratta per via di Teoria et di Practica del maneggio e dell'uso delle armi.*   4°. Sienna. 1621.

——*Della vera pratica e scienza d'armi* . . . . . *etc.* *Opera di* SALVATOR FABRIS.
                                             Folio. Padova. 1624.
    Per Pietro Paolo Tozzi.

——GIO. ANTONIO LOVINO : *Sull'arte di ben maneggiare la spada.*
Dedicated to Enrico III.
This book is mentioned, as having existed, in Mr. F. W. Foster's list of books on sword-play.

——*Il torneo di* BONAVENTURA PISTOFILO, *Nobile Ferrarese, Dottor di Legge e Cavaliere nel Teatro di Pallade dell'ordine Militare et Accademico.*   4°. Bologna. 1627.
    In Bologna per il Ferrone. Con Licenza de Superiori.
Frontispiece and 114 copperplates, fifteen of which relate to the graceful management of the sword. No text. In the South Kens.

——A second edition of NICOLETTO GIGANTI's work (see 1606) was published in Padua.   Oblong 4°. 1628.
    Printed by Paolo Frambotto. Dedicated to the *illust*ᵐᵒ *Sig. Lazaro Stubicka da Koenigsten.*

——*Giuoco d'arme da* TORELLI.   4°. Venetia? 1632.

——*La Scherma di* F. ALFIERI, *Maestro d'Arme dell' Ill*ᵐᵃ *Accademia Delia in Padova. Dove, con nuove Ragioni e con Figure, si mostra la perfezione di quest'Arte, e in che modo, secondo l'arme e il sito, possa il Cavaliere restar al suo nemico superiore.*
                                      Oblong 4°. Padova. 1640.
    *Dedicata all' Illu*ᵐ *SS. della sopra det·a Accademia. Per Seb. Sardi, con licenza.*
Portrait of the author and 37 copperplates after the manner of Callot. Alfieri wrote also a treatise on the two-handed sword.
    (See 1653.)

——*L'Esercizio della Spada, regolato con la perfetta idea della Scherma et insegnato dalla Maestra-mano di* TERENZIANO CERESA, *Parmegiano, detto l'Eremita. Opera utile e necessaria a chiunque desidera uscire vittorioso dalli colpi della Spada nemica.*   4°. Ancôna. 1641.
    Dedicata al Sig. Tomaso Palunci, nobile Anconitano. Ancôna, per M. Salvioni. Con licenza de' superiori.

——A second edition of F. ALFIERI's work (see 1640) was published in Ancona.
                                             4°. 1645.

——*L'arte di ben maneggiare la Spada, di* FRANCESCO ALFIERI, *maestro d'arme dell'*
illustrissima academia Delia in Padova.   Obl. 4°.   Padova.   1653.
Many copperplates.   In the Brit. Mus.

——*Lo Spadone di* F. ALFIERI, *Maestro d'Arme dell Ill*ma *Academia Delia in Padova.   Dove*
si mostra per via di Figura il maneggio e l'uso di esse.   4°.   Padova.   1653.
Per Sebastiano Sardi.   Con licenza de Superiori.
Seventeen copperplates, many of which are repeated.   In the Brit. Mus.
(See also 1640.)

——*Il vero maneggio della Spada, d'*ALESSANDRO SENESIO, *gentil'huomo bolognese.*
                                                        Folio.   Bologna.   1660.
Dedicato al Sereniss. Principe Fernando Carlo, Arciduca d'Austria.   Per l'Herede di Benacci.
Fourteen copperplates, out of the text.

——*Quesiti del Cavaliere instrutto nell arte della Scherma.*   8°.   Padova.   1664.

——FRANCESCO ANTONIO MATTEI.   *Della Scherma Napoletana.*
Novello de Bonis.   4°.   Foggia.   1669.

——*La Scherma Illustrata, composta da* GIUSEPPE MORSICATO PALLAVICINI, *Paler-*
mitano, Maestro di Scherma, per la di cui teorica, e prattica si puo arrivare con facilita alla difesa ed
offesa necessaria, nell occasioni d'assalti nemici.   Opera utilissima alle persone che si dilettano di questa
professione, con le Figure della, Scienza prattica, dichiarate coi loro discorsi.
                                                        Folio.   Palermo.   1670.
Per Domenico d'Anselmo.   Imp. Cuzolinus G. & V. G. Imp. de la Torre R. P.   Con
privilegio per anni X.
Dedicated *All' ill. Signore D. Francesco Statella et Caruso, Marchese di Spaccafurno, etc.,* etc.
Frontispiece containing the arms of the Marchese di Spaccafurno, and thirty-one copperplates.   In the Brit. Mus.

——*Trattato di Scherma Siciliana, ove si monstra di seconda intentione, con una linea retta : Difendersi*
di qual si voglia operatione di resolutione, che operata per ferire a qualunque, o di punta, o taglio, che
accadesse in accidente di questionarsi.   Aggiunto da GIUSEPPE VILLARDITA.   *Con expressione*
di tutte le regole che nascono di seconda operatione.   12°.   Palermo.   1673.
In Palermo per Carlo Adamo.   Imp. Cuz. G. Lu. Imp. R. Ioppulus P.

——*La seconda parte della Scherma Illustrata, ove si dimostra il vero maneggio della Spada e Pugnale,*
et anco il modo come si adopera la Cappa, il Brochiero, e la Rotella di notte, le quali regole non sono state
intese da nessuno Autore.   Composta da GIUSEPPE MORSICATO PALLAVICINI, *Maestro*
di Scherma Palermitano.
                                                        Folio.   Palermo.   1673.
Per Domenico d'Anselmo, etc.
(See 1670.)

Dedicated : *All. Ill. Sign. e padrone colendissimo il Signor Don Girolamo del Carretto e Branciforte, etc., etc., de' duchi di Sassonia.*

Frontispiece, containing the arms of the Conte di Racalmuto, and thirty-six copperplates. In the Brit. Mus.

——*La Scherma Napolitana di* FRANCESCO MONICA.   4°.   Parma.   1680.

——A second edition of F. F. ALFIERI's *Arte di ben mannegiare la Spada* (see 1653) was published by Sardi, in Padova.   Obl. 4°.   1683.

——*Regole della Scherma insegnate da Lelio e Titta Marcelli, scritte da* FRANCESCO ANTONIO MARCELLI, *figlio e nipote, e Maestro di Scherma in Roma.   Opera non meno utile che necessaria a chiunque desidera far profitto in questa professione.   Dedicata alla sacra Real Maesta di Christina Alessandra, Regina di Suetia.*

Parte Prima: Regole della Spada sola.
Parte Seconda : Regole della Scherma.

Nella quale si spiegano le Regole della Spada e del Pugnale, insegnate da Titta Marcelli ; con le regole di maneggiar la Spada col Brocchiere, Targa, Rotella, Cappa, Lanterna ; col modo di Giocar la Spada contro la Sciabola.   4°, in two parts.   Roma.   1686.

Frontispiece containing the portraits of the Marcelli who were fencing-masters, seven in number.   Copperplates in the text from designs by the author himself.   In the Brit. Mus. and Bodl.

——*La Spada Maestra di me* BONDI DI MAZO, *da Venetia.   Libro dove si trattano i vantaggi della Nobilissima Professione della Scherma, si del caminare, girare e ritirarsi, come del ferire sicuramente e difendersi.*   Obl. 4°.   Venetia.   1696.

Dedicato agl' Illustrissimi e Eccellentissimi Signori Conti di Collalto e San Salvatore.   In Venetia per Dominico Louisa à Rialto, a spese dell' Auttore.   Con Licenza de' Superiori e privilegio.

Eighty copperplates.   In the Brit. Mus.

——MS.   British Museum.   Additional, No. 23223.   A treatise on fencing, in Italian. Forty-seven folios.   Date, about the end of the seventeenth century.

——*Scienza prattica necessaria all' huomo, overo modo per superare la forza coll'uso regolato della Spada.*

Parte Prima, opera di C. CALARONE, *detto l'Anghiel : Maestro di Scherma Messinese.*
                                                   4°.   Roma.   1714.

Dedicata all' Eccellentissimo Signor Don Ignazio Mighaccio de' Principi di Baucina, Principi di Malvagna, Duca di Galizia, etc.   Nella stamparia di Luca Antonio Chracas.   Con licenza de' Superiori.

Portraits of the Duca di Galizia and of the author, engraved on copper, out of the text. Woodcuts in the text.

——*Ragionamenti Accademici intorno all'arte della Scherma di* DI MARCO, *professore di Scherma, Napoletano.*   8°.   Napoli.   1758.

——*Discorsi instruttivi ne quali si tratta in particolare intorno all'arte della Scherma, da* A. DI MARCO.   8°. Napoli. 1759.

——*Riflessioni fisiche e geometriche circa la misura del tempo ed equilibrio di quello e della natural disposizione ed agilità dei competitori, in materia di scherma, e regolamenti essenziali per saggiamente munirsi da ogni inconsiderato periglio sul cimento della spada nuda; da* ALESSANDRO DI MARCO, *Professore di Scherma Napolitano, maestro de' due nobili Collegy Capece e Macedonio, e d'altri cavalieri.*   12°. Napoli. 1761.

    Dedicato all ill. ed exc. Signore Francesco Capece Minutolo, Patrizio Napolitano. Con licenza de' Superiori.

    (See also 1758-9.)

——PICARD ALESSANDRO BREMOND. *Trattato sulla Scherma: traduzione dalla francese nella lingua toscana.*   8°. Milano. Pirola. Date ?

    This book is mentioned, as existing, in Mr. F. W. Foster's list of books on sword-play, but without date.

    The French original seems to be altogether unknown.

——GUIDO ANTONIO DEL MANGANO. *Riflessioni filosofiche sopra l'arte della scherma.*   8°. Pavia. 1781.

——MICHELE MICHELI. *Trattato in lode della nobile e cavalleresca arte della Scherma. Diretto ai Nobili e Cittadini Toscani.*   Small 8°. Firenze. 1798.

    Nella Stamperia granducale. Con approvazione.

——*La Scienza della Scherma esposta dai due amici* ROSAROLL SCORZA, *Capit. dei Zappatori Ital. Agg. allo Stato Magg. del Genio, e* GRISETTI PIETRO, *Capitano di Artiglieria Ital.*   4°. Milano. 1803.

    . . . . . . *Romane, memento*
           Haec tibi erunt artes . . . . . .

  Nella Stamperia del Giornale Italico.
  Ten lithographed plates.

GERMAN.

——HANS LEBKOMMER. *Der Altenn Fechter an fengliche Kunst.*

4°. Franckfurt am Meyn. 1529-36 (?)

Woodcuts from drawings of Albert Durer, by Hans Brosamer, in the text.

——*Fechtkunst, die Ritterlich, mennliche Kunst und Handarbeit Fechtens und Kempfens.*

4°. Franckfurt. 1558.

——*Grundliche Beschreibung der Freyen, Ritterlichen unnd Adelichen Kunst der Fechtens in allerley gebreuchlichen Wehren, mit vil schonen und nutzlichen Figuren gezieret und furgestellet, durch* JOACHIM MEYER, *Freyfechter zu Strasburg.* Oblong 4°. Strasburg. 1570.

At the end : *Getruckt zu Strasburg bey Thiebolt Berger com Weynmarkt zum Treubel.* Numerous woodcuts. In the Bodl.

——A. GUNTERRODT. *De veris principiis artis dimicatoriæ.* 4°. Wittemberg. 1579.

——*Sechs Fechtschulen (d. i. Schau- und Pries-fechten) der Marxbruder und Federfechter, aus den Jahren* 1573 *bis* 1614 ; *Nurnberger Fechtschulreime v. J.* 1579, *una Rosener's Gedicht : Ehrentitel un Lobspruch der Fechtkunst,* 1589.—*Mit einer Abbildung aus Leckuchner's Handschrift uber das Messer (Tesak)—Fechten.* 8°. 1573-1614.

Buchhandlung von Karl Groos.

Published at Heidelberg, 1870.

——A second edition of JOACHIM MEYER's work (see 1570) appeared in Augsburg.

Oblong 4°. 1610.

Getruckt zu Augspurg bey Michael Mauger, in verbegung Eliae Willers. Seventy-three woodcuts. In the Brit. Mus.

——*Ein new Kunstlich Fechtbuch im Rappier zum Fechten und Balgen, u. s. w.* Durch MICH. HUNDT. 4°. Leipsig. 1611.

——*New Kunstliches Fechtbuch, das ist aussfuhrliche Description der Freyen Adelichen und Ritterlichen Kunst dess Fechtens in den gebreuchlichsten Wehren, als Schwerdt, Dusacken, Rappier, &c., &c. Durch den Wolerfahrnen und beruhmten Freyfechtern* JACOB SUTORIUM, *von Baden.*

4°. Franckfurt. 1612.

Gedruckt zu Franckfurt am Mayn durch Johann Bringern. In Verlegung Wilhelm Hoffmans.

Ninety-four woodcuts in the text.   In the Brit. Mus.

A facsimile reproduction of this work was brought out at Stuttgart, by J. Scheible, in 1849.

———*Neues Kunstliches Fechtbuch des Weitherumten und viel erfahrnen Italienischen Fechtmeister* HIERONIMO CAVALCABO, *von Bononien Stievorn, aus dem geschrieben welschem Exemplar durch monsieur de Villamont, Ritter des Ordens zu Jerusalem, etc., etc., in französiche Sprache transferirt. Nun aber allen Loblichen Fechtkunst Liebhabern zu gefallen aus gemelter französischer Sprach verdenselt durch Conrad von Einsidell.*   Oblong 4°. Jena. 1612.

Six copperplates, out of the text.   In the Brit. Mus.

———GARZONII *Allgemeiner Schauplatz.*   Franckfurt. 1619.

———KÖPPEN's *Cours v. d. Fechtkunst.*   Small folio.   Magdeburg.   1619.

———*Der Kunstreichen und weitberumeten Fechtmeisters* S. FABRIS *Italianische Fechtkunst.*
                                      Folio.   Leyden.   1619.

Printed by Isaack Elzevier, and dedicated by the same to Gustavus Adolphus.
The copperplates of the first edition are replaced by woodcuts (192).

———KOPPEN. *Newer Diskurs von der rittermässigen und weitberuhmten Kunst des Fechtens, u. s. w.*
                                Small folio.   Magdeburg.   1619.

———*Grundtliche und eigentliche Beschreibung der freyen Adelichen und Ritterlichen Fecht Kunst im einfachen Rappir und im Rappir und Dolch, nach Italianischer Manir und Art, in zwey underschiedene Bucher ferfast, un mit* 670 *schoenen und nothwendigen Kupfferstucken gezieret und for Augen gestellt. Durch* HANS WILHELM SCHÖFFER, *von Dietz, Fech-Meister in Marpurg. Getruckt zu Marpurgk bey Johan Saurn.*   Oblong 4°.   Marpurg.   1620.

———Another edition of GIGANTI's *Theatre* (see Italy, 1606, France, 1619) appeared, as a French and German translation, in Francfurth.   Obl. 4°.   1622.

In the Brit. Mus.

———*Neu Kunstlich Fechtbuch zum dritten mal auffgelegt und mit vielen schoenen Stucken verbessert. Als des Sig. Salvator Fabri de Padua und Sig. Rud. Capo di Ferro, wie auch anderer Italienischen und Französischen Fechter. Durch* SEBASTIAN HEUSSLER, *Kriegsmann und Freyfechter von Nurnberg. Gedruckt zu Nurnberg durch Simon Halbmayerr.*   Oblong 4°.   Nurnberg.   1630.

In Verlegung Balthasar Gaymoren.
Sixty-two copperplates. (See also 1665.)   In the Brit. Mus.

——SALGEN's *Kriegsubung u. s. w. den frischanfahenden Fechtern und Soldaten fur erst nutzlich und nöthig zu wissen.*   1637.

——MS.   British Museum : Additional, No. 17533.—Three treatises in German on the Art of Fencing, as taught by Signor Sieg. Salvator and Signor Moman, by H. A. V.
                                                              Folio, ff. 127.
Ninety-three figures, drawn by the hand in Indian ink, copied from Fabris' plates.
Date, middle of the seventeenth century.

———THIBAULD.   *Ars digladiatoria.*   Folio.   Amsterdam.   1650.

——A third edition of JOACHIM MEYER's work (see 1570) appeared in Augsburg.
                                                    Oblong 4°.   1660.

——*Von* JOHANN GEORG. PASCHEN.   *Kurze, jedoch deutliche Beschreibung handelnd vom Fechten auf den Stoss und Hieb.*   Folio.   Halle in Sachsen.   1661.
(See also 1664, 1667, 1673, 1683.)

——*Deutliche und Grundliche Erklärung der Adelichen und Ritterlichen freyen Fechtkunst.*
Durch J. D. L'ANGE, *Fechtmeister.*   Oblong 8°.   Heidelberg.   1664.
Getruckt zu Heidelberg bey Adrian Meingarten.
Portrait of Daniel L'Ange, by Metzger, and sixty-one copperplates.

——A second edition of PASCHEN's work (see 1661) appeared in Halle.
In the Brit. Mus.   Folio.   1664.

——JO. GE. TRIEGLER's *neues Kunstliches Fechtbuch.*   4°.   Leipsig.   1664.

——*Kunstliches Abprobites und Nutzliches Fecht-Buch von Einfachen und doppelten Degen Fechten, damit ein ieder seinen Leib defendirn kan.*
      Durch SEBASTIAN HEUSSLER.   Oblong 4°.   Nurnberg.   1665.
      Bey Paulus Fursten, Kunsthandler.
      124 copperplates.
      (See also 1630).

——J. G. PASCHEN.   *Vollstandige Fecht- Ring- und voltigier Kunst.*
                                                    Small folio.   Leipsig.   1667.
      In verlag Johann Simon Fickens und Johann Polycarp Seubolds.

——*Grondige Beschryvinge van de Edele ende Ridderlijcke Scherm-ofte, Wapen Konste, etc.*
Vytgegeven ende aen den Dagh gebracht door JOHANNES-GEORGIUS BRUCHIUS, *Scherm ofte Vecht-Meester der wigt-vermaerde Academie.*   Oblong 4°.   Leyden.   1671.
    Tot Leyden, bi Abraham Verhoef.
Portrait of the author by Van Somer, and 143 copperplates.

——Another edition of PASCHEN's work (see 1667) appeared in Leipsig.
                                    Small folio.   1673.

——*Scienza e pratica d'arme di* SALVATORE FABRIS, *Capo dell' Ordine dei sette cuori.*
Das ist: Herrn Salvatore Fabris, Obristen des Ritter Ordens der Sieben Hertzen, Italianische Fechtkunst.
    Von Johann Joachim Hynitzchen, Exercitien Meister.   4°.   Leipsig.   1677.
    Gedruckt bey Michael Boge.
German translation parallel with the Italian text. The plates are the same as in the original edition, with the addition of one, representing the monument erected to Fabris's memory in Padua, his native town, and of a portrait of a certain Heinrich, who seems to have patronized this reproduction of the great master's work.

——*Der Kunstliche Fechter, oder* THEODORI VEROLINI *Beschreibung des Fechtens im Rappier, Dusacken und Schwerdt.*   4°.   Wurzburg.   1679.

——*Der adelichen gemuthen wohlerfahrne Exercitien-meister, d. i.*
Vollstandige Fecht- Ring- und Voltigier Kunst, von JOH. GEORG. PASCHEN.
    Bei Christian Weidermannen.   Small folio.   Franckfurt und Leipsig.   1683.
This book also appeared in Halle in the same year.

——BORATH.   *Palaestra Succana, ou l'art de l'escrime.*   Folio.   Stockholm.   1693.

——*Der geoffnete Fechtboden, auf welchem durch kurtz gefast Regeln gute Anleitung zum rechten Fundament der Fechtkunst, u. s. w. Mit dazu dienlichen Figuren. Ferfertiget, von* Sr. C.
                                   12°.   Hamburg.   1706.

——A second edition of the Italian and German reproduction of SALVATOR FABRIS's work was published in Leipsig.   4°.   1713.

——*Leib-beschirmende und Feinden Trotz-bietende Fecht-Kunst, oder leicht und getreue Anweisung auf Stoss und Hieb zierlich und sicher zu fechten.*
    Nebst einem curieusen Unterricht vom Voltigiren und Ringen.
   Von JOHANN ANDREAS SCHMIDT, *des H. Rom. Reichs Freyen Stadt Nurnberg, bestellter Fecht-und-Exerciten Meister.*   Obl. 8°.   Nurnberg.   1713.

Nurnberg verlegt und zu finden bey Johann Christoph Weigel. Drukts Johann Michael Sporlus sel. Wittwe.

Portrait of the author in his own fencing school, eighty-four copperplates, in and out of the text.   In the Brit. Mus.

———*Neu Alamodische Ritterliche Fecht-und-Schirm Kunst. Das ist Wahre und nach neueter Franzosicher Manier eingerichtete Unterweisung wie man sich in Fechten und Schirmen perfectioniren und verhalten solle.*

Denen respective Herren Liebhaberen zu besserer Erleuterung mit 60 *hierzu deutlichen Figuren herausgegeben, von* ALEXANDER DOYLE, *aus Irrland geburtig.*

(1) Threr Churfurstl Gnaden zu Maintz verordneten Hof-Fechmeistern.

Obl. 4°.   Nürnberg.   1715.

Nurnberg und Franckfurt zu finden, bey Paul Lochnern, Buchhandlern.
In the Brit. Mus.

———*Méthode très facile pour former la noblesse dans l'art de l'épée, faite pour l'utilité de tous les amateurs de ce bel art, par le sieur* JEAN JAMIN DE BEAUPRÉ, *maître en fait d'armes de Son Altesse S. Electorale de Bavière, à la celebre Université d'Ingolstadt.*

On trouvera en ce livre, rangés en ordre, tous les mouvements généralement bien expliqués qui sont necessaires à bien apprendre et à enseigner à faire des armes, en allemand et en français, avec 25 *planches qui représentent toutes les principales actions, à la dernière perfection. Ce jeu est choisi de l'Italien, de l'Allemand, de l'Espagnol et du Français, et composé de manière, par sa grande pratique, qu'on peut l'appeler le Centre des Armes.*

Dedié à Son Altesse Electorale de Bavière.   4°.   Ingolstadt.   1721.
Gedruckt bey T. Gran.

Twenty-five copperplates, out of the text.

———A second edition of ALEXANDER DOYLE's work (see 1715) appeared in Nürnberg.
Obl. 4°.   1729.

———*Anfangsgrunde der Fechtkunst nebst einer Vorrede von dem Nutzem der Fechtkunst und dem Fortzugen dieser Anweisung heraus gegeben von* ANTHON FRIEDRICH KAHN, *Fechtmeister auf der Georgius Augustus Universitat zu Gœttingen.*   4°.   Gœttingen.   1739.

Gedruckt bey Schultzen, Universitats-Buchdrucker.

Portrait of Kahn and twenty-five copperplates, out of the text, engraved by F. Fritsch.
In the Brit. Mus.

———SCHMIDT (JOHANN ANDREAS). *Fecht und Exercitien Meister. Grundlich lehrende Fecht-Schule.*   8°.   Nurnberg.   1749.

(See 1729.)   In the Bodl.

———SCHMIDT'*s Fecht-Kunst.*   8°.   Nurnberg.   1750.

———SCHMIDT (JOH. ANDRE). *Lehrende Fechtschule.*   8°.   Nurnberg.   1760.
Mit Kpf.

——A second edition of A. F. KAHN's work (see 1739) was printed in Helmstadt. *Bey Christian Friedrich Weygrand.* 4°. 1761.

——*Haupt.* S. WEISCHNER. *Uebungen auf den fürstlichen Sächsischen Hoffechtboden zu Weimar, verb. und vern. Aufl.* Weimar. 1764.

——HOFFMAN. *Ritterliche Geschicklichkeit im Fechten durch ungezwungene Stellungen. Mit* 30 *Kpf.* 4°. Weimar. 1766.

——*Haupt.* S. C. F. WEISCHNER. *Ritterliche Geschicklichkeit im Fechten.* 4°. Weimar. 1766.
Thirty copperplates.

——HEINRICH CHRISTOPH RANIS. *Königl. Commissarii und Fechtmeisters Anweisung zur Fechtkunst. Mit Kupfern.* Brit. Mus. 8°. Berlin. 1771. *Bey August Mylius.* Four copperplates, folded.

——TEMLICH's *Anfangsgründe der Fecht-Kunst.* 8°. Halle. 1776.

——VESTER's *Anleitung zur adelichen Fecht-kunst.* 8°. Breslau. 1777.

——SCHMIDT (JOH. ANDR.). *Fecht-Kunst oder Anweisung in Stoss und Hieb. Wie auch zum Ringen und Voltigiren.* 12°. Nürnberg. 1780. *Mit* 82 *figuren.*

——SCHMIDT. *Fecht-Kunst auf Stoss und Hieb.* 8°. Leipsig. 1780

——HASPELMACHER's *Systematische Abhandlung von den schädlichen Folgen einer nicht auf sichere Regeln gegrundeten Fechtkunst, nebst einer Anweisung wie man solche verweiden kann. Bei Joh. Heinrich Kuhnlin.* 8°. Helmstadt. 1783.

——HEINRICH ROUX (the father). *Versuch über das Contrafechten auf der rechten und linken Hand nach Kreuzler'schen Grundsatzen. Bei Cröker.* 4°. Jena. 1786.

——*Flüchtige Bemerkungen über die verschiedene Art zu fechten einiger Universitäten, von einem fleissigen Beobachter.* Halle. 1791-2.

——SCHMIDT's *Lehrschule der Fechtkunst* 1 *Theil, oder Lehrbuch für die Cavalerie zum vortheilhaften Gebrauche des Säbels.* 4°. Berlin. 1797.

——J. AD. K. ROUX. *Grundtliche und vollstandige Anweisung in der teutschen Fechtkunst auf Stoss und Hieb aus ihren innersten Geheimnissen wissenschaftlich erlautert, u. s. w. mit Kupfern.*
　　In Wolfg. Stahl's Buchdl. 　　　　　　　　　　　　　　　　4°. Jena. 1798.
　　One copperplate, folded, containing several figures.

——J. ROUX. *Grundriss der Fechtkunst als gymnastischer Uebung betrachtet.* 　　Jena. 1798.

——*Theorisch praktische Anweisung uber das Hiebfechten, von* J. ROUX. 　　　　Furth. 1803.

——*L'art de faire des armes réduit à ses vrais principes. Contenant tous les principes nécessaires à cet art qui y sont expliqués d'une manière claire et intelligible. Cet ouvrage est composé pour la jeune noblesse et pour les personnes qui se destinent au métier de la guerre, ainsi que pour tous ceux qui portent l'épée. On y a joint un traité de l'espadon, où l'on trouve les vrais principes de cet art, qui y sont expliqués d'une façon aisée, et qui est rempli de découvertes vraiment nouvelles.*
　　Dédié à S. A. R. Monseigneur l'Archiduc Charles, par M. J. DE SAINT-MARTIN *Maître d'Armes Impérial de l'Académie Thérésienne, et ancien officier de cavalerie. Enrichi de 72 figures pour l'intelligence de l'ouvrage.* 　　　　　　　　4°. Vienna. 1804.
　　Cet ouvrage se trouve chez l'auteur à la Leimgruben, No. 155, au premier etage, a Vienne.
　　Portrait of Saint-Martin, and seventy-two copperplates.

FRENCH.

——*La noble science des joueurs d'espée.* 　　　　　　　　　　4°. Paris. 1533 (?)

——A second edition of the above appeared in Antwerp. 　　　　4°. 1535 (1538?)
　　As a second title: *Icy commence un tres beau livret, contenant la chevaleureuse science des joueurs d'espée, pour apprendre à jouer de l'espée à deux mains et autres semblabes espées, avec aussi les braquemars et aultres courts cousteaux lesquelz lon use à une main. . . . .*
　　At the end: *Imprimé en la ville Danvers par moy, Guillaume Wosterman, demourant à la licorne d'or.*
　　Black-letter. Fourteen whole-page, twelve half-page blocks, woodcut. In the Brit. Mus.

——*Traicté contenant les secrets du premier livre sur l'espée seule, mère de toutes armes, qui sont espée, dague, cappe, targue, bouclier, rondelle, l'espée deux mains et les deux espées, avec ses pourtraictures, ayant les armes au poing pour se deffendre et offencer à un mesme temps des coups qu'on peut tirer, tout en assaillant qu'en deffendant, fort utile et profitable pour adextrer la noblesse et supost de Mars ; redigé par art, ordre et pratique.*

Composé par HENRY DE SAINCT-DIDIER, *gentilhomme provencal.*

Dedié à la Maiesté du Roy tres chrestien Charles neufiesme. 4°. Paris. 1573.

A Paris, imprimé par Jean Mettayer et Matthurin Challenge, et se vend chez Jean Dalier, sur le pont Sainct Michel, à l'enseigne de la Rose blanche.

Avec Privilege du Roy.

Portrait of the author and of Charles IX., and sixty-four woodcuts, in the text. In the Brit. Mus.

———*Traité, ou instruction pour tirer des armes, de l'excellent scrimeur* HYERONIME CAVAL-CABO, *Bolognois, avec un discours pour tirer de l'espée seule, fait par le deffunt* PATENOSTRIER, *de Rome.*

Traduit d'italien en françois par le seigneur de Villamont, chevalier de l'ordre de Hierusalem et gentilhomme de la chambre du Roy. 12°. Rouen. 1609.

Chez Claude le Villain, libraire et relieur du Roy, demourant à la rue du Bec, à la Bonne Renommée.

Dedicated to the Maréchal de Brissac.

———A. VAN BREEN. *Le Maniement d'Armes de Nassau avecq Rondelles, Piques, Espée et Targes ; representez par Figures.* South Kens. Fol. La Haye. 1618.

———*Escrime nouvelle ou Théâtre auquel sont representées diverses manières de parer et de frapper, d'espée seule et d'espée et poignard ensemble, demontrées par figures entaillées en cuivre, publié en faveur de ceux qui se délectent en ce tres noble exercice des armes, par* NICOLAT GIGANTI, *Venetien, et traduit en langue française par Jacques de Zeter.* Oblong 4°. Francofurti. 1619.

Apud Ja. de Zeter.

Portrait of the author, and forty-two copperplates, out of the text. In the Brit. Mus.

——— *Academie de l'espée . . . . . à pied et à cheval, de* GIRARD THIBAUST.

Paris. 1626 (?)

———*Academie de l'Espée de* GIRARD THIBAUST *d'Anvers, où se demonstrent par reigles mathématiques, sur le fondement d'un cercle mystérieux, la théorie et pratique des vrais et jusqu'à present incognus secrets du maniement des armes, à pied et à cheval.* Folio. Leyde. 1628.

Frontispiece, portrait of Girard Thibaust. Nine plates containing the coats-of-arms of nine kings and princes who patronized this work. Forty-six copperplates, drawn and engraved by Crispin de Pas, Gelle, Nicol Lastman, Andreas Stockins, Ad. Mœtham, T. Van Paenderen, Role Beaudouc, Iselburg, Wilhelm Delff, P. Sherwontors, Bolsworth, Crispian

Queborn, Salomon Saurius, Schelderie, Egbert a'Paondoron, Petrus de Todo, Jacobus a'Borch, Scheltus, W. Jacobi.

Privileges of Louis XIII., dated 1620, and of the States General of the Low Countries, dated June the 5th, 1627.

The name of the printers and the place of impression is only to be found in a few rare copies, bearing on the last page this notice announcing the death of the author :—

Un advertissement au lecteur.

Le lecteur sera adverti que l'autheur, ayant eu le dessein de produire la science de l'escrime à cheval avec celle à pied, comme il eu est fait mention au frontispice de ce livre, la mort l'ayant prévenu, ne l'a pu mettre en effect ; mesme l'impression du present livre eu a esté retardé iusques à present.

A Leyde, imprimé en la Typographie des Elzeviers, au mois d'Aoust l'an cɪɔɪɔcxxx.

——*L'Exercice des armes ou le Maniement du fleuret par* JEAN BAPTISTE LE PERCHE DU COUDRAY. Folio. Paris. 1635 (?)

——*Le Maistre d'arme libéral, traittant de la théorie de l'art et exercice de l'espée seule, ou fleuret, et de tout se qui s'y peut faire et pratiquer de plus subtil, avec les principales figures et postures en taille douce ; contenant en outre plusieurs moralitez sur ce sujet.*

Fait et composé par CHARLES BESNARD, *breton originaire, habitant la ville de Rennes et y monstrant le susdit Exercice.* 4°. Rennes. 1653.

Dédié à Nosseigneurs des Estats de la province et duché de Bretagne.

A Rennes, chez Julien Herbert, imprimeur et libraire, rue St. Germain, à l'image S. Julien. Avec Privilège du Roy.

Four copperplates, out of the text.

——A second edition of the *Academie de l'Epée* of GIRARD THIBAUST (see 1628) appeared in Brussels. Folio. 1668.

——*Les vrays principes de l'espée seule, dediéz au Roy, par le Sieur* DE LA TOUCHE, *Maistre en faits d'armes à Paris et des pages de la Reyne, et de ceux de la Chambre de son Altesse Royale, Monseigneur le duc d'Orléans.* Oblong 4°. Paris. 1670.

A Paris, de l'imprimerie de Francois Muguet, rue de la Harpe.

Portrait of La Touche, thirty-five copperplates out of the text.

——*L'exercice des armes ou le maniement du fleuret. Pour ayder la mémoire de ceux qui sont amateurs de cet art, par* LE PERCHE. Oblong 4°. Paris. 1676.

Se vand à Paris chés N. Bonnard, rue St. Jacques, à l'Aigle.

Thirty-five copperplates.

This book is sometimes alluded to by bibliographers as a second or even a third edition.

——*Le Maistre d'armes, ou l'exercice de l'espée seulle dans sa perfection. Dédié à Monseigneur le duc de Bourgogne par le sieur* DE LIANCOUR. Obl. 4°. Paris. 1686.

*Les attitudes des figures de ce livre ont ésté posées par le sieur de Liancour et gravées par A.
Perrelle. A Paris, chez l'auteur, faux-bourgs St. Germain, rue des Boucheries.*
Portrait of Liancour by Langlois, from a picture by Monet. Fourteen copperplates out
of the text. (See also 1692.) In the Brit. Mus

——LABAT. *L'art de l'Epée.* 12°. Toulouse. 1690.
Copperplates.
(See also 1696.)

——A second edition of DE LIANCOUR's work (see 1686) was produced in Amsterdam.
Obl. 4°. 1692.

——MS. Sloane, No. 1198. Folio 40. Twenty-three lines.
British Museum. Date, about the end of the seventeenth century.

——*L'art en fait d'armes, ou de l'épée seule, avec les attitudes; dedié à monseigneur le Comte
d'Armaignac, Grand Ecuyer de France, &c., par le Sieur* LABAT, *Maître en fait d'armes, de la
ville et Académie de Toulouse.* 8°. Toulouse. 1696.
*Chez J. Boude, imprimeur du Roy, des Estats de la Province de Languedoc, &c., &c. Se
débitent chez l'auteur, prez les Jacobins.*
Twelve copperplates by Simonin, out of the text.
(See also 1690.)

——*Questions sur l'art en fait d'armes, ou de l'épée, dédié à monseigneur le duc de Bourgogne, par le
Sieur* LABAT, *Maître au dit Art de la Ville et Académie de Toulouse.* 4°. Toulouse. 1701.
*Chez M. G. Robert, maître-ès-arts et imprimeur à la rue Sainte Ursule. Avec Permission. Se
débitent chez l'Autheur*

——*L'Art de tirer des Armes, réduit en abrégé méthodique. Dédié à monseigneur le Maréchal duc de
Villeroy par* J. DE BRYE, *Maistre en fait d'armes.* 8°. Paris. 1721.
*Chez C. L. Thiboust, imprimeur juré de l'Université de Paris ; place de Cambrai. Avec appro-
bation et privilège du Roy.*
Frontispiece and a medallion portrait of the Dauphin.

——A second edition of DE BRYE's work (see 1721) was published in Paris. 1731.

——*Nouveau Traité de la Perfection sur le fait des armes, dédié au Roi, par le Sieur* P. J. F.
GIRARD, *ancien officier de marine. Enseignant la manière de combattre, de l'épée de pointe seule, toute
les gardes etrangères, l'espadon, les piques, hallebardes, etc., tels qu'ils se pratiquent aujourd'hui dans l'art
militaire de France. Orné de figures en taille douce.* Oblong 4°. Paris 1736-7.
Frontispiece and 116 copperplates, out of the text, engraved by Jacques de Favanne. In
the Brit. Mus.

——*Le Maistre d'armes, ou l'abrégé de l'exercice de l'épée, par le sieur* MARTIN, *Maistre en fait d'armes de l'Académie de Strasbourg.   Orné de figures en taille-douce.*   12°.   Strasbourg.   1737.
  Chez l'auteur, au Poel des Marechaux.
  Sixteen copperplates, out of the text.
  Approbation of the professed masters of Paris.

——A second edition of the work of LE PERCHE (see 1676) was published by one of his descendants in Paris.   Oblong 4°.   1750.
  With the addition of five plates.
  Chez la veuve Chereau.

——In the second edition of DE CHEVIGNY's *Science des personnes de cour et d'épée,* which appeared in Amsterdam, 1752, there is one chapter dedicated to fencing (tome vii., chap. x.), containing eight folded copperplates.   In the Brit. Mus.   12°.

——*Principes et quintessence des armes.   Dedié à S. A. Jean-Theodore, duc des Deux-Bavières, cardinal de la sainte Eglise romaine, evêque et prince de Liége, etc., par* GERARD GORDINE, *capitaine et maître en fait d'armes.*   4°.   Liège.   1754.
  Chez S. Bourguignon, imprimeur de la noble Cité, rue Neuvice.   Avec privilège de sa Serenissime Eminence.
  Twenty copperplates, out of the text, by Jacoby.

——*L'escrime pratique ou principes de la science des armes par* DANIEL O'SULLIVAN, *maître en fait d'armes des Académies du Roi.*   8°.   Paris.   1765.
  Chez Sébastien Jorry, imprimeur-libraire, rue, et vis-à-vis, la Comédie Française, au grand Monarque.

——*L'art des armes, ou la manière la plus certaine de se servir utilement de l'épée, soit pour attaquer, soit pour se défendre, simplifiée et demontrée dans toute son étendue et sa perfection, suivant les meilleurs principes de théorie et de pratique adoptés actuellement en France.   Ouvrage nécessaire à la jeune noblesse, aux militaires et à ceux qui se destinent au service du Roy, aux personnes même qui, par la distinction de leur état ou par leurs charges, sont obligées de porter l'épée ; et à ceux qui veulent faire profession des armes. Dedié à son altesse Monseigneur le Prince de Conty.*
  Par M. DANET, *Ecuyer, Syndic Garde des Ordres de la Compagnie des Maitres en fait d'armes des Académies du Roi en la Ville et Faubourgs de Paris.*   8°.   Paris.   1766.

  Tome second, contenant la réfutation des critiques et la suite du même Traité.
                                                                        8°.   Paris.   1767.
  Prix des deux volumes: 12 livres, reliés.   Avec approbation et privilège du Roy.
  Frontispiece and forty-three copperplates, out of the text, engraved by Taraval from designs by Vaxeillère.   In the Brit. Mus. and South Kens.

——*Observations sur le traité de l'art des Armes, pour servir de défense à la verité des principes* *enseignés par les Maîtres d'Armes de Paris par* M. * * * (LA BOËSSIÈRE), *Maître d'Armes des Académies du Roi, au nom de sa Compagnie.* 8°. Paris. 1766.

——*Traité de l'Art des Armes, par* DE LA BOËSSIÈRE. 8°. Paris. 1766 (?).

——*La théorie pratique de l'escrime, pour la pointe seule, avec des remarques pour l'assaut par* BATTIER. 12°. Paris. 1770.

——*La Théorie pratique de l'Escrime pour la pointe seule, avec des remarques instructives pour l'assaut et les moyens d'y parvenir par gradation. Dedié A. S. A. S. Monseigneur le Duc de Bourbon par le sieur* BATIER. 8°. Paris. 1772.
   A Paris, de l'imprimerie de la veuve Simon et fils, imprimeurs-libraires de LL. AA. SS. le Prince de Condé et le duc de Bourbon, et de l'Archeveché, Rue des Mathurins. L'auteur demeure rue de la Coutellerie, maison de Madame Nivelle, vis-à-vis de M. Miret, marchand de vins du Roi, quartier de la Grève. Le prix est de 30 sols, broché, et se vend chez Charles de Poilly, libraire, quai de Gêvre, au Soleil d'or.
   One engraving, drawn by Janinet.

——*L'art de vaincre par l'épée, dédié à messieurs les Gardes-du-Corps du Roi, de la Compagnie de Noailles, par* M. C. NAVARRE, *Maître d'armes de la première Compagnie de la Maison du Roi. Prix: 24 sols.* 18°. Paris. 1775.
   A Paris, chez les libraires du Palais-Royal et du quai de Gesvres; à Versailles, chez les libraires de la galerie des Princes. Avec approbation de la Compagnie.

——*Maximes et instructions sur l'art de tirer des armes, par le Chevalier* DE FREVILLE. 8°. Petersbourg. 1775.

——Reproduced in Leipsig. 8°. 1776.

——*Nouveau traité de l'art des armes, dans lequel on établit les principes certains de cet art, et où l'on enseigne les moyens les plus simples de les mettre en pratique. Ouvrage necessaire aux personnes qui se destinent aux armes, et utile à celles qui veulent se rappeler les principes qu'on leur a enseignés; avec des figures en taille-douce. Par* M. NICOLAS DEMEUSE, *Garde-du-Corps de S. A. S le Prince-Evêque à Liége, et Maître en fait d'armes.* 12°. Liége. 1778.
   Chez Desoer, imprimeur, sur le pont d'Isle, et chez l'auteur derrière le Palais.
   Fourteen copperplates, out of the text.

——A second edition of NICOLAS DEMEUSE's work (see 1778) was published by Desoer in Liege. 12°. 1786.

——*L'Art des Armes, ou l'on donne l'application de la theorie à la pratique de cet Art, avec les principes methodiques adoptés dans nos Ecoles Royales d'Armes.*
   Ouvrage aussi utile que necessaires . . . . etc. (See 1766.)

Par M. DANET, *Ecuyer, Syndic-Garde des Ordres de la Compagnie des Maîtres en fait d'Armes des Académies du Roi en la Ville et Fauxbourgs de Paris, aujourd'hui Directeur de l'Ecole Royale d'Armes.*   8°. Paris. 1787.

Avec approbation et privilège du Roi.

——In "the year vi. of the Republic," Bélin, rue St. Jacques, reproduced the work of DANET in Paris.   Two vols. 8°. 1798.

——A third edition of DE FREVILLE's *Maximes* was published in Leipsig.   8°. 1799.

—— A third edition of NICOLAS DEMEUSE's work (see 1786) was issued from the Imprimerie de Blocquel, in Lille and Paris.   12°.   1800.

The plates, the same in number, are different in character. To the original text is added a *Dictionnaire de l'Art des Armes.*

ENGLISH.

——GIACOMO DI GRASSI, *his true Arte of Defence, plainlie teaching by infallable Demonstrations, apt Figures, and perfect Rules the manner and forme how a man, without other Teacher or master may safelie handle all sortes of Weapons as well offensive as defensive. With a treatise of Disceit or Falsinge : and with a waie or meane by private industrie to obtaine Strength, Judgment and Activitie.*

First written in Italian by the foresaid Author, and Englished by J. G. gentleman.

Printed at London for J. G. and are to be sold within Temple Barre at the sign of the Hand and Starre.   4°. London. 1594.

In the Bodl.

——VINCENTIO SAVIOLO. *His practise, in two bookes ; the first intreating of the use of the Rapier & Dagger, the second of honour and honourable quarrels.*   4°. London. 1595.

Printed by John Wolfe.

Dedicated to the Earl of Essex.

Six woodcuts, in the text.   In the Brit. Mus. and Bodl.

——GEORGE SILVER, (*Gentleman*). *Paradoxe of Defence, wherein is proved the true ground of fight to be in the short aunctent weapons, and that the Short Sword hath the advantage of the long sword or long rapier, and the weaknesse and imperfection of the rapier fight displayed   Together with an admonition to the noble, ancient, victorious, valiant and most brave nation of Englishmen, to beware of false teachers of defence and how they forsake their own naturall fights ; with a brief commendation of the noble science or exercising of arms.*   8°. London. 1599.

In the Brit. Mus. and Bodl.

——*Mars His Feild or The Exercise of Armes, wherein in lively figures is shewn the Right use and perfect manner of Handling the Buckler, Sword and Pike. With the wordes of Command and Brefe instructions correspondent to every Posture.*

And are to be sold by Roger Daniell at the Angel in Lombard Streete.

12°. London. 1611.

Sixteen copperplates, with explanatory legends. No text. In the Bodl.

——*The Schoole of the Noble and Worthy Science of Defence. Being the first of any English-mans invention, which professed the sayd Science; So plainly described that any man may quickly come to the true knowledge of their weapons with small paines and little practise.*

Then reade it advisedly, and use the benefit thereof when occasion shal serve, so shalt thou be a good Common-wealth man, live happy to thy selfe and comfortable to thy friend.

Also many other good and profitable Precepts for the managing of Quarrels and ordering thy selfe in many other matters. Written by JOSEPH SWETNAM. 4°. London. 1617.
Printed by Nicholas Okes.

Dedicated to Charles, Prince of Wales.

This treatise bears great resemblance to that of Saviolo. Seven woodcuts. In the Bodl.

——*Pallas armata: the gentleman's armorie, wherein the right and genuine use of the rapier and the sword is displaied.* 12°. London. 1639.

——MS. British Museum, Additional, No. 5540. Folios 122–123.
The names of yor Pushes as they are to be learned gradually.

Date, middle of the seventeenth century.

——*The shield single against the sword double, by* HENRY NICCOLI.

4°. London. 1653 (?)

——*Scots Fencing Master, or Compleat small-swordman, in which is fully Described the whole Guards, Parades and Lessons belonging to the Small-Sword, etc.* (See 1692.)
By W. H. *Gent.* 8°. Edinburgh. 1687.
Printed by John Reid.

Twelve copperplates, out of the text.

——*The Sword-Man's Vade-Mecum, or a preservative against the surprize of a sudden attaque with Sharps. Being a Reduction of the most essential, necessary and practical part of Fencing; into a few special Rules. With their Reasons: which all Sword-Men should have in their Memories when they are to Engadge; but more especially if it be with Sharps.*

With some other Remarques and Observations, not unfit to be known, by W. H., *Gentleman* (William Hope). 12°. Edinburgh. 1691.
Printed by John Reid.

——*The Compleat Fencing-Master: in which is fully Described the whole Guards, Parades and Lessons, belonging to the Small-Sword, as also the best Rules for Playing against either Artists or others, with Blunts or Sharps. Together with Directions how to behave in a single Combat on Horse-back: illustrated with figures Engraven on Copper-plates, representing the most necessary Postures. The Second Edition.*

By SIR W. HOPE, *Kt.* (See 1687.) 8°. London. 1692.

London, Printed for Dorman Newman, at the King's-Arms in the Poultrey.

Twelve copperplates, out of the text.

This book, with a different title, is in every other respect a reproduction of the *Scots Fencing Master.* (See 1687.)

——A second edition of the *Sword-man's Vade Mecum* (see 1691) by SIR WILLIAM HOPE, Kt., appeared in London.   8°.   1694.

Printed and are to be sold by J. Tailor, at the Ship in St. Paul's Church-yard and S. Holford at the Crown in the Pall Mall.

The title of the second edition only shows a little difference in the spelling.   In the Brit. Mus.

——*The English Fencing Master, or the Compleat Tutor of the Small-Sword. Wherein the truest Method, after a Mathematical Rule, is plainly laid down. Shewing also how necessary it is for all Gentlemen to learn this Noble Art. In a Dialogue between Master and Scholar. Adorn'd with several curious postures.* By HENRY BLACKWELL.   4°.   London.   1705.

(See also 1730.)

Printed for F. Sprint, at the Blue Bell, in Little Britain; and H. Montgommery, at the Looking Glass in Cornhill, near the Royal Exchange.

Five woodcuts, in the text.   Twenty-four copperplates, out of the text, folded.

Dedicated to C. Tryon, Esq., of Bullick, Northants.   In the South Kens. and Brit. Mus.

——*A New, Short and Easy Method of Fencing: or the Art of the Broad and Small Sword, Rectified and Compendiz'd, wherein the Practice of these two weapons is reduced to so few and general Rules, that any Person of indifferent Capacity and ordinary Agility of Body, may, in a very short time, attain to, not only a sufficient Knowledge of the Theory of this art, but also to a considerable Adroitness in Practice, either for the Defence of his life, upon a just Occasion, or preservation of his Reputation and Honour in any Accidental Scuffle, or Trifling Quarrel.*

By SIR WILLIAM HOPE OF BALCOMIE, *Baronet, Late Deputy-Governour of the Castle of Edinburgh.*   4°.   Edinburgh.   1707.

" *Gladiatura, non solum ad Honoris, Vitæque Conservationem; sed etiam at Corporis, atque Animæ Relaxationem, per quam necessaria.*"

Printed by James Watson, in Craig's Closs, on the north-side of the Cross.

One large folded sheet containing sixteen figures engraved on copper.

——*The English Master of Defence or the Gentleman's Al-a-mode Accomplishment. Containing the True Art of Single-Rapier or Small Sword, withal the curious Parres and many more than the vulgar Terms of Art plainly exprest; with the Names of every particular Pass and the true performance thereof; withal the exquisite Ways of Disarming and Enclosing, and all the Guards at Broad-Sword and Quarter-Staff, perfectly demonstrated; shewing how the Blows, Strokes, Chops, Thro's, Flirts, Slips and Darts are perform'd; with the true Method of Travesing. Also etc. etc.*

The like was never Publish't before by any Man in England but by ZACH. WYLDE.

Printed by John White, for the Author.   8°.   York.   1711.

——*Hope's New Method of Fencing, or the True and Solid Art of Fighting with the Back-Sword, Sheering-Sword, Small-Sword, and Sword and Pistol; freed from the Errors of the Schools.*

Wherein the Defence and Pursuit of these Weapons, both on Foot and a Horseback, and that against all kind of Edged or Pointed Weapons whatsoever, are not only compendiz'd and reduc'd to few and general Rules, that . . *etc.* (See 1707.)

But also the nicest Theory of the whole Art is so interspersed with these most easy and useful Rules, that it will at once instruct the greatest Ignorant, and gratify the most Critical and Curious Artist. So that it may be asserted that, by this new Method, the Art of defence with the Sword alone is, by Mathematical Demonstration, brought to the utmost perfection Humane Nature is capable of; and that this assertion is in no ways vain or Chimerical; the Author is ready to deffend the same, either by Argument or Practice, before any Two understanding Sword-men, against any Fencing Master who shall impugn it.

Second edition.

By SIR WILLIAM HOPE OF BALCOMIE, *Baronet, etc.*

" *Gladiatura non solum, etc., etc.*"

4°. Edinburgh. 1714.

Printed by James Watson . . . *etc., etc.* (see 1705). *Sold by Geo. Strahan, at the Golden Ball, over against the Royal Exchange in Cornhill.*

——*A Vindication of the True Art of Self-Defence, with a proposal, to the Honourable Members of Parliament, for erecting a Court of Honour in Great Britain.*

Recommended to all Gentlemen, but particularly to the Soldiery. To which is added a Short but very Useful Memorial for Sword Men.

By SIR WILLIAM HOPE, *Baronet, late Deputy-Governour of Edinburgh-Castle.*

8°. Edinburgh. 1724.

" *Certamen festinantium incendit Ignem Et his festinans effundit Sanguinem. Magno Ingenio turpe non est, sed honorificum Errorem fateri simpliciter.*"

Printed by William Brown and Company.

The same plate that is contained in the work published by Sir W. Hope in 1707, and frontispiece, representing the badge *Gladiatorum Scoticorum.* In the Brit. Mus.

——*Observations on the Gladiators' Stage-Fighting, by* SIR WILLIAM HOPE, *Baronet, etc.*

8°. London. 1725.

——*The expert sword-Man's companion: or the True Art of self defence, with an account of the Author's life and his transactions during the wars with France. To which is annexed the art of gunnerie. By* DONALD McBANE.

12°. Glasgow. 1728.

Printed by James Duncan, and are to be sold at his shop in the Salt-Market, near Gibson's Wind.

Portrait of McBane, and twenty-two plates, out of the text.

——A second edition of SIR WILLIAM HOPE's *Vindication, etc.* (see 1724), was *printed and sold by W. Meadowes, at the Angel in Cornhill,* in London.

8°. 1729.

Same plate and frontispiece.

Dedicated to *the Right Honourable Robert Walpole.*

——*The Art of Fencing, as practised by Monsieur* VALDIN. *Most humbly dedicated to his Grace the duke of Montagu.*   8°. London. 1729.
     Printed for J. Parker in Pall Mall. In the Brit. Mus.

——H. B. (HENRY BLACKWELL) (see also 1705). *The Gentleman's Tutor for the Small Sword; or the Compleat English Fencing Master.*
     Containing the truest and plainest rules for learning that noble Art; shewing how necessary it is for all gentlemen to understand the same in 13 *various lessons between Master and Scholar. Adorn'd with several curious postures.*   Small 4°. London. 1730.
     Printed for J. & T. W. and Sold by T. Jackson at St. James: A. Dodd, without Temple Bar; and E. Nutt, under the Royal Exchange. Price 1s.
     Six woodcuts. In the Bodl.

——*The Art of Fencing, or the Use of the Small Sword. Translated from the French of the late celebrated Monsieur* L'ABBAT, *Master of that Art at the Academy of Toulouse, by Andrew Mahon, Professor of the Small Sword.*   12°. Dublin. 1734.
     Printed by James Hoey, at the sign of Mercury in Skinner Row.
     Twelve copperplates, out of the text. In the Brit. Mus.

——A second edition of Mahon's translation of L'ABBAT's work (see France, 1696) appeared in London.   12°. 1735.
     Printed by Richard Wellington, at the Dolphin and Crown, without Temple Bar.

——A treatise on fencing by Captain J. MILLER, in the shape of an album of fifteen copperplates, engraved by Scotin, with one column of text.   Folio. 1738.

——*A Treatise upon the useful Science of Defence, connecting the Small and Back-Sword, and shewing the Affinity between them. Likewise endeavouring to weed the Art of those superfluous, unmeaning Practices which over-run it, and choke the true Principles, by reducing it to a narrow Compass, and supporting it with Mathematical Proofs. Also an Examination into the Performances of the most Noted Masters of the Back-Sword, who have fought upon the Stage, pointing out their Faults, and allowing their Abilities. With some Observations upon Boxing, and the Characters of the most able Boxers, within the Author's Time.*
     By Capt. JOHN GODFREY.   4°. London. 1747.
     Printed for the Author, by T. Gardner, at Cowley's Head opposite St. Clement's Church in the Strand.

——An album of copperplates representing various attitudes in fencing.
     Oblong 4°. Date about 1750.

——*L'Ecole des Armes, avec l'explication générale des principales attitudes et positions concernant l'Escrime.*

Dediée à Leurs Altesses Royales les Princes Guillaume-Henry et Henry-Frédéric par M. ANGELO. Oblong folio. Londres. 1763.
A Londres, chez R. & J. Dodsley, Pall Mall.
Forty-seven copperplates, out of the text. In the Brit. Mus. and South Kens.

——A second edition of M. ANGELO's work (see 1763), containing the same plates, but with two columns of text, in French and English, was printed by S. Hooper in London.
In the Bodl. Oblong folio. 1765.

——A third edition of M. ANGELO's work (see 1763) appeared in London.
Oblong folio. 1767.

——*The Fencer's Guide, being a Series of every branch required to compose a Complete System of Defence, Whereby the Admirers of Fencing are gradually led from the First Rudiments of that Art, through the most complicated Subtilties yet formed by imagination, or applied to practice, until the Lesson, herein many ways varied, also lead them insensibly on to the due Methods of Loose Play, which are here laid down, with every Precaution necessary for that Practice.*
In four parts.
Part I and II contains such a general explanation of the Small Sword as admits of much greater Variety and Novelty than are to be found in any other work of this kind.
Part III shews, in the Use of the Broad Sword, such an universal Knowledge of that Weapon, as may be very applicable to the Use of any other that a Man can lawfully carry in his hand.
Part IV is a compound of the Three former, explaining and teaching the Cut and Thrust, or Spadroon Play, and that in a more subtile and accurate manner than ever appeared in Print.
And to these are added Particular Lessons for the Gentlemen of the Horse, Dragoons, and Light Horse, or Hussars, with some necessary Precautions and an Index, explaining every term of that Art throughout the book.
The Whole being carefully collected from long Experience and Speculation, is calculated as a Vade-Mecum for Gentlemen of the Army, Navy, Universities, &c.
By A. LONNERGAN, *Teacher of the Military Sciences.*
Hic Juvenis punctim, Cæsimque docentur ab arte
Pellere bellipotens Crimen et Ense Tegi. 8º. London. 1771-2.
Printed for the Author, and sold by W. Griffin, in Catharine Street.

——*Fencing Familiarized, or a new treatise on the Art of Sword Play. Illustrated by Elegant Engravings, representing all the different Attitudes in which the Principles and Grace of the Art depend; painted from life and executed in a most elegant and masterly manner.*
By Mr. OLIVIER ; *Educated at the Royal Academy of Paris, and Professor of Fencing, in St. Dunstan's Court, Fleet Street.*
Sine Regula, sine Delectatione. 8º. London. 1771-2.
Printed for John Bell, near Exeter Change in the Strand, and C. Hetherington, at York.
Facing the above title is its exact translation into French. The text is in both languages.
Frontispiece and eight folded plates, engraved by Ovenden. In the South Kens.

1

——A second edition of OLIVIER's work (see 1771-2), dedicated to the Earl of Harrington, was published by J. Bell, in the Strand. 8°. London. 1780.

Same frontispiece as in the first edition, but the plates are different, being drawn by J. Roberts, and engraved by D. Jinkins, Goldar, W. Blake, and C. Grignon.

——*The Army and Navy Gentleman's Companion; or a New and Complete Treatise on the Theory and Practice of Fencing, displaying the Intricacies of Small Sword Play, and reducing the Art to the most Easy and Familiar Principles by regular progressive Lessons.*

Illustrated by Mathematical Figures and Adorned with elegant Engravings after paintings from Life, executed in the most masterly Manner, representing every material Attitude of the Art.

By J. McARTHUR, *of the Royal Navy.* Large 4°. London. 1780-1.

Content if hence th' Unlearned their wants may view,
The learned reflect on what before they knew.

(*Pope's Essay on Crit.*)

Printed for James Lavers, No. 10, Strand.

Frontispiece, engraved by J. Newton from a drawing by Jas. Sowerby, and eight plates, drawn by the author, and engraved by Jas. Newton.

——Another edition of McARTHUR's work was printed *for J. Murray, No. 32 Fleet Street.* 4°. London. 1784.

Dedicated to *John, Duke of Argyll.* In the South Kens.

——*The Art of Fencing, or the use of the small Sword.*
Collected, revised and enlarged by JAMES UNDERWOOD, *of the Custom House.*
Printed by T. Byrne, Parliament-Street. 8°. Dublin. 1787.
Dedicated to His Grace, Charles, Duke of Rutland. In the Brit. Mus.

——*The School of Fencing, with a general explanation of the principal attitudes and positions peculiar to the Art.*
By Mr. ANGELO. Oblong 4°. London. 1787.
Translated by Rowlandson.
This work of Henry Angelo was translated into French and reproduced, together with the plates, under the head " Escrime," by Diderot and D'Alembert in their " Encyclopédie." In the Brit. Mus.

——*Anti-Pugilism, or the Science of Defence exemplified in short and easy lessons, for the practice of the Broad Sword and Single Stick.*
Illustrated with Copper Plates.
By a Highland Officer.
Whereby Gentlemen may become Proficients in the use of these Weapons, without the help of a Master, and be enabled to Chastise the Insolence and Temerity, so frequently met with, from those

fashionable Gentlemen, the Johnsonians, Big Bennians, and Mendozians of the present Day; a Work perhaps, better calculated to extirpate this reigning and brutal Folly than a whole Volume of Sermons.

8°. London. 1790.

Printed for J. Aitkin, No. 14, Castle-Street, corner of Bear Street, Leicester Square. Entered at Stationer's Hall.

Four copperplates, drawn by Cruikshank. In the Brit. Mus.

——*Rules and Regulations for the Sword Exercise of Cavalry.*

Royal 8°. London. 1796.

Twenty-nine folding plates. In the Brit. Mus. and South Kens.

——*The Art of Defence on Foot with the Broad Sword and Sabre, uniting the Scotch and Austrian Methods, into one regular system.*

To which are added remarks on the Spadroon.

By C. ROWORTH, *of the Royal Westminster Volunteers. The second edition.*

8°. London. 1798.

Printed for T. Egerton, at the Military Library, near Whitehall. In the Brit. Mus.

——*Hungarian and Highland Broad Sword. Twenty-four plates, designed and etched by* T. ROWLANDSON, *under the direction of Messrs.* H. ANGELO *and Son, Fencing Masters to the Light Horse Volunteers of London and Westminster, dedicated to Colonel Herries.*

Oblong folio. London. 1798-9.

Printed by C. Roworth, Bell Yard, Fleet Street. For T. Egerton, at the Military Library, near Whitehall. In the Brit. Mus.

——A second edition of Rowlandson's translation of ANGELO's work (see 1787) appeared in London.

8°. 1799.

——*Sword Exercise for Cavalry, with 6 engravings.* 8°. London. 1799.

——*Cudgel-playing modernised and improved; or the Science of Defence exemplified in a few short and easy lessons for the practice of the Broad Sword or Single Stick on foot.*

Illustrated with Fourteen Positions. By Capt. SINCLAIR *of the 42ᵈ Regᵗ.*

8°. London. 1800.

An attentive perusal of this work will qualify the Reader to handle a sword or stick with Grace, enable him to correct abuse, repel Attack, and secure himself from unprovoked insult.

Printed and sold by J. Bailey, 116 Chancery Lane. Sold also by Champante and Whitrow, Aldgate, Wilmott and Hill, Borough, Lumsden and Sons, Glasgow.

——*The Art of Defence on foot with the Broad Sword and Sabre.*

Adapted also for the Spadroon, or cut and thrust sword.

Improved and augmented with the ten lessons of Mr. JOHN TAYLOR, *late Broadsword Master to the Light Horse Volunteers of London and Westminster.*

Illustrated with plates by R. K. Porter Esq.   8°.   London.   1804.

This is merely a reproduction of Roworth's book (see 1798).   In the South Kens.

————*A treatise on the utility and advantages of fencing, giving the opinions of the most eminent Authors and Medical Practitioners on the important advantages derived from a knowledge of the Art as a means of self defence, and a promoter of health, illustrated by forty-seven engravings.   To which is added a dissertation on the use of the broad sword (with six descriptive plates).*

Memoirs of the late Mr. Angelo and a biographical sketch of Chevalier St. George, with his portrait.

Published by Mr. ANGELO, *Bolton Row, and at his fencing academy, Old Bond Street.*

Folio.   London.   1817.

Containing the same plates as the " Ecole des Armes " of the author's father, a portrait of St. George, engraved by W. Ward from a picture by Bronn, and six plates engraved and designed by Rowlandson, under the care of Angelo himself, in 1798-9.

INDEX.

References in Roman numerals will be found in the bibliography following p.248.

BARCA (F. A. de E. y), xxiii, 173.

Académie d'Armes, 144, 171.

—— coat granted to, 146, 171.

Adarga, 236.

Agocchie (G. dell'), xxv, 61.

Agrippa, C., xxv, xxvi, 45.

Alfieri (F.), xxviii, xxix, xxx, 131.

Anelace, 54, 229, Plate IV.

Angelo (D. T. M.), xlix, 212.

—— (H.), l, li, lii, 213.

Anonymous works on Fencing—

Album of copperplates representing attitudes in fencing, xlviii.

Anti-Pugilism, &c., l

De la destreza de las Armas, MS., xx.

Fechtkunst die Ritterlich, mennliche Kunst und Handarbeit Fechtens und Kempfens, xxxii.

Fluchtige Bemerkungen uber die verschiedene Art zu Fechten, &c., xxxvii.

La noble science des joueurs d'espée, xxxviii.

Libro del Exercicio de las armas, MS., xx.

Mars His Feild, or the Exercise of Armes, &c., xliv.

Pallas Armata : the gentleman's armorie, &c., xlv.

Quesiti del Cavaliere instrutto nel arte della Scherma, xxix.

Sechs Fechtschulen der Marxbruder und Federfechter aus den Jahren 1573 bis 1614, &c., xxxii.

Sword Exercise for Cavalry, li.

The names of ye Pushes, &c., MS., xlv.

Antonio de Lucha, 37.

Appels (attacks), 101, 155, 167.

Artists, 191, 197.

Assaults (regulations), 159.

Austrian broadsword-play, 220

Ayala (A. de), xx.

Back sword, 187, 208.

Backswording, 209.

Badge of Marxbruder, 29.

—— of Federfechter, 30

—— of Scottish Sword-men, 199.

Basket hilt, 240.

Battery and beating, 192.

Batier (or Battier), xliii.

Beaupré (J. J. de), xxxvi, 184

Becca cesa, 43.

—— possa, 41.

Besnard (C.), xl, 137.

Besson, 205.

Blackwell (H.), xlvi, xlviii, 207.

Blades (variety of), 235

Blunts and sharps, 198.

Bolognese schools, 33.

Borath, xxxv.

Botta, 37.

—— lunga, 113.

Botte coupée, 144.

—— secrète, 5, 55

Braquemar, 54, 229, Plate VI

Breen (A. van), xxxix.

Bremond (P. A.), xxxi.

Broadsword, 240.

" Broken " head, 210.

Broquel or brochiero, 44, 236.

Bruchius (J. G), xxxv.

Brussels Academy, 147.

Brye (de), xli, 156

Buck (T.), 203, 204.

Buckler, 16, 17, 18, 20, 28, 44, 119.
Burton (Capt. R.), 8.

C. (Sr.), xxxv.
Caize, 53.
Cala (C. de), xxi.
Calarone (C.), xxx
Capo Ferro (R), xxvii, 107.
Carmona (L. Mendez de), xxi.
Carranza (J. S.) xix, xx, 67, 172.
Carré (N.), 120
Carvalho (R. de), xxiv
Case of rapiers, 51, 236.
Cassani (G. A.), xxvi.
Cavalcabo (C.), 122.
——— (H), xxxiii, xxxix, 106
——— (Z.), xxvi, 66.
Cavatione or cavazione, 101.
Centre of percussion, 49.
Cercle, 141
——— les ongles en dessus, en dessous, 156.
——— parade de, 167.
——— mysterieux, 123
Ceresa (T.), xxviii.
Chapman (G.), 8.
Cinghiara porta di ferro, 38.
Circular parries, 11, 142, 154.
Claymore, 228.
Cloak and sword, 51, 119, 132.
Coda lunga e stretta, 38.
——————— e alta, 39
——————— e distesa, 40.
——————— e larga, 41.
"Colichemarde," 239.
Commanding the sword, 194.
Compases, 70.
Contracavatione, 101.
Contraguardia, 106.
Contrapostura, 98.
Contratempo, 111.
Contreprinse (disarming), 60.
Contres, 144
Contretemps, 193.
Corporation of Maisters of Defence, 18, 188.
——— des Maîtres en fait d'Armes, 146, 171.
——— of Fencing Masters in Spain, 31, 133, 173.
Coudray (J. B. le Perche du), xl, 136.
Coulé (glizade), 167.
Counter-caveating, 193
Counter-guards (of sword), 230.
Countering, 36, 57, 77.
Coupé, 144, 167.

Coustil à croc, 228.
"Crosse blowes," 81.
Cross hilt, 230.
Crossing, 91.
Cuchillo, 174.
Cudgels, 209.
Cup hilt, 236.
Cutlass, 188, 229.
Cuts (classification), 36.

Dagger alone, 174.
Daggers (fencing), 245.
Danet, G., xlii, xliv, 160.
Delforce (J.), 204.
Démarches, 57.
Demeuse (N.), xliii, xliv.
Demi-contre, 168.
Destreza, 93, 121, 173.
Development, 113, 140.
Disarming, 154, 155.
Distance, 8.
Docciolini (M.), xxvi, 96.
Doyle (A.), xxxvi, 184.
"Dui tempi," 99, 138.
Dusack, 75, 77, 229.

Ecole des Armes, 160, 217.
——— Royale d'Armes, 170.
Einsidell (C. von), xxxiii, 180.
Enclosing, 194.
Encyclopédie, 160, 217.
Engagement, 10.
Eon (d'), 171, 217.
Estoc, 22, 57, 228.
Estocada, 72.
Estocade, 53.
——— de passe, de pied ferme, 140.
Ettenhard (F. A.), xxii.

Fabris (S.), xxvi, xxviii, xxxv
Falchion, 229, 243.
Fallopia (A.), xxvi.
Falsifying, 192.
Feder, 30, 180.
Federfechter, 30.
Feints, 11, 101.
Fendente, 131.
Ferron (J), 120.
Fianconata, 107.
Fig, 204, 206.
Fighting guilds, 14.
Filo (falso o dritto), 35.

Finger loop, 232
Firme (M. M), xxiv.
Flail, 15.
Flaman (le), 120.
Flamberg, 192, 228, 237
Flanconnade, 137, 194.
Foil-play, 7.
Foils, 139, 144.
—— (Italian), 179.
Freville (de), xliii, xliv.

Gaiani (G. B.), xxvii, 131.
Gallici (M.), 133.
Ganancia, 72.
Garcia (F. F.), xix.
Garzonius, xxxiii, 180.
German play (Angelo), 184.
Giganti (N.), xxvii, xxxiii, xxxix, 107.
Girard, xli, 156.
Gladiators, 16, 187.
Godfrey (Capt. J.), xlviii, 204.
Gordine (G), xlii, 159
Gorman, 203.
Grados al perfil, 68.
Grassi (G. di), xxv, xliv, 49
Gray (G.), 202.
Grisetti e Rosaroll, xxxi, 177.
Guadagnare di spada, 72.
Guard (definition), 109.
—— (Spanish), 69, 175.
—— For special guard, see under various
    authors.
—— of sword, 230.
Gunterrodt (A.), xxxii.

Half-circle, 138, 140.
Half-hangers, 220.
Hamlet (fencing scene), 3
Hanger, 229.
Hangetort, 76.
Harris (J.), 202
Haspelmacher, xxxvii.
Hesgate (T.), 202.
Heussler (S.), xxxiii, xxxiv, 180.
Hiebcoment, 185.
Hoffman, xxxvii.
Hope (Sir W.), xlv, xlvi, xlvii, 190.
Hundt (M.), xxxii, 180.
Hutton (Capt. A.), 8.
Hynitzchen (J.), xxxv, 183.

"Ignorants," 191.

Imbracciatura, 44.
Imbroccata, 83.
Incartata, 84.
Inquarto, 178.
"Instances," 125.
Intagliata, 178.
Intrecciata, 136.
Italian art of fencing, 179.
—— foil, 179.
—— guard (Angelo), 179

Jarnac (coup de), 53.
Jena, 183.
Jeronimo, 24.
Johnson (Mr), 204

Kahn (A. F.), xxxvi, xxxvii, 182.
Keys (Dr.), 215.
Knuckle-bow, 230, 233.
Konigsmark, 239.
Koppen, xxxiii, 180
Kreussler (W.), 182.
—— (G.), 183.
—— (H.), 183.

Labat, xli, xlviii, 152.
La Boëssière, xliii, 164, 169.
Landsknecht's sword, 78, 229.
Lange (J. D.), xxxiv, 181
Lanistæ, 31.
Lara (A. de), xxii.
La Tousche, xl, 141.
Lebkommer (H.), xxxii, 74.
Left hand (use of), 83, 114, 195
—— arm as counterpoise, 108.
Le Perche, xl, 136, 141
Liancour (de), xl, 143.
Linea perfetta e retta, 133.
Lineas infinitas, de contingencia, 69.
Lines, 9.
Long sword, 18, 228.
Lonnergan (A), xlix, 218
Lovino (G. A.), xxvii, xxviii.
Luis (T.), xxii.
Luxbruder, 31

Machrie (W.), 197.
Mahon (A.), xlviii, 207.
Maindraict, 57.
Maistres en fait d'armes, 147.
Malchus, 228.
Manciolino (A), xxiv, 34.

Mandabolo, 135.
Mandoble, 71.
Mandritti, 36, 81.
Mangano (G. A. del), xxxi.
Marcelli (F. A), xxx, 135.
Marco (A. di), xxx, xxxi.
Marozzo (A.), xxiv, xxv, xxvii, 35, 44.
Martin, xlii, 156.
Marxbruder, 29.
Masks, 159, 169, 246.
Mathews, 189.
Mattei (F. A.), xxix.
Mazo (B. di), xxx.
McArthur (J.), l, 219
McBane (D), xlvii, 204.
McTurk (W.), 212.
Measure, 8.
Medio reves, medio tajo, 72.
Mendoza (L. P. de), xxi.
Menessiez, 161.
Meyer (J.), xxxii, xxxiv, 75-77.
Mezza cavazione, 101.
Mezzo cerchio, 178.
—— dritto, 130.
—— tempo, 96.
Michelangelo, 45.
Micheli (M.), xxxi.
Millar or Miller (J.), xlviii, 203, 207.
Misericorde, 244.
Misura larga, 99, 107.
—— stretta, 99, 107.
Moman, xxxiv.
Moncio (P.), xxiv.
Monica (F.), xxx.
Montante, 135, Plate IV.
Morentin (A. A. y), xxiii.
Motet, 217.
Mysterious circle, 123.
Mur (tirer au), 166.

Narvaez (Don L. P. de), xx, xxi, xxii, 69,
    73, 172.
Niccoli (H.), xlv.
Noveli (N. R.), xxiii.
Numerical nomenclature, 10, 161.

Oath, in Italian schools, 44.
—— in Spanish schools, 32.
Oberhut, 74.
Ochs, 76.
Octave, 138.
Olivier, xlix, 218.

Opposition, 11.
—— of the hand, 148, 150, 152.
O'Sullivan, xlii, 160.

Pagano (M. A.), xxv.
Palladini (C.), xxvi.
Pallavicini (G. M.), xxix, 133.
Paradoxes of Defence, 22.
Parkes (of Coventry), 202, 205.
Parries (eight natural), 10.
—— in rapier-play, 112.
Paschen (J. G.), xxxiv, xxxv, 181.
Pas d'âne, 231.
Passata, 84.
Passes, 112, 168.
Passing, 48, 61, 70.
Passot (épée de), 229.
Patenostrier, xxxix, 105.
Pater, 136.
Paz (S de la), xxiii.
Pembroke (Lord), 217.
Peralta (M. C. y.), xxiii.
Perinat (J. N.), xxiv, 175.
Pepys's account of a stage-fight, 189.
Peso, 132.
Petit Jean, 120.
Pflug, 76.
Pistofilo (B.), xxviii.
Pizarro (J. F.), xx.
" Plain thrust," 199.
Plastrons, 134.
Pompée, 53.
Pona (or Pons) (J.), xix.
Porres (G. A. de), xxi.
Porta di ferro, 39.
Position of hand, 9, 165.
Postura, 98.
Prime, 137, 157.
Prinse (seizing), 59.
Prize-fight, 188.
Prizes, 18, 188.
Pronation, 10.
Punta dritta, riversa o rovescia, 64, 84.
Punta sopramano, 66.

Quarte or carte, 11, 137.
Quarte coupée, 144.
Quarter-staff, 247.
Quarting, 193.
Quatriangle, 57.
Quillons, 231.
Quinte, 10, 140, 156.

Quintino (A.), xxvii.
Quixada (M. P. de M. y), xxii.

Rada (L. de), xxiii.
Ranis (H. C.), xxxvii.
Rapier, 5, 21, 234.
Rebated swords, 7, 134, 246.
Redas, 217.
Renvers, 57.
Reprise, 138.
Reverence, 139.
Reves, 72.
Ricasso, 236.
Ricavazione, 101, 136.
Riposte, 138, 141.
Rocco, 23.
Rocheford (Mons. J. de), account of stage-fight, 189.
Roger le Skirmizour, 17.
Roman (F.), xix.
Rosaroll e Grisetti, xxxi, 177.
Rotella, 44, 119.
Rousseau (A.), 171.
Roux (H.), xxxvii.
—— (J. A. K.), xxxviii.
Roversi, 36.
Rovescio, 64, 130.
Rowlandson, li, 219.
Roworth, li, 219.

Sainct-Didier (H. de), xxxviii, 56.
Saint-Martin (J. de), xxxviii, 171.
Salgen (G.), xxxiv.
Salute, 139, 230.
Salvator (S.), xxxiv.
Saviolo (Vincent), xliv, 26, 79.
Saxe (Marshal), 171.
Sbasso, 104, 178.
Scannatura, 115.
Schlaeger-play, 185.
Schmidt, xxxvi, xxxvii.
—— (J. A.), xxxv, xxxvi, xxxvii, 184.
Schoffer (H. W.), xxxiii, 180.
Schranckhut, 76.
Schwerdt, 15, 76, 77, 181, 228.
Scots' play, 191.
Seconde, 10.
—— tierce en seconde et quarte en seconde, 137.
—— pour le dessus, pour le dessous, 141.
Senese (or Senesio) (A.), xxix, 132.
Sentiment du fer, 127.

Septime, 10, 138, 141.
Shearing sword, 187.
Shell hit, shell dagger, 230.
Sherlock (Mr.), 205.
Side-ring, 231.
Silva (G. de), xix.
Silver (G.), xliv, 22.
Silvie, 53.
Sinclair (Capt.), li.
Single-sticks, 209, 247.
Sixte, 10, 138.
Slip, slipping, 192.
Small sword, 239.
Small-sword play, 6, 149.
Sosa (M.), xxiv.
Spadone, 76, 228.
Spadroon, 207, 243, 247.
—— German, 184.
—— guard, 219.
"Spanish fight," 92.
—— Angelo's description of, 175.
Staff, 247.
Stage-fight, 188, 201.
—— Steele's account of, 203.
Steccata, 226.
"Stesso tempo," 99, 138, 176.
St. George (Chevalier de), 171.
St. George's guard, 220.
St. Michel (Confrérie de), 148.
Stoccata, 84.
—— lunga, 113.
Stock or stuck, 22.
"Stoss und Hieb," 180.
Stramazone, 41.
Stramazoncello, 135.
Strasburg (Académie de), 147.
Striccio, 136.
Students' duels, 181, 185.
Supination, 10.
Sutor (J.), xxxii, 77.
Sutton, 204.
Swashbuckler, 19.
Swetnam (J.), xlv.
Sword, 19.
—— dancers, 15.
—— old and modern, 225.
—— and buckler, 16, 20, 28, 48, 119.
Sword-men, 16.
Swordsmen (Society of Scottish), 199.
Sylva (D. R. de), xxiii.

Tajo, 72.

Tappe de Milan, 105.
Target (hand buckler), 18, 28, 38.
—— (practice at), 36, 75.
Taylor (J.), lii.
Teillagory, 171, 212.
Temlich, xxxvii.
Tempo indivisibile, 132.
Terrewest (J.), 205.
Thibauld, xxxiv.
Thibaust (G.), xxxix, xl, 122.
Thumb-ring, 234.
Tierce, 10, 137, 141
Time, 8, 84, 100, 107.
Tobar (M. de), xxi.
Tocchi di spada, 49.
Torelli, xxviii.
Torquato (E.), xxvii, 130.
Torre (P. de la), xix.
Toulouse Academy, 147.
Transition period, 227.
—— rapier, 238.
Triangle, 57.
Triangular blades, 238.
Triegler (J. G.), xxxiv, 138.
Trovare di spada, 103
Tucke, 22.

Under-counter, 194.
Underwood (J.), l.
Universal parries, 5, 65, 119, 167.
Universities (German), 181.

Vade-Mecum (Swordsman's), 195.
Valdin (Mons.), xlviii, 207.
Verdun, 235.
Verolinus (T.), xxxv, 181.
Vester, xxxvii.
Viedma (D. de), xxi.
Vigeant (Mons.), Bibliography, xvii
Viggiani (Vizani) (A.), xxv, xxvi, 61.
Villardita (G.), xxix.
Volt-coupe, 194.
Volte, 104, 154, 168.

Waster, 209, 247.
Weischner (S. C. F.), xxxvii.
West Smithfield, 20.
Westwicke, 189.
Wylde (Z.), xlvi, 207.

Yorke (Rowland), 21, 208

Zeter (J.), xxxix, 180.
Zweyhander, 76, 228.